Income Distribution and
High-Quality Growth

Income Distribution and
High-Quality Growth

Income Distribution and High-Quality Growth

edited by Vito Tanzi and
Ke-young Chu

The MIT Press
Cambridge, Massachusetts
London, England

This book was set in Palatino on the Monotype "Prism Plus" PostScript Imagesetter by Asco Trade Typesetting Ltd., Hong Kong.

Printed and bound in the United States of America.

Library of Congress Cataloging-in-Publication Data

Income distribution and high-quality growth / edited by Vito Tanzi and
  Ke-young Chu.
     p.   cm.
  Includes bibliographical references and index.
  ISBN 0-262-20109-7 (alk. paper)
  1. Income distribution. 2. Equity. 3. Economic development.
  I. Tanzi, Vito. II. Chu, Ke-young, 1941–
  HC79.I5I483   1998
  339.2—dc21   97-22967
                                                         CIP

3 2280 00618 8262

Contents

Preface

In 1993, the managing director of the International Monetary Fund (IMF), Michel Camdessus, who has always strongly urged IMF member governments to pursue policies designed to promote high-quality economic growth, suggested that the IMF host a major international conference on income distribution and economic growth. This book contains the papers presented at that conference, held in Washington, D.C., June 1–2, 1995. We hope that the analyses and policy ideas contained in this book prove useful to policymakers, scholars, and others interested in exploring the vital question of how distributional equity and economic growth are intertwined.

The chapter authors and discussants came from governments, academia, research institutions and international organizations and from industrial, developing, and transition countries on all continents. They prepared well-focused papers and comments for the conference. Many IMF staff members provided useful advice that was essential for the success of the conference. Camdessus himself provided substantial input into the design of the conference.

We are especially thankful to the staff members of the Fiscal Affairs Department's Expenditure Policy Division (EPD). They contributed to the preparatory work for the conference, and after the conference, many of them assisted cheerfully in the work for the publication of the book. In this regard, we should mention particularly EPD chief Sanjeev Gupta and EPD members Elliott Harris, Manfred Koch, Alex Mourmouras, Edgardo Ruggiero, and Jerald Schiff for their careful reading of the manuscript. Special thanks are due to Lawrence Hartwig, who assisted in handling the considerable amount of correspondence with the conference participants and performed the massive task of dealing with the successive drafts of the chapters and comments on the word processor. And Diane Cross's painstaking reading of the entire manuscript led to substantial editorial and stylistic improvements.

We thank the MIT Press for its interest in the book and for the professional preparatory work that led to its publication. We add the usual disclaimer that the views expressed in the chapters and comments by all participants are their own and do not necessarily reflect those of the IMF, the MIT Press, or the institutions for which the participants work.

Finally, we note with sorrow the untimely death of Michael Bruno, who, together with Lyn Squire and Martin Ravallion, contributed actively to the productive and lively discussion at the IMF conference. His paper, in this volume, has much to offer to those who seek new insights into the relationship between income distribution and economic growth.

Introduction

Although the majority of the people in the industrial world and some in the developing world enjoy unprecedented affluence, a much larger number of the people in low-income countries continue to live in abject poverty. And although several developing countries are achieving rapid economic growth and poverty reduction, most former centrally planned countries are struggling to implement market-oriented reforms in the midst of economic deterioration and rising poverty.

The high level of living standards that economic growth has brought to the industrial world has made the need to reduce the poverty in low-income countries more imperative. This poverty points to income inequality as a pressing policy issue. In many low-income countries, the income share of the households that belong to the poorest quintile ranges between 2 and 6 percent, while those in the richest quintile enjoy an income share of between 40 and 60 percent.

Transition economies face the demanding task of strengthening macroeconomic performance, introducing market institutions, and reforming social programs. Many of them suffer not only from a major reduction in output, an increase in income inequality, and the consequent increase in poverty but also from economic dislocations arising from the breakup of political unions and foreign trading arrangements.

The situation is less dramatic, but still pressing, in many industrial countries, where a relatively small but significant share of the population lives in poverty. A large number of jobless workers rely on unemployment benefits. In some of these countries, social security programs have succeeded in reducing poverty but have become a major financial burden for the governments, crowding out productive activities, discouraging work effort, and contributing to large fiscal deficits.

To reduce poverty, the world needs to achieve sustained and balanced economic growth. Low-income countries and the former centrally planned countries must raise their growth rates toward those enjoyed by the more dynamic economies of the developing world. To this end, industrial countries should maintain sustainable economic growth, providing themselves and the rest of the world with both capital for productive investment and markets for goods and services. The unequal income distribution in many countries is clearly a major factor contributing to poverty, but government may not be able to achieve significant income redistribution immediately.

A number of questions remain unresolved among economists regarding the complex linkages between growth and distribution:

• How does income distribution interact with economic growth in the short and the long runs?

• To what extent can government use transfer programs to increase the incomes of the poor?

• How can government use broader social programs to help the poor increase their income-earning capacity over time?

• Does distributional inequality, by limiting the capacity of the poor to increase their human capital, create an obstacle to this longer-term poverty reduction? Or is distributional inequality a necessary means of achieving economic growth, since it is assumed to promote saving and since government's attempts to redistribute income may discourage work effort and create costly bureaucracies?

• How does the inequality of opportunity affect income distribution?

The issue of equity also emerged as a result of the widespread external payments difficulties that heavily indebted countries faced in the 1980s and the economic transformation efforts of the former centrally planned economies in the 1990s. In implementing wide-ranging economic reform programs, these countries confront the short-run adverse distributive effects of some reform measures.

The International Monetary Fund (IMF) cooperates with its member countries worldwide to promote sound international monetary cooperation and domestic macroeconomic policies. It conducts periodic consultations with member countries on a range of economic policy issues, provides the countries with financial assistance aimed at addressing external payment difficulties, and provides technical assistance for improving economic policies and institutions. In this regard, the IMF is interested in improving its understanding of how countries can increase their chances for achieving high-quality economic growth, that is, sustainable economic growth that contributes to poverty reduction and distributive equity.

Against this background, on June 1–2, 1995, the IMF held a conference on income distribution and sustainable growth at its headquarters in Washington, D.C. Forty-five scholars and policymakers from academic institutions, governments, and international organizations around the world attended. These participants, joined by staff members of the IMF, discussed various issues concerning income distribution and economic growth.

This book presents the papers delivered at the conference and the discussants' comments. Michel Camdessus, the IMF managing director, begins by elaborating on why the IMF is concerned about income distribution. Enrique Iglesias, the Inter-American Development Bank (IDB) president, draws policy lessons from the growth experiences of Latin America.

The other chapter authors take a close look at several interrelated aspects of the process of equitable economic growth. Joseph Stiglitz provides a framework for analyzing government's role. Andrea Brandolini and Nicola Rossi; Michael Bruno, Martin Ravallion, and Lyn Squire; and John Flemming discuss relevant policy issues for, respectively, industrial, developing, and transition countries. Arnold Harberger and Jagdish Bhagwati discuss, respectively, domestic and external sector policies that promote equitable growth. Alberto Alesina analyzes the political aspects of reform and redistributive policies. Finally, Manuel Guitián and Vito Tanzi discuss the equity and growth implications of the IMF's policy advice.

Promoting Equitable Economic Growth: Conceptual Issues

The chapters touch on a number of conceptual issues that are pertinent to an informed discussion of strategies for equitable growth:

Poverty and Income Distribution
Policymakers should clarify whether their primary goal is to reduce poverty or to achieve greater income equality per se. These two goals may require different policies. In a country where most of the people are poor, income distribution between the poor and the ultrapoor can become an important issue. The polarization of income groups is often as important an issue as poverty.

Pretax and Posttax Distributions of Income
Income distribution analysis has typically taken the pretax (and pretransfer) distribution of income as a given, focusing on how tax and

transfer policies affect the distribution of disposable income. This approach has only limited usefulness. The analysis should also assess how government can change the pretax (and pretransfer) distribution of income through appropriate economic policies, such as by promoting employment, and encouraging the accumulation of human capital over time on changing regulations, which may have given special advantages to some groups.

Equality of Opportunity and Equality of Outcome

The fairness of an economic system cannot be assessed only in terms of the degree of inequality of outcomes at a given point in time (e.g., as measured by the Gini coefficient) because temporary factors may have an influence on outcome. The questions of whether individuals are able to move up the economic ladder and whether income or wealth is acquired justly also play a large role in shaping the perceived fairness of a given distribution of income.

Policies for Equitable Economic Growth

A general policy conclusion is that there need not be a trade-off between growth and equity over the long run. Rather, the impact of growth on income distribution depends on the interrelated policies used to achieve growth and distribute the fruits of this growth. Sound macroeconomic and structural policies are consistent with sustainable economic growth, reduced poverty, and improved equity over the longer term. However, an attempt by government to influence income distribution dramatically through large-scale tax and transfer programs can have a negative impact on growth.

Government has a crucial role to play in any strategy that seeks to pursue growth and equity by securing macroeconomic stability and the appropriate level of investment, including in infrastructure and human capital. To this end, it is crucial that government's productivity, in all its dimensions, be increased.

Because of the small share of total income that the truly poor receive, reductions in inequality can have a large direct effect on poverty. In addition, a more equitable income distribution may encourage growth over the long term. The increased social stability resulting from reduced inequality encourages investment in physical and human capital and may help government avoid using inefficient redistributive policies that it might be forced to adopt in a divisive political climate arising from excessive income inequality. This reinforces the notion that equity and growth may go hand in hand over time.

In the short run, however, macroeconomic adjustment with major structural reforms may increase unemployment and worsen inequality while boosting growth prospects. Privatization, a reduction in the size of the civil service, and labor shedding by private firms release labor that cannot be absorbed immediately by the rest of the economy. In addition, the demand for different skills changes; those who possess scarce new skills gain, while others may lose. Well-targeted social safety nets are crucial to protect the most vulnerable from transitory shocks.

Government policies, such as the sale of state assets at prices below their market values, create rents, leading to opportunities for the acquisition of income and wealth in a manner that is perceived as unjust. Once entrenched in the system, these rents, which often are associated with corruption, are difficult to eliminate. Government policies nevertheless should aim at eliminating existing rents and preventing new ones from emerging.

Fiscal Policy

It is difficult for a country to have a tax system that is both efficient and progressive. This is particularly true for countries without a well-developed tax administration. Even a progressive tax system may have a limited impact on income distribution. In addition, the burden of corporate taxes may, in a world of mobile capital, fall largely on labor, limiting the government's ability to redistribute income through the tax system. Therefore, government should seek to determine a distribution of tax burdens seen as broadly fair rather than use the tax system to achieve a drastic income redistribution. Tax policy should be aimed at moving toward a system of easily administered taxes with broad bases and moderate marginal rates.

On the expenditure side, there is more room for government to affect income distribution. Universal access to basic health care, education, and social infrastructure tends to improve the well-being of the poor and economic growth by increasing either their income-earning capacity or their direct consumption of public goods, or both. However, such policies may be fiscally costly. In the context of structural adjustment programs entailing fiscal retrenchment, protecting social expenditures or reducing less productive spending to provide basic health and education services can both benefit low-income groups and support economic growth. In the short run, targeted transfer programs can help cushion the potential short-run adverse effects of economic reform on the poor.

Monetary Policy

Over the longer term, low and stable inflation contributes to higher growth and increased equality. Inflation distorts the price system and inhibits the efficient allocation of resources. Fiscally induced inflation also crowds out private capital formation. The negative effect of high inflation falls particularly heavily on the poor, who cannot protect the real value of their few assets during inflation.

Low inflation and appropriately tight monetary policy are favorable for the poor over the longer term; nevertheless, a tightening of monetary policy can induce a recession and reduce employment in the short term, resulting in a temporary increase in income inequality.

Trade Policy

For low-income countries, an outward-oriented strategy is closely associated with increased efficiency and higher growth. This higher growth arises from exploiting comparative advantage, as well as from the increased efficiency of capital, including the capital formed through direct foreign investment. In addition, such a policy stance would likely induce a shift in trade and production toward labor-intensive goods, increasing both employment and real wages and contributing to a more equitable distribution of income in developing countries.

For the industrial world, there has been fear of the adverse impact of expanded trade with developing countries on low-skilled wages and employment. However, whether or not trade has adversely affected sectors producing goods intensive in unskilled labor is still a matter of debate; for example, the relative price of goods produced in industrial countries with unskilled labor does not appear to have declined since the mid-1980s. Rather, technological change appears to be responsible for at least part of the increased wage inequality in industrial countries.

Government's Limitations

Much of the analysis and policy prescription presented in this book recognizes government's political and administrative constraints, and it makes distinctions between what is more feasible and less feasible. In many cases, sound economic policy is politically beneficial. Thus, there is increasing evidence of a negative effect of excessive income inequality on social cohesion and the political feasibility of sound economic policies. Therefore, policies seeking to promote distributional equity often improve a government's ability to pursue sound economic policies. Properly targeted social safety nets can mitigate the adverse effects of economic reform measures without an excessive fiscal burden, thus reducing the political opposition to reform.

Sound economic policies are not always easy to implement. Powerful and well-entrenched vested interest groups can leave a well-intentioned government severely weakened, unfocused, and paralyzed. These groups can force the government to introduce inequitable and macroeconomically destabilizing allocative distortions in the form of tax exemptions, budgetary subsidies, and price controls.

Conclusions

Income distribution has become a key economic issue. The paramount importance of achieving poverty reduction worldwide is forcing economists and economic policymakers to focus on improving their understanding of how income distribution and economic growth interact. The globalization of the markets for products and capital has also heightened their interest in the distributional implications of economic policy.

We hope that this book will help economists, government officials, and all others who are concerned about this vital issue to sort out the various arguments and to promote policies that bring about equitable growth.

1

Income Distribution and Sustainable Growth: The Perspective from the IMF at Fifty

Michel Camdessus

Although the closer integration of markets across countries promises an unprecedented opportunity to achieve greater efficiency and higher economic growth worldwide, it is clear that we face a much more volatile global market environment—a place where risks are higher than before and where the best way for countries to avoid financial crises such as that experienced by Mexico at the end of 1994 is to adopt strict policy discipline to guard against adverse market reaction. Our own reflections at the International Monetary Fund have already suggested several avenues for renewed efforts to avoid Mexico-like adverse market reactions in this evolving global environment:

• Strengthen our surveillance to help member countries prevent economic crises, especially those that could pose risk to the international monetary system.

• Find ways to help member countries deal effectively with crises when they do occur.

• Help member countries achieve conditions for growth that is sustainable, respects the environment, brings lasting full employment and poverty reduction, and fosters greater equity through increased equality of opportunity.

In this regard, the IMF's experience in working with member countries for half a century has provided valuable lessons—in particular, that the pursuit of these goals requires a sound mix of policies, with attention given to the distributional implications of these policies, for example, through cost-effective social safety nets aimed at helping the poor during periods of reform and adjustment.

But in this approach, we face an old issue: how income distribution is related to economic growth. Particularly, we face three related questions that are likely to stay with us into the next century:

1. Why is income distribution an important policy issue?

2. What are the implications of income distribution for economic growth?

3. What are the implications of our concern about income distribution for IMF operations?

Let us look at each of these questions. First, income distribution is an important policy issue because of its relevance to efforts to reduce poverty. There is no question that sustained economic growth is a crucial condition for reducing poverty; however, growth alone may not necessarily reduce poverty. Poverty reduction achieved only through growth may not be fast enough, particularly when the initial distribution of wealth, including land, is highly uneven. Therefore, a strategy for the alleviation of poverty should focus on both growth and reduced income inequality.

Income distribution also relates to social justice and to perceptions of social justice, which can affect harmony among different social groups and the political sustainability of economic policy. Broad public support is more likely to come for a wise and sustained course of adjustment and reform when the distribution of income and opportunities to attain economic advancement are seen as relatively fair, or at least not outrageously biased toward privileged groups.

The second question, on the implications of income distribution for economic growth, seems to have two competing views. The view stressing equity-growth trade-offs is a long-held one that policies that reduce income inequality affect growth adversely for at least two reasons:

1. Transfers and taxes used to redistribute income may create distortions and disincentives. Moreover, the resources required for redistributive programs may reduce the funds available for public and private investment in physical and human capital.

2. Since high-income groups tend to save a larger portion of their income, greater distributional equality is likely to decrease aggregate savings and, thus, investment.

The other view stresses equity-growth complementarity. There is growing recognition that an excessively unequal income distribution may itself be detrimental to sustainable growth. Perhaps cost-effective programs aimed at reducing excessive income and consumption inequality, in the context of macroeconomic stability and allocative efficiency, may promote, not deter, sustainable economic growth. Three well-recognized channels provide insights into how economic policies are intertwined with social issues and the political process. The recognition of these channels forces us to think about the broader implications of, and necessary preconditions for, sound economic policies.

The first channel is the positive effect of such policies on the efficient use and development of human resources. For example, many East Asian countries have achieved remarkably high economic growth and declining income inequality by pursuing good macroeconomic policies and high investment in physical and human capital, with heavy emphasis on primary education. The second channel is the positive effect of such policies on public and private savings. Sound macroeconomic, budgetary, and financial policies that avoid excessive distributional inequality also create conditions for sustainable growth through higher rates of savings and investment. The third channel is the positive effect of reduced income inequality on the political process and on social cohesion. A highly unequal distribution of income, or the lack of opportunity for large segments of the population, may lead to political and social instability and impede efficient economic activity. Moreover, in a democratic society, a highly unequal income distribution could generate political pressures for unsound economic policies. This is the most fertile soil for populism to flourish. Greater income equality achieved through well-designed income transfers (including social safety nets) can help secure support for policies crucial for economic reform and sustainable growth.

The third and final question concerns whether the IMF, as a macroeconomic policy institution, should be interested in income distribution. What are the implications of the linkages between income distribution and economic growth for the IMF's operations? De facto, by trying to create conditions for high-quality growth, IMF policy advice often has implicitly a distributional content. For example, in the surveillance process, in conducting a comprehensive analysis of the general economic situation and policy strategy of a member, discussions deal frequently with labor market and unemployment issues, as well as with the effectiveness and efficiency of social expenditures. As such, the IMF cannot but call the attention of the country and the IMF membership to income inequality and its potential adverse consequences for the social fabric and sustainable growth. As another example, IMF-supported reform programs include targeted safety nets aimed at shielding the most vulnerable groups from the short-run adverse effects of economic reform measures. The IMF also provides technical assistance in this area. In collaboration with the World Bank, these reform programs are seeking increasingly to improve the economic participation of the poor in the growth process.

Is this the proper way for the IMF to address distributional concerns? Is this sufficient for achieving growth with equity? Or does it need to amend its policy advice?

Considering the world situation, I feel that there is perhaps a need and potential to do more, for at least two reasons: high-quality growth is still elusive in many countries, and unemployment and poverty are more persistent worldwide than they could and should be.

Certainly the IMF must proceed with caution to ensure it does not stray from its central mandate, remains realistic about what it can achieve with regard to these sensitive issues while respecting member countries' sovereign choices, and considers staffing constraints and other priorities. The IMF must seek imaginative ideas, however, in treading a narrow path to optimizing the mutually supportive interaction between growth-oriented adjustment strategies and a thoughtful approach to distributional issues.

2 Income Distribution and Sustainable Growth: A Latin American Perspective

Enrique Iglesias

Latin America has the most unequally distributed income in the world. This is not a new phenomenon. Data from twenty or even thirty years ago clearly show the same relative inequality patterns. Even more troubling, the poor have fallen further behind the rich since 1980.

This chapter examines why the distribution of income in Latin America is so unequal; what we can expect to happen to inequality as Latin American countries emerge from adjustment and more onto a long-run growth path; under what conditions a more equitable distribution could lead to a higher growth rate; and what these countries can do to speed up the transition to a more equitable distribution of the benefits of economic activity.

2.1 Background

Latin America has always had a highly unequal distribution of income and a high level of poverty relative to its income. Analysis of recent household surveys makes it clear that in most countries, the recessions that accompanied the adjustment process during the 1980s increased both earnings inequality and poverty.

Tables 2.1 and 2.2 give, respectively, the distribution of household income from national surveys conducted around 1970 and comparative data over the 1980s. Where possible, they show both the Gini coefficient and the share of income going to the bottom 40 percent of households.[1] Note that in table 2.2, there are urban data only for several countries, which means that these observations are not strictly comparable to countries with a national sample. However, each row in the table represents an internally consistent time series of income distribution statistics over the decade.

Table 2.1 gives an idea of relative income concentration across the region. Argentina and Uruguay had a relatively equitable distribution,

Table 2.1
Distribution Statistics in Latin America, circa 1970

Country	Date	Gini coefficient	Share of bottom 40 percent
Argentina	1961	0.42	0.173
Brazil	1970	0.55	0.095
Colombia	1971	0.51	0.113
Chile	1971	0.46	0.131
Costa Rica	1971	0.46	0.131
Guatemala[a]	1979–1981	0.48	
Honduras[b]	1967–1968		0.073
Mexico	1968	0.52	0.106
Panama	1970	0.57	0.070
Peru	1971	0.58	0.059
Uruguay	1967	0.42	0.143
Venezuela	1971	0.49	0.103

Source: Altimir (1992a), except as noted.
Note: All data refer to distribution of household income.
a. Fields (1990).
b. Anand and Kanbur (1993).

while Brazil, Colombia, Honduras, Mexico, Panama, Peru, and Venezuela had very high levels of inequality. Chile and Costa Rica were in the middle.

To get an idea of just how unequally distributed income is in Latin America relative to other countries, note that in Korea, Pakistan, and Taiwan in the 1960s, the bottom 40 percent received around 20 percent of income, while in Egypt and India, that group got around 15 percent (Anand and Kanbur 1993). Clearly the high relative inequality of Latin America is not recent.

Consider next what happened to inequality over the 1980s (see Table 2.2). For the countries for which we have Gini estimates for the beginning and end of the decade, there was a substantial rise in inequality in most cases. That means that recessions in the 1980s hit the poor harder than the rich.[2] But rising inequality was not universal. In Colombia, Costa Rica, Uruguay, and Paraguay, inequality went down.

Cycles in inequality appear to have been significantly influenced by cycles in economic growth and per capita income over the decade. During the 1980s, Latin America struggled to adjust to a severe balance of payments crisis brought about by overborrowing and unfavorable external shocks. Every country in the region had at least one recession, and many faced two or three. In every case for which we have evidence, these recessions were associated with increased inequality, and in almost every case, subsequent recoveries were equalizing. Recessions under Latin American conditions were inequitable in that the burden of falling incomes had an especially heavy impact on the people who started with the least income. That is especially true when the recessions were accompanied by hyperinflation, as was the case in Argentina and Brazil in 1989, Bolivia in 1985, and Peru in 1990. Recoveries had the opposite effect: Not only did the poorest gain more than the better off, but in Colombia, Costa Rica, Paraguay, and Uruguay, they even improved their relative position.

In other words, inequality was countercyclical during the 1980s in Latin America, rising during recessions and falling during recoveries. In the twenty-seven cases for which we have comparable before and after data, only two do not show this positive relationship between equality and the state of the economy. A hypothesis for this strong relationship is that recession under conditions common in Latin America during the 1980s created severe downward pressure on wages and employment for those at the bottom of the income pyramid. With insignificant levels of unemployment insurance, workers were forced to accept large real wage reductions, unemployment, or work in the informal sector. For new entrants, the choices were equally stark. This group comprised the bulk of rising unemployment, and for those who did find work, the evidence suggests a rise in the age-wage differential in most countries.[3]

Although changes in overall income distribution tend to be dominated by what happens within the wage distribution, changes in the factor shares of labor and capital must also have played a part in the rising inequality in Latin America during the 1980s. Recessions in developed countries have a large impact on profits because of the stickiness of wages and the tendency to stockpile labor when reductions in aggregate demand are expected to be temporary. No such safeguards to labor income seem to have been present in Latin America. There may have been some stockpiling of labor, but the reduction in real wages in most countries was so large that it swamped any reduction in profits that took place at the same time. As a result, for almost every country for which there are data, there was a fall in the share of wages in gross domestic product (GDP) during the 1980s.[4]

In addition to wage repression, another factor that contributed to increasing the share of capital was a dramatic rise in real interest rates over the decade in some countries, particularly Brazil. Many countries had established internal bond markets during the 1970s, so as the financial picture

Table 2.2
Gini Coefficients in Latin America, 1979–1992

Country and source	1979	1980	1981	1982	1983	1984	1985	1986	1987	1988	1989	1990	1991	1992
Argentina (Buenos Aires)														
Psacharopoulos et al. (1993)		0.41									0.48			
Fiszbein (1989)		0.40	0.43	0.40	0.40		0.40		0.43	0.45				
Bolivia (urban)														
Psacharopoulos et al. (1995)					0.52		0.52							
Brazil (total)														
Barros et al. (1993)	0.59		0.58		0.59	0.59	0.59	0.59	0.60	0.61	0.63	0.61		
Chile														
Mújica and Larrañaga[a] (1993)	0.52	0.53	0.52	0.54	0.54	0.55	0.53	0.54						
Pardo et al. (1993)								0.53	0.53		0.54		0.47[b]	
Colombia (urban)														
Psacharopoulos et al. (1993)		0.58									0.53			
Costa Rica (total)														
Gindling and Berry (1992)		0.40	0.40	0.42	0.38	0.38	0.37	0.36	0.42	0.42				
Psacharopoulos et al. (1993)			0.48								0.46			
Guatemala (total)														
Psacharopoulos et al. (1993)								0.58			0.59			
World Bank (1991)			0.48					0.53			0.57[c]			
Mexico (total)														
Psacharopoulos et al. (1993)						0.51					0.52			
Mckinley and Alarcón (1994)						0.43					0.47			0.47
Paraguay (Asunción)														
Psacharopoulos et al. (1994)					0.45							0.40		

Peru							
GRADE (1992)[d]	0.34						0.41	0.44
Panama (total)							
Psacharopoulos et al. (1993)		0.45	0.39	0.40	0.39		0.56	
Uruguay (urban)							
Psacharopoulos et al. (1993)	0.44						0.42	
Venezuela (total)							
Márquez et al. (1993)	0.40			0.44		0.46		0.44
Psacharopoulos et al. (1993)	0.43			0.44			0.44	

Note: All Gini coefficients are from Psacharopoulos et al. (1993); they are based on household income per capita.

a. Greater Santiago.
b. Based on distribution of wage income only.
c. Taken from IDB data worksheets.
d. Salary income in metropolitan Lima only.

of their governments worsened, they had to borrow to cover their deficits. Prior to 1982, some of that borrowing was external. Afterward, governments borrowed increasingly from their own citizens, and that forced up the real interest rate. This situation had the effect of pushing several governments into a fiscal vicious circle in which the rise in their interest costs exacerbated their deficits, which in turn required increased borrowing, which caused a further increase in the real interest rate. Effectively, such countries resorted to raising taxes, most of which are levied on salaries and paid by the middle and working classes, to compensate bondholders who are at the top of the income distribution.

There was also strong upward pressure on real interest rates as a consequence of the need to attract foreign capital to finance current account deficits or to stem capital outflow. In effect, the better integration of Latin America into world capital markets meant that Latin societies had to pay owners of capital a rate reflecting what they could earn elsewhere, including compensation for the perceived higher risk of operating in Latin America.[5]

2.2 Four Questions

Why Is the Distribution of Income in Latin America Unequal?

The market distributes income across the economically active population, and the family distributes that income across all the members of the society. The focus here is on the distribution of income across those who earn or receive it. The two basic determinants of the distribution in this sense are differences in returns across skills and between factors and differences in the ownership of capital, both physical and human. Of these various causal factors, wage differentials in the labor market and differences in education among workers are the most important. Many studies find that differences in education are the biggest determinant of variations in income across the labor force.

Factor shares going to capital and labor, or the return to capital relative to the average wage, play a lesser role because the owners of capital are so few relative to the number of workers. Thus, an understanding of the distribution of income and the forces that are likely to change it begins with the labor market.

Two features of the labor market are critical: the skill differential and the relative size of the skilled labor force. Put another way, what matters is the return to human capital and the distribution of human capital across the labor force. If the skill differential is high but there are few skilled workers, the distribution will be relatively equitable. That will also be the case if the skill differential is high and almost everyone is skilled. High levels of inequality occur when there is a large return to skill and an unequal distribution of skills—precisely the conditions present in most Latin American countries. In Brazil and Mexico, skill-intensive growth has raised the skill differential, and a relatively successful industrialization strategy has enlarged the number of skilled workers. But the modern skill-using economy is like an island surrounded by a large body of poorly educated and untrained labor toiling in agriculture or in the urban informal sector at very low wages. The result is a dualistic economy with a high degree of income inequality. Note that the size of the modern sector is crucial to this pattern of inequality.

Argentina and Uruguay have relatively modern economies and equitable distributions of income because they have relatively few uneducated, unskilled workers. Paraguay has an equitable distribution for the opposite reason: a relatively small modern sector.

Wage differentials are determined primarily by supply and demand. Skill-intensive growth raises the differential, and a rise in the share of the skilled in the labor force should lower it. But there are several other important factors as well. One is the distribution of land in the agricultural sector. Countries with a large agricultural sector and an unequal distribution of land will have an inequitable distribution because the wages of the unskilled will be driven down by the excess supply of landless day labor in agriculture. Different land tenure arrangements and distributions are important causes of the wide differences in income inequality between Colombia and Costa Rica, on the one hand, and Bolivia and Guatemala, on the other.

Another factor is the degree of integration of the national economy. In small, integrated economies, all sectors and regions tend to move together. The benefits of growth tend to be dispersed throughout the economy, thereby making the distribution more equal. Contrast that with large economies like Brazil or Peru, which are not well integrated. Both have a modern sector separated from a backward area by geographic and cultural barriers. Growth that typically starts in the modern sector (in Lima or the southeast of Brazil) does not trickle down fast enough to the backward sector to permit it to keep up. As a result, growth tends to produce rising inequality, not because the backward area gets any poorer but because the income differential widens between the two regions.

Another dimension of this phenomenon is cultural separation. Typically, indigenous people are not well integrated into the modern economy, one of the reasons for their significantly higher levels of poverty than non-indigenous people in every country in the region. The most striking example is Mexico, where the rate of poverty is over 80 percent for the indigenous group compared to only 18percent for the nonindigenous group (see Psacharopoulos and Patrinos 1994, p. 207). Where the share of indigenous people in the population is large, as it is in Bolivia, Ecuador, Guatemala, Mexico, and Peru, growth will tend to produce rising inequality simply because, with rare exceptions, the indigenous people are not well integrated into the modern economy.

All of these factors help to explain the significant differences between income distribution in East Asia and in Latin America. Korea and Taiwan both had a significant land reform after World War II, and both are geographically compact, well-integrated economies. Brazil, Mexico, and Peru are large, have a poor distribution of land, and have a modern sector only weakly linked to a significant part of the economically active population. These are the conditions that tend to produce inequitable growth.

What Will Happen to Income Distribution on a Long-Run Sustainable Growth Path?

For the past decade, policymakers in Latin America have had to worry primarily about balance of payments crises and structural adjustment. They could not be too preoccupied with the long run. That is changing. Policymakers in many of the economies of the region now face the question of what is likely to happen to income distribution in the context of sustainable growth.

This is a fundamentally different question from the relationship between distribution and income during the recovery phase of an economic cycle. I noted in section 2.1, the strong evidence that inequality is countercyclical, rising in recession and falling in recovery. The return to a long-run growth path from a recession helps the poor more than everyone else. In a recession, there is a sudden reduction in the demand for labor of all sorts. But the structure of labor supply is fixed. What happens to the distribution of income depends on a complex process of bumping down, in which more skilled or educated workers replace the less skilled. Typically, the least skilled in Latin America have suffered the largest wage reductions, and the distribution of income has become more unequal. Recoveries have tended to reverse the process.

What is different about long-run growth is that both demand and supply change. Basically, the impact on income distribution is determined by how much demand changes relative to supply and the relative shares of skilled and unskilled labor. The final relationship between growth and income distribution depends on both the structure of the economy and the growth strategy. In other words, the relationship is ambiguous and depends on conditions particular to each country.

In countries such as Brazil or Peru, which have large and relatively unintegrated backward regions, growth is likely to exacerbate inequality. Unless there is a change in the growth strategy or the government takes effective steps to increase the links between regions, little of the growth will be reflected by progress in the backward regions. Instead, growth is likely to produce what Edmar Bacha years ago called Belindia, a country with a modern Belgium on one side and a backward India on the other. This process is already evident from the recent data for Peru. To prevent this outcome, explicit steps must be taken to improve the productivity of the backward regions and increase their links with the leading sectors.

Several other countries in Latin America (Argentina, Costa Rica, and Uruguay) have a well-educated labor force and a relatively small unskilled, uneducated labor force. In such cases, growth is likely to be equalizing for two reasons. First, even if growth is skill intensive, the demand for unskilled labor will tend to narrow the skill differential. If that does not happen, there will still be an increase in the size of the modern skilled sector, which will draw people from the shrinking backward sector. When the skilled sector is already large, this movement will be equalizing because it means that fewer and fewer are left behind.

The ambiguity in the relationship between growth and income distribution will be most acute in the countries that are relatively integrated and still have a large supply of unskilled labor. Here we have countries on the rising portion of the Kuznets curve, where growth in the modern sector is likely to increase inequality. But this will be a transition process that lasts only until the modern sector grows large enough to absorb most of the low-wage, unskilled labor. Consider the experience of Chile. It has always been an economy with a fairly high degree of inequality and a wide skill differential, primarily because it had a relatively small modern sector. However, Chile now appears to have passed through the transition period. Thanks to a very successful growth strategy, accompanied by a massive commitment to education, Chile has raised its per capita income by 37 percent since 1987. Between 1987 and 1990, that growth increased inequality (see table 2.2). But two more years of growth changed the picture dramatically. Wages began to rise rapidly for the unskilled, and the Gini coefficient fell from 0.54 to 0.47, a very sharp decline indeed. The combination of reductions in the supply of unskilled labor through

education, increases in the demand for unskilled labor because of rapid
growth, and changes in the relative size of the modern and traditional
sectors all played a part in producing equalizing growth.

Does a More Equitable Income Distribution Lead to a Higher Growth Rate?

There has been a recent revival of interest in the reverse causal link between equity and growth. Work by Alesina and Rodrik (1994), Birdsall,
Ross, and Sabot (1995), Fishlow (1995), and Persson and Tabellini (1994)
has examined whether inequality can have a significant negative effect on
growth. In this literature, the comparison of Latin America and East Asia
figures prominently because of East Asia's high growth and low inequality in contrast with the opposite combination in Latin America.

The traditional, pessimistic view, based on the work of Kaldor and
others, was that growth would be deterred by redistribution because
growth requires investment, and the savings to finance that investment
came from the rich. A more recent variant on this theme is that in a world
of highly mobile capital, low wages are required to make a country attractive to investors, both foreign and domestic. If workers demand higher
wages or governments attempt to tax capital or lower interest rates,
investors will leave, and the country will stagnate.

Recent distribution and growth evidence from a cross section of developing countries shows that many countries, particularly in East Asia, have
both an equitable income distribution and very high growth rates. Why?
First, they saved and invested, belying the notion that only the rich save.
Second, they invested heavily in education and based their growth on
exports, which at least at the outset were not particularly skill intensive.
The result was favorable to income distribution in two ways. High investment and rapid growth in exports permitted these countries to grow
faster than they otherwise would have because they never faced severe
foreign exchange or capital constraints. At the same time, investments in
education reduced the supply of unskilled labor. The result was a sharp
narrowing of wage differentials and a fall in indexes of inequality. Growth
benefited the poor as well as the rich, and a pro-growth economic policy
also turned out to be pro-poor.

An interesting political economy reason that a pro-equity policy may
also be pro-growth is that countries with an acceptable distribution of income are more likely to avoid periods of destructive populist policy (see
Persson and Tabellini 1994 and Alesina and Rodrik 1994). They do not

have to distort market incentives and divert scarce government revenue into programs to favor the poor and the disadvantaged. Democratic countries with a highly unequal distribution of income or large numbers of poor are likely to face demands for redistribution and policies to achieve it that cannot be afforded. When populist governments respond to this demand, the result has been a fierce battle over income shares. In a market economy, these populist episodes have often led to hyperinflation.

In Argentina, Brazil, and Peru during the 1980s and in Chile in the early 1970s, government attempted to raise real wages and run large fiscal deficits, mainly to finance social and transfer programs helpful to the poor. In each case, the demand stimulus caused hyperinflation, recession, and a disastrous decline in well-being for everyone, particularly the poor. Latin American experience demonstrates that the enemy of sustainable growth has been populist governments' attempts to satisfy demands for greater equity. Countries smart enough or lucky enough to find a growth strategy in which benefits do trickle down will be able to avoid the problem of stop-and-go policy cycles caused by political pressures.

Capitalist economies can produce results so inequitable that any positive efficiencies from the market are more than offset by periodic bouts of populism. It should be government's role to find a way to get the benefits of market incentives and private sector efficiency while avoiding the destructive battles over distribution that are generated by inequitable growth. Social investments in education and health are two government policies that work in this regard. They enhance the efficiency of the private sector and raise the growth capacity of the economy while they improve the distribution of income.

There are other measures, such as early childhood programs and investments in backward regions, that the government can adopt to increase both productivity and distribution. What the government should not do is to tax the productive sector to make pure welfare transfers to the poor. If such programs are large enough to be significant, they are generally unsustainable, and they have often led to hyperinflation as well.

Evidence from Latin America on whether countries with more equitable distribution of income grow more rapidly is ambiguous. Costa Rica has a low level of inequality and has grown relatively rapidly. In contrast, Brazil and Mexico were able to grow rapidly for two decades, although they had two of the highest levels of income inequality in the world. Chile and Colombia performed very well in the 1980s, despite having high levels of inequality at the outset of the decade. Argentina and Uruguay grew slowly, although they had fairly equitable distributions and the best-educated labor forces in Latin America.

What Can Countries Do to Speed Up the Transition to a More Equitable Distribution?

Most Latin American countries are not yet at the transition stage. Their modern sectors are too small and their pools of unskilled labor are too large for there to be much hope that growth will be equalizing in the short run. The solution for them, obviously, is not to stop growing. Even in the absence of any complementary measures, growth, if it is fast enough, eventually will be accompanied by falling inequality.

Governments do not have to be passive bystanders in this process. They can speed up the transition from inequitable to equitable growth with policies aimed at changing the supply of unskilled and skilled labor relative to demand.

First, countries should choose a growth strategy that favors products that can be produced by the poor. Import substitution was a particularly poor strategy in this regard because it discriminated against agriculture and exports, both of which tend to engage unskilled labor. The import substitution strategy was reversed in the 1980s in favor of exports, and the favorable results of that change are already clear in many countries. During the 1980s, poverty and inequality declined in only four countries in Latin America (Colombia, Costa Rica, Paraguay, and Uruguay). Each had a large agricultural sector that grew rapidly, partly as a result of real devaluations during the period.

Second, countries should increase their commitment to education. Increasing education levels should do more than anything else to reduce the level of inequality in a society, since it increases the supply of skilled labor and raises labor productivity. It is the one government policy that simultaneously should increase the long-run growth rate and speed up the transition to the point where growth is equalizing. The experience of both Costa Rica and Chile is instructive and encouraging in this regard. Both countries have a relatively well-educated labor force or a good distribution of human capital. Both countries protected their commitment to education during their adjustments. And both acquired flexibility and an ability to develop new and promising export opportunities, thus facilitating rapid growth and rising real wages for those at the bottom of the labor pyramid.

Third, governments should implement meaningful land reform. As already noted, countries such as Colombia and Costa Rica have a large agricultural sector and a relatively equitable distribution of land. Not coincidentally, they also have an equitable distribution of income. The wage at the floor of the income pyramid is determined by the wage for day labor in agriculture. If most farmworkers are farm owners, that wage will have to be equal to what the worker could have earned farming his own land. The larger that minimum landownership is, the higher the floor is on the minimum wage. In the opposite case, where many farmworkers have no land, the minimum wage tends toward the subsistence level and landowners reap high profits.

In Latin American countries, land reform has been a politically explosive issue for decades. Short of war or revolution, these countries have found it exceptionally difficult to bring about a significant redistribution of land. Urban industrialization defused the demand for land by offering rural migrants better opportunities in the expanding urban sector. It is no accident that the most powerful demand for land reform in recent years has come from countries that were unable to provide an urban growth alternative.

Finally, in those countries that have a backward region with weak links to the modern sector, the government should develop a regionally targeted development strategy designed to deepen the interaction of the region with the rest of the economy so that future growth stimulates a greater production response in the backward region. Such a program will require investments in education and infrastructure, encouragement of the private sector, and the elimination of regional disincentives to investment.

2.3 Conclusions

The conclusion I draw is that the relationship between distributional equity and economic growth depends on the conditions in each country and the policies each government follows. A strategy of heavy investment in education and export promotion seems a good choice in all circumstances. It will reduce the supply of unskilled labor, improving equity and increasing the growth rate and the productivity of the economy. Another important point is that in many countries, structural factors and the educational profile of the labor force imply that growth will not be equalizing in the short run. Despite their best efforts, many countries will move up the Kuznets curve, at least in the short run. But that is only a transitional stage. Everyone will gain from the education-export strategy outlined in this chapter, even if the distribution of income does not seem to improve in the short run.

Notes

1. The Gini coefficient is a measure of inequality. It goes from zero for perfect equality in which each person has the same income, to one for maximum inequality in which one individual has all the income.

The household survey data on which this discussion is based are of variable quality. In all cases total income is substantially underreported, forcing some sort of adjustment. To make matters worse for those interested in income distribution, the underreporting of profits and interest income in larger than the underreporting of wages. The Economic Commission for Latin America and the Caribbean (ECLAC) made an attempt to correct for underreporting by comparing average profit and wage income with national accounts figures. The World Bank used the ECLAC adjustments in its estimates. Given this high degree of underreporting, one should take the Gini estimates as broad indicators of trends rather than exact estimates of the degree of inequality.

2. In developed countries, the profit share goes up in booms because of a tendency to stockpile labor during recessions that are expected to be temporary, and wages do not reflect cyclical changes in productivity.

3. For further evidence on the age-wage differential during the 1980s see Morley and Alvarez (1991, 1992a, 1992b) and Morley (1992).

4. Data on the labor share can be derived from the national accounts. Data are available for ten countries for the entire 1980–1990 period. The labor share falls in seven, rises slightly in Costa Rica and Panama, and rises by an improbably large amount in Uruguay. Unfortunately the labor share excludes the wages of the self-employed. For most countries, however, the data are consistent with the inequality trends shown in table 2.1. Where the labor share rose, as in Costa Rica and Uruguay, the distribution became more equal. Where it fell, as in Argentina, Mexico, Peru and Venezuela, inequality increased. See ECLAC, *Statistical Yearbook for Latin America and the Caribbean* (various years).

5. There is a wide divergence in real interest rates across countries in Latin America. The country that comes close to the hypothetical case described in the chapter is Brazil, where the real rate rose to over 65 percent for a short period in 1988. The real rate also rose in Bolivia, Costa Rica, and Mexico, because of both internal government deficits and capital outflows. Other countries such as Argentina, Uruguay, and Venezuela never had a significant positive real interest rate, at least according to the interest rate series reported over the decade.

References

Alesina, Alberto, and Dani Rodrik. 1994. "Distributive Policies and Economic Growth." *Quarterly Journal of Economics* 108:465–490.

Altimir, Oscar. 1992a. "Crecimiento, distribución del ingreso y pobreza en América Latina: algunos hechos estilizados." Mimeo. Washington, D.C.: Inter-American Development Bank.

Altimir, Oscal. 1992b. "Cambios en las Desigualdades de Ingreso y en la Pobreza en América Latina." Mimeo.

Altimir, Oscal. "Income Distribution and Poverty Through Crisis and Adjustment." 1994. *ECLAC Review* 52 (December): 7–31.

Altimir, Oscal. N.d. "Latin American Poverty in the Last Two Decades." Mimeo. Santiago, Chile. Economic Commission for Latin America and the Caribbean.

Anand, Sudhir, and S. M. R. Kanbur. 1993. "Inequality and Development." *Journal of Development Economics* 41:19–45.

Birdsall, Nancy, David Ross, and Richard Sabot. 1995. "Inequality as a Constraint on Growth in Latin America." In David Turnham, Colm Foy, and Guillermo Larrain, eds., *Social Tensions, Job Creation and Economic Policy in Latin America.* Paris: OECD.

Chenery, Hollis. 1974. *Redistribution with Growth: Policies to Improve Income Distribution in Developing Countries in the Context of Growth.* London: Oxford University Press.

Economic Commission for Latin America and the Caribbean (ECLAC). 1990. "Magnitud de la pobreza en América Latina en los años ochenta." Santiago, Chile: ECLAC. Mimeo. May.

Economic Commission for Latin America and the Caribbean. 1992. "Latin American Poverty Profiles for the Early 1990s." LC/L 716. Santiago, Chile: ECLAC.

Economic Commission for Latin America and the Caribbean. 1993. *Panorama Social de América Latina: Edición 1993.* LC/G 1768. Santiago, Chile: ECLAC.

Fishlow, Albert. 1995. "Inequality, Poverty and Growth: Where Do We Stand?" Paper prepared for Annual World Bank Conference on Development Economics, May.

Fiszbein, Ariel. 1989. "An Analysis of the Size Distribution of Income in Argentina, 1974–1988." Ph.D. dissertation, University of California.

Gindling, T. H., and A. Berry. 1992. "The Performance of the Labor Market During Recession and Structural Adjustment: Costa Rica in the 1980s." *World Development* 20:1599–1617.

Grupo de Aná lisis para el Desarrollo (GRADE). 1992. "Gestión Pública y Distribución de Ingresos: Tres Estudios de Caso para la Economía Peruana." Mimeo.: GRADE, January.

Márquez, Gustavo, Joyita Mukherjee, Juan Carlos Navarro, Rosa Amelia González, Robert Palacios, and Roberto Rigobon. 1993. "Fiscal Policy and Income Distribution in Venezuela." In Ricardo Hausmann and Roberto Rigobon, eds., *Government Spending and Income Distribution in Latin America.* Washington, D.C.: Inter-American Development Bank.

Mckinley, Terry, and Diana Alarcón González. 1994. "Widening Wage Dispersion Under Structural Adjustment in Mexico." Paper presented at Conference on the Impact of Structural Adjustment on Labor Markets, San Jose, California, September.

Morley, Samuel A. 1992. *Policy, Structure and the Reduction of Poverty in Colombia: 1980–89.* Working Paper no. 126. Washington, D.C.: Inter-American Development Bank, June.

Morley, Samuel A. 1994. *Poverty and Distribution in Latin America: Evidence from the Past, Prospects for the Future.* Washington, D.C.: Overseas Development Council.

Morley, Samuel A., and C. Alvarez. 1991. *Recession and the Growth of Poverty in Argentina.* Working paper no. 125. Washington, D.C.: Inter-American Development Bank.

Morley, Samuel A., and C. Alvarez. 1991. *Poverty and Adjustment in Costa Rica.* Working Paper no. 123. Washington, D.C.: Inter-American Development Bank.

Morley, Samuel A., and C. Alvarez. 1992b. *Poverty and Adjustment in Venezuela.* Working Paper no. 124. Washington, D.C.: Inter-American Development Bank.

Mújica, Patricio, and Osvaldo Larrañaga. 1992. "Políticas Sociales y Distribución del Ingreso en Chile." Mimeo. January. Santiago, Chile: Instituto Latino Americano de Doctrina, Estudios Sociale (ILADES).

Paes de Barros, Ricardo, Rosane Mendonca, Lauro Ramos, and Sonia Rocha. 1992. "Welfare, Inequality, Poverty and Social Conditions in Brazil over the Last Three Decades." Mimeo. Washington, D.C.: Brookings.

Pardo, Lucia V., Felipe Balmaceda M., and Ignacio Irarrazaval Llona. "Pobreza, Crecimiento y Políticas Sociales." In *Comentarios sobre la Situación Económica 1992, Taller de Coyuntura*, pp. 139–170. University of Chile. Santiago, Chile.

Persson, Torsten, and Guido Tabellini. 1994. "Is Inequality Harmful for Growth?" *American Economic Review* 84:600–622.

Psacharopoulos, George, Samuel Morley, Ariel Fiszbein, Haeduck Lee, and Bill Wood. 1993. *Poverty and Income Distribution in Latin America: The Story of the 1980s.* Human Resources Report no. 27. Washington, D.C.: World Bank.

Psacharopoulos, George, and Harry Antonio Patrinos. 1994. *Indigenous People and Poverty in Latin America.* Washington, D.C.: World Bank.

World Bank. 1991. *Guatemala: Country Economic Memorandum.* Report no. 9378-GU. Washington, D.C.: World Bank.

3

The Role of Government in the Contemporary World

Joseph E. Stiglitz

Since the mid-1980s, the world has seen dramatic change: from the end of the cold war and the collapse of the command and control systems, to increasing unemployment in Europe and increasing inequality in the United States.[1] Corresponding to these changes are changes in intellectual perspectives: the demise of the socialist and planning paradigms as alternatives to the market or mixed economy. The East Asia miracle firmly established that rapid development is possible, but whether it has served more to buttress the free market approach or the managed market approach remains a subject of controversy.[2] There are other changes as well: an increased awareness of the importance of environmental considerations and the limitations of the global resource base; a globalization of the world economy, associated with more extensive international trade; more rapid diffusion of technology; and larger international movements of capital.

In the face of all this change, some things remain unchanged. Even with increases in average per capita incomes, poverty rates remain high, and in some countries they are increasing; even with a cleaer understanding of market economies, at least periodically, many governments have been unable to sustain high levels of employment, and many countries face high inflation.

In the light of all of these changes, there is an increasing demand throughout the world for a reexamination of the role of government. Within many countries, including the United States, there are great debates not only about the appropriate scope of government but how government should carry out its activities and at what level—federal (national), state (provincial), or local—they should be carried out.

In this chapter, I outline some answers to the questions of the appropriate economic role of government, based on both modern economic theory and recent historical experiences.[3] The principal theses can be summarized as follows:

• Government has a distinctive role to play in the economy in promoting performance at both the macroeconomic and microeconomic levels. Markets are the best way of organizing the production and dissemination of goods and services, but there are important instances where they fail to produce efficient outcomes. Many of the most successful examples of development, however, have entailed governments' responding to these failures not by replacing markets but by working with them, complementing them, and even helping to create them.

• Government has an important role in promoting equity, but modern views emphasize the importance of individual responsibility in an environment that ensures economic opportunity to provide resources and opportunities. Appropriately designed policies, such as those promoting education and training, can increase equity at the same time that they promote economic efficiency; there need not be a trade-off. And indeed the countries of East Asia have shown that equalization policies that promote equality can be growth enhancing.

• Changes in economic circumstances (technology) necessitate changes in the role of government.[4]

• Not only what the government does has to be reexamined, but so too how it does it. Recent attempts within the United States to "reinvent government" provide striking examples of how government can be made more effective in promoting not only efficiency (correcting market failures) but also equity.

• Among the major lessons derived from the experience of the economies in transition are that government has an essential role in establishing and maintaining the institutional (including legal) infrastructure that market economies require to function effectively and that systemic transformation—including establishing this institutional infrastructure—places heavy demands on public policy.

• While market failures are more prevalent in less developed countries, government's ability to remedy these failures may be more circumscribed. Both what the government does and how it does it must be carefully tailored to prevent abuses, such as those commonly associated with rent seeking. Reforms in the ways in which government conducts its business can improve its efficiency and its efficacy.

The topic of this chapter is a vast one, with a large literature extending over a long period of time. Rather than provide a summary of this literature, I have chosen to focus on what some of the more salient recent developments in how this question—one of the oldest facing any society —is approached. There have been marked changes in views of the role of the government in the past quarter-century. Some were driven by changes in the world (the changes to which I referred earlier, including the end of the cold war, the success of the countries of East Asia, changes in technology that reduced transportation and communication costs and led to the globalization of the economy), some were driven by changes in our understanding of the world (such as the circumstances under which markets produce efficient outcomes), and some were driven by changes in values (which themselves may be affected by changes in the world and how we come to understand it).

The factors that are at play in one country may be markedly different from those in another. Given differences across time and over countries in both trade-offs and values, it is not surprising that views about the appropriate role of government should change over time and differ across countries. Thus, my task here is not to provide a simple answer to the question of what should be the role of government, applicable to all countries and for all times, but rather to provide a framework that may be useful in approaching that question. That framework leads me to certain conclusions concerning the role of government in the United States, and I frequently illustrate my analysis with examples drawn from the United States, because I have focused so much of my attention on this issue recently. At the same time, differences in values in empirical judgments about the magnitude of the trade-offs may lead one to quite different conclusions.[5]

3.1 The Interaction Between Government and Markets

Although the jargon of economics has increasingly entered into political discourse, there still remains a large gulf between popular discussions of the role of government and technical discussions within the economics profession. To be sure, there is some parallel of topics covered—education, health, research, the environment, and others. Popular discussions focus on some observed deficiency in the world, such as inadequate education opportunities, the health of the poor, or the slow pace of innovation. In the past, the presumption was that these inadequacies of the market economy could be remedied by appropriate government action. Technical discussions, on the other hand, begin by asking why the market does not yield efficient outcomes. Is there any reason to believe that the government can remedy these seeming failures? Or, on the contrary, are there reasons to believe that government might actually make matters worse?

Since at least the 1950s, the point of departure has been the fundamental theorems of welfare economics, the formal articulation of Adam Smith's invisible hand theorem: *Markets provide an efficient allocation of resources, provided certain basic conditions are satisfied.* Thus, analytic discussions begin with identifying circumstances when those conditions are not satisfied.

Traditional Market Failures

Traditional discussions focused on three market failures, that is, three circumstances in which government action was required if the economy was to be (Pareto) efficient.

Public Goods   The most obvious was public goods, such as national defense.[6] In the absence of public provision, there will be an undersupply —or no supply—of these goods.

Goods with Externalities   These are the goods for which the benefits or costs are not fully received or are borne by those purchasing the good. Markets provide too little of some goods—those for which there are positive externalities (spillovers), such as research and development—and too much of other goods—those for which there are negative externalities, like air and water pollution. In the former area, government has long recognized its responsibilities. The beginning of the telecommunications industry, for example, can be traced back to U.S. government support of the first telegraph line between Washington, D.C., and Baltimore in 1842, and the enormous increase in agricultural productivity in the United States can be traced to the federally supported program of research and extension services, dating to the Morrill Act of 1863. And while economists from Francis Edgeworth and A. C. Pigou onward wrote about the imperative of government intervention to correct pollution and congestion externalities, it has only been in the last quarter-century—when these market failures could no longer be ignored, as air in many major cities became unbreathable and as rivers and lakes became so polluted that no species could survive in them—that governments undertook strong actions to remedy them. Although there is an ongoing debate about the most effective way of addressing these externalities, there are few who seriously question that government should do something.

To be sure, there are some circumstances in which individuals can, in the absence of government intervention, arrive at an efficient solution, *provided government assigns property rights clearly and enforces those property rights.* This was one of Coase's (1960) major insights. But it is now recognized that those circumstances are highly circumscribed, for example, entailing strong and unrealistic assumptions concerning information about preferences of individuals.[7] Moreover, Coasian bargaining may entail large transactions costs, making governmental solutions (Pigouvian taxes) preferable.

Competition   Markets provide efficient resource allocations if there is perfect competition, but competition is seldom perfect in the way envisaged in the fundamental theorems of welfare economics, and in some cases, it is very imperfect or even absent. Adam Smith recognized the proclivity of those engaged in the same business or trade to conspire to raise prices at the expense of consumers. Firms may more greatly increase their profits by trying to reduce the degree of competition than by producing goods more efficiently. Government policies to increase competition—both structural policies that inhibit competition-reducing mergers and policies aimed at reducing restrictive and collusive practices—not only strengthen the efficiency and innovativeness of the economy but ensure that the benefits are passed on to consumers in the form of lower prices.[8]

In some areas—natural monopolies—there are sufficient returns to scale that competition is not viable. Here, government regulation or ownership is required for efficiency.

The thinking about competition policy has gone through three revolutions since the mid-1970s. The first suggested a much more circumscribed role for government. The contestability doctrine, for instance, argued that so long as there was potential competition, there did not have to be actual competition. If any firm charged a price higher-than-average cost, a new entrant would enter and steal its customers. Airlines were given as the classic example. There might be only one airline flying a given route, but if it charged more than average cost, a potential competitor would divert its planes and pick up the passengers. The "Chicago" school (Posner) not only argued that market dominance was not a problem—so long as there was *potential* competition—it also contended that restrictive practices (such as vertical restraints) were efficiency enhancing and would not survive otherwise.

The second revolution not only overturned these doctrines; it suggested that competition may be even more fragile than had previously been thought. For instance, theory and evidence cast doubt on the contestability of this doctrine. If there are even epsilon sunk costs, it has been shown that an incumbent can maintain his monopoly position, and furthermore, resources may be wasted in the attempt to preempt entry (Stiglitz 1981). The long periods during which airline prices in markets with limited actual competition remain substantially above average costs serve to corroborate these theoretical views (Borenstein 1992). Similarly, a vast literature has shown that vertical restraints may not only effectively reduce competition, they may even reduce economic efficiency (Rey and Stiglitz 1995).

Today the contestability doctrine cannot be regarded as grounds for government to ignore its responsibilities to ensure a competitive environment. But it has become increasingly clear that there is more scope for actual competition than regulators (and economists) had previously recognized. This was the third revolution. There are large parts of the telecommunications and electricity generating industry in which competition is viable.[9] There is still an important role for government: making sure that the remaining elements of monopoly or near monopoly (such as the last mile of telephone service) are not leveraged. And indeed, in the United States, courts were convinced that the variety of devices by which those in control of the last mile might be able to do so were so vast and complicated that regulation itself could not adequately cope with the problem, and structural separation was required.[10]

There is another important change: The remarkable reduction in transportation costs and other barriers to trade has led to larger markets. As the size of the market has increased, even when there are some increasing returns, there are more viable competitors. Thus, as countries open up their economies to competition from abroad, the ability of large domestic firms to exercise market power may be circumscribed, and the role of government competition authorities may be lessened.

The New Market Failures
More recently, attention has centered on two other market failures, which are more pervasive but for which the government response is frequently less clear. Often hidden in discussions of the fundamental theorem of welfare economics are the assumptions of a complete set of markets and of perfect information (or, more accurate, that information is not affected by any action which any agent can take.) The Greenwald-Stiglitz theorem

essentially established that whenever markets were incomplete or information imperfect (essentially always), the economy was not constrained Pareto optimal (where the term *constrained Pareto optimal* serves simply as a reminder that the costs of information and of establishing markets have been taken into account in the analysis in establishing that there are government interventions that can make some individuals better off without making anyone else worse off). While the fundamental theorem of welfare economics established a presumption that markets were efficient—and that when markets failed, there were well-identified, targeted interventions, largely using market mechanisms, which could remedy the failure—the Greenwald-Stiglitz theorem reversed that presumption. It showed that the Arrow-Debreu analysis of competitive economies was not robust; introducing even a slight degree of information imperfection fundamentally altered conclusions. The theorem, however, was too strong, for it provided too little guidance for what the government should do. The pervasiveness of market failures made it clear that government could not correct every failure, and it seldom had sufficient statistical knowledge concerning the structure of the economy to know with precision what it should do (even if we were to ignore the political economy issues, to be discussed below). It did, however, provide the intellectual basis for the pragmatic approach to the role of the state in economic policy, in which, when assessing the appropriate role of the state, the strengths and weaknesses of the public and private sectors are balanced, in the light of actual institutional arrangements within each. Before discussing this approach in greater detail, I want to note several instances of government policy aimed directly at remedying the market failures of incomplete markets and imperfections of information.

Absence of Markets   There are many missing markets, and the absence of markets often provides an important rationale for government action. The absence of a student loan market provided the motivation for the establishment of student loan programs. (In many countries, the response to the absence of educational opportunities was more sweeping: providing free higher education.) This is an example of where the economists' approach tends to be distinctive: Economists try to tailor the solution narrowly to the market failure. In this case, the market failure is an imperfection of the capital market, and hence the solution is improved access to capital markets.

Although the absence of risk and capital markets provides perhaps the most widespread context for governments to "correct" missing markets

—from the securitization of mortgages in the United State, to the establishment of long-term lending institutions in many developing countries, to the provision of a range of social insurance in almost all advanced industrialized economies—there are other "missing markets," which give rise to the often-noted problem of coordination failures: intermediate goods that are not developed because there is no demand for their output and industries that would use the intermediate goods but do not develop for lack of availability of these crucial inputs. (If there were a complete set of markets, prices would be such in equilibrium that intermediate goods would be produced, and the industries that used those intermediate goods would be established.) Indicative planning represented a by and large unsuccessful attempt by government to provide the information that a more complete set of futures markets would have given.[11]

Careful studies of the role of government in addressing the problem of missing markets try to push the analysis back a step by asking why a market is absent. Sometimes the answer is simple: Market "failures" often lead to insufficient innovation, including "market" innovations, government can perform an entrepreneurial role in creating a market,[12] and once the market is created, it functions well on its own. This appears to be the case for the market for securitized mortgages. In other cases, there are adverse selection and moral hazard problems, which inhibit the creation of a viable market. In these cases, government needs to be attentive to these problems, but it is still the case that the nature of the problem facing the government can be markedly different from that facing the private sector.[13]

Imperfect Information   Imperfect information gives rise to moral hazard and adverse selection problems, which themselves have strong consequences for the performance of labor, capital, and product markets. But there are a number of situations where imperfections of information provide the direct rationale for government action. Firms on their own might have inadequate incentive to disclose the health and safety consequences of their products or their workplaces. They might, for instance, use toxic pesticides that increase agricultural productivity but at the same time increase the incidence of cancer among both agricultural workers and consumers. Health and safety, like the environment, are important, though often unmeasured, aspects of our standard of living.

Arenas with Multiple Market Failures

Many of the arenas in which government has been most active are marked by multiple market failures (combined, in many cases, with concerns about income distribution). Here, I focus on four of the more important.

Macroeconomics   Of all the failures of the market, none is more important in its economic and social consequences than the macroeconomic failures: the periodic failures of the economy to utilize its resources fully, often on a massive scale, such as during the Great Depression. Markets by themselves do not necessarily ensure full employment, and it is now widely recognized that macroeconomic policy can contribute to stability. Although the reasons for these massive market failures remain a source of dispute, there is increasing consensus that they are related to one or more of the market failures already described (e.g., absence of futures markets, imperfections of capital markets).[14]

Technological Change   The fundamental theorems of welfare economics began with the assumption of a given technology. Yet the essence of development is the transformation of an economy, including the absorption of more advanced technology. And within developed countries, the defining characteristic of modern capitalist economies is technological change, as Schumpeter (1942) emphasized so forcefully. But there are reasons to believe that the market by itself will underinvest in research, particularly basic research. Basic research has both of the essential properties of a pure public good, but even much of so-called applied research has significant externalities. The developers of the laser and transistor reaped but a small fraction of the total benefits that have accrued to society as a result of their innovations. Thus, the debate over whether the government should support technology—suggesting that the government is not as well placed for picking winners as the private sector—is focused on the wrong issue. Government has a role in technology not because of its superior ability to pick winners but because in many areas there are large spillovers, and without government support, there will be underinvestment in those areas.

Financial Markets   Throughout the world, financial institutions have exhibited enormous fragility; their failure not only causes economic disruption and misery in the lives of the affected individuals, but the resulting lack of confidence in financial institutions can impede the functioning of this sector of the economy, and thus the efficient allocation of scarce capital resources. Regulation of financial institutions to strengthen their safety and soundness can increase the effectiveness of this vital sector of the economy, and today most governments assume this responsibility. (The failure of this sector to perform on its own in an ideal way can be related to several of the market failures already discussed. Imperfections of information and free rider problems lead to imperfect monitoring. Banks cannot divest themselves of some of the risks, including macroeconomic risks, which often are important factors contributing to their failure. For a fuller discussion, see Stiglitz 1993.)

Growth Governments everywhere are concerned with economic growth, not because it is an end in itself but because it is necessary to attain other, more fundamental objectives, such as increasing living standards and alleviating poverty. And all of the arenas described earlier (as well as several to which I turn shortly, such as education) have profound effects on long-term economic growth. Well-designed financial markets can increase the mobilization of capital and the efficiency with which it is allocated, increased expenditures on education raise the pace of human capital formation, and government support of research and technology increases the pace of technological change. These three factors (human and physical capital accumulation and technological change) represent the main sources of economic growth. [15]

3.2 Equity

Equity has long been a major concern of government policy. Even well-functioning market economies may yield outcomes in which large proportions of the population live in poverty. The first fundamental theorem of welfare economics only ensured the Pareto efficiency of the economy; it said nothing about the desirability of the distribution of income (welfare) that emerged from market processes. (The second fundamental theorem did, however, argue that if one disliked the distribution of income, there was a simple way to correct the problem: lump-sum redistribution of endowments. Market mechanisms could then be resorted to, to ensure the efficiency of outcomes.)[16] In virtually all countries today, government assumes some responsibility for redistribution. But what it does, and both popular and economists' perceptions of what it ought to do, have changed markedly.

Equity-Efficiency Trade-off
Earlier discussions focused on the trade-off between equity and efficiency. The East Asia miracle has called into question these traditional views.[17]

Recent studies show not only that they were able to attain rapid rates of growth while maintaining relatively high levels of equity but even suggest that their egalitarian policies may have played an important role in boosting their growth rates. Appropriately designed egalitarian policies may also promote political and economic stability and social cohesion, societal attributes which are conducive to economic growth. (At the microeconomic level, a sense of fairness within the firm can elicit greater effort and worker efficiency.) [18]

Policies Promoting Economic Efficiency and Equity
One of the other reasons that egalitarian policies may be efficiency enhancing is that the burden of some market failures is not felt uniformly across the population.

Education   Capital market failures may have an impact on poor individuals more than richer ones. Education represents one arena in which today all governments take on a responsibility, one that simultaneously promotes equity and efficiency.[19] Indeed, governments have played a large role in education for a long time. (In the United States, the Northwest Ordinances of 1785 and 1787 committed the government to support education, devoting the revenues of the sales of certain lands to that purpose.)

Among societies' most valuable resources are its human resources. But imperfections in capital markets mean that many poorer people will not be able to invest in themselves or their children at an efficient level. (Appropriability problems also imply that firms will have insufficient incentives to invest in the training of their workers.) Policies that improve the accessibility of education to all can thus both lessen inequality and promote overall economic growth and efficiency.

Health   Health has come to be viewed as a public responsibility much more recently than education has. Again, the main motivation may be equity, as reflected in the concept of specific egalitarianism (Tobin 1970) holding, in this case, that the right to live should not be subjected to the dictate of the marketplace. Still, there is evidence galore of market failures. With third parties paying for much of health care, consumers have little incentive to conserve on resources. And information problems are legion; after all, one of the things that consumers are buying is the physician's information, with the buyer having to rely extensively on the seller's judgment about the returns to different expenditures.

Social Insurance
Much of what falls under the rubric of equity policies should really be
thought of as policies to improve living standards far more broadly. This
is particularly true of programs referred to as social insurance. Individuals
are risk averse. Reducing the risks or the impacts of the risks is an important component in raising living standards. Unfortunately, markets have,
at least in the past, failed to provide (or have provided only at high cost)
insurance against many of the most important risks individuals face. These
market failures explain at least in part the role of government in providing
unemployment insurance, disability insurance, health insurance (particularly for the aged), and annuities.[20] More broadly, downward economic
mobility in modern societies is sufficiently great that a significant fraction
of the population ends up availing itself of the safety net.[21] To put it still
another way, individuals value economic security, security is an important
aspect of living standards, and government programs can do, and have
done, much to improve economic security, though there is more that
could be done. There are indirect benefits as well: Increasing the capacity
to accept and absorb risk can increase overall output and efficiency.

3.3   Reinventing Government: Efficiency

Recent experiences have made us increasingly aware of the limitations of
government, as well as its strengths. To some extent, these perceptions of
limitations are an outgrowth of excessive expectations. Government may
not be able, for instance, to eliminate cyclical fluctuations in the economy;
nevertheless, it may be successful in moderating them.[22] And government
may not be able to eliminate poverty, but it can reduce it, or at least mitigate its worst manifestations.[23]

Some of these limitations are, or may be, a reflection of inherent
properties of government or the way it has been traditionally organized. Inherent limitations arise from the fact that government has both
limited information about and control over the private sector. Other inherent limitations arise from constraints on government imposed to ensure
that it does not abuse its powers and its inability to make long-term
commitments.[24]

Improving Government by Increasing Competition
Although some of the inefficiency of government may be an outgrowth
of the inherent problems already described, government can be designed
in such a way as to increase the likelihood of efficiency.

Traditionally, government enterprises face little competition. Competition forces firms to be both efficient and responsive to their customers; the absence of competition in the public sector often results in a lack of efficiency and customer responsiveness.[25] In some contexts, competition can be fostered, even within the public sector, at relatively little cost.

Improving Government by Increasing Incentives

In some countries, government bureaucracies pursue objectives more related to the interests of the bureaucrats (a manifestation of the principal-agent problem) or the special interests that have captured them than to a broader conception of national interests (such as addressing the problems discussed in the previous two sections.) Of course, large enterprises too face problems in controlling their bureaucracies.[26] Part of the process of reinventing government has been the application of the lessons learned within the private sector to the public sector by making government more customer driven and performance oriented. Too often public organizations focus on intermediate objectives rather than ultimate goals, and in doing so they may actually impede the attainment of those ultimate goals. Enforcement agencies, for example, may count the number of cases tried, but the ultimate goal is legal compliance, and the manner in which enforcement actions are brought may actually impede compliance.

Other Examples of Market Mechanisms

Although market mechanisms do not work in many of the areas where government is active (that is why the government is in that area), government nevertheless can make more extensive use of market mechanisms. For instance, some government action is required to reduce pollution; rather than employing command and control mechanisms, government can employ systems of tradable permits and pollution taxes, which can attain pollution abatement in a more efficient manner. Private markets may not provide adequate safety or health standards on their own, but bonded and certified private auditing agencies may be substituted for direct government inspection.

Every area of government activity needs to be looked at from the perspective of whether efficiency can be increased. Consider the issue of procurement. We used to think that the best way of ensuring that the taxpayer was not cheated was to have a competitive bidding process. But to have a fair bidding process, one has to specify precisely what is being bid on. Even a fairly simple commodity, like a T-shirt, may require pages upon pages of specifications. Compliance with bidding regulations was so difficult that there were relatively few bidders in many cases. Buying off-the-shelf items—relying, in effect, on the market mechanism, where reputation and competition ensure that prices are in line with quality—may actually save government substantial sums of money.

Privatization and Corporatization

The issue of what government finances versus what it produces also needs to be reexamined. Discussions since the early 1980s have produced the mantra of privatization: The government should produce as little as possible. Even when there is a natural monopoly, private ownership combined with regulation is preferable to government ownership. Without disputing the overall tenor of that conclusion, there are two general observations. First, in the absence of effective government regulation, when privatization results in a monopoly, there is no presumption that resources will be efficiently allocated overall, since (especially when the good produced is an intermediate good) the monopolist will charge an excessively high price. Second, in the absence of competition, there is not even an assurance that the privatized enterprise will be efficient, particularly when privatization means the sale of a state-owned enterprise to the president's cousin. With competition, even a government enterprise may be efficient (as evidenced by the experience with Canadian railroads).[27] There is, in fact, no general theorem assuring us that privatization is welfare enhancing.[28]

(There has been a similar mantra concerning deregulation. Most of those discussions completely ignore the underlying problems, which provide the rationale for government action. For instance, there is a legitimate issue concerning the extent to which safety should be ensured by reputation and disclosure (whether voluntary or involuntary) mechanisms; tort actions, which focus, ex post, on consequences; or regulation. Ironically, some participants in the recent debates seem to want to reduce the effectiveness of both liability and regulatory mechanisms.)

3.4   Reinventing Government: Equity

Some of the changes that I alluded to in the beginning of this chapter have necessitated a reexamination of the role of government in redistribution. The renewed interest in equity issues within both the academic and political worlds is in part a consequence of all three changes discussed: changes in the world, changes in our perceptions, and changes in values. We have already examined one aspect of the changed perceptions:

The view that there *necessarily* is a trade-off between efficiency and equity, or within the developing countries, between growth and equity, has been discredited, both theoretically and by the East Asia experience. Earlier views emphasized the role of physical capital as opposed to human capital and assumed that rich individuals have a higher saving rate than poor and that these saving rates are immutable. The East Asia experience shows that human capital is at least as important as physical capital, saving rates can be changed, and even poor individuals can save at very high rates.

Changed Circumstances: The Increase in Inequality
Not only has the trade-off changed, but the point from which we begin the analysis has changed significantly. Inequality in the United States (and some other countries) has increased markedly over the past quarter-century.

Research within the United States strongly suggests that the reasons for the increased inequality are multiple and lie largely with factors like technology, beyond the direct purview of government.[29] However, critics of existing redistributive programs who contend that they have been ineffective in reducing poverty do not ask the appropriate counterfactual: But for these programs, what would have been the incidence of poverty? For the United States, studies show that existing programs have a marked positive effect and that the weakening of union power (partly as a result of a changed legal climate) and the declining real value of the minimum wage may have contributed substantially to the increase in inequality. Nonetheless, there is little doubt that government programs have failed to address adequately the underlying fundamental problems, which relate to resources and incentives.

Changes in technologies have increased the skill premium. Real wages of low-skilled workers have actually decreased in the United States.[30] In a world of perfect markets, there would be a self-correcting mechanism, the increased wage differential would provide incentives for more individuals to acquire the requisite skill. As more acquired these skills, wages of skilled workers would fall relative to those of unskilled workers, until the wage differential just compensated for the cost of obtaining the requisite skills for the marginal individual. Given the distribution of abilities (at acquiring the skills valued highly by the market) across the population, even after adjustment, there may be increased inequality, but less than at the current time. But the irony is that just at the time when obtaining skills is more important, the ability to afford the skills is reduced; real incomes at the bottom have declined. The consequence for the United

States is the possibility of the poor remaining in poverty longer. With lower real incomes, increased real tuition, and declining real government assistance to students, there has been an increase in the disparity in enrollment rates between children from poor and rich families.[31] Society is becoming even more fragmented. Government has a vital role to ensure access to education, which will contribute to both equity and economic efficiency.

Changed Perspectives

Earlier literature emphasizing the role of government in redistribution took the pretax distribution of income as given. The new emphasis is on how government can change the pretax distribution of income. Such policies, which include improving education and job training opportunities for the poor, boost economic efficiency in two ways: through the direct effect of ensuring that all individuals live up to their full economic potential and through the indirect effect of a reduced burden on redistributive taxation.[32]

Government has other instruments to change the pretax distribution of income; one of the more controversial is the minimum wage. Recent econometric evidence and economic theory suggest that the minimum wage, provided it is not set too high, can have positive employment, equity, and efficiency effects.[33]

The earned income tax credit, which was greatly expanded in 1993, has as its objective ensuring that all individuals who work full time, even at the minimum wage, attain a level of income sufficient to raise the family above the poverty level. The credit increases the return to workers who are participating in the labor force ("making work pay") but does not increase the employer's cost of labor.[34]

Changing Perspectives: The Increased Stress on Opportunity and Individual Responsibility

In going from the pretax to the posttax situation, economists have long discussed the importance of incentives. In current popular discussions, the economists' concept of incentives is translated into that of individual responsibility,[35] and the key issue is how to combine individual responsibility with social justice.[36]

In current analytic discussions, the focus has shifted from evaluating outcomes to evaluating opportunities. If identical twins are afforded identical opportunities, and one chooses a life of leisure and low income and the other a life of hard work and high income, there is today widespread sentiment that the government should not redistribute income from the richer brother to the poorer. Both had the same opportunities but made different choices. (To be sure, one could argue at a philosophical level that the brother who chose the life of leisure lacked an "endowment" for hard work, but treating individual preferences as part of endowments represents a fundamental shift in the traditional way economists have approached normative issues.)

Although we can never observe each individual's opportunity set, in practice the focus on opportunities translates into a greater focus on the transition matrix describing the evolution of incomes over time (across generations). A society in which children of poor parents almost surely end up poor themselves is viewed to be unjust in a fundamental sense.[37]

In the current view, society should provide individuals with the opportunities and resources with which they can attain a decent standard of living—provided they exercise individual responsibility. Government should make sure that all individuals have access to educational opportunities (resources) to develop fully their capabilities. When workers are displaced from their existing job, government can provide information and transitional assistance to facilitate the movement to a new job.[38] In the end, however, responsibility rests with the individual to make the best of these opportunities.

This leaves three problems. First, what should happen to those who, for one reason or another, fail to avail themselves of these opportunities? Judgments about how this question should be answered are likely to vary across countries and over time. Today I sense that the prevailing mood is predicated on the belief that there are limits to government's responsibility. What is at issue is not just possible adverse incentive effects but fundamental moral judgments.[39] (A more subtle but related issue concerns those whose "upbringing" results in a predilection not to seize opportunities that are offered. To what extent should government be responsible for inequities in society that give rise to differences in patterns of preferences? Such predilections could result in transition matrices with low levels of mobility, even if government provided equal educational opportunities or went still further and provided poorer individuals with extra educational opportunities to compensate for differences in home educational background.)

This brings us to the second major problem: To what extent should children be made to suffer for the failure of their parents to exercise their responsibilities? Here there seems to be a growing consensus that government should take on a larger role in forcing parents to live up to their individual responsibility.[40]

The third problem is what should happen to those who, through no fault of their own, even were they to avail themselves of all the opportunities, simply lack the ability (perhaps because they are disabled) to sustain employment, even at the minimum wage. Here I believe that compassion dictates that society provide a certain minimal standard.[41] Yet a problem has arisen in many societies that many claim that they are disabled (in this sense) who probably are not. Modern technology has again markedly changed the nature of the problem. With technology, many individuals can overcome their disabilities, for example, by compensating for lack of sight or hearing. Too many countries have viewed disability as a dichotomous variable: One is either able to work or not. With appropriate resources, individuals can be made productive members of the labor force. Policies need to be designed to provide both resources and incentives.[42]

3.5   Transition Economies and Developing Countries

Special issues are raised by economies in transition from socialism and the market and developing economies.

Transition Economies

In most countries, market economies have evolved gradually over time, but in transition economies, there is an attempt to put a market economy into place virtually overnight. These economies have thus challenged our basic understanding of how market economies function,[43] and each country has had to ask: What should be the role of government?

Reform efforts, at least in their initial stages, emphasized the need to reduce the role of government and shrink the state sector. What was not originally appreciated is the heavy burden that transition places on the state, and not only in carrying out policies such as privatization.

Reform efforts, in particular, have made clear the importance of the underlying legal infrastructure, which we all too often take for granted: the set of laws that enforce contract enforceability, provide for bankruptcy, ensure fair and effective competition, and ensure the protection of private property. Contract enforceability is particularly important for capital markets, and without capital markets, long-term investments and the agglomeration of capital are greatly circumscribed. (The absence of contract enforceability shows up in less developed economies in part as a heavy dependence on earnings from commerce, as opposed to manufacturing, and on family-based organizations.)

The problems facing the economies in transition have also highlighted the importance of other aspects of our institutional infrastructure, including the financial institutions (and the requisite government supervision) that enable financial markets to allocate scarce capital efficiently and monitor its use effectively and the fiscal administration, particularly tax collection, without which government cannot effectively function.

These countries are in the position of needing to strengthen government in these areas at the same time that they make it less pervasive and intrusive in others.

Developing Countries

The modern theory assessing the economic role of government recognizes both the strengths and limitations of markets, as well as those of the public sector. Almost by definition, "market failures" are more pervasive in the less developed economies. One of the ways that these economies are less developed is that certain markets (e.g., financial markets) typically are less developed. This by itself might suggest a wider role for government, but at the same time, the limitations on government may also be more pronounced. It is ambiguous whether, on balance, government should have a more or less circumscribed role. But what the government does and how it does it have to be examined in light of the country's particular capacities in the public sector and market development in the private.

There may not be general answers, but certain aspects merit comment. In the case of many countries, particularly those of East Asia, governments played an instrumental role in promoting economic growth.[44] For instance, they helped create financial markets and institutions, promoted exports and the absorption of advanced technology, promoted education and provided essential infrastructure, and played an entrepreneurial role in economic situations where there seemed to be a dearth of private entrepreneurs.

In other countries, government efforts have been less effective or even, apparently, counterproductive. Government has certain powers that private (voluntary) organizations do not, including powers of compulsion and taxation. Those powers can be and often are abused, promoting special interests at the expense of the general interest. Economists have focused on the concept of rent seeking, and while some of the rents represent simply transfer payments, the distortions induced into the economy represent sizable economic losses, which less developed countries can ill afford. Economic reform and transformation programs must consider measures to address rent seeking and corruption. For instance, full price liberalization, particularly of energy and credit, limits the ability of government to allocate rents, as does voucher, as opposed to transaction-based, privatization. Open auctions not only typically maximize the amount of revenue to the public fisc but provide for transparency, thus diminishing opportunities for corruption. Reducing regulations, including reducing the number of permissions and approvals needed for undertaking any given action, and creating competition among jurisdictions may also reduce the scope for official extortion.

I have already noted changes in perceptions concerning the appropriate role of government. Nowhere is this more marked than in those less developed countries where the planning paradigm used to dominate. Today it is recognized that governments do not seem to have a comparative advantage in planning, that markets (firms) do engage in extensive planning, and that the kind of information produced by national plans was neither detailed enough for project selection nor complete enough to rely on for price setting. A typical list of responsibilities of government, beyond planning the overall economy, would start with providing the infrastructure. Today even that role is questioned. Private firms can provide roads and telecommunications, given an appropriate institutional (regulatory) structure. The ability to finance a project out of revenues provides a market test for projects, and although there may well be infrastructure projects with positive consumer surplus that fail this test (call them "errors of omission"), there is a widespread perception that too many projects with negative net consumer surplus—projects that would never have met the market test—have been undertaken. Moreover, placing infrastructure projects in the private sector may increase the likelihood of efficiency and decrease the likelihood of corruption.

China may be the exception that proves the rule. China seems to have taken a markedly different course from most of the other economies making a transition to the market. Rather than focusing on privatizing existing enterprises, it is has focused on developing new enterprises. The success of these new enterprises has provided competitive pressures to reform the more stagnant public enterprises. While economists have long emphasized the importance of strong property rights and transparent regulatory and other policies, China has succeeded—so far—with often seemingly ambiguous property rights and nontransparency. There remains a debate about whether eventually these problems will hinder China's progress, but there is little doubt that the growth that has been sustained since the early 1980s has already had an enormous impact on living standards.

3.6   Devolution

I have focused on what activities should be undertaken by government, not the level of government at which they should be undertaken. Not only is there a great debate in the United States about the role of government, there is also a debate about the appropriate role of the federal government relative to state and local governments. There is a large literature on the general principles of fiscal federalism.[45] Just as the Arrow-Debreu theorem and the fundamental theorem of welfare economics provide the benchmark for evaluating market economies, the Tiebout (1956) model provides the benchmark in this area. The issue is, Will the decentralized provision of local public goods (that is, public goods whose benefits are limited to a particular geographic locality) result in Pareto efficiency?[46] The intuition behind Tiebout's conjecture was similar to that behind Adam Smith's: If some community provides local public goods more efficiently or an array of public goods more to the liking of those within the community, individuals will migrate there. Just as individuals vote with their dollars in conventional markets, they vote with their feet in local public goods. The discipline of competition makes the market for local public goods work, just as it makes the market for private goods work. Unfortunately, just as when economists tried to prove Adam Smith's conjecture rigorously, they discovered that it was not true except under idealized conditions that frequently were not satisfied—the market failures with which I have been concerned in this chapter—so too when economists tried to prove Tiebout's conjecture rigorously, they discovered that it was not true except under idealized conditions. There were some major differences. The conditions under which Tiebout's conjecture was true appeared even more restrictive and less likely to be satisfied, and when satisfied, they had strong (and clearly not satisfied) implications for voting patterns: There would be unanimity among all voters.[47]

Some of the major lessons that seem relevant to the current political debate may be summarized as follows:

• Where population and capital are highly mobile, the scope for redistribution at the local (provincial) level is highly circumscribed.

• Federal action is appropriate for the provision of national public goods, for remedying externalities that have cross-boundary effects, and for setting standards and taking other actions that facilitate interstate commerce.[48]

• There may be better information and a greater sense of responsibility when actions are taken at as grass roots a level as possible. (Public good problems may be attenuated and a sense of participation in decision making enhanced.) On the other hand, the relevant mix of political actors may differ across levels of government, and some of the differences in outcomes with devolution may be attributable to this rather than to a greater responsiveness to the needs of the affected parties.

Much of the current debate on devolution within the United States seems less motivated by a concern for efficiency than by other considerations. The debate does not begin by asking which goods should be supplied at the federal level and which at the local level. Much of the debate has been over the supply of redistributive payments—precisely the category that theory suggests are least suitable for devolution. There remains a concern about the specter of a race to the bottom.[49]

Both the literature and the political debate have focused on limiting cases, that is, which goods should be the responsibility of which level of government. In theory and practice, there is a continuum of both financial and operational responsibilities. Just as government subsidies are an appropriate way to deal with (positive) externalities generated by the private sector, matching payments may be an appropriate way to deal with externalities associated with the local provision of certain public goods.[50]

3.7   The Role of Government in an International Setting

Governments traditionally have taken a large role in international commerce, whether by levying tariffs to raise revenues or to protect domestic industries, or by pursuing conventional mercantilist policies or modern export promotion. The recognition of the disastrous consequences of the beggar-thy-neighbor policies of the Great Depression led to the concerted attempt in the post–World War II era to establish a set of international institutions within which a so-called liberal trade and economic regime can flourish.

Today these questions are approached within much the same framework that has been used to discuss the role of government in national economies and the interactions between states and localities within a federalist structure. There is a recognition that just as competitive markets domestically result in efficient outcomes, so too do competitive markets internationally. Just as externalities can generate problems domestically, so too can problems arise in an international setting. Beggar-thy-neighbor policies represent one example of an externality.

There are some important differences, however. At the international level, the potential for competition is larger simply because of the large scale of the market. While the size of many economies is such that returns to scale and scope imply that there might be a single efficient producer, at the international scale there are few industries for which world production would be efficiently supplied by one or two producers. While each country benefits from free international trade (and it benefits if it opens up its borders unilaterally), not everyone within a country benefits, and in many countries there are no existing redistributive mechanisms to cope with these effects.

Governments can take actions that either encourage or discourage the creation of a liberal trade regime. They can, for instance, enact programs that facilitate adapting to trade-induced shocks. On the other side, they can enact regulations that serve as protectionist barriers, and they can fail to enforce effective competition laws, thus contributing to the maintenance of barriers to, in particular, entry into their markets by new foreign producers. The kind of world economic environment that emerges over the next quarter-century will depend on how each of the major governments answers these questions.

In my discussion of fiscal federalism, I referred to local public goods. There is a corresponding concept of international public goods, the benefits of which accrue (in some measure or another) to those residing in all countries. In a sense, the liberal economic trading regime can be thought of as an international public good. There are at least three other important examples: international environmental goods (such as those associated with global warming arising from the increased concentration of greenhouse gases), international security, and the provision of basic research. One of the main established rationales for government activity is the provision of public goods. Without government provision, there will be an undersupply because of the free-rider problem. The globalization of the international economy has elevated the importance of international public goods as a policy issue. Without cooperative action on the part of all the principal economies of the world, we risk an undersupply of international public goods.

3.8 Theory and Dogma

The modern analysis of the economic role of government assesses the strengths and limitations of markets and government; it sees the two as complements, with roles assigned on the basis of comparative advantage.

Advocates of a minimalist role for government make three assertions, none of which is established on the basis of theory or evidence.

First, they assert that anything the government can do, the private sector can do better. This assertion ignores the distinctive difference between government and all other organizations in society, arising from the state's essential properties of universal membership and the associated powers of compulsion and proscription. (The inherent limitations of government arise from some of the same attributes. In order to reduce potential abuses, a variety of constraints, such as those pertaining to hiring, wages, and equitable treatment, are imposed. Moreover, while the government enforces private contracts, there is no outside party to enforce government commitments.)

Second, they assert that anything the government does can and will be undone by the private sector. Although there are some highly idealized models (typically involving rational expectations) where certain actions of the government can be undone (an increase in money supply is undone by an increase in the price level), most government actions are, at best, only partially undone. Thus, while certain lump-sum redistributions might (in a Barro world) be undone, changes in relative prices in general cannot be undone, and most government policies have effects on relative prices. To be sure, government needs to pay attention to private sector responses to its actions, but this does not imply that the government is powerless.

Third, they assert that when government policies do have effects, they are more often deleterious than beneficial. This assertion is made not as a theoretical proposition but as a historical generalization, and as a historical generalization, it seems to be little more than an article of religious faith. There is a long list of positive government programs—from the agricultural extension and research programs that did so much to boost agricultural productivity in the United States over the past century, to the establishment of the Internet, which has formed the basis of a modern communications revolution—for which relatively small investments have produced huge returns. This is not to say that all investments have been productive, nor should one expect them to be in a world with imperfect information and uncertainty. Nor are they in the private sector, as the savings and loan bailout and investments in certain other sectors in the U.S. economy bear testimony.

3.9 Conclusion

There is an old joke about economics: The questions stay the same; only the answers change. The question I have addressed, concerning the role of the government, has been posed throughout our profession's history in one form or another. The changing world—and changing ideas about this changing world—have necessitated our asking this question again. Government does have a vital role to play in promoting sustainable economic growth, protecting the environment, promoting safety and health, and contributing to economic security. Governments have played, and continue to play, a constructive role. But by refocusing attention and rethinking not only what government does but how it does it, we can create a government that is a more effective partner and better able to work together with citizens, businesses, and the myriad of other institutions that make up our complex society, to pursue policies that promote both economic and noneconomic objectives.

Notes

1. The standardized unemployment rate for the European Union rose from 8.2 percent in 1991 to 11 percent in early 1996. Between 1979 and 1993, real family income in the United States in the bottom fifth fell by 15 percent, while the income of the top fifth rose by 18 percent.

2. See, for instance, World Bank (1993).

3. I set out some of my views on these issues in a lecture delivered in Amsterdam in 1988 (see Stiglitz 1988b and the accompanying comments of the discussants). For subsequent amplifications and modifications, see Stiglitz (1990), and my 1992 Barcelona lecture (Stiglitz, 1992).

4. For instance, changes in technology may enable there to be viable competition in a sector in which there previously was a natural monopoly. This has been the case, for example, in long-distance telephone service and electricity generation.

5. There is a long and sound tradition in economics of delineating descriptive statements from value statements and the normative consequences that are drawn from them. It is worth noting, however, that there is a curious correlation between those whose values seem to emphasize efficiency over equity concerns and those who believe that there are large supply elasticities. To put it another way, there is a curious correlation between those who believe that the marginal cost of enhanced equity is large (a descriptive statement) and those who believe that the marginal benefit of enhanced equity is small (a value statement).

6. The concept of *pure* public goods was defined by Samuelson (1954); they were goods for which exclusion was prohibitively costly and for which consumption was nonrivalrous. Many publicly provided goods are *impure*, possessing one or the other of these properties in some degree. There are some public goods that possess neither of these properties; these are often referred to as *publicly provided private goods*.

7. See, for example, Farrell (1987). Consider the familiar problem of determining whether smoking should be allowed in a room. In large groups, each individual has an incentive to free-ride on the actions of the others; providing a smoke-free room is a public good that benefits all nonsmokers. Although the theoretical literature has identified a number of incentive-compatible revelation mechanisms, most suffer from one problem or another (e.g., budget balancing); perhaps these deficiencies explain why none has been employed in practice.

8. A large literature suggests that monopolies are less innovative (Arrow 1962; Stiglitz 1986), even when faced with the threat of competitive entry (Stiglitz 1987). At the same time, with highly competitive markets, problems of appropriability may reduce incentives to invest in research and development. The conflict between dynamic and static efficiency represents one of the main challenges to modern competition policy. However, the argument that companies must be large to compete effectively in the international innovation arena is belied by the success of the myriad of smaller firms in several highly innovative areas, including computers and biotechnology.

9. The recently announced open access rule attempts to create a competitive market for electricity generation in the United States. The state of California and the U.K. government have gone further in attempting to create competitive markets in retailing, leaving the transmission services as the one "natural monopoly" component of the industry. For a more extended discussion of these issues, see *The Economic Report of the President* (1996).

10. In the U.S. telephone industry, the recently passed Telecommunications Act combines regulatory oversight with structural safeguards, striking a somewhat different balance from that provided under the consent decree that had governed the industry since the breakup of AT&T in 1984.

11. Participants had little incentive to reveal their plans honestly. Moreover, since plans are often state contingent, the fact that indicative plans typically did not provide for many, or even most, of the relevant contingencies meant that the entire exercise was intrinsically flawed.

12. There are theoretical reasons to expect private underinvestment in some entrepreneurial activities, especially when the "product" is not protected by patents. Products that are successful will be quickly imitated, and their profits eroded.

13. For instance, there may exist no competitive equilibrium in markets with adverse selection problems, as new entrants attempt to skim the cream. Government can force a pooling equilibrium and can proscribe or discourage cream-skimming practices (e.g., in the health insurance market, by using risk adjusters.)

14. For a survey of recent theories, see, for example, the symposium in vol. 7, no. 1, *Journal of Economic Perspectives*, including papers by Mankiw and Greenwald and Stiglitz (1993). Some of the New Keynesian models emphasize price and wage rigidities; while some of these rigidities are related to costs of adjustment (Mankiw 1985), others arise out of imperfections of information and capital market imperfections (Greenwald and Stiglitz 1991). Other theories (Greenwald and Stiglitz 1992) emphasize the absence of certain markets, such as equity markets, which is the result of incomplete and costly information; in these models

increased price and wage flexibility may actually lead to greater economic instability. Still other models emphasize coordination problems that arise from incomplete markets.

15. A large literature describes the breakdown of growth into its components (see, e.g., Solow 1957 and Denison 1972). More recent calculations suggest an increasing role for human capital accumulation (see, e.g., Romer 1994).

16. The limitations on that theorem have been extensively discussed elsewhere (see, e.g., Mirrlees 1971; Stiglitz 1994).

17. See, for example, World Bank (1993), Amsden (1989), Wade (1990), and Alam (1989), and Stiglitz (1996).

18. This is an important aspect of the efficiency wage theories, which have been developed since the mid-1970s. See, for example, Stiglitz (1986) and Akerlof and Yellen (1986).

19. Or at least this is their stated intent. In some cases (countries), the benefits of public provision accrue disproportionately to the children of the well off. And resource allocations within education may not be designed to maximize society's overall return.

20. A large literature explains these market failures in terms of adverse selection, moral hazard, and transaction costs.

21. The "insurance" interpretation of broad redistributive policies (including safety nets) was emphasized by Lerner (1944).

22. Like so many other conclusions in economics, even this one has been questioned recently (see C. Romer 1986). Still, the weight of opinion is that economic fluctuations are smaller than they were fifty years ago.

23. The Luxembourg data show that after-tax/subsidies inequality is lower than the before-tax/subsidies inequality in all of the major industrialized countries included in their data set.

24. These constraints include those attempting to ensure that government acts in an equitable manner and does not violate its fiduciary responsibilities. Examples include civil service and procurement laws. Although some constraints on employment and procurement are inevitable, this does not mean that there do not exist modifications in these rules that will contribute to efficiency without impairing other governmental objectives.

The government enforces commitments of private parties, but who is there to enforce the commitments of government? Note, however, that the political process can impose transaction costs, which have the effect of being at least partial commitments.

25. Competition has other benefits; it provides not only incentives but also yardsticks against which performance can be judged, and relative competencies assessed for purposes of selection. See Nalebuff and Stiglitz (1983).

26. A large literature has developed exploring what has come to be called the principal agent literature (see Stiglitz 1974a, Ross 1973). For applications to organizations, see the symposium in the *Journal of Economic Perspectives* (spring 1991).

27. See Daves and Christensen (1980).

28. The most general theorem on privatization is that of Sappington and Stiglitz (1987).

29. For a summary, see the *Economic Report of the President, 1995.*

30. In traditional parlance, technological change has, in this perspective, been "Pigou unskilled labor savings."

31. Between 1980 and 1994 real tuition at public four-year colleges in the United States increased by 86 percent; at two-year colleges by 70 percent (see ERP 1996).

32. Recent advances in the theory of optimal tax and expenditure policy have emphasized this role (see, for example, Diamond and Mirrlees 1971 and Stiglitz 1987).

33. See Card and Kreuger (1995). Theoretical work has supported their conclusions that small increases in the minimum wage may have small effects on unemployment (and of an ambiguous sign). Efficiency wage theories emphasize the productivity-enhancing effects, which, even if not large enough to offset the wage increase fully, mitigate its employment effects. (The well-documented ripple effect—even low-wage workers whose wages exceed the minimum wage typically receive wage increases when the minimum wage is increased—is consistent with the importance of the efficiency wage effect.) With imperfections of competition in labor markets, a minimum wage increase may even lead to positive employment effects.

34. The earned income tax credit has two disadvantages, which account for why it can only be part of an overall strategy to reduce poverty. First, it has direct budgetary costs, a major disadvantage since most governments are attempting to reduce their deficit. Second, there is always a phase-out of incomes; that is, at some point the government wage subsidy must be reduced to zero. Since subsidies are reduced over the phase-out range, there is, in effect, a "tax"; more precisely, the marginal return to working is actually lower than the wage. To reduce the budgetary impact, governments are often tempted to have the subsidy phase out fairly rapidly, and this results in high marginal tax rates—in some recent congressional proposals in the United States, in excess of 50 percent.

35. There is a distinction. One of the reasons for emphasizing individual responsibility is that it enhances individual incentives, but there are those who believe that even if, say, the elasticity of labor supply were zero, individual responsibility would be important because it is a value in its own right.

36. Social justice, like individual responsibility, is typically not precisely defined in popular discussions. Economists use an egalitarian social welfare function (one in which a mean-preserving spread of consumption equivalents, taking into account forgone leisure, reduces social welfare) to evaluate the (after-tax subsidy) distribution of income. In modern public finance, tax and subsidy policies are evaluated in two stages. First, are they Pareto efficient? That is, can anyone be made better off without making someone else worse off given the information constraints (e.g., government's capacity to observe and verify an individual's abilities directly, rather than relying on inferences based on, say, earned income)? Second, what is their impact on the social welfare function, where the social welfare function is defined as being egalitarian, so mean-preserving increases in inequality reduce social welfare?

37. One can define social welfare functions over transition matrices rather than over distributions of income. The problems of ranking transition matrices are far more complex than even the problems of ranking distributions of income.

38. The role of government in this area is partially motivated by the market failure arising from the absence of private markets for "transitional insurance." There may be good reasons for the absence of such a market, related to problems of moral hazard and adverse selection; in designing transitional assistance programs, the government will need to take the former into account.

39. The magnitude of these may be sensitive to social context and thus may be particularly prone to changing over time and across countries. Peer monitoring and social pressure, combined with more detailed knowledge of individual circumstances, may make adverse incen-

tive effects from intrafamily redistribution much smaller than comparable redistributions at the government level (see Arnott and Stiglitz 1991). Changes in society may, however, affect the scope of intrafamily redistribution.

I sense the dominant view in the United States is that although background conditions may be relevant for understanding why individuals might not exercise their individual responsibility, in the end, individuals do have the capacity to make choices. But there are also those who hold that there are circumstances where special dispensation may be warranted, particularly when the background conditions are related to past social injustices.

40. Economists have long taken an individualistic approach to evaluating social outcomes; the principle of consumer sovereignty argued that outcomes should be evaluated using the individual's own preferences (see Bergson 1966). Nonindividualistic approaches (and discussions of merit goods and bads) were criticized for being paternalistic governmental intrusions into what should be individual prerogatives. But such approaches never dealt satisfactorily with children, who do not make choices for themselves in any case. The issue there is, *Who* should make choices on their behalf? There is a growing consensus that when parental choices are likely to have adverse societal consequences (e.g., a high likelihood of crime or dependency), the state has a legitimate right to intervene.

41. This is a conclusion based on my values, and one with which other economists, employing other social welfare functions, might well disagree. (Disagreements are also likely to arise among those who see a high social cost to such compassion. The number of individuals who seem to be disabled or lack the ability to earn an income may increase greatly in response to providing even a minimal living standard.)

42. I have emphasized individual incentives, but I should also emphasize the importance of bureaucratic incentives. Those responsible for making the social welfare system work should provide and be provided the incentives and resources appropriate to the conditions of each individual (see section 3.9).

43. See, for instance, Stiglitz (1994). In particular, they have helped clarify the ways in which the basic perfect information-perfect competition paradigm may be very misleading.

44. See, for instance, World Bank (1993) and Stiglitz (1996), and Stiglitz and Uy (1996).

45. For textbook renditions, see for instance, Musgrave and Musgrave (1976) and Stiglitz (1988a).

46. The theory of clubs emphasizes that the beneficiaries of a public good may be defined on bases other than geography. The principles of decentralization are the same in either case.

47. Stiglitz (1983a) established the conditions under which decentralization would result in the efficient supply of local public goods (and efficient community size). Stiglitz (1983b) developed some of the peculiar implications that arise when there is heterogeneity of skills and preferences. Stiglitz (1977) discusses a variety of the "market failures" that arise, for example, when there are a limited number of communities, so that each community is not a "utility taker" for individuals of any particular set of skills. Milleron (1972) provides a rigorous analysis of the theory of local public goods.

48. As distinct from local public goods, the benefits of which accrue to only those who reside in the local community.

49. Within the U.S. fiscal structure, there are further problems. Since most states have constitutional provisions requiring some form of a balanced budget, they are ill prepared to increase expenditures on welfare payments in the event of an economic downturn. This

has been recognized in recent debates by calling for the provision of "rainy day funds," but the magnitude of the funds seems to fall far short of the magnitude of the needs (given past patterns of economic fluctuations).

Some suggest that the race to the bottom is indeed the objective of the proposed devolution of these welfare programs. The dynamic forces for reducing welfare payments will be stronger than the political forces that so far have maintained support for such payments at the national level.

50. The zeal for block granting with low standards of accountability may be attributed to the natural desire of state and local governments to receive increased lump-sum payments from the federal government. With no constraints on how such funds are expended, economic models predict that the marginal effect on public expenditures on the "desired" area would be no different from what it would be with a lump-sum grant. For the most part, federal expenditures on block-granted welfare would simply substitute for state and local expenditures, with overall expenditures decreasing from the current level (which has been determined on the basis of matching grants). Some econometric evidence, however, suggests that the substitution may be somewhat smaller than the theoretical models predict; there appears to be a "flypaper effect," with a substantial fraction of the money allocated to, say, education or welfare actually going where it is intended.

References

Akerlof, G., and J. Yellen eds. 1986. *Efficiency Wage Models of the Labor Market.* Cambridge: Cambridge University Press.

Alam, M. S. 1989. *Governments and Markets in Economic Development Strategies.* New York: Praeger.

Amsden, Alice H. 1989. *Asia's New Giant.* Oxford: Oxford University Press.

Arnott, R., and J. E. Stiglitz. 1991. "Moral Hazard and Nonmarket Institutions: Dysfunctional Crowding Out or Peer Monitoring." *American Economic Review* 81(1):179–190.

Arrow, K. J. 1951. "An Extension of the Theorem of Classical Welfare Economics." In J. Newman, ed., *Proceedings of the Second Berkeley Symposium on Mathematical Studies and Probability.* Berkeley: University of California Press.

Arrow, K. J. 1962. "Economic Welfare and the Allocation of Resources for Invention." In *The Rate and Direction of Economic Activity*, pp. 609–625. Princeton, N.J.: Princeton University Press.

Atkinson, A. B., and J. E. Stiglitz. 1980. *Lectures on Public Economics.* New York: McGraw-Hill.

Bator, Francis M. 1958. "The Anatomy of Market Failure." *Quarterly Journal of Economics* 72:351–379.

Baumol, W. J. 1982. "Contestable Markets: An Uprising in the Theory of Industrial Structure." *American Economic Review* 72:1–15.

Baumol, W. J., John C. Panzar, and Robert D. Willig. 1982. *Contestable Markets and the Theory of Industry Structure.* New York: Harcourt Brace Jovanovich.

Bergson, Abram, 1966. "A Reformulation of Certain Aspects of Welfare Economics," *Quarterly Journal of Economics*, 1938 (Feb.). Reprint, in Abram Bergson, ed. *Essays in Normative Economics.* Cambridge, Mass.: Harvard University Press.

Borenstein, Severin. 1992. "The Evolution of U.S. Airline Competition." *Journal of Economic Perspectives* 6(2):45–73.

Buchanan, James M. 1965. "An Economic Theory of Clubs." *Economica* 32:1–14.

Buchanan, James M., and Charles Goetz. 1972. "Efficiency Limits of Fiscal Mobility: An Assessment of the Tiebout Model." *Journal of Public Economics* 1:25–43.

Card, D., and A. B. Krueger. 1995. "Time-Series Minimum-Wage Studies: A Meta-Analysis." *American Economic Review* 85(2):238–242.

Coase, Ronald H. 1937. "The Nature of the Firm." *Economica* 16:386–405.

Coase, Ronald H. 1960. "The Problem of Social Cost." *Journal of Law and Economics* 3:1–44.

Daves, D. W., and L. R. Christensen. 1980. "The Relative Efficiency of Public and Private Firms in a Competitive Environment: The Case of Canadian Railroads." *Journal of Political Economy* 88:958–976.

Debreu, G. 1952. *The Theory of Value*. New York: Wiley.

Demsetz, Harold. 1970. "The Private Production of Public Goods." *Journal of Law and Economics* 13:293–306.

Denison, E. 1972. "Classification of Sources of Growth." *Review of Income and Wealth* (March): 1–25.

Diamond, P., and J. Mirrlees. 1971. "Optimal Taxation and Public Production, II: Tax Rules." *American Economic Review* 61:261–278.

Economic Report of the President. 1995, 1996. Washington, D.C.

Farrell, J. 1987. "Information and the Coase Theorem." *Journal of Economic Perspectives* 1 (2).

Greenwald, Bruce, and Joseph E. Stiglitz. 1986. "Externalities in Economies with Imperfect Information and Incomplete Markets." *Quarterly Journal of Economics* 101(2):229–264.

Greenwald, Bruce, and Joseph E. Stiglitz. 1991. "Information, Finance, and Markets: The Architecture of Allocative Mechanisms." Working Paper no. 3652. Cambridge, Mass.: National Bureau of Economic Research.

Greenwald, Bruce, and Joseph E. Stiglitz. 1992. "Towards a Reformulation of Monetary Theory: Competitive Banking." Working Paper no. 4117. Cambridge, Mass.: National Bureau of Economic Research.

Greenwald, Bruce, and Joseph E. Stiglitz. 1993. "New and Old Keynesians." *Journal of Economic Perspectives* 7(1):23–44.

Leibenstein, H. 1966. "Allocative Efficiency and X-Efficiency." *American Economic Review* 56:392–415.

Lerner, A. P. 1944. *The Economics of Control*. New York: Macmillan.

Mankiw, N. Gregory. 1985. "Small Menu Costs and Large Business Cycles." *Quarterly Journal of Economics* 100:529–537.

Mankiw, N. Gregory. 1993. "Symposium on Keynesian Economics Today." *Journal of Economic Perspectives* 7(1):3–4.

Milleron, J. C. 1972. "Theory of Value with Public Goods: A Survey Article." *Journal of Economic Theory* 5:419–477.

Mirrlees, J. 1971. "An Exploration in the Theory of Optimum Economic Taxation." *Review of Economic Studies* 38:175–208.

Musgrave, R. A., and P. B. Musgrave. 1976. *Public Finance in Theory and Practice.* 2d ed. New York: McGraw-Hill.

Nalebuff, B., and J. E. Stiglitz. 1983. "Prizes and Incentives: Towards a General Theory of Compensation and Competition." *Bell Journal of Economics* 14:21–43.

Oakland, William. 1987. "Theory of Public Goods." In A. Auerbach and M. Feldstein, eds., *Handbook of Public Economics*, vol. 2. New York: North-Holland.

Pigou, A. C. 1932. *The Economics of Welfare.* 4th ed. London: Macmillan.

Pigou, A. C. 1947. *A Study in Public Finance.* 34th ed. London: Macmillan.

Posner, Richard A. 1992. "The Chicago School of Antitrust Analysis." In G.-H. Burgess, Jr., ed., *Antitrust and Regulation*, pp. 159–182. International Library of Critical Writings in Business History no. 4. Aldershot, U.K.:Elgar.

Rey, P., and J. E. Stiglitz. 1995. "The Role of Exclusive Territories in Producers' Competition." *Rand Journal of Economics* 26(3):431–451.

Romer, Christina D. 1986. "Is the Stabilization of the Post War Economy a Figment of the Data?" *American Economic Review* 76(3):314–334.

Romer, Paul. 1994. "The Origins of Endogenous Growth." *Journal of Economic Perspectives* (8)1:3–22.

Ross, S. 1973. "The Economic Theory of Agency: The Principal's Problem." *American Economic Review* 63:134–139.

Samuelson, P. A. 1954. "The Pure Theory of Public Expenditure." *Review of Economics and Statistics* 36:387–389.

Samuelson, P. A. 1958. "Aspects of Public Expenditure Theories." *Review of Economics and Statistics* 40:332–338.

Sappington, D., and J. E. Stiglitz. 1987. "Privatization, Information and Incentives." *Journal of Policy Analysis and Management* 6(4):567–582.

Schumpeter, J. 1942. *Socialism, Capitalism, and Democracy.* New York: Harper.

Solow, Robert. 1957. "Technical Change and the Aggregate Production Function." *Review of Economics and Statistics* 39:312–320.

Stiglitz, J. E. 1974a. "Incentives and Risk Sharing in Sharecropping." *Review of Economic Studies* 41:219–255.

Stiglitz, J. E. 1974b. "Theories of Discrimination and Economic Policy." In G. Von Furstenburg et al. eds., *Patterns of Racial Discrimination*, pp. 5–26. Lexington, Mass.: Lexington Books.

Stiglitz, J. E. 1977. "The Theory of Local Public Goods." In M. S. Feldstein and R. P. Inman, eds., *The Economics of Public Services*, pp. 274–283. London: Macmillan.

Stiglitz, J. E. 1981. "Potential Competition May Reduce Welfare." *American Economic Review* 71:184–189.

Stiglitz, J. E. 1983. "The Theory of Local Public Goods Twenty-five Years After Tiebout: A Perspective." In Zodnow, George R., ed. *Local Provision of Public Services: The Tiebout Model Twenty-five Years Later*, pp. 17–53. NBER Reprint 489. New York: Academic Press.

Stiglitz, J. E. 1986. "Theories of Wage Rigidities." In J. L. Butkiewicz et al., eds., *Keynes' Economic Legacy: Contemporary Economic Theories*, pp. 153–206. New York: Praeger.

Stiglitz, J. E. 1987. "Pareto Efficiency and Optimal Taxation and the New Welfare Economics." In Alan Auerbach and Martin Feldstein, eds., *Handbook of Public Economics*, pp. 991–1042. Amsterdam: North-Holland.

Stiglitz, J. E. 1988a. *Economics of the Public Sector*. 2d ed. New York: W. W. Norton.

Stiglitz, J. E. 1988b. "The Economic Role of the State." In A. Heertje, ed., *The Economic Role of the State*, pp. 9–85. Cambridge, Mass.: Basil Blackwell and Bank Insinger de Beaufort NV.

Stiglitz, J. E. 1990. "The Economic Role of the State: Efficiency and Effectiveness." In T. P. Hardiman and M. Mulreany, eds., *Efficiency and Effectiveness*, pp. 37–59. New York: Institute of Public Administration.

Stiglitz, J. E. 1991. "Symposium on Organization and Economics." *Journal of Economic Perspectives* 5:15–24.

Stiglitz, J. E. 1992. "Rethinking the Economic Role of the State: Publicly Provided Private Goods." Lecture delivered at University Pompeu Fabra, Barcelona, November 15.

Stiglitz, J. E. 1993. "The Role of the State in Financial Markets." In *Proceedings of the World Bank Annual Conference on Development Economics*, pp. 19–52. Washington, D.C.: World Bank.

Stiglitz, J. E. 1994. *Whither Socialism?* Cambridge, Mass.: MIT Press.

Stiglitz, J. E. 1996. "Some Lessons from the Asian Miracle." Background paper for *The Asian Miracle*. Washington, D.C.: World Bank.

Stiglitz, J. E. 1996. "Some Lessons from the East Asian Miracle." *The World Bank Research Observer* 2(2):151–177.

Stiglitz, J. E., and M. Uy. 1996. "Financial Markets, Public Policy and the East Asian Miracle." *The World Bank Research Observer* 2(2):249–276.

Tiebout, C. M. 1956. "A Pure Theory of Local Expenditures." *Journal of Political Economy* 64:416–424.

Tobin, J. 1970. "On Limiting the Domain of Inequality." *Journal of Law and Economics* 13(2):263–277.

Wade, R. 1990. *Governing the Market: Economic Theory and the Role of Government in East Asian Industrialization*. Princeton: Princeton University Press.

The World Bank. 1993. *The East Asian Miracle: Economic Growth and Public Policy*. Oxford: Oxford University Press.

Comments

Alberto Giovannini

Stiglitz displays solid economics, insight, and an effective attack on the intellectual fads that too often underlie policy debates in many countries. Especially since the collapse of the communist bloc, there has been a sea change in economic policymaking throughout the world. Old ideas supporting a pervasive role of government in society, the ideas behind the welfare state in the Western countries, and the ideas behind the socialist state in the communist bloc have been replaced. The replacement came from free market liberalism, supply-side economics, and mainstream U.S. academic macroeconomics.[1]

Stiglitz is concerned that this powerful intellectual trend might lead to problems and imbalances in the future. He wants to set the intellectual record straight on the role and the limits of government in modern societies, to avoid a wholesale rejection of institutions whose elimination might have dire consequences in the future.

Microeconomic Analysis of Governments' Role

Most appealing is Stiglitz's use of solid microeconomic theory to attack many questions regarding the role of government, and the proof that such an application can go very far. In this sense, the economic profession can provide an important contribution to political debates in many countries by reducing a number of issues that were previously, and often still are, the domain of rhetoric and political horse trading to problems for technicians to deal with, using the careful, solid, and effective analysis Stiglitz and others developed over the years. This is, in my view, the purist form of technical progress in economic analysis.

The broad case for government is well presented by Stiglitz and is hard to quibble with. I do not want take issue on his specific points, but I do see a risk that his careful analysis can be superficially used as rhetorical ammunition by the large constituency of those who are happy with the status quo. Those who do not recognize the profound innovation in Stiglitz's approach to the analysis of the role for government might take a narrow view and conclude that government still has an important role to play and the elimination of government will be damaging. I believe that, in many countries, maintaining the status quo is equally damaging because I suspect the status quo is far from the normative optimum that Stiglitz presents.

Paying Attention to Dynamic Problems

In the spirit of these observations, I want to address one problem that I believe is central to Stiglitz's analysis but might have been dwarfed by the very large questions that he addresses. In the normative analysis of the role of government in a democratic society, I find the dynamic problems the most interesting and challenging. One well-known example of these dynamic problems is the question, posed by McKinnon, about the proper sequence of liberalization of goods and financial markets in previously constrained economies. I want to address here a more general question, which I will introduce with a fact and an anecdote.

The fact was documented by Richard Musgrave and Peggy Musgrave (1976), and is shown in figures 3.1 and 3.2., which illustrate the level of government spending as a percentage of gross national product (which I will call "the size of government") in the United Kingdom, the United States, and Germany and over the 1890–1980 period. These well-known figures show a strong upward trend in all countries and are viewed as an illustration of Wagner's law on the continuing growth of government in modern industrial societies. I do not address Wagner's theories here but, rather, consider another phenomenon illustrated by the figures. The phenomenon is hysteresis: In all three countries, the largest accelerations in the size of government occur in correspondence with the wars. In Germany, the size of government increases without interruption from World War I until the beginning of World War II. Then it decreases appreciably after the wars' end. Of course, the historical experience in the three countries is quite different; two of them won both world wars and one lost both (with effects on the pattern of military spending after the wars); one country was much more involved in the cold war military buildup than the other two; and so on. Yet the pattern illustrated in the figures suggests a tendency for government spending to remain at high levels after the military buildups. (The experience of the United States during the

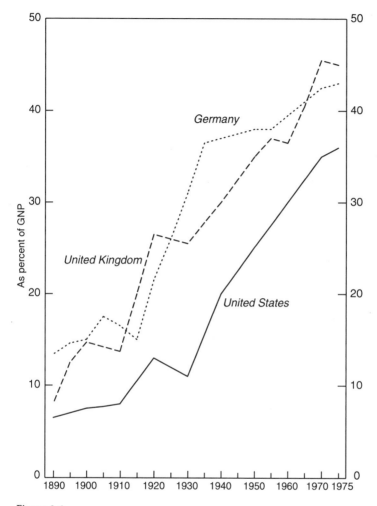

Figure 3.1
Public expenditure. Source: Musgrave and Musgrave (1976).

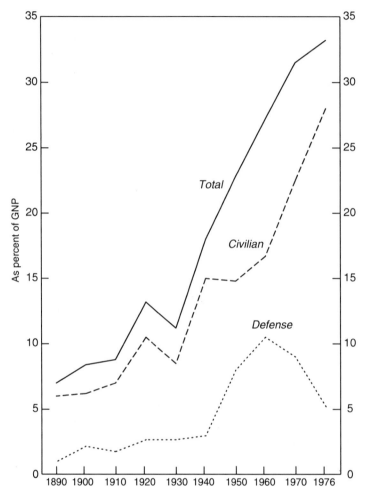

Figure 3.2
U.S. civilian and defense expenditures. Source: Musgrave and Musgrave (1976).

1970s as it appears in figure 3.2 nicely illustrates this point: During that time, a decrease in military spending was accompanied by an acceleration of civilian spending.)

It is said that World War II brought the English aristocracy (and therefore the political elite) in close contact with the proletariat as they sought shelter from German bombings. The sight of the appalling conditions (health and otherwise) of the English poor apparently led many aristocrats to become supporters of welfare laws after the war.

The hysteresis suggested by the fact and the anecdote about the aristocracy and the proletariat could be dismissed as an interesting but limited phenomenon. There are many reasons that nonmilitary spending should increase following an increase in military spending; the reconstruction efforts and assistance to war veterans are obvious examples. I suspect, however, that more general and more challenging problems are raised by the experience of the United Kingdom, the United States, and Germany. The problems can be posed as a question: What makes governments fluctuate in size and scope?

The problem of the dynamics of government is central from both a theoretical and a practical perspective. Theoretically it is important to determine the forces that affect the changes in size and scope of government, because it is important to determine what will move government from an equilibrium situation to another. As Samuelson (1947) pointed out, for comparative statics analysis to yield fruitful results, we must develop a theory of dynamics. The practical relevance of this problem is hard to miss: Whoever advocates change in the role of government in modern democracies wants to know which forces push for that change and which forces resist it.

Slow Government Adaptation to Changes in External Circumstances

The problem can be studied by considering the classic tools of comparative statics. Consider an economy where the government plays the roles outlined by Stiglitz and, according to Stiglitz's criteria, has reached an optimum. Now subject that economy to some sort of shock, say, a technological shock, such that the size and scope of government are no longer adequate. What forces will move government to the right place?

At this point, it is useful to contrast the case of a full-information economy without market imperfections, and therefore without government.

In that economy, an exogenous shock generates economic incentives for individuals to adapt to the new situation; individuals see a private (I want to stress the point here: monetary) gain in changing their pattern of production, investment, and consumption to adapt to the new situation. Their adaptation will bring about, in equilibrium, the new optimum. That is, in the new equilibrium, resources will be allocated efficiently, given the new circumstances (this is, of course, the first welfare theorem).

Now one can easily see that the monetary incentives to adapt to a new situation are not present in the case of the government. The optimal change in the role and scope of government to new circumstances occurs not because of prospective economic gains accruing to some actors but because some enlightened technician like Stiglitz has come up with the new optimal role of government and has succeeded in convincing democratic institutions that the changes should be carried through.

Stiglitz has effectively and convincingly criticized the assumptions behind the adaptation of a market economy to changed circumstances as I have described them.[2] I am sure that he would share with me a lot of doubts that the mechanisms leading to adaptation of governments are reliable and work with acceptable speed.

The general conjecture that I offer therefore is the following: Because direct economic incentives to adaptation do not characterize governments, their adaptations to changes in the external environment occur much more slowly than they would in an efficient world. Such changes are not guaranteed to bring governments to more efficient outcomes.

My conjecture should not be taken only as a negative one. I am convinced that, over time, the lack of adaptation of governments causes very visible and ultimately unacceptable waste and that democracies have the mechanisms in place to react to these situations. Yet the inefficiencies of government are not always so visible, the constituencies resisting change are often immensely powerful, and the checks and balances that such constituencies can use in the defense of their own special interests are numerous.

Indeed, Stiglitz's own work can be applied to some extent to study the forces resisting adaptation by governments to efficient outcomes. For example, information problems, among others, plague decision making of governments. The distribution of information in government bureaucracies and the use of information by bureaucrats can give rise to perverse incentives and suboptimal outcomes in government decision making.

Thus, I trust that economic analysis in the style of Stiglitz can and will further our understanding of the forces underlying the adaptation of governments to changes in the economic environment. This analysis will greatly improve the techniques of economic policymaking.

Notes

1. I would characterize this as a blend of monetarism and neo-Keynesianism with some addition of rational expectations.

2. See, for a nice and comprehensive illustration, Stiglitz (1994).

References

Musgrave, Richard A., and Peggy B. Musgrave. 1976. *Public Finance in Theory and Practice.* New York: McGraw-Hill.

Samuelson, P. A. 1947. *Foundations of Economic Analysis.* New York: Atheneum.

Stiglitz, Joseph E. 1994. *Whither Socialism?* Cambridge, Mass.: MIT Press.

Comments

Jean-Claude Milleron

Here I organize my comments and questions along two main avenues: the quest for efficiency through the market or (and) through sound economic policies, and the equity aspects. Stiglitz has two main messages. First, because of many advances in economic analysis (mainly the new information paradigm), we should realize that policies have limits, which does not necessarily mean that Stiglitz presents a plea for more state intervention. Second, the traditional trade-off between equity and efficiency might have to be reconsidered, which implies, according to Stiglitz, that more attention should be paid to some instruments that have not been studied sufficiently.

Toward an Efficient Allocation of Resources

The demonstrations of existence are crucial for the consistency of economic analysis. If the concepts we are talking about (e.g., competitive equilibrium) do not have a good chance of coming to fruition, we may do better devoting our time to other kinds of activities.

The first question to address is, The existence of what? There are important views in various pieces of work by Stiglitz, in particular, in *Whither Socialism*, in which the concept of equilibrium itself has to be made relative.

It seems to me that there is a basic difficulty in the Arrow-Debreu definition of equilibrium that Stiglitz does not mention. I have in mind the case of correspondence, or multivalued demand and supply functions. On the production side, such a case is not only a refinement for mathematicians, since it covers all the constant return to scale cases. In such a case, in order to ensure consistency, the decision maker at the firm level needs information not only on prices but also on the level of demand and the production programs of fellow entrepreneurs. This case is a good example because it does not refer to some external economy type of inefficiency. It raises the following questions: How should the decisions at the production level be made? Who should make them? This remark certainly does not imply that the government is the best for undertaking marketing surveys (the Plan, in France, was considered something like that; Pierre Massé talked about the planning process as a "generalized marketing study"). However, when discussing developing countries in a global market, for instance, is there not some room for more information on the strategy of the players? Who should provide this information? This is my first question.

But existence is not only the result of fixed-point theorems. Existence of some institutions is often required, and it is well known that the Arrow-Debreu theorem calls for the existence of future contingent markets for any good or commodity traded in the economy. Again, the nonexistence of such markets does not imply that the government should intervene directly, but it might be advisable for the government to make more extensive use of market mechanisms.

It seems that a lot of interesting new developments are related to the analysis of the specification of commodities. Interesting developments in industrial economics address the question of the choice of qualities (considered a crucial parameter in the strategy of the firm). Stiglitz mentions the difficulty of defining sufficient specifications in a competitive bidding process.

My second question is, Isn't there also an important difficulty in defining the states of nature, such as defined in the theory? This is a well-known point in private contracts. Isn't there room for a kind of forum (and this might be true at the international level also) in which the possible states of nature could be examined and the different beliefs confronted? This was also a possible interpretation of the role of some planning agencies in the past. Should we abandon this sort of idea?

Efficiency is certainly important; however, we can live with second-best situations. Stability is too often forgotten; instability may have terribly harmful consequences. There are so many possible structures of instability that it is difficult to make a general point.

Stiglitz rightly reminds us that macroeconomic policy can enhance economic stability. I also remember that from Samuelson-Solow to the school of rational expectations, there is an old debate on long-run dynamics, and I share Stiglitz's skepticism on the possible existence of a unique "socially optimal path."

My third question relates to the following aspect: In the literature, there exist some nonpathological examples in which it may happen that, for some values of the parameters characterizing the economy, competitive equilibrium is not unique. In such cases, it may happen that during development, the economy has to jump from one equilibrium to another, a jump that may be accompanied by important changes in the welfare distribution and in the level of prices. Therefore, my third question is, What importance should we attach to such cases? And there are related questions: Are these cases just unusual examples to be studied by specialists? Is there a possible link between such cases and the use of a minimum wage by the state that Stiglitz discusses?

Location is a difficult issue that implies various kinds of nonconvexities that the Arrow-Debreu model does not like. Stiglitz mentions the issue of local public goods, which is important for discussions about devolution.

More generally, we all have in mind models of location in which, because of some nonconvexities, the equilibrium solution is of a "bang bang" type, and maybe nonoptimal. These cases concern the location of people and activities as well.

At this stage, I have a fourth question: Should the government also have a completely hands-off policy on issues related to location? Clearly there are a lot of risks in rent-seeking situations, and even corruption behind such policies where they are applied. Does silence on these issues mean that the best approach would be a kind of benign neglect?

Governments will have to pay more and more attention and devote more means to the global allocation of resources. Stiglitz emphasizes the importance of the now well-identified global public goods problem and gives convincing examples. Here, my fifth question relates to Stiglitz's comments on the specific character of government with its powers of compulsion and prescription. The counterparts of such powers correspond to the provision of some public goods at the national level. If such a compulsion does not exist, a misallocation of resources would appear because of a free-rider problem. Now let us go to the provision of global public goods. Is there a risk of an underprovision of such public goods? If the answer is yes, then how should it be overcome?

Equity-Efficiency Trade-off

My first point is that the scoop here would be that the old equity-efficiency trade-off is over. From a political point of view, it would be very important news. I am afraid that I am not yet fully convinced. Perhaps it is a matter of clarification.

Stiglitz says that earlier literature emphasizing the role of government in redistribution took the pretax distribution of income as a given. I am not so sure that I agree. I would say that the distribution of capabilities (or individual productivities) was considered as a given. And the kind of policy that Stiglitz considers in order to act on pretax distribution of income, an interesting idea, aims at changing the distribution of capabilities. As a consequence, the indirect result of such a change would be a change in the pretax distribution of income.

At this stage, I am not sure that I would throw the baby out with the bathwater. Let me summarize my views on this point. First, it is probably necessary to have a good conceptual framework to address some difficult tax issues like the optimal progressivity of income tax. Is it true that the Atkinson-Mirrlees model is still the best alternative? Second, if my interpretation is correct, changing the distribution of qualifications takes time. It might be true that there remains a short- to medium-term trade-off between efficiency and equity and a medium-long term complementarity. The arguments that Stiglitz presents on this point are rather convincing. Finally, is it not correct to say that in many transition economies the changes toward more efficiency were accompanied by an increase in inequality in the distribution of income and welfare? Is it not also broadly accepted today that in many developing countries the adjustment policies that are being implemented may be rather harmful for the weakest members of the population, thereby increasing inequality in the distribution of income?

Having presented my views, here is my sixth question for Stiglitz: Do you agree that the mechanisms you have in mind are mainly medium to long term and that they should be presented as such?

My second point on distribution is very brief. It might also be a matter of clarification. There is some ambiguity on the question of the treatment of the people with the lowest qualifications. As a consequence, my seventh question is, Does Stiglitz imply a minimum wage or the provision of some level of minimum resources (overall?)? There is a kind of Rawlsian point here. Is Stiglitz suggesting some possibly negative income tax, such as that discussed in the economic literature of the 1970s?

My final point is related to the approach proposed for the disabled in our society, whom I refer to as the disabled of the world. I like the warning on disability defined as "a dichotomous variable: one is able to work or not." We should be capable of proposing some fresh ideas from this point of view as a follow-up to debates that took place in various forums and in particular in Copenhagen at the 1995 World Summit on Social

Development. There is something missing in the "neoclassical" paradigm: the feeling that most people have of belonging to various entities, groups, countries, and regions that represent more than themselves. The contrary of such a belonging could be called exclusion. And with Stiglitz's approach, I found for the first time something that an economist can use to address this concept of exclusion. Perhaps in the future we may have to elaborate along these lines.

Reference

Stiglitz, J. 1994. *Whither Socialism*. Cambridge, Mass.: MIT Press.

4

Income Distribution and Growth in Industrial Countries

Andrea Brandolini and
Nicola Rossi

Effective work [in the study of the economic growth of nations] calls for a shift from market economics to political and social economy.
—Kuznets (1955, p. 28)

In the early 1950s, taking the United States as the yardstick, the degree of concentration of before-tax incomes was lower in Denmark and the Netherlands and higher in Italy and Japan; it was about the same in Canada and Great Britain (Kravis 1960). Two decades later, around 1970, the share of posttax income appropriated by the bottom 20 percent of the population ranged between 4 percent in France and about 8 percent in Japan; the corresponding Gini coefficients fell from over 41 percent in France to about 30 percent in Norway and Sweden (figure 4.1). Along with France, Italy, the Federal Republic of Germany, and the United States showed the highest inequality, whereas the United Kingdom, Australia, and Japan shared with the Scandinavian countries the lowest. Scattered information confirms that economic inequality was far from constant in the postwar years. Significant reductions in the concentration of income were observed in the Scandinavian countries, as well as in the Federal Republic of Germany, Japan, and the Netherlands, in conjunction with the extraordinary and prolonged acceleration of growth and near full employment experienced by industrialized countries since the early 1950s.

As for income distribution, growth too was far from uniform, even in those golden years. As Maddison (1991) noted, European countries and Japan were able to seize the postwar opportunities more than other countries. In the early 1950s, labor productivity in European countries was about half of that observed in the United States, and a decade later, it was about six-tenths. Interestingly, catching up did not prove to be stronger

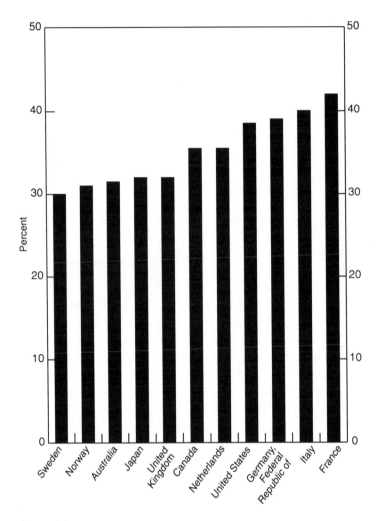

Figure 4.1
Selected OECD countries: Gini coefficients circa 1970. Based on posttax, unadjusted income,
household weight. Source: Sawyer (1976, table 6).

in poorer countries; among European countries, the Federal Republic of Germany and the Benelux countries were apparently better placed for it.

By the early 1970s, the golden age was coming to an end, replaced by a rather sluggish performance of both output and employment. Production and productivity leveled off around the secular trend, with several countries experiencing negative growth rates in the 1970s and again in the early 1980s and 1990s. Unemployment rates almost tripled in the 1980s relative to the 1960s. The ranking in terms of inequality of member countries of the Organization for Economic Cooperation and Development (OECD) that had remained much the same in the second half of the 1970s (figure 4.2) showed some marked difference by the mid-1980s, with the Anglo-Saxon countries (Australia, Canada, the United Kingdom, and, most notably, the United States) moving toward the top of the scale, the deutsche mark area approaching the low-inequality Scandinavian countries, and Mediterranean countries (Italy, Spain, Portugal, and, to a lesser extent, France) being somewhat in the middle (figure 4.3).

The available evidence for the latest decade (e.g., Gottschalk 1993; Fritzell 1993) indicates that the various factors affecting income distribution combined differently across countries in determining the evolution of inequality in the past decade. In fact, most countries experienced a rise in inequality of pretax and transfer income, the largest increase in earnings dispersion being in countries with less centralized wage-setting institutions, such as the United States. The increasing inequality of labor market outcomes was effectively, if partially, offset by active redistributive policies in Australia, Canada, France, the Federal Republic of Germany, and Sweden. In the United States and the United Kingdom, on the contrary, the redistributive impact of transfers and taxes worked in quite the opposite direction. For these two countries, the many changes to the welfare system implemented in the 1980s may have not only failed to mitigate the underlying market forces, but probably reinforced them in widening income distribution (Gramlich, Kasten, and Sammartino 1993; Johnson and Webb 1993; Atkinson 1996).

Excessive emphasis on the picture drawn so far may be undue for at least two reasons. First, the points in time of figures 4.1 through 4.3 correspond to markedly different macroeconomic conditions. Economic growth and (un)employment levels may be expected to affect the level and trend in absolute and relative earnings, as well as the pattern of property incomes, while inflation is quite likely to influence the real value of nonindexed sources of income.

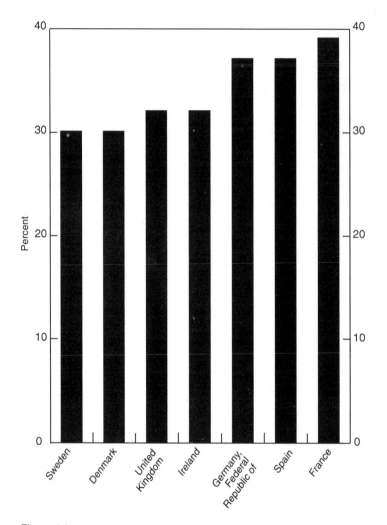

Figure 4.2
Selected OECD countries: Gini coefficients circa 1975. Based on posttax and transfer income, adjusted to national accounts, household weights; imputed rents included in Spain, Sweden, and the United Kingdom. Source: Van Ginneken and Park (1984, table 1).

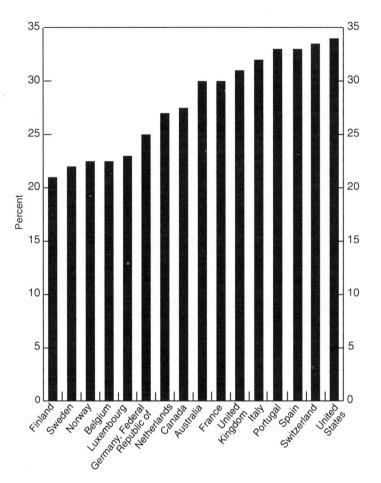

Figure 4.3
Selected OECD countries: Gini coefficients circa 1985. Based on posttax and transfer equivalent income, person weights. Source: Atkinson, Smeeding, and Rainwater (1995).

Second, and more important, whereas the trends in productivity appear to be well established, the described pattern of inequality over time and across countries rests on rather shaky foundations. Unlike national accounts, statistics on income distribution still lack a generally recognized and internationally accepted framework, and very few countries, if any, are likely to abide by the *Provisional Guidelines on Statistics of the Distribution of Income, Consumption, and Accumulation of Households* set by the United Nations (1977). Also, matters are made particularly difficult by institutional differences, such as the organization of pension plans, health, housing, education, and taxation. Because the statistical information is drawn from such heterogeneous sources, their degree of comparability is generally, questionable, a point clearly understood in the studies referred to above. Van Ginneken's and Park's (1984) study was significantly entitled *Generating Internationally Comparable Income Distribution Estimates*, whereas Atkinson, Rainwater, and Smeeding (1995, p. 13) stated at the beginning of their OECD report, "Issues of methodology are central to this investigation. Any comparison of income inequality in two or more countries is only comprehensible by referring to the methods employed. Published comparisons are frequently based on different source types or distributions defined in different ways. Distribution of annual household income per capita in country A cannot be directly compared with that of family income unadjusted for family size in country B, nor is it possible to eliminate all differences in definition. It is therefore necessary to understand how differences affect findings regarding inequality." We fully subscribe to this statement, and it is one of our central contentions here that neglecting such methodological issues may lead to misleading conclusions.

Nonetheless, pooling together the evidence of these major and widely used international comparisons may provide an initial set of working hypotheses, which may then be proved or disproved by research. That said, the prima facie evidence suggests that a major reranking might have taken place, with countries of the continental Europe faring much better than the United Kingdom and the United States in terms of income inequality. Interestingly, a similar reranking apparently took place with regard to labor productivity, with the United Kingdom approaching the United States at a much slower pace than other European followers (notably, the Scandinavian countries and those of the deutsche mark area). Such simultaneous reshuffling of relative positions in income distribution and productive capacity poses a number of important questions:

• Was the economic performance in any way linked with the state of income distribution prevailing in the aftermath of World War II?

• Was the subsequent evolution of income distribution in different countries a mere consequence of the growth acceleration and slowdown taking place since the 1950s? In other words, did the United Kingdom grow at a slower pace because of its initial rather fair distribution, or did the rising inequality of the 1980s lead to a lower sustainable growth path? Did continental Europe rapidly catch up because of its initial sizable inequality, or were social policies in continental Europe capable of associating a fairer distribution of income with higher growth? In short, did continental Europe pay a price, in terms of economic growth, for more egalitarian outcome? And if not, why?

In tacking these questions, we begin with a review of the many recent theoretical developments questioning the perceived trade-off between equality and growth and conclude that although much progress has been achieved, the issue still escapes a general consensus, and it remains in many respects an empirical question. We then come back to issues of conceptual and statistical comparability, submitting that their neglect undermines most of the available empirical on the growth-equality relationship, and we provide fresh evidence on the subject, drawing on relatively unexplored sources of information. Finally, after summarizing the main results, we offer some admittedly speculative comments on policy implications.

4.1   What Does Economic Theory Tell Us About the Growth-Inequality Relationship?

Setting the Problem Right

Before discussing the new theories linking economic growth to income distribution, it is necessary to set the problem at hand in a somewhat more precise way. A useful abstraction, on a theoretical ground, is to distinguish between two key aspects: the economic mechanism underlying the production of goods (and services) and the set of rules governing its distribution among people (Brandolini 1992). Macroeconomists have been overwhelmingly concerned with constructing models describing the economic mechanism; distributive issues have always been at the margin. At most, some attention has been devoted to factor shares, but they can hardly be regarded as a proxy for the personal income distribution;

in contemporary industrialized economies, the classical identification between income sources and social classes is, to say the least, somewhat
blurred. An understanding of the division of the product among people
demands specifying the entitlement rules, which state who receives what
and in which proportion. The notion of entitlement rules is broader than
that of property rights; it extends to encompass all those social norms that
govern the appropriation of resources without necessarily being set by law
(e.g., when primogeniture is the socially prevailing way of transmitting
wealth between generations in the absence of any specific legislation).

The recognition that the appropriation of the product is governed by
rules established to some extent outside the purely economic sphere has
far-reaching consequences. First, aggregation matters. The inadequacy of
the basic hypothesis of modern macroeconomics, the representative agent
hypothesis, becomes manifest. If people are different in the extent to
which they are entitled to enjoy the fruits of the economic system, there
is much less space to model the aggregate behavior as that of the average
agent. To put it differently, if individual saving decisions depend not only
on standard economic variables such as income and wealth but also on the
individual's relative position in the income scale (i.e., social status; see
Duesenberry 1949 and Cole, Mailath, and Postlewaite 1992), the aggregate saving cannot be evidently modeled as that of the average individual. The departure from the representative agent hypothesis need
not be so radical, however. Focusing on recent analytical contributions
on the growth-inequality relationship, the economy's capacity to save is
influenced by the fraction of credit-constrained individuals in theories
of capital market imperfections or by the decision of the median agent
(voter) in the new political economy—the minimal, if clever, departure
from the average representative agent hypothesis. In brief, setting entitlement rules determines the personal income distribution and allows its
feedback into the economic mechanism.

In the second place, one is forced to think about the different institutional arrangements in a more careful way. A good case in point is provided by the institutional features of unemployment insurance schemes.
As Atkinson (1992) has argued, unemployment benefits are characterized
not only by their amount but also by "the conditions under which benefits are paid, their link to labor market decisions, the contributory basis of
unemployment insurance, and the limited duration of insurance benefit";
accounting for all these features may well lead to conclusions about, say,
the effect of the scheme on employment, rather different from those ob-

tained by simply assuming that the benefit is a constant fraction of the wage rate. Extending Atkinson's conclusion to our framework, it is fairly obvious that the definition of such institutional features influences the personal income distribution. This suggests that the role of the political and administrative forces shaping institutional arrangements such as unemployment insurance should be made explicit, and the results of models should be seen as conditional on the assumed institutional structure. The contributions of the new political economy to the topics at hand are an intriguing attempt to meet these conditions.

Exogenous and Endogenous Growth Models
In probing more deeply into the nexus between inequality and growth, the obvious starting point is represented by the class of neoclassical growth models stemming from work by Solow (1956) and Swan (1956). In these models, income distribution has no role in determining aggregate savings, and aggregate savings have no influence on the long-term growth of the economy, irrespective of the way the propensity to save is determined, whether exogenously or as the result of an optimal decision (Bertola 1994). As Stiglitz (1969, p. 384) pointed out, the independence of aggregate capital accumulation from the distribution is a result of the linear relationship between savings and income (or wealth); adopting Kaldor's (1955–1956) hypothesis of a higher propensity to save out of profits than out of wages would not alter the result. In this framework, Stiglitz (1969) showed the existence of an intrinsic tendency of wealth to become more evenly distributed when the economy is on a balanced growth path.

By construction, in the steady state of Stiglitz's model, all per capita variables increase at the exogenously determined rate of technical progress, ruling out at the beginning any influence of aggregate savings. A different perspective is offered by the recently developed theories of endogenous growth, where accumulation is positively related to the aggregate (optimal) saving rate, paving the way for income distribution to play a role. Consider the "knowledge spillover" model, one of the simplest in this class: Society is supposed to accumulate over time a stock of knowledge whose return cannot be privately appropriated and spreads out across all members of the community. The working hypothesis is that the amount of received knowledge is proportional to the stock of physical capital and unfolds by augmenting labor productivity. The production function then shows diminishing returns to labor and capital at the firm level, but it exhibits constant returns to capital in the aggregate. Under this and other standard hypotheses on the utility function, the higher the propensity to save, the more intense the growth.

Because the representative agent hypothesis has not been abandoned yet, the distribution of resources is unimportant. The dynamics of wealth inequality, on the other hand, implies that individual wealth paths will endlessly diverge. This, however, does not impede the movement toward an even distribution, whose speed is positively dependent on the propensity to save. In summary, the basic results Stiglitz (1969) obtained in extending Solow's growth model carry over to the knowledge-spillover endogenous-growth model: In the absence of frictions, there is a tendency of the distribution of wealth (and income) to become more egalitarian; unless aggregate savings cease to be a linear function of income, wealth inequality has no effect on aggregate growth. The latter is the key point: When saving and investment decisions are one and the same, which is the case in the type of growth models we are studying, distribution matters to the extent that wealth is a determinant of people's saving behavior. It is to this last point that we turn our attention.

Political Institutions Approach
Whether growth is exogenous or endogenous, Stiglitz's framework focuses on the economic mechanism with perfect markets and identical preferences. With endogenous growth, assuming different preferences is a simple way to make economic performance dependent on wealth distribution. In particular, if the propensity to save rises with wealth, a more unequal wealth distribution leads to higher aggregate investments. This type of class behavior is an easy, if unattractive, way to rationalize the popular idea that higher inequality fosters growth. It hints, however, that while maintaining equal preferences, mechanisms generating social segmentation (e.g., credit market imperfections) may actually create a link between growth and distribution. Before dealing with this approach, we focus on a second way of departing from the baseline in Stiglitz's case, one incorporating a political mechanism in an otherwise perfect market framework.

The endogenizing of political mechanisms with reference to the growth-inequality link is associated with work by Alesina and Rodrik (1992, 1994), Alesina and Perotti (1996), Bertola (1993), Perotti (1992), Persson and Tabellini (1992, 1994), and Saint-Paul and Verdier (1992, 1993) and critically reviewed by Perotti (1993, 1994, 1996) and Alesina and Perotti (1994).

Consider, for instance, a simple endogenous growth model with overlapping generations, modified to embody redistributive taxation and a political mechanism along the lines suggested by Persson and Tabellini (1992, 1994). Typically in such models, people work when young and accumulate capital to sustain their consumption when old. Let the tax-benefit structure comprise a direct tax levied on wealth held by the old generation and a uniform benefit paid to the same generation. This system is purely redistributive in the sense that it takes away from those investing more than the average to give to those investing less.

As the tax rate rises, the adverse incentive to accumulation is less and less mitigated by the higher transfers to households that the higher tax revenue allows to pay. Consequently, the higher the tax rate, the lower the rate of growth of the economy. In the extreme, when the tax rate is unity, all returns from investment are entirely paid as taxes, the incentive to wealth accumulation vanishes, at least to the extent that individuals do not take into account the effect of their behavior on the aggregate stock of capital, and current income is wholly consumed. Because no accumulation takes place, the original distribution of wealth persists forever.

It is clear that individuals have well-defined preferences over the tax-benefit schedule. Understandably, those richer than the average would not levy any tax on wealth, thus maximizing the rate of growth of the economy. But the people with wealth below the average would balance the gain from a wider redistribution with the loss due to the slower growth, choosing a tax rate between zero and unity. Redistribution would become more and more attractive as individual wealth falls. Below a certain threshold (determined by preferences and technology), people would be so poor as to choose a tax rate equal to unity at the cost of hindering any growth; as a by-product, they would make income distribution among the old perfectly even.

Suppose now that the tax-benefit structure is chosen by a democratic voting process. Since preferences are well defined and single-peaked, the median voter theorem can be applied. Therefore the tax rate will be set at the level preferred by the median voter. In the empirically relevant case, wealth (and income) distribution is skewed to the right, and the median is less than the mean. It follows that the closer that median wealth is to mean wealth, the lower the tax rate and the higher the rate of growth of the economy. To the extent that the distance between the mean and the median is a good measure of inequality—which is not strictly the case, as shown, for instance, by Wolfson (1994)—Persson and Tabellini (1992, 1994) can conclude that inequality is harmful for growth.

Persson and Tabellini's conclusion is subject to a series of qualifications. First, it is possible to show that the evolution of the model over time is rank preserving, implying that the median voter always belongs to the same dynasty. This has the important implication that a tax rate between zero and one eventually chosen by the median voter at time 0 cannot be sustained in the long run (except for a case with probability zero). If the wealth of the median voter dynasty grows more quickly than the average, the tax rate gradually approaches zero: Economic growth tends to a maximum and inequality to a minimum. In the opposite case, where the median voter dynasty fails to keep the pace of the average, the economy converges to the no-accumulation and maximum-inequality long-run equilibrium. At the end of the day, what matters is the inequality of the original distribution of wealth, its role being limited to selecting the long-run equilibrium.

Second, the impact of inequality on growth requires a democratic one-person, one-vote system. If political rights are restricted so that the median voter is in the upper half of the population, the link disappears. At the other extreme, it may well happen that the distribution is so skewed as to imply a tax rate on wealth above unity—that is, expropriation of capital. In this case, the political mechanism would fail to provide an institutional way out to the distributional conflict, paving the way to changes of governments, changes of regimes, and, more generally, political instability, as suggested by Alesina and Perotti (1996) and Perotti (1994, 1996).

Third, Persson and Tabellini's (1992, 1994) result crucially depends on the policy mix as well as on the stage of development of the economy (Perotti, 1992). The result that inequality is bad for growth is also obtained by Alesina and Rodrik (1992, 1994) in a model where capital-income taxation finances the provision of productive ("law and order") public services, but the opposite result is found by Saint-Paul and Verdier (1992, 1993) in a model where public education is funded with nondistortionary taxes. Bertola (1993) similary shows that the rate of growth preferred by capital-poor (with respect to the average) median voters is lower than the social optimum when capital-income subsidies are financed by labor-income taxes, but may well be larger when investment subsidies are financed by indirect consumption taxes (Bertola uses "capital" and "labor" as shorthand for "reproducible" and "nonreproducible" factors, respectively). Perotti (1993), on the other hand, suggests that income distribution affects growth differently in rich and poor economies. In a model combining a political mechanism with imperfect capital markets, preconditions for higher growth are a more even distribution in high-income countries, but concentration of resources in the upper class in low-income countries.

Social Institutions Approach
The starting point of the political institutions approach is that some relevant economic variables are set through a political procedure, which conveys outcomes different from those achieved, for instance, by a social planner. No market failure or coordination problem is supposed to impair the economic system, and the inequality-growth link stems entirely from the specification of entitlement rules in the form of political rights.

Conversely, the assumption of some kind of market imperfection is at the origin of an alternative approach to the growth-distribution nexus. An extensively studied example (e.g., Galor and Zeira 1993) is that of an economy where education holds the key to better-paid jobs but is costly. If capital market imperfections prevent the worse off from attaining a sufficiently high level of education, preferred-skill jobs could actually be beyond their reach.

More specifically, suppose that people are given the choice between working as unskilled or studying to increase their work ability by paying a fee and then earning the skilled wage rate. Production occurs in two sectors differing for technology: one using capital and skilled labor, the other relying on unskilled labor only. Both sectors are assumed to benefit from the accumulation of knowledge, and labor productivity in both is proportional to the stock of physical capital. Moreover, the education fee is indexed to the skilled wage rate.

To have people investing in education, its opportunity cost must be smaller than the wage differential between skilled and unskilled jobs. When such a condition is met and all people can borrow any amount at the current interest rate, everybody chooses to study and the model collapses to the simple endogenous growth models already discussed. However, in the absence of credit markets, only people with initial wealth higher than the education fee have access to education; the others are forced to work in the unskilled sector. The level of the education fee splits the population into two classes that differ in both job status and income and also their ability to accumulate physical capital. Such class behavior affects the aggregate wealth dynamics: the higher the employment share of the skilled sector, the stronger the pace of accumulation. Wealth distribution, on the other hand, determines the sectoral composition of the labor force, since skilled workers are all people having at time 0 wealth higher than the education fee. In the long run, only the level of per capita wealth will differ across people, whereas the rates of growth will converge to a common value.

The society turns out to be divided into two broad classes: the "poor," that is, people with initial wealth too small to allow them to accumulate human capital, who will eventually settle on the lower steady state, and the "rich," who are born with an endowment sufficient to incur the cost of education and whose wealth will converge to the upper steady state. As a result, inequality tends asymptotically to a positive value, the sign of the long-run tendency being dependent on the initial degree of concentration. Two different phenomena are at work. Within-group inequality is unequivocally diminishing as all the poor, on one side, and all the rich, on the other, are converging to their respective level of per capita wealth; between-group inequality, on the contrary, is bound to persist and, in the end, it will explain all the long-run inequality.

This simple story captures several aspects of the growth-inequality relationship. First, it highlights how the existence of capital market imperfections leads naturally to establishing an influence of the distribution of resources on accumulation. In the story, wealth distribution would be irrelevant for the aggregate behavior of the economy if the credit market were perfect; in the absence of such a market, the distribution would matter in that the exclusion of some people from education because of their insufficient initial endowment would lower the steady-state growth rate. The result survives by allowing for some less drastic imperfection. Galor and Zeira (1993) and Torvik (1993) model the imperfection of the credit market as a wedge between the interest rates paid by borrowers and received by lenders, arising from the cost that the latter must incur to avoid defaulting by the former. In Aghion and Bolton (1992, 1993), the imperfection stems from the "debt-overhang problem," whereby the poor need to borrow more funds than the rich to be able to invest; the higher the repayment they owe to lenders, the less effort they supply to increase the probability of success of their project. Below a certain wealth level, incentives are so distorted that lending is unprofitable, even if these very poor individuals are not necessarily credit constrained, as they might prefer being lenders rather than borrowers. In Ferreira (1995), loan arrangements require a collateral, which indirectly sets a credit ceiling proportional to borrowers' wealth. In general, the possibility of borrowing gives rise to a "middle class" made up of those whose inheritances are large enough to make education worthwhile, but at the cost of becoming borrowers. However, in the models by Galor and Zeira (1993) and Torvik

(1993), the middle class is bound to disappear; in the long run, the off-spring of some of its members will succeed and join the rich, and the others will experience a decline in wealth from generation to generation until they join the poor. The relative size of the two groups eventually will depend on the initial wealth distribution. Differently, in the models by Aghion and Bolton (1992, 1993) and Ferreira (1995), the economy converges under certain conditions to a unique invariant income distribution, independent of the initial conditions.

Second, the emphasis on education provides a clear example of how the link between growth and inequality might change with different institutional arrangements. Studies by Glomm and Ravikumar (1992), Bénabou (1996a), and Garcia-Peñalosa (1995) examine the issue of private versus public schooling, finding that the latter can yield higher per capita incomes or growth rates when the initial income inequality is sufficiently high. On the other hand, Bénabou (1996a) and Fernandez and Rogerson (1994) show that moving from local to national funding of education raises average income. The large international differences in the organization of educational systems suggest that the impact of inequality on economic performance might greatly vary across countries.

Third, market imperfections need not be limited to capital markets. For instance, Agell and Lommerud (1993) consider a model with imperfect labor mobility across sectors. Because of their locational preferences, workers do not move toward the areas where the modern high-productivity businesses are based. In the absence of active public policies, competitive wage premiums arise, and growth is dampened; social institutions taking the form of central bargaining may implement egalitarian wage policies, which compress wage differentials and stimulate labor reallocation from low- to high-productivity sectors. This has the dual effect of speeding up growth while establishing a more even distribution of wages and income. Acemoglu (1996) analyzes a model where matching in the labor market is costly and mobility costs are high. In this framework, more human capital heterogeneity increases the level of social mismatch and lowers output; as heterogeneity depends on the distribution of income, inequality is harmful for growth. In related work, Bénabou (1994, 1996b) shows how a high degree of stratification may be brought about by small differences in wealth, even in the absence of capital market imperfections; in turn, local segregation makes income inequality more persistent and slows growth.

Market imperfections redesign entitlement rules by restricting differently agents' opportunity sets. From a positive point of view, this means that the development of social institutions aimed at removing market imperfections may simultaneously reduce inequality and raise productivity. From a normative point of view, it paves the way for a positive role for public policies aiming at equalizing opportunities "by letting all agents have access to profitable activities on similar terms" (Aghion and Bolton 1993, p. 34). At the end of the day, both the political institutions approach and the social institutions approach regard the relationship between inequality and growth as negative, but according to the former, increased inequality translates into pressure for more redistribution, which hurts people's incentives to invest, whereas for the latter it implies that fewer people have access to all investment opportunities. As Bénabou (1996c) pointed out, a rather different view of government lies behind the two approaches: Public policies are distortionary in the political institutions approach but lead to positive efficiency gains in the social institutions approach.

4.2   Unequal Inequalities

The theoretical debate is hardly over and, as Lindert and Williamson (1985, p. 342) pointed out, is quite likely to persist for at least two reasons: "First, highly politicized debates tend to have long lives. Government policies which involve a possible redistribution of income create opposing self-interests, and each side can be counted on to promote its cause by economic arguments that are hard to falsify. Second, the issue is exceedingly difficult to resolve with evidence. Certainly, the trade-off cannot be assessed by simple correlations between growth and inequality."

Notwithstanding Lindert's and Williamson's warning, inferences based on simple (cross-country partial) correlations are still the keystone of most empirical studies dealing with the subject and, to some extent, this chapter is not an exception.[1] Their drawbacks have been outlined elsewhere (Levine and Renelt 1992) and need not be recalled here except to note that they might be exacerbated in the case at hand. To clarify the issue, it may be worth considering the standard layout of recent empirical studies, whose main ingredient is a Cobb-Douglas production function, augmented to embody human capital H_{jt},

$$Q_{jt} = K_{jt}^{\alpha} H_{jt}^{\kappa} (A_{jt} L_{jt})^{1-\alpha-\kappa} \tag{4.1}$$

where Q_{jt}, K_{jt}, L_{jt}, and A_{jt} are the output, the capital stock, the labor input, and the efficiency factor, respectively, and j and t refer to country and time. Let k_{jt} and h_{jt} indicate the investment in physical and human capital, respectively, as a share of output, and let γ and δ be the constant (across countries and capital goods, and over time) exogenous technical progress and depreciation rates. In the neighborhood of the steady-state path, labor productivity, defined as the ratio of Q_{jt} to L_{jt} evolves according to the following equation (Mankiw, Romer, and Weil 1992):

$$\ln\left(q_{jt+1}/q_{jt}\right) = \gamma + [1 - \exp(-\lambda_{jt})]\left[\ln A_{j0} + \gamma t + \frac{\alpha}{1 - \alpha - \kappa}\ln k_{jt}\right.$$

$$+ \frac{\kappa}{1 - \alpha - \kappa}\ln h_{jt} + \frac{\alpha + \kappa}{1 - \alpha - \kappa}\ln(n_{jt} + \gamma + \delta) - \ln q_{jt}], \quad (4.2)$$

where $\lambda_{jt} = (n_{jt} + \gamma + \delta)(1 - \alpha - \kappa)$ and the "time length" between observations has been normalized to unity. In equation 4.2, the difference (in brackets) between steady-state labor productivity and its current value affects the future labor productivity growth rate and induces conditional convergence toward the stochastic (across countries and over time) steady-state equilibrium path, given by a linear function of the population growth rate (n_{jt}), the time trend, and suitable proxies for the investment rates in physical and human capital. Augmented versions of equation 4.2 allow for an efficiency variable A_{j0}, depending (directly or indirectly) on technological progress as well as on additional variables, such as measures of the role of the public sector in the economy, the degree of openness of the domestic economy to foreign trade, political instability, or economic inequality.

The theory behind equation 4.2 does not impose any specific time unit. As pointed out by Cellini (1997), neoclassical growth models embody, in the econometric terminology, an "error correction mechanism," whereby convergence toward the steady state occurs if $-1 < -[1 - \exp(-\lambda_{jt})] < 0$. Because such a convergence mechanism is independent of the time unit, it should show up in the data at any frequency. It follows that the very nature of equation 4.2 suggests abandoning the usual practice of looking at long-term averages and exploiting, when available, the wealth of information, if available, embodied in higher frequency data.[2]

The important point to note is that the constant term of the linear functions defining steady-state labor productivity allows for country-specific and time-specific effects. The latter may be accounted for, in principle, by the term γt, while the former are embodied in the term $\ln A_{j0}$, which approximates the initial state of the technology and all the unobserved elements determining the efficiency of production. In this setting, country-specific effects (including the structure of taxation, and the regulation of international trade, and the provision of public services) may well be correlated with the other explanatory variables considered in the model.[3]

When confined to cross-sectional data, the above setup is bound to ignore country-specific effects, while time-specific effects become irrelevant and the story told by equation 4.2 boils down, in the simplest case, to a simple regression of average (per capita or per worker) productivity growth rates against average population growth rates, initial physical and human capital proxies, and initial productivity levels.

Consider now augmenting the simplified setup with measures of income distribution. First, different theoretical views of the growth-inequality relationship imply different concepts of the distribution of economic resources (e.g., wealth versus income, inequality versus polarization). Second, measures of the distribution of economic resources within a given population may widely differ as to the definition of economic resource, the unit of analysis, the degree of comparability across basic units, and the implied attitude toward inequality. To date, cross-sectional analyses have been mixing up measures of inequality with a questionable degree of logical and statistical comparability. As a result, the cross-country variability of inequality measures may have accounted for country-specific effects ruled out by assumption in the cross-sectional context.[4]

In short, the conceptual and statistical heterogeneity of inequality measures should be taken seriously and full comparability ensured whenever possible. This rather difficult task has been made possible recently by the important work undertaken since the early 1980s at the Luxembourg Income Study (LIS).[5] The LIS group has assembled and, as much as possible, homogenized national micro-data-sets to create a unified database for household incomes. Using the LIS database, possibly in conjunction with country studies, Gottschalk (1993), Atkinson, Rainwater, and Smeeding (1995), Fritzell (1993), and Gottschalk and Smeeding (forthcoming), among others, have recently provided insightful analyses of distributional changes in a number of OECD countries, attempting to trace the causes of such changes. In the following sections we will shed further light on the growth-inequality debate by applying the standard cross-sectional time-averaged methodology to the LIS database and subsequently exploiting the panel information coming from national sources. It is worth underlining that for the reasons explained above, we regard the first research strategy as hardly informative and report the relevant results mostly for comparative purposes.

4.3 Empirical Evidence

LIS Database
Standardized income inequality measures are provided in Atkinson, Rainwater, and Smeeding (1995) for seventeen OECD countries (sometimes for more than one year) and lend themselves naturally to analyses of the kind attempted by Alesina and Rodrik (1992, 1994), Persson and Tabellini (1992, 1994), and Perotti (1994b) in estimating a reduced-form relationship between some inequality measure at some point in time and the subsequent average growth rate of gross domestic product (GDP) per capita.

Because all countries in the sample are democracies, the LIS database provides an ideal environment to test the political institutions channel, which should entail a negative relationship between initial inequality and subsequent growth. At the same time, all countries in the sample possess sufficiently developed capital markets, which makes it unlikely that a correlation between equality and growth comes from this channel.[6] Because the countries in the sample have rather different institutional structures and standards of social policy, the social institutions approach should emerge only with selected sections of the sample.

In the following regressions, based on an augmented linear unrestricted version of equation 4.2,

$$\ln(q_{jt}/q_{jt-5}) = \pi_0 + \pi_1 \tau + \pi_2 \ln k_{jt-5} + \pi_3 \ln h_{jt-5}$$

$$+ \pi_4 \ln(n_{jt-5} + 0.05) + \pi_5 G_{jt-5} + \pi_6 \ln q_{jt-5}, \qquad (4.3)$$

two alternative measures of income inequality (G_{jt-5}) have been considered: a summary measure of inequality (the Gini coefficient; table 4.1) and the income share of the third quintile of the distribution (table 4.2). Their sampling date (reported in appendix 4.1) varies by country, and for a few countries, more than a sampling date is available; in general, information can be grouped around 1979 and 1984. Consequently, the dependent variable—the growth rate of GDP per worker—was computed over five-year periods starting with those two years. In addition to a time dummy (τ) and a constant term, the regression included (in logarithm) the level of GDP per worker (q_{jt-5}), the share of fixed investment over GDP (k_{jt-5}), the share of the relevant age group attending secondary school in the same years (h_{jt-5}), and the sum of the rate of growth of population (n_{jt-5}), the rate of technological progress, and the rate of depreciation (estimated at 0.05).

Table 4.1
Estimates of Equation 4.3: Dependent Variable: Growth Rate of GDP per Worker. Income Distribution Variable: Gini Coefficient, LIS Database

	Heteroskedasticity adjusted	Error in variables	Robust regression
Constant ($\hat{\pi}_0$)	0.2070 (0.1672)	0.2127 (0.1857)	0.4490 (0.1494)
Time dummy ($\hat{\pi}_1$)	0.0035 (0.0008)	0.0035 (0.0008)	0.0023 (0.0007)
Gini coefficient ($\hat{\pi}_5$)	−0.0031 (0.0464)	−0.0177 (0.2424)	0.0574 (0.0498)
Initial labor productivity ($\hat{\pi}_6$)	−0.0301 (0.0162)	−0.0304 (0.0128)	−0.0514 (0.0145)
R-squared	0.5312	0.5313	
Root mean squared error	0.0128	0.0127	
Number of observations	27	27	27

Note: Standard errors in parentheses.

Table 4.2
Estimates of Equation 4.3: Dependent Variable: Growth Rate of GDP per Worker. Income Distribution Variable: Income Share of third Quintile, LIS Database

	Heteroskedasticity adjusted	Error in variables	Robust regression
Constant ($\hat{\pi}_0$)	0.2296 (0.1684)	0.3094 (0.1719)	0.3834 (0.1677)
Time dummy ($\hat{\pi}_1$)	0.0035 (0.0008)	0.0034 (0.0008)	0.0025 (0.0008)
Income share for thrid quintile ($\hat{\pi}_5$)	−0.2387 (0.2370)	−1.0154 (1.4080)	−0.1435(0.3095)
Initial labor productivity ($\hat{\pi}_6$)	−0.0280 (0.0165)	−0.0217 (0.0146)	−0.0417 (0.0167)
R-squared	0.5408	0.5723	
Root mean squared error	0.0127	0.0122	
Number of observations	27	27	27

Note: Standard errors in parentheses.

Estimating equation 4.3 by ordinary least squares (OLS), out of the several variables included, only the initial level of GDP per worker, the time dummy (catching time-specific effects), and the constant survived the initial specification search. Tables 4.1 and 4.2 therefore report the restricted estimates allowing for White's (1980) heteroskedasticity consistent standard errors in the first column, Greene's (1993) error-in-variables adjustment in the second column, and a treatment of outliers (as suggested by Li 1985) in the third column.

As tables 4.1 and 4.2 show, the coefficients of the basic variables (the time trend and the catch-up variable) have the expected sign, are reasonably significant, and explain a large fraction of the variance in growth. However, contrary to recent literature, neither the Gini coefficient nor the income share of the third quintile plays a significant role in the regressions. If anything, both income distribution variables seem to revive the time-honored growth-equality trade-off. As the second and third columns of tables 4.1 and 4.2 indicate, the disappointing result cannot be imputed to measurement errors in the inequality indicators or to the few outlying observations, and reverse causation is clearly ruled out by the timing of the variables. In addition, it is worth noting that the zero impact of income inequality on growth is not a consequence of investment's playing a major role in the regression, which would be the case if inequality affected growth through accumulation, as the share of fixed investment never survived the specification search.[7]

In short, when inequality measures are selected so as to ensure a reasonable degree of comparability (and to rule out spurious country-specific effects), the following points are worth noting: Simple (cross-section partial) correlations do not support the idea that growth is inversely related to inequality, and if anything, income inequality at the start of the period has a positive effect on subsequent growth. In the light of previous remarks on the informational content of the LIS database, these results cast some doubts on the political institutions approach, which would have implied a significantly negative impact of initial inequality on growth.

National Sources

A viable alternative to the standardized LIS database is given by national sources providing inequality measures—possibly heterogeneous across countries, but homogeneous over time in a given country. As table 4A.1 suggests, the statistical information available translates into an unbalanced panel extending over nine developed countries (Australia, Canada, Finland, the Federal Republic of Germany, Italy, Norway, Sweden, the United Kingdom, and the United States) and, on average, over a twenty-three-year period, from the late 1960s to the early 1990s.

The results of estimating equation 4.2 on the whole sample by ordinary least squares (OLS), allowing for fixed effects, are reported in table 4.3.[8] It should be noticed that the (linear unrestricted) estimated version of equation 4.2 adds to the basic specification the inequality measure (as given by the Gini coefficient) and the logarithm of the share of government consumption over GDP (g_{jt}),[9] and it allows for a number of differenced regressors designed to filter the short-run movements of labor

Table 4.3
Estimates of Equation 4.4: Dependent Variable: Growth Rate of GDP per Worker. Income Distribution Variable: Gini Coefficient (Whole National Sample, Fixed Effects)

	Specification	Specification	Specification
Constant $(\hat{\pi}_0)$	0.7289 (0.2153)	0.4278 (0.1943)	0.3708 (0.1792)
Long-run effects			
Time trend $(\hat{\pi}_1)$	0.0012 (0.0005)	0.0007 (0.0004)	0.0004 (0.0004)
Physical capital $(\hat{\pi}_2)$	0.0067 (0.0151)	0.0186 (0.0135)	0.0217 (0.0132)
Human capital $(\hat{\pi}_3)$	−0.0172 (0.0132)	−0.0153 (0.0105)	
Population growth $(\hat{\pi}_4)$	−0.0392 (0.0157)	−0.0480 (0.0106)	−0.0529 (0.0108)
Income distribution $(\hat{\pi}_5)$		−0.0136 (0.0575)	0.0054 (0.0522)
Initial labor productivity $(\hat{\pi}_6)$	−0.0821 (0.0206)	−0.0584 (0.0180)	−0.0527 (0.0165)
Government consumption $(\hat{\pi}_7)$		−0.0335 (0.0184)	−0.0288 (0.0171)
Short-run effects			
Physical capital $(\hat{\pi}_8)$	0.2251 (0.0238)	0.0922 (0.0186)	0.0939 (0.0185)
Human capital $(\hat{\pi}_9)$	−0.0048 (0.0236)	0.01178 (0.0190)	
Population growth $(\hat{\pi}_{10})$	−0.0443 (0.0112)	−0.0580 (0.0124)	−0.0603 (0.0123)
Income distribution $(\hat{\pi}_{11})$		−0.0438 (0.0689)	
Government consumption $(\hat{\pi}_{12})$		−0.5733 (0.0472)	−0.5030 (0.0522)
R-squared	0.6072	0.8158	0.8132
Root mean squared error	0.0171	0.0118	0.0118
Number of observations	201	201	201

Note: Heteroskedasticity-corrected standard errors in parentheses.

productivity,

$$\ln(q_{jt}/q_{jt-1}) = \pi_0 + \pi_1 t + \pi_2 \ln k_{jt-1} + \pi_3 \ln h_{jt-1} + \pi_4 \ln(n_{jt-1} + 0.05)$$
$$+ \pi_5 G_{jt-1} + \pi_6 \ln q_{jt-1} + \pi_7 \ln g_{jt-1} + \pi_8 \Delta \ln k_{jt} + \pi_9 \Delta \ln h_{jt}$$
$$+ \pi_{10} \Delta \ln(n_{jt} + 0.05) + \pi_{11} \Delta G_{jt} + \pi_{12} \Delta \ln g_{jt}, \tag{4.4}$$

where all other variables are defined as before. In table 4.3, column a reports on the estimation of equation 4.4 in its basic version, column b presents its augmented version, and column c constrains to zero a few badly determined coefficients. As before, White's (1980) corrected standard errors take care of heteroskedasticity.

With the exception of the human capital proxy, equation 4.4 seems to track reasonably well the movements of labor productivity. Abstracting

Table 4.4
Estimates of Equation 4.4: Dependent Variable: Growth Rate of GDP per Worker. Income Distribution Variable: Gini Coefficient (Whole Sample, Fixed Effects, Sensitivity Analysis)

	Error in variables	Robust regression	Weighted regression
Constant ($\hat{\pi}_0$)	0.3265 (0.5436)	0.3702 (0.1809)	
Long-run effects			
Time trend ($\hat{\pi}_1$)	0.0004 (0.0009)	0.0004 (0.0004)	0.0011 (0.0004)
Physical capital ($\hat{\pi}_2$)	0.0200 (0.0240)	0.0228 (0.0143)	0.0760 (0.0198)
Human capital ($\hat{\pi}_3$)			
Population growth ($\hat{\pi}_4$)	−0.0520 (0.0148)	−0.0439 (0.0101)	−0.0529 (0.0122)
Income distribution ($\hat{\pi}_5$)	−0.0355 (0.3533)	−0.0138 (0.0541)	0.0228 (0.0608)
Initial labor productivity ($\hat{\pi}_6$)	−0.0487 (0.0491)	−0.0479 (0.0162)	−0.0573 (0.0161)
Government consumption ($\hat{\pi}_7$)	−0.0249 (0.0483)	−0.0157 (0.0199)	−0.0270(0.0272)
Short-run effects			
Physical capital ($\hat{\pi}_8$)	0.0943 (0.0168)	0.0965 (0.0165)	0.2020 (0.0233)
Human capital ($\hat{\pi}_9$)			
Population growth ($\hat{\pi}_{10}$)	−0.0599 (0.0103)	−0.0461 (0.0094)	−0.0609 (0.0132)
Income distribution ($\hat{\pi}_{11}$)			
Government consumption ($\hat{\pi}_{12}$)	−0.0566 (0.0636)	−0.5938 (0.0417)	−0.3678 (0.0560)
R-squared	0.8132		0.8521
Root mean squared error	0.0118	0.0118	0.0104
Number of observations	201	201	201

Note: Heteroskedasticity corrected standard errors in parentheses.

from short-run effects, a conditional convergence effect (as given by $\hat{\pi}_6$) shows up quite strongly, together with a positive effect on growth of a high ratio of investment to GDP ($\hat{\pi}_2$), a negative effect of population growth ($\hat{\pi}_4$), and a negative effect from overly large government ($\hat{\pi}_7$). However, income distribution (as measured by the Gini coefficient) always makes a very poor showing (the coefficient $\hat{\pi}_5$ is never significant and takes positive as well as negative values), strongly suggesting that, prima facie, the steady-state equilibrium path of labor productivity does not depend on income inequality.

This result is not driven by measurement errors in the inequality indicator or by one or two outliers. Table 4.4, column a, allows for mismeasurement in the Gini coefficient; the implied downward bias in the estimate of the coefficient of the inequality indicator does not appreciably change the results. Accounting for a few outliers, as in column b, casts doubts on the role of government consumption but yields estimates otherwise quite close to the ordinary least squares ones. Finally, column c applies weighted least squares (with weights inversely proportional to population) to investigate further the issue of heteroskedasticity, again without changing the substance of the results. In all cases, $\hat{\pi}_5$ would entail a growth-equality trade-off, but it is never significantly different from 0.

In brief, when inequality measures are observed over time so as to allow country dummies to capture differences in sources, definitions, and measurement, we confirm all the relevant results found using the LIS database: no evidence of a negative effect of inequality on growth—which is, if anything, positive—and little support for the political institutions approach (see also Perotti 1994, 1996); however, in table 4.4, the impact of income inequality might well be captured by the role of investment in physical capital.

Should this evidence be taken as conclusive? Not necessarily. While raising doubts about the political institutions approach, the empirical evidence does not do justice to the social institutions approach, which may be expected to have results, depending on the institutional context. This, as a matter of fact, is the message of table 4.5, where the estimates of equation 4.4 for different subsamples are reported.

In particular, columns a and b in table 4.5 split the sample between European and non-European countries and show that equation 4.4 provides a reasonable description of the evolution of labor productivity in both subsamples. Conditional convergence is apparently slower in Europe, where the economy moves halfway to the steady state in about seven years, as opposed to less than three years in the case of North America and Oceania (given the formula for λ, these estimates look rather sensible). Moreover, the impact of basic determinants of the steady-state growth path is largely comparable among the two areas, with one single (and striking) exception: income distribution. In fact, Gini coefficients apparently play opposite roles: Higher inequality leads to lesser growth in Europe and to higher growth in North America and Oceania. Notice also that income distribution affects productivity growth in both areas, in spite of the significant contribution of the share of fixed investment in all regressions. However, as columns c and d of table 4.5 suggest, geography might not be the root of the problem, the watershed being not the Atlantic Ocean but possibly the social institutions and norms prevailing in continental Europe as opposed to Anglo-Saxon countries.

Table 4.5
Estimates of Equation 4.4: Dependent Variable: Growth Rate of GDP per Worker. Income Distribution Variable: Gini Coefficient (National Subsamples, Fixed Effects)

	Europe	North America and Oceania	Continental Europe	North America, United Kingdom, and Oceania	Scandinavia
Constant ($\hat{\pi}_0$)	0.440 (0.217)	1.102 (0.424)	0.433 (0.241)	0.969 (0.310)	0.797 (0.168)
Long-run effects					
Time trend ($\hat{\pi}_1$)	0.001 (0.001)	−0.002 (0.001)	0.000 (0.001)	0.001 (0.001)	
Physical capital ($\hat{\pi}_2$)	0.028 (0.013)		0.033 (0.015)	0.052 (0.021)	0.041 (0.014)
Human capital ($\hat{\pi}_3$)		0.090 (0.037)			0.124 (0.040)
Population growth ($\hat{\pi}_4$)	−0.067 (0.015)	−0.099 (0.019)	−0.071 (0.015)		
Income distribution ($\hat{\pi}_5$)	−0.105 (0.066)	1.154 (0.174)	−0.186 (0.070)	0.167 (0.081)	−0.099 (0.068)
Initial labor productivity ($\hat{\pi}_6$)	−0.067 (0.023)	−0.185 (0.046)	−0.063 (0.026)	−0.095 (0.029)	0.067 (0.015)
Government consumption ($\hat{\pi}_7$)	−0.063 (0.024)	−0.078 (0.023)	−0.061 (0.027)		
Short-run effects					
Physical capital ($\hat{\pi}_8$)	0.069 (0.020)	0.173 (0.018)	0.057 (0.020)	0.172 (0.023)	0.035 (0.016)
Human capital ($\hat{\pi}_9$)		−0.133 (0.067)			
Population growth ($\hat{\pi}_{10}$)	−0.067 (0.014)	−0.094 (0.024)	−0.069 (0.014)	−0.041 (0.022)	−0.052 (0.021)
Income distribution ($\hat{\pi}_{11}$)					
Government consumption ($\hat{\pi}_{12}$)	−0.643 (0.061)	−0.334 (0.055)	−0.703 (0.063)	−0.398 (0.058)	−0.771 (0.048)
R-squared	0.8187	0.8896	0.8443	0.8285	0.8802
Root mean squared error	0.0115	0.0096	0.0111	0.0112	0.0096
Number of observations	141	60	112	89	59

Note: Heteroskedasticity corrected.

Different subsamples tell largely different and conflicting stories, which offset each other in the whole sample. The equality-growth trade-off seems to be alive and well in English-speaking countries while equality seems to be conducive to growth in Europe, most notably in continental Europe. Interestingly, as column e of table 4.5 shows, the latter finding does not depend on the performance of the Scandinavian countries. Our estimates suggest that a 5 percentage point decrease in the Gini coefficient might lead, ceteris paribus, to a percentage point increase in steady-state labor productivity in the nations of continental Europe. The opposite result would prevail in the Anglo-Saxon countries, with a 5 percentage point increase in the concentration index stimulating growth by 1 percentage point.

Coefficient estimates also hint that the way income equalization is arrived at may be crucial, since the positive impact of equality on growth in continental Europe is partially offset by the negative effect of government consumption. In other words, while suggesting that social institutions increasing the size of government may imply lower growth rates, the evidence also indicates that public spending (possibly on social transfers) may actually be growth enhancing. In this respect, we fully endorse Atkinson's (1995) view: What matters most is the fine institutional structure, which eventually sets the balance between distributional outcomes and public finance implications.

4.4 Conclusion

Empirical work on the growth-inequality relationship is admittedly difficult. The typical problems arising from the limited amount of information available on long-term growth compound with a host of statistical and methodological issues plaguing the measurement of inequality. We explicitly attempted to tackle these difficulties by adopting two strategies, the first favoring a high degree of comparability across countries and the second exploiting the gains from using inequality measures homogeneous over time at the country level. In this respect, our approach is likely an improvement over the existing empirical literature, but we hardly need to stress that our results, as suggestive as they might be, are little more than guidance for further research of a more structural nature. On the one side, the theoretical links between inequality and growth are to be better understood and tested through modeling strategies more adequate than reduced-form regressions, whose information content is very limited. On the other side, highly stylized analyses, like the one performed here, have to be substantiated by the wealth of information, now available for many countries and produced by researchers investigating the many aspects of the evolution of income distribution over time.

Nevertheless, some concluding, if speculative, comments are in order. In the face of the relatively homogeneous nature of the political institutions and the similar placing in the international per capita income scale of the countries in our sample, the evidence presented does not lend much support to the political economy explanation of the growth-inequality link but suggests that the recent emphasis on political institutions might be partly misplaced. The markedly different response of economic performance to changes in the distribution of income across countries calls for a broader view; the observed wide differences in the social institutions that characterize different countries might be a useful starting point.

The paramount importance of social institutions also permeates recent views of the European postwar economic performance (e.g., Crafts and Toniolo 1996). For instance, Eichengreen (1996, p. 41) remarks that European "postwar growth benefitted from the presence of institutions singularly well suited to reconstruction and growth. Those institutions solved commitment and coordination problems in whose presence neither wage moderation nor the expansion of international trade could have taken place." He adds that institutions were not equally well suited to the needs of growth in all European countries and "these different institutional responses go a fair way toward accounting for variations across countries and over time in European growth performance." Eichengreen's idea that institutions are a device to create credible commitments points to the role of long-term contracts; social pacts between labor, management, and government; statutory wages and price controls; and centralization of sectoral wage negotiations as "mechanisms used to precommit unions to wage moderation and to thereby induce management to invest."

When, around 1970, it became less and less feasible to sustain the distributional environment that had made possible high investment rates and high productivity growth, the postwar social pact began to crumble in a number of European countries (notably France and Italy), and the institutions developed to solve the postwar commitment and coordination problems went only halfway to meet the new circumstances, showing a lack of flexibility that possibly contributed to the dramatic rise of unemployment and the decline of labor force participation rates. Nevertheless, as Freeman (1994) forcefully argues, in the 1970s and 1980s, European labor institutions and social protection schemes were apparently still better suited than North American ones for improving productivity. In particular, Germany (and Japan) outperformed the United States, still preserving a significant institutional presence in market adjustment. Institutions preventing excessive market failures, mandating cooperative attitudes, and insuring people against extreme fluctuations fostered growth and did not reduce it.

These cursory remarks are consistent with the working hypothesis put forward in this chapter that productivity growth, rather than being reduced, might be stimulated by the presence of equality-enhancing institutions. Social institutions—from those framing labor market relations, to those removing obstacles to the efficient accumulation of human and physical capital, to social protection schemes—do not necessarily prevent markets from satisfactorily functioning and may actually solve commitment and coordination failures reasonably well. On the contrary, generic social spending cuts may be costly and ineffective, leading to slower growth and undesirable social outcomes, when their implementation disregards their impact on the net of social bounds originated by the interaction of agents, markets, and social institutions.

At the same time, social institutions are neither ahistorical nor uniquely defined entities, a point neatly made by Esping-Andersen (1990) with regard to the welfare state. The highly differentiated performance of social institutions across time and space asks for a reconsideration of social policy and suggests the need to redesign substantially the network of social institutions so as to meet the requirements of the incoming century, an issue that is vividly present in Stiglitz (this volume, chap. 3) as well as in the recent effort of the British Commission on Social Justice (1994). While postwar industrial societies felt a responsibility for providing social insurance against the sudden loss of earning power, future industrial societies will have to concentrate instead on the provision of resources and opportunities to help people cope with more frequent changes in work or residence. The focus will be on quality services such as training, child care, and elder care rather than cash benefits and on poverty prevention through education rather than poverty relief.

Appendix 4.1

Inequality Measures: The LIS Database

The main objective of LIS is to create a database containing social and economic data collected in household surveys of different countries. LIS reorganizes original national micro-data-sets in order to increase the degree of cross-national comparability. The LIS database we have used draws on the work by Atkinson, Rainwater, and Smeeding (1995). In this study, a number of inequality measures (distribution by percentile as well as summary measures) are provided for the distributions of total family incomes (after-tax and cash transfers) in the mid- to late 1980s in seventeen OECD countries. To compare households of different sizes and compositions, all income figures are adjusted by an equivalence scale. Details on the LIS database, the quality and consistency of the LIS data sets, and its major limitations are also outlined in the study. Table 4A.1 lists the OECD countries for which comparable inequality measures are available in the LIS database; it also indicates the nature (and years) of the underlying surveys and the agencies responsible for them. It reports as well the quality level of each LIS country data set. Quality level 5 indicates that the basic information consists in the amount of income actually reported by the population. Quality level 4 refers to edited income data, whereby all item nonresponse is corrected. Quality level 3 refers to the amount of income recorded in information taken from tax records. Income data at quality level 2 are grossed up to the total amount recorded by some administrative government agencies. Finally, information at quality level 1 would include the underground economy.

Inequality Measures: National Sources
Along with comparable cross-country information on income distribution, Atkinson, Rainwater, and Smeeding (1995) extensively review the available evidence contained in national studies of income inequality; further information is provided by Atkinson (1996). National studies are based on different definitions, sources, and timing and are much less comparable across countries. For nine countries, it proved possible to use the available information to construct consistent yearly time series spanning the periods listed in table 4A.2. Whenever needed, missing figures were replaced by estimates based on other distributional indicators (Italy, Norway, Sweden, and the United Kingdom) or, in some cases, a linear time trend (Australia, Canada, Finland, and the Federal Republic of Germany).

Other Variables
Variables other than the above inequality measures have been drawn from Penn World Table, Version 5.5.

Table 4A.1
LIS Database on the Distribution of Household Equivalent Incomes

Country	Years	Type of survey	Main source	Data quality
Australia	1981/82, 1985/86	Income survey	Australian Bureau of Statistics	4
Belgium	1985	Panel study	Centre de Politique Sociale	4
Canada	1981, 1987	Income survey	Statistics Canada	4
Finland	1987	Survey and administrative records	Central Statistical Office	2
France	1979, 1984	Income tax records	Institut National de la Statistique et des Etudes Economiques (INSEE)	3
West Germany	1984	Panel study	Deutsches Institut für Wirtschaftsforschung (DIW)	4
Ireland	1987	Income survey	Economic and Social Research Institute (ESRI)	4
Italy	1986	Income survey	Banca d'Italia	4
Luxembourg	1985	Panel study	Centre d'Etudes de Populations, de Pauvreté et de Politiques Socio-Economiques (CEPS)	4
Netherlands	1983, 1987	Income survey	Central Bureau of Statistics	5
Norway	1979, 1986	Income tax records	Statistics Norway	3
Portugal	1980/81, 1989/90			
Spain	1980/81, 1990/91			
Sweden	1981, 1987	Survey and administrative records	Statistika Centralbyran	2
Switzerland	1982	Income survey	Volkswirtschaftliches Institut, Universität Bern	5
United Kingdom	1979, 1986	Expenditure survey	Central Statistical Office	4
United States	1979, 1986	Labor force survey	Bureau of the Census	4

Source: Atkinson, Rainwater, and Smeeding (1995, tables 3.1, 3.3).

Table 4A.2
National Sources

Country	Income definition	Income unit	Period	Main source
Australia	Household	Household	1969–1990	Saunders (1992)
Canada	Household	Household	1971–1983	Wolfson (1986)
Finland	Equivalent	Person	1966–1990	Uusitalo (1989)
West Germany	Household	Household	1960–1990	Guger (1989)
Italy	Household	Household	1967–1993	Brandolini and Sestito (1994)
Norway	Equivalent	Person	1970–1990	Ringen (1991)
Sweden	Equivalent	Person	1975–1991	Gustafsson and Palmer (1995)
United Kingdom	Household	Household	1961–1991	Goodman and Webb (1994)
United States	Household	Household	1967–1992	U.S. Department of Commerce (1993)

Note: In some cases, data were derived by Atkinson (1996) and Atkinson, Rainwater, and Smeeding (1995) and not by the original sources.

Notes

We thank Alberto Alesina, Anders Björklund, Michael Deppler, Assar Lindbeck, Peter Saunders, Tim Smeeding, and two anonymous referees. We are also grateful to Liliana Pulcini for careful editing. Estimations were performed by using the econometric package Stata. The views expressed herein are those of the authors and do not necessarily reflect those of the Bank of Italy.

1. Barro (1991) and Barro and Lee (1994) are probably among the best examples in the field at large. Cross-country evidence on the growth-equality trade-off based on reduced-form regressions is provided by Alesina and Perotti (1996), Alesina and Rodrik (1992, 1994), Clarke (1995), Perotti (1992, 1994, 1996), and Persson and Tabellini (1992, 1994).

2. A different problem arises in overlapping-generation models such as Persson and Tabellini's (1994), where the logical time unit is a generation. In such a case, the theoretical time scale is lost in real data in the process of aggregation across generations. As a consequence, time lags may lose their original meaning, the growth-inequality relationship may show up over relatively shorter periods of time, and taking long-run averages may be a very inappropriate way of filtering short-run dynamics.

3. Cellini (1997), Knight, Loayza, and Villanueva (1993), and Islam (1995) explicitly account for country-specific effects in testing theories of economic growth. They do not deal with the growth-inequality issue.

4. For instance, the "political institutions approach" actually refers to polarization (see Wolfson 1994 and Esteban and Ray 1994) rather than inequality measures of the distribution of wealth among individuals. In testing that approach, though, the literature thoughtlessly uses polarization and concentration measures of income (personal or family) before tax. Moreover, it is sometimes recognized that income units and income concepts may vary across countries. It is no wonder, then, that adding continental dummies to cross-country regression washes out the effect of income distribution. The comparability issue is explicitly recognized by Perotti (1996), who attempts to adjust inequality figures to ensure partial comparability, at least as far as the definition of recipient unit and the coverage of the underlying survey are concerned. The supposedly higher degree of comparability apparently allows him to pinpoint more precisely the impact of income distribution on growth.

5. The LIS project began in 1983 under the joint sponsorship of the government of Luxembourg and the Centre d'Etudes de Populations, de Pauvreté et de Politiques Socio-Economiques of the International Network for Studies in Technology, Environment, Alternatives, Development (CEPS/INSTEAD). It is now funded on a continuing basis by CEPS/INSTEAD and by annual contributions of its member countries. Membership includes countries in Europe, North America, Asia, and Oceania. At the beginning of 1997, the database contained information for twenty-five countries for one or more years, ranging from the late sixties to the mid-nineties.

6. This is not to say that capital market imperfections are absent altogether. See, for example, Jappelli and Pagano (1989, 1994).

7. Allowing for a measure of liquidity constraints (the maximum loan-to-value ratio as reported in Japelli and Pagano 1994) or for its interaction with the income distribution variable leaves the results entirely unchanged.

8. Allowing for fixed effects as in table 4.3 may result in inconsistent estimators because of the presence of a lagged-dependent variable in the right-hand side of the regression equa-

tion. The asymptotic bias of the fixed-effects estimator typically shows up in panels with a large number of individuals (or, for that matter, countries), but only a few time observations. This is not the present case, though, and the bias might well be ignored.

9. The degree of openness of the economy failed as an additional regressor, and lack of data prevented the use of political instability indicators.

References

Acemoglu, D. 1996. *Matching, Heterogeneity and the Evolution of Income Distribution*. Discussion Paper, no. 1345. London: Centre for Economic Policy Research.

Agell, J., and K. E. Lommerud. 1993. "Egalitarianism and Growth." *Scandinavian Journal of Economics* 95:559–579.

Aghion, P., and P. Bolton. 1992. "Distribution and Growth in Models of Imperfect Capital Markets." *European Economic Review* 36:603–611.

Aghion, P., and P. Bolton. 1993. *A Theory of Trickle-Down Growth and Development with Debt-Overhang*. Discussion Paper no. 170. London: London School of Economics, Financial Markets Group.

Alesina, A., and R. Perotti. 1994. "The Political Economy of Growth: A Critical Survey of the Recent Literature." *World Bank Economic Review* 8:351–371.

Alesina, A., and R. Perotti. 1996. *Income Distribution, Political Instability, and Investment*. *European Economic Review* 40:1203–1228.

Alesina, A., and D. Rodrik. 1992. "Distribution, Political Conflict, and Economic Growth: A Simple Theory and Some Empirical Evidence." In A. Cukierman, Z. Mercowitz, and L. Leiderman, eds., *Political Economy, Growth, and Business Cycles*. Cambridge, Mass.: MIT Press.

Alesina, A., and D. Rodrik. 1994. "Distributive Politics and Economic Growth." *Quarterly Journal of Economics* 109:465–490.

Atkinson, A. B. 1992. "Institutional Features of the Unemployment Insurance and the Working of the Labor Market." In P. Dasgupta, D. Gale, O. Hart, and E. Maskin, eds., *Economic Analysis of Markets and Games*. Cambridge, Mass.: MIT Press.

Atkinson, A. B. 1995. *The Welfare State and Economic Performance*. Discussion Paper no. WSP/109. London: London School of Economics, STICERD.

Atkinson, A. B. 1996. *Seeking to Explain the Distribution of Income*. In J. Hills, ed., *New Inequalities*. Cambridge: Cambridge University Press.

Atkinson, A. B., L. Rainwater, and T. M. Smeeding. 1995. *Income Distribution in OECD Countries: The Evidence from the Luxembourg Income Study*. Paris: OECD.

Barro, R. 1991. "Economic Growth in a Cross Section of Countries." *Quarterly Journal of Economics* 106:407–443.

Barro, R., and J. Lee 1994. Sources of Economic Growth. *Carnegie-Rochester Conference Series on Public Policy* 40:1–46.

Bénabou, R. 1994. "Human Capital, Inequality, and Growth: A Local Perspective." *European Economic Review* 38:817–826.

Bénabou, R. 1996. *Heterogeneity, Stratification, and Growth*: Macroeconomic Implications of Community Structure and School Finance. *American Economic Review* 86:584–609.

Bénabou, R. 1996b. "Equity and Efficiency in Human Capital Investment: The Local Connection." *Review of Economic Studies* 63:237–264.

Bénabou, R. 1996c. "Unequal Societies." Working Paper no. 5583. Cambridge, Mass.: National Bureau of Economic Research.

Bertola, G. 1993. "Factor Shares and Savings in Endogenous Growth." *American Economic Review* 83:1184–1198.

Bertola, G. 1994. "Theories of Savings and Economic Growth." *Ricerche economiche* 48:257–277.

Brandolini, A. 1992. *Nonlinear Dynamics, Entitlement Rules, and the Cyclical Behaviour of the Personal Income Distribution*. Discussion Paper no. 84. London: London School of Economics, Centre for Economic Performance.

Brandolini, A., and P. Sestito. 1994. "Cyclical and Trend Changes in Inequality in Italy, 1977–1991." Mimeo.

Cellini, R. 1997. "Implications of Solow's Growth Model in the Presence of a Stochastic Steady State." *Journal of Macroeconomics* 19:101–125.

Clarke, G. R. G. 1995. "More Evidence on Income Distribution and Growth." *Journal of Development Economics* 47:403–427.

Cole, H. L., G. J. Mailath, and A. Postlewaite. 1992. "Social Norms, Savings Behavior, and Growth." *Journal of Political Economy* 100:1093–1125.

Commission on Social Justice. 1994. *Social Justice: Strategies for National Renewal*. London: Vintage.

Crafts, N., and G. Toniolo, eds. 1996. *Economic Growth in Europe Since 1945*. Cambridge: Cambridge University Press.

Duesenberry, J. S. 1949. *Income, Savings and the Theory of Consumer Behavior*. Cambridge, Mass.: Harvard University Press.

Eichengreen, B. 1996. "Institutions and Economic Growth: Europe After World War II." In N. Crafts and G. Toniolo, eds., *Economic Growth in Europe Since 1945*, pp. 38–72. Cambridge: Cambridge University Press.

Esping-Andersen, G. 1990. *The Three Worlds of Welfare Capitalism*. Princeton: Princeton University Press.

Esteban, J.-M., and D. Ray. 1994. "On the Measurement of Polarization." *Econometrica* 62:819–851.

Fernandez, R., and R. Rogerson. 1994. *Public Education and Income Distribution: A Quantitative Evaluation of Education Finance Reform*. Working Paper no. 4883. Cambridge, Mass.: National Bureau of Economic Research.

Ferreira, F. H. G. 1995. *Roads to Equality: Wealth Distribution Dynamics with Public-Private Capital Complementarity*. Discussion Paper no. TE/95/286. London: London School of Economics, STICERD.

Freeman, R. 1994. *Working Under Different Rules*. New York: Russell Sage Foundation.

Fritzell, J. 1993. "Income Inequality Trends in the 1980s: A Five-Country Comparison." *Acta Sociologica* 36:47–62.

Galor, O., and J. Zeira. 1993. "Income Distribution and Macroeconomics." *Review of Economic Studies* 60:35–52.

García-Peñalosa, C. 1995. "The Paradox of Education or the Good Side of Inequality." *Oxford Economic Papers* 47:265–285.

Glomm, G., and B. Ravikumar. 1992. "Public Versus Private Investment in Human Capital: Endogenous Growth and Income Inequality." *Journal of Political Economy* 100:818–834.

Goodman, A., and S. Webb. 1994. *For Richer, for Poorer: The Changing Distribution of Income in the United Kingdom, 1961–1991*. Commentary no. 42. London: Institute for Fiscal Studies.

Gottschalk, P. 1993. "Changes in Inequality of Family Income in Seven Industrialized Countries." *American Economic Review* 83:136–142.

Gottschalk, P., and T. M. Smeeding. forthcoming. "Cross National Comparisons of Earnings and Income Inequality." *Journal of Economic Literature*.

Gramlich, E. M., R. Kasten, and F. Sammartino. 1993. "Growing Inequality in the 1980s: The Role of Federal Taxes and Cash Transfers." In S. Danziger and P. Gottschalk, eds., *Uneven Tides: Rising Inequality in America*. New York: Russell Sage Foundation.

Greene, W. H. 1993. *Econometric Analysis*. New York: Macmillan.

Guger, A. 1989. *The Distribution of Household Income in Germany*. WIFO Working Paper no. 35. Vienna: Austrian Institute of Economic Research.

Gustafsson, B., and E. E. Palmer. 1995. Changes in Swedish Inequality: A Study of Equivalent Income 1975–1991. Gothenburg: University of Gothenbury. Mimeo.

Islam, N. 1995. "Growth Empirics: A Panel Data Approach." *Quarterly Journal of Economics* 110:1127–1170.

Jappelli, T., and M. Pagano. 1989. "Consumption and Capital Market Imperfections: An International Comparison." *American Economic Review* 79:1088–1105.

Jappelli, T., and M. Pagano. 1994. "Saving, Growth, and Liquidity Constraints." *Quarterly Journal of Economics* 109:83–109.

Johnson, P., and S. Webb. 1993. "Explaining the Growth in UK Income Inequality." *Economic Journal* 103:429–443.

Kaldor, N. 1955–1956. "Alternative Theories of Distribution." *Review of Economic Studies* 23:94–100.

Knight, M., N. Loayza, and D. Villanueva. 1993. Testing the Neoclassical Theory of Economic Growth. *IMF Staff Papers* 40:512–541.

Kravis, I. B. 1960. "International Differences in the Distribution of Income." *Review of Economics and Statistics* 42:408–416.

Kuznets, S. 1955. "Economic Growth and Income Inequality." *American Economic Review* 45:1–28.

Levine, R., and D. Renelt. 1992. "A Sensitivity Analysis of Cross-Country Growth Regression." *American Economic Review* 82:942–963.

Li, G. 1985. "Robust Regression." In D. C. Hoaglin, F. Mosteller, and J. W. Tukey, eds., *Exploring Data Tables, Trends, and Shapes.* New York: Wiley.

Lindert, P. H., and J. G. Williamson. 1985. "Growth, Equality, and History." *Explorations in Economic History* 22:341–377.

Maddison, A. 1991. *Dynamic Forces in Capitalist Development.* Oxford: Oxford University Press.

Mankiw, N. G., P. Romer, and D. N. Weil. 1992. "A Contribution to the Empirics of Economic Growth." *Quarterly Journal of Economics* 107:407–437.

Perotti, R. 1992. "Income Distribution, Politics, and Growth." *American Economic Review Papers and Proceedings* 82:311–316.

Perotti, R. 1993. "Political Equilibrium, Income Distribution, and Growth." *Review of Economic Studies* 60:755–776.

Perotti, R. 1994. "Income Distribution and Investment." *European Economic Review* 38:827–835.

Perotti, R. 1996. "Growth, Income Distribution, and Democracy: What the Data Say." *Journal of Economic Growth* 1:149–187.

Persson, T., and G. Tabellini. 1992. "Growth, Distribution and Politics." *European Economic Review* 36:593–602.

Persson, T., and G. Tabellini. 1994. "Is Inequality Harmful for Growth?" *American Economic Review* 84:600–621.

Ringen, S. 1991. "Households, Standard of Living, and Inequality." *Review of Income and Wealth* 37:1–13.

Saint-Paul, G., and T. Verdier. 1992. "Historical Accidents and the Persistence of Distributional Conflict." *Journal of the Japanese and International Economies* 6:406–422.

Saint-Paul, G., and T. Verdier. 1993. "Education, Democracy and Growth." *Journal of Development Economics* 42:399–407.

Saunders, P. 1992. "Poverty, Inequality and Recession." *Economic Papers* 11(3):1–22.

Sawyer, M. (1976). *Income Distribution in OECD Countries.* OECD Economic Outlook, Occasional Studies. Paris: OECD.

Solow, R. M. 1956. "A Contribution to the Theory of Economic Growth." *Quarterly Journal of Economics* 70:65–94.

Stiglitz, J. E. 1969. "Distribution of Income and Wealth Among Individuals." *Econometrica* 37:382–397.

Swan, T. W. 1956. "Economic Growth and Capital Accumulation." *Economic Record* 32:334–361.

Torvik, R. 1993. "Talent, Growth and Income Distribution." *Scandinavian Journal of Economics* 95:581–596.

United Nations. 1977. *Provisional Guidelines on Statistics of the Distribution of Income, Consumption, and Accumulation of Households.* Studies in Methods, Series M, no. 61. New York: United Nations.

United States. Department of Commerce. 1993. *Money Income of Households, Families, and Persons in the United States: 1992.* Current Population Reports, Series P-60, no. 184. Washington, D.C.: Government Printing Office.

Uusitalo, H. 1989. *Income Distribution in Finland.* Helsinki: Central Statistical Office of Finland.

van Ginneken, W., and J. Park. 1984. *Generating Internationally Comparable Income Distribution Estimates.* Geneva: International Labor Office.

White, H. 1980. "A Heteroskedasticity-Consistent Covariance Matrix Estimator and a Direct Test for Heteroskedasticity." *Econometrica* 48:817–830.

Wolfson, M. C. 1986. "Stasis Amid Change—Income Inequality in Canada, 1965–1983." *Review of Income and Wealth* 32:337–369.

Wolfson, M. C. 1994. "When Inequalities Diverge." *American Economic Review Papers and Proceedings* 84:353–358.

Comments

Michael Deppler

Brandolini and Rossi address directly the issue of whether there is a trade-off between growth and inequality. After a series of twists and turns, the answer is: Take your pick. In Anglo-Saxon countries, there is a trade-off; in continental European countries, there is complementarity. Moreover, the difference in results is sharp and statistically significant, namely, the coefficient π_5 in columns 3 and 4 in table 4.5.

Income Distribution, Growth, and Social Institutions in Continental Europe

For a European social chartist, which the authors tend to be, there is plenty of evidence for this case. But this also applies if you are Reagan, Clinton, Thatcher, or Blair; there is something for everyone here.

The authors, however, focus on only one aspect of their results: the European one. Their conclusion is that social institutions that promote social peace and cohesion lead to both greater equality and greater productivity. The institutional structures that underlie this social cohesion are not entirely clear but include minimum wage laws, restrictions on hiring and firing, income support systems, and centralized wage bargaining—in general, all matters that in other contexts are often viewed as rigidities.

There is much in the chapter that I find appealing. Anyone familiar with postwar Anglo-Saxon and continental European economies cannot but be aware of the much greater weight that social arrangements bring to bear on European than Anglo-Saxon economies, on the one hand, and of the generally stronger productivity performance of the former group of countries during the postwar period, on the other. Against that background, I find the featured result of the study broadly intuitive. For much of the postwar period, the more social-minded systems generated the highest productivity growth, and conversely. It is this stylized, if "non-classical," fact that Brandolini and Rossi capture. However, they focus on only one aspect of their argument: that steps to strengthen social cohesion have been growth inducing in Europe. They do not explore the implications of the contrasting result that in Anglo-Saxon countries, it is steps taken toward more market-oriented frameworks and greater inequality that have had growth-inducing effects. Why is this so? What is it that ostensibly makes steps toward more socially minded institutions have such different effects across economies? This is an aspect they do not explore.

Although I find the broad result historically plausible, the pertinent policy question is whether, in thinking about policies for Europe looking forward, one can be confident that the result these authors posit will hold in the future.

It is in such a context that I think of a country like Sweden. The welfare state did very well by Sweden during much of the postwar period, and by the early 1970s Sweden was at the top of the OECD's per capita income tables. Today, however, Sweden is very much in the lower half of those tables. The question is whether the social measures underlying the welfare state—measures that could be afforded during a period of rapid catch-up in productivity growth—are still adapted and affordable today. For instance, has the compression of wages as a result of centralized bargaining in Sweden contributed to a lack of creativity, mobility, and competitiveness that is hindering per capita income growth today even if it might once have been growth enhancing?

In another case, Belgium has, in the name of social cohesion and social peace, had a full indexation of the economy for many years. The IMF has accepted this as a constraint on policy formulation. But recently, because of their increasing commitment to a fixed exchange rate, the Belgian authorities have introduced the so-called competitiveness law—a law that gives the authorities the power to control nominal wages once these threaten competitiveness. So now one rigidity (indexation) has been countered by another distortion, a law that constrains nominal wages. As economists and policymakers, how do we approach this? Do we say social cohesion means that we should live with this, or that this compounding of rigidities will unduly constrain the productive system in time?

Similar issues come to mind when thinking about pension entitlements in Europe. In the past, these systems generated large positive real rates of return, which helped ensure social cohesion and peace and, according to Brandolini and Rossi, more growth. Looking forward, however, rates of return are likely to be much lower. Is this to mean even less growth, or the adoption of policies that presume a trade-off, rather than complementarity, between equality and growth? Again, this is an issue where the implications of the chapter need to be more fully thought through.

Understanding Non-European Experiences

In the same vein, it would be useful to link the authors' results to another stylized fact: that Anglo-Saxon countries have generally experienced much lower average levels of unemployment over the past decade than have continental European countries. The question is, Why? Is there, in fact, a trade-off between equality and unemployment because of insider-outsider relationships? More broadly, as policymakers, should we worry more about income equality or unemployment?

In sum, Brandolini and Rossi present an interesting study. It captures a stylized difference in the postwar functioning of Anglo-Saxon and continental European economies and provides food for thought. What the differences mean and whether they can be presumed to persist, however, remain very much open questions.

Comments

Assar Lindbeck

Distribution of Factor Income and Productivity Growth

The relation between income equality and productivity growth depends on how a certain distribution of income has come about. Suppose that we want to study the relation between the initial equality of factor income, that is, pretax and pretransfer income, and subsequent productivity growth. The likelihood of a positive relation must be greater if a certain degree of equality of labor income is a result of an equal distribution of human capital than if it has come about by way of regulation of relative wages. A positive relation must also be more likely if a certain degree of equality of factor income is the result of dispersed ownership of financial and real capital assets rather than of low profits because of regulations of prices or an overvalued currency. It must also be important how the existing distribution of real and financial capital has come about. In one country, a rather dispersed distribution of financial and real capital assets may be the result of a historical process of large and widely dispersed private saving among individuals. In another country, it may be the result of the fact that the government owns the bulk of the stock of real and financial capital. Most observers would probably argue, as I do, that the incentive structure is more conducive to rapid productivity growth in the former country because private entrepreneurship is more likely to flourish. After all, private entrepreneurship requires private equity capital, and this presupposes private wealth, and hence private saving, for a prolonged period of time.

Distribution of Disposable Income and Productivity Growth

So far I have commented on the importance for productivity growth of how a certain distribution of factor income has come about. Similar points are relevant when we look at the relation between disposable income and productivity growth. An equalization of disposable income may improve productivity growth by mitigating liquidity constraints for investment in human capital among low-income groups. It is often also hypothesized that such redistributions stimulate productivity growth by reducing social conflicts and perhaps even by increasing the tolerance among citizens for the market system. Attempts to equalize the distribution of disposable income relative to the distribution of factor income are, however, bound to reduce the connection between effort and economic reward, because of tax and benefit wedges between the social and private return on work, saving, investment, and entrepreneurship. But the size of the disincentive effects of these wedges depends crucially on the methods used to reduce the dispersion of disposable income.

This discussion suggests that a satisfactory analysis of the relation between income equality and productivity growth requires a rather elaborate specification of factors that influence the distribution of income, such as the detailed structure of taxes, benefit systems, regulations, and institutions. Obvious examples are the size of various marginal tax wedges; the asymmetries in the taxation of different types of income and assets; the construction of various welfare state benefit systems (including work requirements and coinsurance); the form of governmental regulations of private investment and production in the private sector; the size, structure, and conditions for subsidies to firms; the trade policy regime; regulations on the hiring and firing of labor; the system of wage bargaining; the character and degree of competition policy in the product market; the obstacles to the entry and exit of firms; and others. Several of these variables are bound to influence both the distribution of income and the rate of productivity growth, and it is unlikely that all of them are orthogonal to overall measures of the distribution of income, such as the Gini coefficient, in regression with productivity growth as the dependent variable.

Methodological Hazards

More generally, these considerations reflect the hazards of regressing productivity growth on broad explanatory variables, such as the size of aggregate public sector spending or taxes, the investment share, or resources devoted to education. The result of such regressions would also be expected to be extremely fragile with respect to the alternative specifications of the regression equations. Such fragility has indeed been established in the literature. Levine and Renelt (1992), for example, suggest that the results of such regressions are also quite fragile with respect to the choice of countries and data sets.

In studies of the relation between the distribution of income and the rate of productivity growth, it is also rather dubious to assume monotonicity and, hence, to use linear regression equations. It is likely that public sector spending enhances productivity growth but that the marginal return will fall sooner or later and subsequently become negative. Moreover, conventional microeconomic theory tells us that the negative incentive effects of distortionary taxes on economic efficiency increase, on the margin, by higher marginal tax rates. The joint effects of these forces may well be a positive relation between the equality of disposable income and productivity growth at low levels of equality, but a negative relation above a certain level of income equalization when this has been brought about by taxes, transfers, or regulations.

The consequences of initial income inequality for subsequent redistribution policy may also lack monotonicity. Up to a point, a more compressed distribution of income may contribute to social peace and reduced political incentives to redistribute income by implementing distortionary taxes. As the distribution of disposable income is made more even by the help of political interventions, the political discussion may become increasingly focused on distributional issues, and this may, in fact, increase income conflicts and the pressure for further redistributions. One reason is that the distribution of income may then become regarded as "arbitrarily" decided by political forces rather than fulfilling some economic function in the market system. It is my impression that conflicts over the distribution of income in Sweden have never been so sharp as during the past two decades, when the distribution of disposable household income has been exceptionally even. Indeed, de Tocqueville speculated in the nineteenth century that the more income is redistributed by political means, the more dissatisfied people will be with the remaining inequalities.

These reflections should accentuate our skepticism about the reliability of existing linear regressions between broad measures of income inequality (such as the Gini coefficient) and the rate of productivity growth. The point is relevant also when evaluating Brandolini and Rossi's chapter, which is in the tradition of such broad econometric studies. Indeed, the authors share this skepticism, at least in the beginning of the chapter.

Contributions of the Chapter and Unresolved Issues

The main contribution of this chapter is the authors' use of two new data sets: the Luxembourg Income Study (LIS) for seventeen OECD countries and a collected data set from national sources for nine developed countries. The only statistically significant explanatory variables for labor productivity growth in the LIS data set are a time dummy and the initial level of labor productivity (the latter reflecting the catch-up mechanism). The same explanatory variables survive in the second data set, where, in addition, investment in real assets appears with a positive sign and population growth and government consumption with negative signs. In neither data set do measures of initial inequality of factor income have much explanatory power. Indeed, to the extent that such influence may be detected in the study, it appears with a positive (though insignificant) sign.

There are, as always, technical problems in studies like this. For instance, the time trend is an important "explanatory variable" that does not really explain much from an economic or political point of view. It might have been useful to see how much Brandolini and Rossi's model had explained after deducting the influence of the time trend. Another problem with the analysis is that while an interpretation in terms of causality perhaps may make sense in their regressions between initial inequality and subsequent productivity growth during a subsequent five-year period, such an interpretation is more doubtful in their regressions (on the basis of national statistics), with only one-year lags between the dependent and the independent variables, even though a distinction between long-run and short-run effects is made using an error-correction mechanism.

The authors find some comfort in getting significant results from subsamples with European continental and Anglo-Saxon countries—with a positive influence of one-year lagged income equality on productivity growth in the former countries and a negative influence in the latter. (The authors' skepticism about cross-country studies with broad aggregate variables seems to subside somewhat when they report these results.) I do not know what to make of this result. The first group consists of only five countries and the second group of only four. This small sample should caution us about generalizations and intuitive explanations of the results.

The attempted explanation these authors make is that cooperative labor relations and the commitment to welfare state provisions on the European Continent after World War II equalized income, reduced social conflicts, and moderated wage demands and that these features have stimulated productivity growth. One possible objection to this attempted explanation is that the asserted real wage restraints have not been strong enough to prevent stagnating employment in Europe since the mid-1970s, and a dramatic rise in unemployment and a fall in labor force participation as a result. Real wage moderation has, in fact, been much more pronounced in the United States than on the European Continent since the mid-1970s, which may help explain the lower unemployment rate in the United States during the past decade or two.

The authors' results also raise problems about the relevant definition of labor productivity growth. Suppose that labor productivity is defined as value added per employed (or per hour of work). With this definition, labor productivity growth has certainly been faster in continental Europe than in the United States during the past two decades. This is hardly true, however, if we instead define labor productivity with the size of the working-age population in the denominator. Maybe the second measure of labor productivity is more relevant than the former, when we want to judge the ability of the economic system to provide more goods and services to the population—at least if unemployment and withdrawals from the labor force are results of aggressive wage pressure by unions or of various distortionary taxes, benefits, or regulations.

The authors claim that their results give "little support" to the "political institutions approach," taken by Persson and Tabellini and by Alesina and Rodrik, in explaining the relation between initial income equality and subsequent productivity growth. This claim is not obvious, since these studies are confined to the influence of initial income equality via the political process, and this influence may be counteracted by various direct disincentive effects in connection with the creation of the initial distribution of income.

Brandolini and Rossi end with some speculation that productivity growth, "far from being reduced, might be enhanced by the presence of equality-enhancing institutions." Is this assumed to be a monotonic relation, and if not, which countries are today on the positive and negative branches of this relation? The authors also argue that "generic social spending cuts may be costly and ineffective, leading to slower growth and undesirable social outcomes when implemented, failing to realize their impact on the net of social bounds originated by the interaction of agents, markets, and social institutions." This may be true, but spending cuts may in some countries be necessary to save the welfare state, by preventing it from undercutting its own economic foundations because of various disincentive effects.

Future Research

Evaluations of the relation between income equality and productivity growth have to rely on much more detailed specification than studies have thus far provided. We have to look at the effects on productivity growth of specific policy instruments, mechanisms, and institutions rather than confine the studies to the effects of overall measures of income equality and broad institutional characteristics. The attempted short-cuts that have been used in recent studies should be regarded at best as the starting point for more serious, detailed studies. I believe that Brandolini and Rossi also take this position.

Studies in which the policy instruments are specified in detail nevertheless are also hazardous because of the difficulties of finding good measures of the instruments, our limited knowledge about the functioning of the economic and political system, and the risk of running out of degrees of freedom in the statistical studies. Indeed, when economists make statements about complex economic and social processes, such as the relation between policy actions that influence equality and productivity growth, we should probably approach the issue as a judge in a court proceeding does, trying to use all available information. We should then rely not just on economic theory and various econometric studies but also on other types of relevant quantitative and qualitative empirical indicators, as well as on common sense and the keen observation of everyday life.

Reference

Levine, R., and D. Renelt. 1992. "A Sensitivity Analysis of Cross-Country Growth Regression." *American Economic Review* 82:942–963.

5

Equity and Growth in Developing Countries: Old and New Perspectives on the Policy Issues

Michael Bruno, Martin Ravallion, and Lyn Squire

Do the poor lose, either absolutely or relatively, from policies that promote aggregate economic growth? Does the answer differ between middle-income newly industrialized economies and low-income developing countries? These questions are not new and were very much at the center of the development debate some twenty years ago in the discussion of how to achieve redistribution with growth (Chenery et al. 1974). They have recently achieved renewed prominence as many countries adjust from the growth crises of the past two decades and as others switch from centrally planned systems to market-based ones. The claim has been made that growth-oriented reform policies of the kind usually advocated by the international financial institutions (IFIs) have worsened the lot of the poor.

We begin by reviewing recent evidence indicating that although income inequality differs significantly across countries, there is no discernable systematic impact over time of growth on inequality. There are exceptions, but generally sustainable economic growth benefits all layers of society, and the gain is roughly in proportion to the initial level of living. Based on the evidence of the past three decades, there seems to be no credible support for the Kuznets hypothesis. And there have been few cases of immiserizing growth.

We then switch from long-run growth to issues of adjustment and transition. Here we argue that the key components linking growth, as a necessary condition for sustained poverty reduction, and adjustment, (stabilization plus structural reform) as a necessary condition for aggregate growth recovery, come out strengthened from the recent growth crises and associated reform efforts. Obviously necessity is not sufficiency, and we do not argue that growth *always* benefits the poor or that *none* of the poor loses from any pro-growth policy reform. But we do contend that macroeconomic adjustment and structural reform are essential for sustainable growth recovery, which in turn is necessary for a sustained reduction in aggregate poverty.

The first two sections of this chapter support and strengthen the case for policies conducive to broad-based economic growth as part of a comprehensive poverty-reduction strategy, as argued in the *World Development Report* on poverty (World Bank 1990) and the associated policy paper (World Bank 1991), *Assistance Strategies to Reduce Poverty*. But a macropolicy environment conducive to growth is not enough. The second part of the poverty-reduction strategy outlined *World Development Report*—promoting universal access to basic education, health, and social infrastructure (as well as the adoption of social safety nets, particularly in the process of recovery from a low-level growth crisis)—has received added support from new research on the reverse linkage from initial distribution of assets and income to subsequent growth. We review the evidence that high-inequality countries, such as a number in Latin America and Africa, have lower growth and remain inegalitarian, whereas low-inequality countries, such as many in East Asia, remain egalitarian and achieve rapid poverty reduction from the process of growth.

The theoretical underpinnings of this reverse linkage are only gradually being understood. Some lines of argument originate from political economy considerations: Concentration of wealth, such as in land or human capital, leads to policies that protect sectarian interests and impede growth for the rest of society; inequality may also contribute to political instability. Another argument has to do with credit market imperfections, whereby investment in human and physical capital is confined to the owners of initial wealth. The policy implication is that reducing inequality, such as through securing wide access to basic education and health, benefits both the poor immediately and everyone through higher growth. We end by drawing out implications for domestic policy and the IFIs.

5.1 The Effect of Growth on Distribution

Recognizing that we are concerned about how the benefits of growth in aggregate incomes are distributed, the question arises as to whether there is any systematic tendency for inequality to change in the process of rising average affluence.[1] This is a long-standing issue in development economics. A still widely held view is that economic growth in low-income countries will necessarily be inequitable, and this view has had considerable influence on thinking about development policy among both advocates and critics of redistributive interventions. By this view, "the rich are usually the first to reap the benefits of national income growth" (Watkins 1995, p. 34). Here we review the theories and evidence, and provide new results on more recent and improved data.

Kuznets Hypothesis

In his influential argument as to why we might expect inequitable growth in poor countries, Kuznets (1955) claims that inequality will increase in the early stages of growth in a developing country, and after some point it will begin to fall; that is, the relationship between inequality (on the vertical axis) and average income (horizontal) will trace out an inverted U. Kuznets did not set out a formal theory of why this might happen, but sketched an argument, which has subsequently been formalized. As typically presented, the Kuznets hypothesis assumes that the economy comprises a low-inequality and low-mean rural sector and a richer urban sector with higher inequality. Growth occurs by rural labor's shifting to the urban sector, such that a representative slice of the rural distribution is transformed into a representative slice of the urban distribution. Thus (by assumption), distribution is unchanged within each sector. Starting with all the population in the rural sector, when the first worker moves to the urban sector, inequality must increase. And when the last rural worker leaves, it must clearly fall again. Between these extremes, the relationship between inequality and average income will follow an inverted U.[2]

Kuznets himself was tentative about the hypothesis, yet it has found many supporters since, to the point of being deemed "fully confirmed" by Oshima (1970), a "stylized fact" by Ahluwalia (1976), and an "economic law" by Robinson (1976). Claims of support for the hypothesis can be found in a literature spanning twenty-five years.[3] We shall argue that the evidence from cross-country data sets has been misleading because of omitted country-level effects. New studies using panel data and within-country time-series data do not support the hypothesis.

Cross-Country Studies. There have been innumerable tests of the Kuznets hypothesis on cross-country data sets, by regressing a measure of inequality against a suitable function of average income and seeing if that function follows an inverted U. We shall not review the earlier literature here and note only that these tests have typically been ad hoc, with no clear link to the assumptions of the hypothesis. Instead, we focus on a nagging concern about all the tests using cross-country data: that there may be important country-level determinants of inequality (including past inequality) that are correlated with current income levels, and so lead to biased estimates. Indeed, such biases could arise solely from differences in the type of data. For example, income is a more common measure for inequality in many middle-income developing countries, notably in Latin America, whereas consumption is more common elsewhere, including among the Asian economies, many of which were closer to the bottom of the income ladder twenty to thirty years ago when the data used to test the hypothesis were set up. And since consumption inequality is bound to be lower than income inequality due to consumption smoothing, these differences alone would tend to yield an inverted U relationship even if none existed using the same welfare measure. With strong, latent country-level effects, there can be no guarantee that differences at one point in time will reveal how inequality will evolve with growth.

If such country-level effects were not in fact a problem, then one would expect to see the inverted U reappearing in later country cross-sections. So what do data since the mid-1980s suggest about the Kuznets hypothesis? Using data from sixty-three surveys spanning 1981 through 1992 covering forty-four countries,[4] we tried replicating a number of the specifications for testing the hypothesis typically found in the literature.[5] This was done for both levels and changes over time, to eliminate the country-level fixed effect. In no case was there evidence of an inverted U, and in no case could one reject the null hypothesis that the regression coefficients were jointly zero. This also confirms earlier results for smaller samples reported by the World Bank (1990), Fields (1989), and Ravallion (1995).[6]

It appears, then, that the cross-country inverted U found in many earlier tests of the hypothesis, mainly using compilations of distributional data for the 1950s to early 1970s, may well have become blurred, or even vanished, over time. This probably reflects how various omitted variables have evolved. The new data confirm earlier concerns that these omitted variables were creating an appearance of a cross-country inverted U that had little to do with the hypothesis. We would conjecture that with the growth seen in much of Asia, and the lack of it in much of Africa, the poor and low-inequality countries of twenty to thirty years ago have split into two, blurring the old inverted U but quite possibly better revealing the true relationship.

Further Intertemporal Evidence. To avoid confusing the effects of independent country-specific characteristics (initial conditions) with those of intertemporal changes of policies or economic conditions, arguments for or against the existence of a Kuznets process should ideally be based on time-series evidence. Here we report on two exercises using time-series data. The first draws on data covering forty-five developed and developing countries for the years 1947 to 1993. It contains 486 observations on Gini indices.[7] The second makes use of the most extensive time-series data for any single developing country, India.[8]

Table 5.1 gives decade averages of the Gini indices for each of the forty-five countries for which reasonably comparable estimates are available for four or more surveys. Although there is clearly variation over time (some of which could be differences between surveys or measurement errors), the data suggest substantially greater variation in inequality across countries at a given time than over time for a given country. Indeed, 87 percent of the variance in Gini indices by country and date is accounted for by cross-country variation, whereas only 6 percent is accounted for by variation over time.

The inequality rankings of countries are thus highly stable over the decades; between the 1960s and 1980s, the rank correlation coefficient is 0.85 (table 5.1). Figure 5.1 plots the average Gini index for either the 1980s or 1990s against that for the 1970s. The last column of table 5.1 also gives the direction of the trend;[9] a zero in the final column indicates that the coefficient on time is not significantly different from zero at the 5 percent level, while a plus (or minus) sign indicates that it is significantly positive (negative). Only seventeen countries out of forty-five have a significant trend in inequality one way or another, and in twelve of the cases its value is small (+ or −0.4 a year).

It would not be correct to conclude from these data that that distribution does not change over time. Even when there is no trend, there is variation, and even seemingly small changes may matter to assessments of overall social progress, including poverty reduction.

What is plain from table 5.1 is that there are strong country effects in inequality, which could well entail appreciable biases in standard tests of the Kuznets hypothesis.[10] For example, if, as table 5.1 suggests, past inequality is an important predictor of current inequality and past inequality influences current incomes, then the standard cross-country regressions used to test the inverted U will be biased.

All this lends support to the view that failure to allow for country effects could be serious. The search for a general law linking growth and inequality must confront the fact that the vast bulk of the variation is among countries, not over time. Further statistical tests on the data set

Table 5.1
Gini Indices: Decade Averages, 1960 to Date

Country	Observations	1960s[a]	1970s	1980s	1990s	Trend[b]
Czechoslovakia	10	22.6	20.9	21.1		(−)
Bulgaria	25	22.1	21.9	23.0	27.3	0
Hungary	7	24.4	22.2	22.8		0
Poland	7			25.2		0
Spain	6			25.7		0
United Kingdom	31	25.0	24.3	27.3	32.4	(+)
Former Soviet Union	4			26.0		(+)
Netherlands	9		28.1	28.6		(+)
Taiwan	26	31.2	29.3	29.0	30.5	0
Finland	6		30.7	31.0		0
Canada	23	31.6	31.6	31.5	27.6	0
India	29	31.5	30.9	31.4	31.1	(−)
China	12			31.5	36.2	(+)
New Zealand	11		31.4	34.1		(+)
Sweden	14		33.1	33.7	32.3	0
Indonesia	7		36.6	33.4	33.1	0
Pakistan	6		35.5	33.4		0
Norway	7	36.8	35.3	31.0		(−)
Korea	10	31.5	36.1	35.6		0
Japan	22	35.6	34.1	34.4	35.0	0
Italy	15		37.4	33.4	32.2	(−)
Bangladesh	9	33.5	34.8	37.3		0
United States	45	34.6	34.5	36.9	37.9	(+)
Australia	10	32.0	36.7	36.2	32.5	0
Belgium	8	36.4	42.0	29.6	35.8	0
Portugal	4		40.6	36.8	36.2	0
Germany, Federal Republic	6		36.0	35.8	45.4	(+)
Cote d'Ivoire	5			39.1	41.4	0
Singapore	6		39.0	40.7		0
Venezuela	4		41.5			(−)
Sri Lanka	7	46.0	38.8	43.7		0
Tunisia	5	42.3	44.0	43.0	41.0	0
Philippines	6	42.9	45.3	40.0		0
Hong Kong	10	47.5	41.9	41.4	45.0	0
France	7	48.0	41.6	37.8		(−)
Thailand	8	42.0	41.7	37.8		(+)
Bahamas	11		48.2	44.4	43.0	(−)
Trinidad and Tobago	4		48.5	41.7		0
Costa Rica	5	52.6	46.1	45.1		0

Table 5.1 (continued)

Country	Observations	1960s[a]	1970s	1980s	1990s	Trend[b]
Malaysia	5		51.5	48.0		0
Colombia	5		52.1	51.2		0
Mexico	4	55.3	49.7			(−)
Honduras	5			54.0	52.7	0
Chile	13			54.8	53.1	0
Brazil	7			59.0	55.6	0

Note: The table includes all countries with four or more observations, based on national household survey data. All Gini indexes are measured for the same indicator (consumption or income) over time for a given country, though it varies between countries. This accounts for some of the cross-county differences, though on adding dummy variables for the type of data in a pooled model, one still finds that the bulk of the variation is between countries rather than over time.
a. Rank correlations of inequality between decades: 1960s–1970s, 0.909; 1970s–1980s, 0.863; 1980s–1990s, 0.849; 1960s–1980s, 0.850.
b. The signs indicate the significance of the Gini time trends (0 indicates no significant trend).

confirm this point. If one allows for country-specific effects, none of the countries in the sample presented in table 5.1 appears to follow the predictions of the Kuznets hypothesis (see Deininger and Squire 1996b for further discussion and analysis).

It is worth reviewing the data for India in more detail because it is one of the most extensive and reliable series and bears on subsequent discussion. At the time of writing, we could construct distributions of real household consumption expenditures per person in India from thirty-three nationally representative and reasonably comparable household surveys spanning the period 1951 to 1992.[11] Figure 5.2 plots India's Gini index and net domestic product per person from 1951 to 1991. There was a trend decrease in inequality up to about the mid-1960s but no trend in either direction after that. There is no sign that growth increased inequality, including during the period of higher growth in the 1980s. On running the Anand-Kanbur test equation appropriate to the Gini index, one obtains not an inverted U but an ordinary U, though for most of the range of the data, inequality falls as average income increases. However, if one takes first differences of the above equation (so that it is the change in the Gini index between surveys that is regressed on the change in average income and the change in its inverse) then the relationship vanishes. There is no sign in these data that higher growth rates in India put any upward pressure on overall inequality.

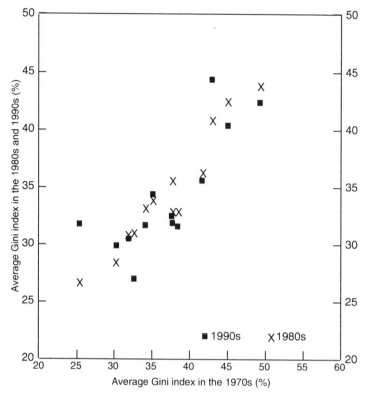

Figure 5.1
Gini indices over time by country

Other Lessons from Tests of the Kuznets Hypothesis. The fact that there are such strong country-level effects in distribution does not mean that distribution is unchangeable. Some of the observed variation (across countries and over time) is clearly due to differences in the underlying data and measurement errors. But the literature on testing the Kuznets hypothesis has also suggested a number of other factors that appear to influence inequality and explains at least some of the omitted country-level effects identified above. Kuznets (1966) speculates on a number of those factors, including shifting intersectoral inequalities, a declining share of (unequally distributed) property income, and policy changes concerning social security and employment. But on all these, the database for testing was weak at the time Kuznets was writing. That has changed.

Higher primary and secondary school enrollment rates tend to be associated with lower inequality, and the significance of the income variables

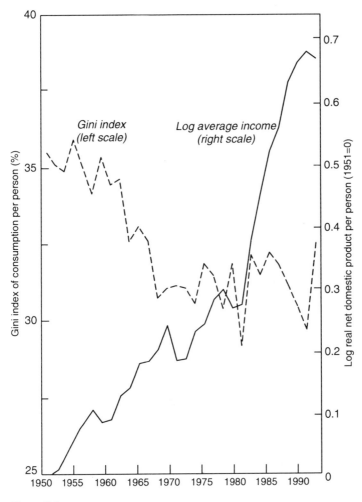

Figure 5.2
Inequality and average income in India, 1950–1992

tends to diminish when education is taken into account. The quantitative importance of this effect suggests that it may be policy relevant: A 20 percentage point increase in the percentage of the labor force that has at least secondary education increases the share of income received by the bottom 60 percent by between 3 percent and 4 percentage points (Bourguignon and Morrisson 1990). Papanek and Kyn (1986) find that primary and secondary school enrollment has a quantitatively important effect on the income share received by the poorest 40 percent. By contrast, it is significant but of low quantitative importance in reducing inequality (as measured by the Gini index). Human capital in primary and secondary education had a significant effect on reducing the Gini coefficient in Korea and increasing the share of the bottom 20 percent, whereas university education slightly increased the Gini and did not significantly affect the bottom share of the income distribution (Jung 1992).

Mineral and agricultural exports would be expected to increase inequality to the degree that they produce concentrated rents. This is confirmed for developing countries where a sizable (greater than 5 percent) contribution of mineral exports to gross domestic product (GDP) was associated with 4 percent to 6 percent decreases of the bottom 40 percent income share (Bourguignon and Morrisson 1990). High importance (greater than 5 percent of GDP) of agricultural exports leads to greater inequality only if such exports are produced on large, rather than on small and medium, farms. By contrast, Papanek and Kyn (1986), using data for developing as well as developed countries, fail to find significant effects, presumably since failure to correct for protection does not allow inferences concerning the international competitiveness of such exports.

Trade theory would predict that protection lowers the reward for the most abundant (most equally distributed) factor of production and increases returns to scarce factors, which are likely to be the more inequitably distributed. Presence of protection indeed seems to worsen income distribution (Bourguignon and Morrisson 1990).

Factor market distortions, whereby there is a wedge between the real wage in the modern sector of the economy and the lower wage in the traditional, mainly agricultural, sector, can also influence the extent of inequality. In cross-country comparisons, Bourguignon and Morrisson (1995) find that the extent of economic dualism, as measured by the labor productivity in agriculture relative to nonagricultural sectors, tends to increase overall inequality.

There is also evidence for India that the sectoral composition of growth has played a role in the evolution of distribution. Recall that at the aggregate level, the data for India reveal little effect of growth on inequality. So which of the Kuznets assumptions do not hold for India? At any one date, both mean that consumption and inequality are higher in urban areas, as Kuznets postulated. The radical departure from his assumptions is in the nature of India's growth process. Growth under the Kuznets hypothesis is driven by rural-to-urban migration, assuming that the means and distributions remain the same within each sector. However, Ravallion and Datt (1996) find that this process has been only a minor source of growth in India, the bulk of which has come from intrasectoral growth; between 1970 and 1990, the Kuznets growth process accounted for only 6 percent of total consumption growth, while growth within the urban and rural sectors accounted for 20 percent and 74 percent, respectively.

Impact of Growth on Absolute Poverty

The still quite widely held pessimism about the scope for reducing poverty through economic growth has rested in large part on the belief that growth would be inequitable in poor countries. We have surveyed past and new evidence on this view and rejected it as a generalization; there have been cases in which growth was associated with rising inequality, but there have been at least as many cases of falling inequality. There does not appear to be any systematic tendency for distribution to improve or worsen with growth. On average, then, absolute poverty will fall. This is confirmed by the results of a number of recent studies (Fields 1989; World Bank 1990; Squire 1993; Ravallion 1995; Ravallion and Chen 1997). How responsive is poverty to economic growth? Regressing the rates of change in the proportion of the population living on less than one dollar per day against the rate of change in the real value of the survey mean for the twenty countries spanning 1984 through 1993, we obtained a regression coefficient of -2.12 (with a t-ratio of -4.67); thus, a 10 percent increase in the mean can be expected to result in roughly a 20 percent drop in the proportion of people living on less than one dollar per day.[12] This reflects in large part the density of people living on around one dollar per day. But if we also consider "higher-order" measures of poverty, the effect is even stronger. For the squared poverty gap index proposed by Foster, Greer, and Thorbecke (1984), the corresponding elasticity is even higher at -3.46 ($t = -2.98$).[13] This indicates that the gains are not confined to those near the poverty line. These results confirm those of Ravallion (1995) on a smaller data set.

Somewhat smaller elasticities, but broadly similar results, are obtained if we look at the evolution of poverty over forty years in India. Over thirty-three household surveys, the elasticity of the proportion of the population below India's official poverty line and mean consumption is -1.33 ($t = 15.19$). For the squared poverty gap, the elasticity is -2.26 ($t = 10.22$) (Ravallion and Datt 1996).[14]

These elasticities are averages. There is a variation between countries and over time in the extent to which absolute poverty measures respond to growth. Initial distribution is an important factor. Ravallion (1997b) studies the effect on poverty of growth in average incomes during sixty-four spells (made up of two comparable surveys) across forth-two countries in the period 1984 through 1994. He confirms that absolute poverty measures typically respond elastically to growth, but also that the elasticity varies markedly with the initial Gini index. A country with a low initial Gini index of about 0.25 can expect an elasticity around -3.3, while a high-inequality country with a Gini of, say, 0.60 could expect an elasticity of only about -1.8.

Growth is only one of the factors that has influenced progress in reducing poverty, albeit it is an important one. Regressions for rates of poverty reduction against rates of growth still leave a sizable share of the variance in country performance unaccounted for by growth. Some of this is measurement error. But measured changes in inequality have a strong independent explanatory power; indeed, rates of poverty reduction respond even more elastically to rates of change in the Gini index than they do to the mean. Regressing the change in the log of the proportion of the population living on less than one dollar per day on the change in the log of the survey mean *and* the change in the log of the Gini index across twenty countries with two reasonably comparable observations in the period 1984 through 1992, one obtains an elasticity to the mean of -2.28 ($t = -6.07$) while the elasticity to the Gini is 3.86 ($t = 3.20$).[15] Even seemingly modest changes in overall inequality can entail sizable changes in the incidence of poverty. When combined with the tests of "augmented" Kuznets hypotheses discussed above, we can postulate a number of other factors that matter through their influence on inequality, including education, the trade regime, and the sectoral composition of growth. We will see whether some or all of these factors might also matter to the poor through their impact on the growth process.

5.2   Distributional Effects of Pro-growth Reforms

So far we have argued that the rate of overall economic growth has no systematic impact on inequality. Yet it has been argued that some of the policy changes advocated as promoting growth increase inequality. For example, real devaluations can promote growth, but they also have an impact on inequality, though the direction of that effect is not obvious on a priori grounds. Here we look more closely at the role played by economy-wide policy changes. In particular, we ask whether the economy-wide factors (including macroeconomic policy changes) that are likely to increase the overall rate of economic growth also have distributional implications.

Adjustment and Transition
For much of the developing world, the 1980s was a period of rapidly rising servicing costs on foreign debt, external terms-of-trade shocks, and fiscal and external imbalances, entailing an unsustainable excess of aggregate demand over supply. Adjustment programs were introduced to help restore macroeconomic balance by combining fiscal contraction—cutting government spending and/or raising taxes—with supply-side measures aimed at reducing inefficiency, such as cutting trade distortions or wasteful parastatals. Unless there is an exceptionally rapid supply-side response, somebody's consumption must fall. The distribution of the burden of adjustment has been one of the most debated issues in development studies over the past decade. The issue has been of even greater significance in the centrally planned economies that are now privatizing and placing much greater reliance on market solutions. What can we say about the impact of adjustment and transition on the poor?

Many countries were not well equipped with relevant household-level data for monitoring welfare impacts of policy reform at the time that adjustment began in the early 1980s. This has improved since. Yet even with good data, it can be difficult to isolate the role played by adjustment. Poverty may have risen during an adjustment period, but it may have risen even further without adjustment. Much of the criticism of adjustment policies may have to do with the observation of real hardships that are temporarily incurred at the stabilization stage, yet in all probability would be much greater were the crisis allowed to deepen further. One of the few clear patterns to emerge from the new household-level evidence on the evolution of poverty indicators during adjustment is that the poverty measures tend to move with the mean consumption or income of households, increasing in recession and falling in recovery (Lipton and Ravallion 1995, sec. 5.3).

What happens to the rate of growth in the adjustment to a deep crisis is crucial. In this respect, an important link to likely outcomes for the poor is evident in recent findings of relatively speedy growth recovery (in GDP though not in investment) after deep inflation (and growth) crisis (Bruno and Easterly 1995). The median per capita growth rate in a group of thirteen countries successfully stabilizing from more than 40 percent inflation shifted from −4 percent in the years up to and including the first year after stabilization, to 1.5 percent in the second year, and to close to 4 percent in the third year and beyond. Even when aggregate growth remains temporarily negative as inflation already falls, it is not at all clear which way the distributional outcome goes; income groups whose nominal income is not tied to inflation or whose income taxes are withheld at the source will gain in relative terms as inflation falls drastically.[16]

The distributional impacts of adjustment depend on the economy's initial conditions, including its openness, and the extent of flexibility in its output and factor markets, thus pointing to the importance of market reforms as an important conditioning environment. Actual experiences in distributional shifts during adjustment have been diverse. In the Philippines, adverse distributional effects resulted in higher poverty despite modest growth in the late 1980s (Balisacan 1993). A small improvement in distribution helped the poor during adjustment in Indonesia during the mid-1980s (Ravallion and Huppi 1991). Dorosh and Sahn (1993) argue that the distributional effects of real devaluations will tend to be pro-poor in a number of African countries, since the rural poor tend to be net producers of tradables.[17] The diversity of initial conditions warns against generalizations on the distributional impacts of adjustment.

A common presumption is that countries under shock face a dynamic trade-off; living standards may fall in the short term during adjustment (relative to nonadjustment), but they will rise in the longer term. This trade-off, however, could well be overstated. For example, Peru initially avoided adjustment, and poverty rose sharply between 1985 and 1990 (Glewwe and Hall 1994). Yet the subsequent period of more orthodox reforms between 1991 and 1994 quickly saw positive growth and falling poverty measures (Favaro and MacIsaac 1995).

Evidence from Three Regions
In this section, we review the evidence now available for sub-Saharan Africa and Latin America, the two regions most closely associated with adjustment, and then turn to the evidence for the transition economies of Eastern Europe and the former Soviet Union.

New, encouraging results have emerged for some countries in Africa. Demery and Squire (1996) use household survey data at two points of

Table 5.2
Macroeconomic Policy and Poverty in Africa

Country	Change in poor (percentage points per annum)	Change in macropolicy (weighted score of macropolicy variables)
Cote d'Ivoire	+5.30	−1.65
Kenya	−0.28	+0.45
Nigeria	−1.27	+1.79
Tanzania	−1.83	+2.76
Ghana	−1.95	+1.35
Ethiopia	−3.60	+0.55

Source: Demery and Squire (1996).

time in the mid-1980s to early 1990s to assess the change in poverty in the six African countries for which such data are available. They find that the five countries experiencing improvement in an index measuring performance in fiscal, exchange rate, and monetary policies also saw poverty decline, whereas the one country in the sample that witnessed a deteriorating policy performance suffered increased poverty (table 5.2).

These results cannot be extrapolated to the rest of the continent; policy implementation varied widely, and on balance poverty has almost certainly increased.[18] Nor can it be concluded that all the poor benefited in the countries that saw declining poverty on average; the surveys reveal that some among the poor suffered greater deprivation. And it cannot be claimed that causality from macroeconomic policy to poverty has been established. Nevertheless, the data do confirm that improvements in macroeconomic policy are consistent with declines in poverty, even in the short run. This is, in turn, consistent with evidence on growth; poverty fell where growth was positive and increased where growth was negative. Indeed, Demery and Squire (1996) show that the change in poverty was determined primarily by the change in mean income, with changes in inequality playing a secondary role and, at least in this sample, working in the opposite direction to growth as far as the poor are concerned.

In the Latin American context, Morley (1994) has similarly recorded a close relationship between growth and outcomes for the poor in the adjustment process. Reviewing periods of recession (falling per capita income for at least two years) and periods of recovery, he finds that poverty increased in fifty-five of the fifty-eight cases of recession and fell in twenty-two of the thirty-two recoveries. Contrary to the results from the sample of six African countries, Morley finds that recessions were accompanied by rising inequality (the poor suffered doubly), while recoveries were associated with falling inequality (the poor benefited doubly). But as in the African sample, the changes in poverty could be attributed mainly to changes in mean income.

Evidence now appearing for the transition economies of Eastern Europe and the former Soviet Union again points to the importance of changes in aggregate GDP but also to a systematic trend toward greater inequality. As might be expected, the large drops in GDP in these countries have been reflected in substantially higher levels of poverty. What is more interesting is the tendency toward greater inequality. These countries began the period with some of the lowest Gini coefficients in the world. The transition has entailed consistent association between growth and inequality: Both they deteriorated (Milanovic 1995; Ravallion and Chen 1997).

Thus, we find evidence of a systematic worsening of inequality in the transition economies as GDP has declined but observe no simple relationship between growth and inequality in the adjusting countries, although the shifts in the Gini coefficient at least in Africa appear to have been larger during the adjustment phase than during periods of stable growth. We conclude that successful adjustment usually leads to growth recovery, which in general will also reduce poverty. We end, though, with two qualifications.

First, the detailed policy response, particularly in the composition of public expenditure cuts, can greatly affect the poverty outcomes of adjustment. In some cases, aggregate budget contraction has been combined with rising shares (and occasionally rising absolute levels) of public spending in the social sectors, including targeted transfers (Ribe et al. 1990; World Bank 1990, chap. 7; Selowsky 1991). In Indonesia, the careful mix of public spending cuts during adjustment and the rapid currency devaluations helped mitigate the short-term consequences for the poor of declining growth (Thorbecke 1991). Maintaining public infrastructure can also be crucial to the success of reform programs. The fiscal crunch often tempts governments to cut these infrastructural sectors. There is another lesson here for the nature of fiscal retrenchment during stabilization.

Second, we have said nothing about other dimensions of poverty, including human development, which may not be adequately reflected in income or consumption-based measures (Sen 1992). It is beyond our scope to go deeply into the nonincome dimensions of welfare. There is evidence that progress in reducing income poverty is instrumentally crucial to progress against most nonincome dimensions of poverty but that incomes are not all that matter. Indeed, for some nonincome dimensions of welfare, command over market goods may well be secondary to command over key, publicly provided social services, notably access to basic health care and schooling.[19] Cross-country comparisons also suggest that public health spending in developing countries generally matters more to the health of the poor than the nonpoor (Bidani and Ravallion 1997). Cuts in key categories of social spending during adjustment can entail heavy burdens on poor people in both the short and the long runs.

5.3   The Effect of Distribution on Growth

So far we have looked at how growth might alter distribution. We now consider the possibility of a reverse causation. There are a number of ways in which this could happen.[20] We focus on two, credit constraints and political economy, which have potential implications for the accumulation of capital, especially human capital, and growth. The first affects the access of the poor to education, and the second affects incentives and the returns to education.

Credit, Distribution, and Growth

By preventing the poor from making productive investments (such as schooling), credit constraints arising, for example, from asymmetric information perpetuate a low and inequitable growth process. Furthermore, the more inequitable the initial distribution (and, hence, the greater the number of poor and typically credit-constrained people), the more severe this effect will be. A number of authors have examined credit market imperfections in general equilibrium models with lumpy investment (Banerjee and Newman 1993; Tsiddon 1992; Saint-Paul and Verdier 1992; Galor and Zeira 1993). The main result is that where credit market constraints prevent the poor from making productive indivisible investments, inequalities in the wealth distribution can have significant negative impacts on growth. What can policy do? Here we review three possible actions: provision of credit, redistribution of assets, and tax-subsidy interventions.

Intervention in credit markets aimed at channeling credit directly to rationed groups by means of subsidized interest rates may well reduce growth even further. In a dynamic perspective, such interventions are likely to cause efficiency-decreasing distortions and rent-seeking behavior, thus further reducing efficiency and equity (Bencivenga and Smith 1991).

An alternative approach entails equalizing the distribution of assets, to increase the poor's ownership of capital directly and their access to credit markets. A large number of analytical models have stressed the importance of the initial distribution of endowments and the potentially large increases in social welfare that could be gained by an initial redistribution of assets (including Banerjee and Newman 1993 and Chatterjee 1991). Evidence from Asian countries (Japan, Taiwan, and Korea), where externally imposed land reform was followed by high growth, appears to support the hypothesis. But in many situations, such redistribution may be possible only with full compensation. Whether, and under what circumstances, such schemes will then pass the scrutiny of careful evaluation has yet to be determined.[21] There are often less ambitious but still potentially important opportunities for giving poor farmers greater security of tenure in places where land rights are ill defined.

If the informational imperfections that cause credit rationing cannot be eliminated, governments can seek ways around them by subsidizing education and taxing future wages. Assuming that higher education is reflected in higher lifetime earnings, governments can provide subsidies to schooling and finance them through a tax on future earnings, without having to deal with the problems involved in identifying individual ability (Hoff and Lyon 1994). It can be shown that policies mandating compulsory schooling, financed by a proportional tax on wage income, increase economic growth and, by redistributing from agents with high human capital endowment to those with less, make the intragenerational distribution of income more equal (Eckstein and Zilcha 1994). Where it is very difficult to identify the type of individual agents ex ante, or if access to credit markets is highly unequal, such policies can be desirable.

Political Economy

The discussion suggests that among economies characterized by credit rationing, those with a more equal distribution of wealth will accumulate more human capital and grow faster than those marked by a more inegalitarian distribution. High inequality will also make it easier to adopt distortionary policies that will negatively affect individuals' investment decisions, stifle growth, and conceivably generate political instability.

The most common mechanism used to establish a link between political forces and economic outcomes is the notion of the median voter. According to this argument, the median voter's distance from the average capital endowment in the economy will increase with wealth inequality, thus leading him or her to support a capital tax rate that is higher the more unequal the distribution of wealth is. This, in turn, would reduce incentives for investment in physical and human capital, resulting in lower growth.

The median voter model, however, is not a plausible description of the political process governing decision making in many developing countries. An alternative mechanism relies on lobbying. Greater wealth allows the rich to spend more resources on lobbying activities to obtain differential treatment. In the extreme form, the ability to lobby would be directly proportional to the amount of economic assets owned by an individual. A model that uses this assumption is provided by Persson and Tabellini (1994), who draw a connection between high concentration of land, landowners' ability to lobby government successfully for preferential tax treatment of this asset, and the ensuing overinvestment in land. Such disproportionate taxation of nonlandowning groups leads to increasing inequality over time and to slower growth.

Inequality of asset ownership is also at the root of the many models that relate inflation to inequality of the distribution of income. The key idea is that inflation imposes losses on certain groups and that such losses are distributed very inequitably. Inflation taxes holders of money assets (the rich), but their access to foreign currency and capital flight allows them to shift the burden of inflation to the poor. This opens not only the possibility for the rich to "park" their assets abroad and then approve inflationary policies (financed by the poor), but it could also form the basis for strategic behavior of the rich (in support of "populist" policies), which could give rise to the typical stop-and-go policy cycles observed in many Latin American countries (Laban and Sturzenegger 1992). Similarly, Özler and Tabellini (1991) model the class struggle of workers, capital, and the government and—based on the capitalists' ability to invest in a risk-free foreign asset at the world interest rate—show a broad range of situations where domestic investment and growth would be negatively associated with inequality in the distribution of assets.

In contrast to median voter models, lobbying models can incorporate dynamic effects and strategic behavior. If politicians are self-interested, the ability of the rich to offer high bribes, and the inability of the poor to resist taxation, can lead to path-dependent equilibria (Brainard and Verdier 1994); for example, industries affected by a negative shock may choose whether to adjust or to lobby for protection, depending on the type of politician in power. Adjustment will be slower the more responsive politicians are to lobbying; in this case, growth-reducing policy interventions would be expected to increase with overall wealth inequality.

Recent models have emphasized that major policy decisions, particularly the adoption of macroeconomic stabilization measures, can be understood in the framework of a bargaining game between different social groups. Many factors beyond the distribution of income can influence bargaining power, but income distribution plays an important role. Models that describe economic stabilization as a strategic game between the rich and the poor show that stabilization, being associated with an increase in aggregate productivity, is more likely to be delayed, the greater the inequality of the income distribution (Alesina and Drazen 1991). The reason is that an unequal distribution of income (or differential access to "financial technology," which could be used to diversify risk) implies that waiting reduces the utility of the rich only marginally while imposing large costs on the poor. This would in turn increase the probability that in the end the poor will give in and shoulder all of the cost of adjustment. The model can also be used to show that even if (often under external pressure or acute fiscal crisis) adjustment measures are adopted, the lack of social consensus or the perception by some groups that they have to pay a disproportionate share of adjustment costs may lead to backsliding as soon as the external pressures subside (Laban and Sturzenegger 1994).

Evidence

The arguments reviewed suggest that greater income inequality will lead to lower investment in physical and human capital and, hence, to slower growth. There have been a number of recent attempts to test this hypothesis. Data quality is unusually worrying here. Although household survey methods have improved greatly in the past ten to fifteen years, a large question mark must be attached to the quality and comparability of the historical data on distribution in the 1950s, 1960s, and 1970s, which have been used to test the impact of initial distribution on growth.[22] Furthermore, unlike the tests of the Kuznets hypothesis, the noisy inequality variable is now on the right-hand side, so there must be a general presumption that standard estimators will give biased results. Although these and other issues of data and econometric specification should not be underrated, they take us beyond our present scope.[23]

The tests that have been reported in recent literature confirm a negative impact of initial inequality on growth in both developed and developing Persson and Tabellini countries (Alesina and Rodrik 1994; Persson and Tabellini 1994; Clarke 1995). For a sample of nine OECD countries, analysis of twenty-year growth rates starting from 1830 shows that the income share of the top quintile is negatively related to growth; it explains about 20 percent of the variance of growth rates across countries, and an increase of one standard deviation in this share decreases the Persson and Tabellini growth rate by half a percentage point (Persson and Tabellini 1994). For a sample of developing and developed countries, Clarke (1995) shows a robust relationship between initial inequality and growth that holds for different econometric specifications. On an expanded and (almost centainly) higher quality data set, Deininger and Squire (1996b) confirm significant adverse effects of higher initial income and (especially) land inequality on subsequent growth rates controlling for other factors normally expected to influence growth rates. The empirical prediction that high inequality in landownership is associated with lower capital accumulation and growth is also confirmed by Persson and Tabellini (1994). There is also evidence from a cross-section of seventy countries for the period 1960 through 1985 that economic inequality increases political instability and reduces physical capital investment (Alesina and Perotti 1993).

But the verdict is not yet in on how strong or robust the impact is of initial inequality on future growth. For example, in one test, Fishlow (1996) reports no significant effect, once one controls for Latin America (with simultaneously high inequality and low growth for much of the period).[24] As in tests of the Kuznets hypothesis, there are some strong regional effects in the cross-sectional relationship, though that fact alone does not mean the relationship is spurious. Like the Kuznets hypothesis, the real test will be in how the regional effects evolve. Further empirical work is needed, and the better distributional data now available should stimulate future research on this issue.

5.4   Conclusions

The "stylized fact" that distribution must get worse in poor countries before it can get better turns out not to be a fact at all. Effects of growth on inequality can go either way and are contingent on a number of other factors. There is little sign in the new cross-country data we assembled of any systematic impact of growth on inequality. Possibly measurement errors are confounding the true relationship, but we think it more likely that the relationship between growth and distribution is by no means as simple as some theories in development economics have postulated.

If distribution is unchanged, then growth will reduce absolute poverty. Indeed, absolute poverty measures typically respond quite elastically to growth in average incomes, and the benefits are certainly not, as a rule, confined to those near the poverty line.

One should be clear about what can and cannot be concluded from our results. It would not be correct to say that growth *always* benefits the poor or that *none* of the poor lose from pro-growth policy reforms. Here we are looking only at broad aggregates. Cases of sufficiently adverse distributional impacts to wipe out the aggregate gains to the poor are unusual, if not rare. But there can be large differences between countries in the extent to which growth reduces absolute poverty. The gains to poor people will tend to be lower the higher the extent of initial inequality. And even in countries with initially low inequality and a growth process that brings rapid and sizable gains to most of the poor, some will not be in a position to take advantage of the new opportunities, and some may well lose. There can be an important role here for compensatory direct interventions, providing they are well integrated into the general policy framework, in keeping with overall fiscal and monetary discipline.

Nor does the evidence suggest that growth is always distribution neutral. Roughly half the time, inequality rises, and half the time, it falls. And it would also be wrong to conclude that changes in distribution are of little consequence. Indeed, we find that poverty measures respond quite elastically to changes in distribution. The point is not that distribution is irrelevant or that it never changes, but rather that its changes are generally uncorrelated with economic growth.

There are arguments as to why initial distribution matters for the nature and extent of subsequent growth. As a general rule, a more equal initial distribution will entail that a given rate of growth will be more pro-poor. It has also been argued that it will result in a higher rate of growth. This link can operate through credit market constraints, by limiting the ability of the poor to invest. The negative effect on growth is strengthened if distortionary policy interventions in favor of the rich further undermine the poor's incentives to invest. The empirical evidence on these effects is as yet mixed, though the recent literature does not support a view that higher initial inequality allows a higher rate of growth. Some studies suggest no effect, and others suggest that high inequality inhibits growth.

Thus, there does not appear to be any intrinsic overall trade-off between long-run efficiency and equity. In particular, policies aimed at facilitating accumulation of productive assets by the poor, when adopted in a relatively nondistorted framework, are also important instruments for achieving higher growth. The problem should not be posed as one of choosing between growth and redistribution.

When we put these two halves together—one on the impact of growth on distribution and one on the reverse causation—we can begin to see the structure and some of the details of a joint model of distribution and growth and, hence, of poverty. The extent to which this is a truly simultaneous model is a moot point; distribution may well affect growth more than growth affects distribution, though this interrelationship is still being researched. There is also a dynamic state-dependent structure to this joint model, in which initial conditions (of average incomes, inequality, and other factors) matter. Within this structure, a common set of policy-relevant explanatory variables can be identified, with basic education one of the more robust predictors of both variables; higher proportions of men and women with good basic schooling entails a better distribution of a larger total income.

Countries that give priority to basic human capabilities in schooling, health, and nutrition not only directly contribute to well-being but are also more likely to see improving income distributions and higher average incomes over the longer term. There are often also ways in which governments can help relieve the credit constraints facing the poor, though even means-tested credit subsidies may not be the best way. Reducing transaction costs and helping people organize themselves have often proved to be better approaches. A more equitable distribution of physical assets, notably land, can also help greatly (both directly and by relieving credit constraints on investment by poor people), though the policy implications are not as straightforward as with health and education. The sectoral composition of economic growth has also been emphasized as an important factor. Sectoral biases against the rural sector in pricing, exchange rates, and public investment are not in the interests of either higher growth or better distribution. Sound macroeconomic policies appear to be essential for sustained growth; they either have no systematic effect on distribution or have potentially adverse short-term impacts that typically are not strong enough to outweigh the gains to the poor from growth. Paying attention to the composition of public expenditures in the adjustment program and to the inclusion of effective safety nets for the poor will help improve the distributional outcome in the transition to a pro-poor growth recovery.

Some of the key factors in achieving an equitable growth path, such as better schooling, also raise the living standards of poor people, in both income and nonincome dimensions. The nature of the dynamic interaction of initial conditions with future growth and distributional change can also have important policy implications. Countries with poor initial conditions (due, in part, to past policies) will tend to diverge from the rest. It may be possible to overcome this only if the lagging countries can get a large enough jump start, and here there may be an especially important role for international development assistance, since private capital flows usually come in only at a later stage of the reform process. There will undoubtedly remain areas of social policy or infrastructure in which private capital will not participate, even after successful reform.

The upshot of all that we know is that promoting growth is good because it is a potentially, and, in most cases, an actually, important vehicle for improving the living standards at all levels, and we now have a better idea about the policies that lead to growth, ranging from the fundamental institutional and market incentives to the promotion of macrostability. These policies should be pursued in all countries, but we suspect that these will be less effective or less well implemented in high-inequality countries. Reducing inequality is good because it will benefit the poor both immediately and in the longer term through a more pro-poor and probably higher growth rate.

Apart from the details of structural and macropolicy interventions that have already been mentioned, there are two major aspects that our analysis highlights for the changing role of the IFIs. First, there is an important implication in the area of greater selectivity among countries. Obviously the IFIs should support growth-promoting policies in all countries, but the focus should be on countries that are clearly committed to reform. It appears that low-inequality countries may well be more likely to be responsive to the need for reforms and more able to implement them in a shared-growth fashion. Testing commitment in high-inequality countries would seem especially important. Actions that are both growth promoting and equity enhancing may be the only realistic solution, but even this solution, experience shows, does not necessarily guarantee sustainability. The second important implication comes from the externality that appears to be associated with improvement in the distribution of assets and income: Future generations benefit because future growth will tend to be higher through better policies and better access to credit markets. If further research establishes the strength and robustness of this result, then it has an important policy implication: The IFIs should be willing to subsidize actions that encourage redistribution, especially investment in basic education and land reform.

Notes

For their helpful comments, we are grateful to the discussants, Jiwei Lou, Jacob Mwanza, and Dani Rodrik, ad well as other conference participants, and to Klaus Deininger, Peter Lanjouw, Andrés Solimano, Jack van Holst Pellekaan, Dominique van de Walle, Holger Wolf, and Shlomo Yitzhaki. The views set out in this chapter are those of the authors and should not be attributed to the World Bank.

1. There are numerous measures of inequality that might be considered compelling, and in principle they can diverge greatly in their assessments of whether distribution has improved. In practice, however, for many of the purposes of measurement, there appears to be considerable congruence among a number of these measures. We will rely heavily here on the most widely used summary statistic on distribution, the Gini index. There is also the question, Inequality of what? Here we focus mainly on current income or consumption inequality; both may diverge from other measures that might be compelling, such as inequality in lifetime utility or inequality in "capabilities" (on the latter, see Sen 1992).

2. See Anand and Kanbur (1993) for a more precise formulation, and necessary and sufficient conditions for the inverted U for six possible inequality measures.

3. An influential early example was Adelman and Morris (1973). At the time of writing, the most recent example we know of is Ram (1995).

4. This is the same data set used in Chen, Datt, and Ravallion (1994), which gives details.

5. We tried regressing the Gini index against a quadratic function of mean consumption (both linear and logs) as well as the Anand and Kanbur (1993) specification in which the Gini is regressed on the mean and the reciprocal of the mean. We also tried the specification proposed by Ram (1955) in which a quadratic function of the mean is used but with the intercept suppressed. This test did suggest an inverted U, but it appears to have very low power to reject the Kuznets hypothesis; indeed, on suppressing the intercept, one will find an inverted U between any two independent random variables with positive means (Ravallion 1996a).

6. The latter allows for fixed country-level effects. Fields and Jakubson (1992) find that the inverted U "flips" to an ordinary U when one allows for fixed effects, but our data do not confirm this finding.

7. See Deininger and Squire (1996a) for further details.

8. See Ravallion and Datt (1996).

9. These are based on ordinary-least-squares estimates of the coefficient on time.

10. These effects may entail either an omitted dynamic effect of past inequality or some other omitted country-level fixed effect in the error term. Either will bias standard tests on cross-sections of country data.

11. The surveys were done by India's National Sample Survey Organization (NSSO). To form the national distributions of real consumption from the NSSO tabulations of nominal expenditure distributions, an allowance was made for urban-rural cost-of-living differences and for differences in the rate of inflation between urban and rural areas (for details, see Datt 1996).

12. It might be argued that this correlation is partly spurious, since both the survey mean and the poverty index were estimated from the same data. If instead we use an instrumental variables estimator, using the growth rate in GDP per capita between the survey dates as the

instrument, then we get a very similar result: an elasticity of -2.15 (t-ratio $= -3.24$). Since the national accounts and census are largely independent of the household surveys, our estimate of the elasticity appears to be robust.

13. The corresponding instrumental variables estimate is -4.11 ($t = -2.36$).

14. Using the rate of growth in consumption per person from the national accounts as an instrument, the instrumental variables estimates are -1.47 ($t = 6.51$) for the head count index and -2.51 ($t = 4.50$) for the squared poverty gap.

15. The elasticity to changes in the Gini index is even higher if one uses a measure of poverty that better reflects distribution among the poor, using the "squared poverty gap" index, the elasticity to the Gini rises to 8.07 ($t = 2.49$), while the elasticity to the mean is -3.79 ($t = -3.61$).

16. This, for example, was the case for wage earners as against profit earners in the Israeli stabilization of 1985. Measurement is complicated by the fact that inflation during the household survey period will generally put an upward bias on inequality measures defined on nominal incomes (Kakwani 1987); conversely, stabilization will impart a downward bias.

17. Lipton and Ravallion (1995) review other recent arguments and evidence on the impacts of adjustment on the poor.

18. See Chen, Datt, and Ravallion (1994), who also show that countries without adequate poverty data tend also to have worse macroperformance, so compilations of available poverty data may well understate the problem.

19. On these issues, see Anand and Ravallion (1993) and Bidani and Ravallion (1997).

20. Generally when markets are incomplete, there will be efficiency implications of changes in distribution (Hoff 1994). Some specific examples in the literature are reviewed in Lipton and Ravallion (1995, sec. 5.1). The following discussion draws in part on Deininger and Squire (1996b).

21. Ongoing World Bank involvement in market-assisted land reform operations in South Africa and Colombia would provide an opportunity to test this empirically.

22. Some of the "data points" in these older compilations were not even based on household surveys but were synthetic estimates, and the quality of the survey data sets used was highly variable. For an overview of these issues see Fields (1994). Recent compilations have gone some way toward eliminating these problems (Chen, Datt, and Ravallion 1994; Deininger and Squire 1996a).

23. The inclusion of the initial average income variable on the right-hand side of these equations explaining the rate of growth also raises concerns about bias in the ordinary least squares estimators widely used in this literature.

24. Although Clarke (1995) and Deininger and Squire (1996b) report that the inequality effect on growth is robust to this and other changes in specification.

References

Adelman, Irma, and Cynthia Taft Morris. 1973. *Economic Growth and Social Equity in Developing Countries*. Stanford: Stanford University Press.

Adelman, Irma, and Sherman Robinson. 1988. "Income Distribution and Development." In H. Chenery and T. N. Srinivasan, eds., *Handbook of Development Economics*, 2: chap. 19. Rotterdam: North Holland.

Ahluwalia, Montek S. 1976. "Income Distribution and Development: Some Stylized Facts." *American Economic Review Papers and Proceedings* 66:128–135.

Alesina, Alberto, and Allan Drazen. 1991. "Why Are Stabilizations Delayed?" *American Economic Review* 81:1170–1188.

Alesina, Alberto, and Roberto Perotti. 1993. *Income Distribution, Political Instability, and Investment*. Working Paper. no. 4486. Cambridge, Mass.: National Bureau of Economic Research.

Alesina, Alberto, and Dani Rodrik. 1994. "Distributive Politics and Economic Growth." *Quarterly Journal of Economics* 109:465–490.

Anand, Sudhir, and S. M. Ravi Kanbur. 1993. "The Kuznets Process and the Inequality-Development Relationship." *Journal of Development Economics* 40:25–52.

Anand, Sudhir, and Martin Ravallion. 1993. "Human Development in Poor Countries: On the Role of Private Incomes and Public Services." *Journal of Economic Perspectives* 7:133–150.

Balisacan, Arsenio M. 1993. "Anatomy of Poverty During Adjustment: The Case of the Philippines." *Economic Development and Cultural Change* 44:33–62.

Banerjee, Abhijit V., and Andrew F. Newman. 1993. "Occupational Choice and the Process of Development." *Journal of Political Economy* 101:274–298.

Bencivenga, Valerie, and Bruce Smith. 1991. "Financial Intermediation and Endogenous Growth." *Review of Economic Studies* 58:195–209.

Bidani, Benu, and Martin Ravallion. 1997. "Decomposing Social Indicators Using Distributional Data." *Journal of Econometrics* 77:125–139.

Bourguignon, François, and C. Morrisson. 1995. *Inequality and Development: The Role of Dualism*. Document 95-32. Paris: DELTA.

Bourguignon, François, and C. Morrisson. 1990. "Income Distribution, Development and Foreign Trade: A Cross-Sectional Analysis." *European Economic Review* 34:1113–1132.

Brainard, S. Lael, and Thierry Verdier. 1994. "Lobbying and Adjustment in Declining Industries." *European Economic Review* 38:586–595.

Bruno, Michael, and William Easterly. 1995. *Inflation Crises and Long-Run Growth*. Policy Research Working Paper no. 1517. Washington, D.C.: World Bank.

Chatterjee, S. 1991. *The Effect of Transitional Dynamics on the Distribution of Wealth in a Neo-classical Capital Accumulation Model*. Working Paper no. 91-22. Philadelphia: Federal Reserve Bank of Philadelphia.

Chen, Shaohua, Gaurav Datt, and Martin Ravallion. 1994. "Is Poverty Increasing or Decreasing in the Developing World?" *Review of Income and Wealth* 40:359–376.

Chenery, H., M. Ahluwalia, C. Bell, J. Duloy, and R. Jolly. 1974. *Redistribution with Growth*. Oxford: Oxford University Press.

Clarke, George R. G. 1995. "More Evidence on Income Distribution and Growth." *Journal of Development Economics* 47:403–427.

Datt, Gaurav. 1996. "Poverty in India 1951–1992: Trends and Decompositions." Mimeo. Washington, D.C.: Policy Research Department, World Bank.

Datt, Gaurav, and Martin Ravallion. 1992. "Growth and Redistribution Components of Changes in Poverty Measures: A Decomposition with Applications to Brazil and India in the 1980s." *Journal of Development Economics* 38:275–295.

Deininger, Klaus, and Lyn Squire. 1996a. "A New Data Set for Measuring Income Inequality." *World Bank Economic Review* 10:565–592.

Deininger, Klaus, and Lyn Squire. 1996b. "New Ways of Looking at Old Issues: Growth and Inequality." Mimeo. Washington, D.C.: Policy Research Department, World Bank.

Demery, Lionel, and Lyn Squire. 1996. "Macroeconomic Adjustment and Poverty in Africa: An Emerging Picture." *World Bank Research Observer* 11(1) (February): 39–60.

Dorosh, Paul A., and David E. Sahn. 1993. "A General Equilibrium Analysis of the Effect of Macroeconomic Adjustment on Poverty in Africa." Mimeo. Ithaca, N.Y.: Cornell University Food and Nutrition Policy Program.

Eckstein, Zvi, and Itzhak Zilcha. 1994. "The Effects of Compulsory Schooling on Growth Income Distribution and Welfare." *Journal of Public Economics* 54:339–359.

Favaro, Edgardo, and Donna MacIsaac. 1995. "Who Benefited from Peru's Reform Program? Poverty Note." Mimeo. Washington, D.C.: Latin America 3 Country Department, World Bank.

Fields, Gary. 1989. "Changes in Poverty and Inequality in Developing Countries." *World Bank Research Observer* 4:167–185.

Fields, Gary. 1994. "Data for Measuring Poverty and Inequality Changes in the Developing Countries." *Journal of Development Economics* 44:87–102.

Fields, Gary, and George Jakubson. 1992. "New Evidence on the Kuznets Curve." Mimeo. Ithaca, N.Y.: Cornell University.

Fishlow, Albert. 1996. "Inequality, Poverty and Growth: Where Do We Stand?" In Michael Bruno and Boris Pleskovic, eds., *Annual World Bank Conference on Development Economics 1995*. Washington, D.C.: World Bank.

Foster, James, J. Greer, and E. Thorbecke. 1984. "A Class of Decomposable Poverty Measures." *Econometrica* 52:761–766.

Galor, Oded, and Joseph Zeira. 1993. "Income Distribution and Macroeconomics." *Review of Economic Studies* 60:35–52.

Glewwe, Paul, and Gillette Hall. 1994. "Poverty, Inequality, and Living Standards During Unorthodox Adjustment: The Case of Peru." *Economic Development and Cultural Change* 42:689–717.

Hoff, Karla. 1994. "The Second Theorem of the Second Best." *Journal of Public Economics* 54:223–242.

Hoff, Karla, and Andrew B. Lyon. 1994. *Non-Leaky Buckets: Optimal Redistributive Taxation and Agency Costs*. Working Paper Series no. 4652. Cambridge, Mass.: National Bureau of Economic Research.

Jung, Jin Hwa. 1992. "Personal income Distribution in Korea, 1963–1986: A Human Capital Approach." *Journal of Asian Economics* 3:57–72.

Kakwani, Nanak. 1987. "Inequality of Income Derived from Survey Data During the Inflationary Period." *Economics Letters* 23:387–388.

Kuznets, Simon. 1955. "Economic Growth and Income Inequality." *American Economic Review* 45:1–28.

Kuznets, Simon. 1966. *Modern Economic Growth*. New Haven: Yale University Press.

Laban, Raul, and Federico Sturzenegger. 1994. "Distributional Conflict, Financial Adaptation, and Delayed Stabilizations." *Economics and Politics* 6:257–276.

Lipton, Michael, and Martin Ravallion. 1995. "Poverty and Policy." In Jere Behrman and T. N. Srinivasan, eds., *Handbook of Development Economics*, 3: chap. 4. Amsterdam: North-Holland.

Milanovic, Branko. 1995. *Poverty, Inequality and Social Policy in Transition Economies*. Research Paper, no. 9. Washington, D.C.: World Bank, Transition Economics Division.

Morley, Samuel A. 1994. *Poverty and Inequality in Latin America: Past Evidence, Future prospects*. Policy Essay no. 13. Washington, D.C.: Overseas Development Council.

Oshima, H. 1970. "Income Inequality and Economic Growth: The Post-War Experience of Asian Countries." *Malayan Economic Review* 15:7–41.

Özler, S., and G. Tabellini. 1991. *External Debt and Political Instability*. Working Paper no. 3772. Cambridge, Mass.: National Bureau of Economic Research.

Papanek, Gustav, and Oldrich Kyn. 1986. "The Effect on Income Distribution of Development, the Growth Rate and Economic Strategy." *Journal of Development Economics* 23:55–65.

Persson, Torsten, and Guido Tabellini. 1994. "Is Inequality Harmful for Growth?" *American Economic Review* 84:600–621.

Ram, Rati. 1995. "Economic Development and Inequality: An Overlooked Regression Constraint." *Economic Development and Cultural Change* 3:425–434.

Ravallion, Martin. 1995. "Growth and Poverty: Evidence for the Developing World." *Economics Letters* 48:411–417.

Ravallion, Martin. 1997a. "On Rati Ram's Test of the Kuznets Hypothesis." *Economic Development and Cultural Change*. forthconing.

Ravallion, Martin. 1997b. "Can High-Inequality Developing Countries Escape Absolute Poverty?". *Economics Letters*, forthcoming.

Ravallion, Martin, and Shaohua Chen. 1997. "What Can New Survey Data Tell Us About Recent Changes in Living Standards in Developing and Transitional Economies?" *World Bank Economic Review* 11(May): 357–382.

Ravallion, Martin, and Gaurav Datt. 1996. "How Important to India's Poor Is the Sectoral Composition of Growth?" *World Bank Economic Review* 10:1–25.

Ravallion, Martin, and Monika Huppi. 1991. "Measuring Changes in Poverty: A Methodological Case Study of Indonesia During an Adjustment Period." *World Bank Economic Review* 5:57–82.

Ribe, Helena, S. Carvalho, R. Liebenthal, P. Nicholas, and E. Zuckerman. 1990. *How Adjustment Programs Can Help the Poor*. World Bank Discussion Paper no. 71. Washington, D.C.: World Bank.

Robinson, Sherman. 1976. "A Note on the U-Hypothesis Relating Income Inequality and Economic Development." *American Economic Review* 66:437–440.

Saint-Paul, Gilles, and Thierry Verdier. 1992. "Historical Accidents and the Persistence of Distributional Conflicts." *Journal of the Japanese and International Economies* 6:406–422.

Selowsky, Marcelo. 1991. "Protecting Nutrition Status in Adjustment Programs: Recent World Bank Activities and Projects in Latin America." *Food and Nutrition Bulletin* 13:293–302.

Sen, Amartya. 1992. *Inequality Re-Examined*. Oxford: Oxford University Press.

Squire, Lyn. 1993. "Fighting Poverty." *American Economic Review, Papers and Proceedings* 83(2):377–382.

Thorbecke, Erik. 1991. "Adjustment, Growth and Income Distribution in Indonesia." *World Development* 19:1595–1614.

Tsiddon, Daniel. 1992. "A Moral Hazard Trap to Growth." *International Economic Review* 33:299–321.

Watkins, Kevin. 1995. *The OXFAM Poverty Report*. Oxford: OXFAM.

World Bank. 1990. *World Development Report*. New York: Oxford University Press.

World Bank. 1991. *Assistance Strategies to Reduce Poverty*. World Bank Policy Paper. Washington, D.C.: World Bank.

World Bank. 1993. *The East Asian Miracle: Economic Growth and Public Policy*. New York: Oxford University Press.

Comments

Jiwei Lou

The relationship between equity and growth is a classic issue in development economics. Regarding this issue, some propositions were once acknowledged as truth. Bruno, Ravallion, and Squire present a strong challenge to the propositions that there exists a systematic link between growth and inequality, that the Kuznets hypothesis is tenable, and that there is a trade-off between efficiency and equity, and thus the two cannot be achieved at the same time. The arguments they present are significant and profound because they refute the long-held propositions that have greatly influenced public policy.

I agree entirely with the authors that there is no systematic link between growth and inequality over time and that equitable growth can be achieved by designing and implementing good public policies in developing countries. The authors present these arguments by using a great deal of time-series and cross-country data. They use time-series data from transitional countries to support their arguments; however, we must be careful when using the data from these countries, which have special problems that are not typical subjects of development economics. In fact, the validity of the authors arguments would not be affected even if these data were not used. My comments here focus on the general issue of income distribution in the transitional economies and on the special issue of the Chinese economy.

Inequality in the Transitional Economies

We are all familiar with the following pretransition features: Enterprises were not profit maximizers; there were general price distortions and industry-entry barriers; most production consumption decisions were made by the state, and the income was directly distributed by the state; the analytical framework did not address some general policy issues in development economics, such as elimination of price distortion, free trade, and the relationship between growth and distribution. In these economies, the Gini coefficient was generally low, from 0.2 to 0.25, but the low Gini coefficient was determined by a mechanism that differed from the one in the developing countries.

The general income distribution issues in the early stage of transition may be summarized as follows:

• Enterprises and individuals must be required to bear the responsibilities for the consequences of their own conduct, to create an incentive mechanism.

• Consumption must be diversified, to support structural changes.

• The huge fiscal subsidies must be reduced, to stabilize the economy.

These policies must be implemented in the transitional economies, but they destroy the extreme egalitarianism and increase the Gini coefficient. Nevertheless, this is a kind of progress.

In contrast, the Gini coefficient is between 0.3 and 0.4 in the market economies. To some extent, the low coefficient is one of the conditions for the market economy to operate. The policies mentioned above brought about economic growth in China but not in other transition countries; clearly growth depends on other factors as well. However, whether policies can bring about growth is not within the scope of the Kuznets hypothesis; therefore, it is not appropriate to use the data from the transitional economies to test the hypothesis.

Income Distribution in China

China's policy of letting a few regions and households get rich first, with the others then following, is a significant factor in the recent increase in inequality.

China is in transition, and it is necessary for it to adopt some policies that are common for transitional economies. In prereform China (1978), in fact, the Gini coefficient was only about 0.21 for rural residents and 0.11 for urban residents. The urban area had a higher degree of central planning and was more inclined toward egalitarianism. This point also shows that the initial distribution of the Gini coefficient in China is the opposite of the initial distribution in the Kuznets hypothesis.

In the initial stage of the reform, the foreign capital China attracted mainly came from the overseas Chinese community, who have blood relationship with the people living in China's coastal areas. For this reason and to attract foreign capital, it was necessary to offer some preferential polices and institutional flexibility to the coastal areas.

Early in the reform period, the reform objectives were not very clear and concrete, and the reform theory was not well thought out. Under these circumstances, it was not possible to have a well-designed overall policy. Instead, China experimented in some areas, and its experience thus gained guided the reform.

On the whole, China's policy has been realistic and successful. The policy has resulted in rapid growth but, inevitably, inequality. This is not a stylized fact, but a result of the policy of inequality that the policymakers chose to adopt.

Inequality with Reform

In general, China chose a gradual approach to reform, though some reform measures were adopted quite rapidly, for instance, the foreign exchange and taxation reforms implemented in 1994. The gradual approach has enabled China to avoid an economic recession, such as those experienced in Eastern Europe and the former Soviet Union. With rapid growth, the nation's living standard has improved, but China has also paid the price of increased inequality.

A number of reform mechanisms have led to unequal income distribution. First, price distortions and a dual-track price system have been maintained in too many areas and for too long—for more than ten years for commodity prices, interest rates, and the foreign exchange rate. The foreign exchange rate was not subject to market forces until 1995. Price distortions and the dual-track price system enabled some people to earn quick profits and resulted in unequal income distribution.

Another problem is that the process of removing entry barriers has been too slow. Approval from different government levels must be obtained to set up a company, apply for a loan, buy foreign exchange, and use land. The restrictions on establishing companies, operating an export and import business, and buying foreign exchange have been greatly eased recently, but they are still excessive. This system has increased transaction costs and led to profiteering and inequality.

Cost distortions in the social welfare system are problematic. The level of social welfare is high and wages are low in the state sector, and the welfare level is low and wages high in the private sector. Cost distortions have created many dual-track families: One partner works in the state sector, enjoying high welfare for housing and medical care; the other partner works in the private sector, enjoying a high wage. In fact, the state sector provides social welfare for both partners. Furthermore, because some state enterprises and institutions carry a heavy welfare burden, they can pay only low wages; as a result, the real living standard of their employees has been lowered.

Finally, a vested interest has been formed. The vested interest accepts the distortions and blocks any change in income distribution. A typical example is the financial arrangement between the central and local governments. In China, local governments control most of the tax revenue. The coastal areas, for example, take in fiscal revenue to maintain their public expenditures, and with a tax rate lower than the national average. As a result, these areas can attract more investment and promote economic growth. Figure 5.3 shows an unusual case in China: Provinces with high per capita GDP have low tax elasticity. In the figure, tax elasticity descends from the left to the right. The first fifteen provinces on the left are all inland provinces, and the ten coastal provinces are all among the second fifteen provinces.

The policy adopted in 1994 unified the taxation system. Under the new system, the central government gained control of most tax income, but it had to compromise substantially. China still does not have any policy whereby financial resources are redistributed among provinces so poor areas have financial assistance for supporting public services.

All of these distortions have worsened income distribution while promoting little growth. The gradual approach to reform allowed these distortions to persist for too long. The inequality caused by these distortions has therefore been linked with reform.

By presenting a great deal of facts, Bruno, Ravallion, and Squire have shown that the Kuznets hypothesis is not tenable, growth in its initial stages is not necessarily associated with inequality, the need for a trade-off between efficiency and equality is questionable, and a good policy in income distribution is favorable to growth.

The so-called stylized fact refers to the process of transforming poor market economies into modern economies. To test the validity of the hypotheses, one should look at the development process of the relevant economies, such as the market economies in which per capita GDP rises from US$200 to US$2,000. Under normal circumstances, the Gini coefficient of the transitional economies will increase when they move from extreme egalitarianism to a common pattern of income distribution in the market economies. This increase, however, is not a stylized fact.

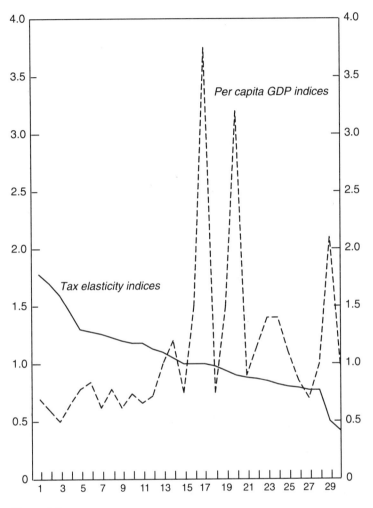

Figure 5.3
Industrial and commercial tax elasticity indices of thirty provinces (indicated by numbers 1–30), China (1986–1991 average)

The main cause for the worsening of income distribution in the transitional economies is policy and institutional distortions. One of the costs of the gradual approach to reform is that it has slowed the process of correcting the distortions and helped to form a vested interest group, which resists any efforts to eliminate the distortions.

If China wants equitable growth, it needs to eliminate price distortion and remove market entry barriers, to rationalize the initial income distribution; increase taxation capacity and improve the income distribution among regions and basic public services; and establish a social security system and a progressive personal income tax system. Based on a justifiable initial income distribution, an improvement in equity should be pursued. In this respect, the general experiences of the developing economies as expressed by Bruno, Ravallion, and Squire are indicative and significant. China still has a long way to go and must speed up the process.

Comments

Jacob M. Mwanza

Bruno, Ravallion, and Squire examine evidence concerning the relation between growth and distribution (or equity), the effect of pro-growth policies on distribution, and the impact of distribution on growth. They review a large volume of recent empirical research, including some of their own analyses. The results support several interesting conclusions.

First, regarding the link between growth and distribution, they note that recent cross-country estimates do not support the Kuznets hypothesis that growth is initially associated with increased inequality; time-series analyses reveal that Gini coefficients for a large number of countries have been stable; and growth does help to reduce absolute poverty. This last result is particularly well illustrated, using time series from India's national sample survey.

Second, with respect to the relation between pro-growth policies and distribution, they found that many countries that are emerging from deep crises have recorded rapid recoveries in growth, and this recovery has been consistent with improvements in distribution. They note as well that transition economies have experienced declines in income *and* worsening inequality. Indeed, the evidence shows that broad-based improvements in macroeconomic policy have a positive effect on distribution and poverty even in the short run.

Third, on the impact of distribution on growth, they find that theoretical work suggests that higher initial inequality reproduces itself (primarily through the political economy of the distribution of assets and opportunities), and tentative results from the as yet limited amount of empirical research suggest that inequality has a negative impact on growth.

They conclude that policies that promote growth are likely to improve distribution and reduce poverty. However, it is more difficult to promote growth in high-inequality countries. From these results, the authors draw two lessons for the international financial institutions (IFIs): emphasis should be given to the countries that are demonstrably committed to reform, and as long-term growth strategy, these institutions should consider methods to subsidize the transfer of assets in high-inequality countries.

All of us are deeply indebted to Bruno, Ravallion, and Squire for their stimulating and provocative work. Their results cast doubt on many deep-seated ideas that have been widely taken as facts throughout the development community.

In my comments, I point to some areas that would benefit from further research and then turn to some specific policy issues that these authors raise.

Further Research

The authors conjecture that "the poor and low-inequality countries of twenty to thirty years ago have split into two, blurring the old inverted U but (quite possibly) better revealing the true relationship." With the data available to the authors, this conjecture could be tested. Two tests seem to be relevant. The first is whether the distribution in countries in each region follows an inverted U once the various country-level determinants of inequality are allowed for. The second is whether the two regions have in fact had two separate experiences, with the high-growth Asian countries becoming more egalitarian and the slow-growth African countries becoming less so.

The databases Bruno, Ravallion, and Squire considered cut across the broadest dimensions of income, consumption, and social groupings, and the results show that growth reduces inequality and poverty. A key question, however, is whether this result applies once the experiences of males and females, as separate groups, are taken into account. Some of the elements of improved distribution are noted—education, access to credit, and a supportive trade regime—yet many microlevel studies have argued that growth has not benefited specific groups, especially women producers and women heads of household. A major theme of gender research has been that women have fared poorly because of the unequal distribution of assets and opportunities. It would be useful if this research could be extended to deal with the role of growth in the inequality and poverty that women experience and whether the pro-growth policies now in place in transitional economies do improve distribution and reduce poverty for women, even in the short run.

These results have clear implications for policy. Gender specialists have been arguing that the women do not benefit fully from growth and bear disproportionate costs of adjustment. Some further research within this framework would help determine the importance of these issues for policy.

I find the evidence on the relative stability of the Gini coefficient over time to be depressing. The implication is that inequality, both high and low, reproduces itself, even in the face of major public programs to improve equity. For years, economists have labored under the Pigovian perception that public sector intervention has a positive role in removing restrictions that inhibit competition and, where the restrictions cannot be removed, providing compensatory payments as a means of improving distribution.

Does the result of a stable Gini coefficient mean that public intervention to improve distribution has been ineffective in the face of class and/or sectional interests? Or has public intervention, despite its stated objectives, been a means of preserving the status quo?

In my view, answers to these questions reflect on some basic premises of development economics. Most of us now accept that national planning of the type that was so popular two decades ago has many drawbacks. For most of us, the reintroduction of planning would be a step back. However, the majority of development economists see some positive role for state intervention, even if it is only to reform macroeconomic policies, sell off the parastatals, repair the basic infrastructure, or improve health and education. For their part, the IFIs favor selected state intervention. Indeed, Bruno, Ravallion, and Squire suggest that the IFIs should subsidize redistribution policies in high-inequality countries.

Thus, I urge that some detailed research be done to highlight the role of state intervention (broadly defined) on the pattern of distribution over time. A useful starting point is the experience of African countries over the past three decades. Among other things, it would highlight the role of the state in the economic decline and the impact of the decline in distribution and poverty. Answers to these questions would help direct the reform efforts now underway in Africa. There has been much talk about "reinventing the state." It would be a major help to know the pitfalls to avoid as this is done.

Policy Issues

The results that Bruno, Ravallion, and Squire present deal with broad trends. Policymakers, however, face issues that are immediate and context specific. Although senior officials who are reforming governments may wish to keep one eye on the broad sweep of history, they have to focus on day-to-day events, especially if they are to meet the range of performance criteria, benchmarks, targets, and conditions agreed on with the international agencies.

Thus, some detailed work is needed to derive concrete policy proposals from the results of Bruno, Ravallion, and Squire's work. One issue arises as a consequence of the stability of the Gini coefficient. Many African countries have regressed substantially over the past two decades. The process has involved a dramatic drop in per capita income combined with the erosion of the capacities of the key economic institutions. It is now well established that poverty has worsened, and I suspect that inequality has intensified as well.

What measures have to be undertaken, as part of a reform package, to ensure that the Gini coefficient does not remain at a permanently higher level? I can think of several. From a distributional perspective, the privatization of state-owned assets involves the widest possible spreading of claims to those assets (as in a voucher system). To do otherwise, for example, through the widely favored procedure of selling off assets to the highest bidder, has the effect of allowing those who prospered during the period of collapse (many by illegal means) to gain and maintain an unwarranted advantage. Other such policies include improving access to land and security of tenure, providing widespread access to education and health, and opening the economy to competition so that the cozy relations enjoyed by those who had access in the old regimes are forced to become efficient or go out of business.

Some of these measures are well known and are being implemented by reforming governments. However, there must be many similar policies; if they are taken during the reform program, they could help reverse some of the deterioration in the distribution of income and assets that occurred in the prereform period.

My fear is that if policies such as these are not implemented, many reforming countries risk locking themselves into a highly unequal system of distribution that, as Bruno, Ravallion, and Squire's research shows, will lead to lower rates of growth in the future.

I am impressed with the range of data that these authors have included in their analysis, but some systematic effects have been excluded. One of these is the internationalization of capital and finance. There is now considerable evidence to show that the very rich and the well-to-do shifted large amounts of resources out of developing countries over the past two or three decades. For these groups, national estimates of their consumption or income (or whatever other index of inequality is used) are distorted. Their income and consumption transcend national boundaries.

In many cases, especially in Africa, this movement of wealth was aided and abetted by the state. Government mechanisms were regularly used to transfer public resources to private individuals, who then transferred the resources abroad. Enough has been written about the dynamics and dimensions of capital flight to begin to raise serious questions about the value of data on national measures of equality, especially in small countries.

How the globalization of income and wealth can be taken into account in the empirical estimates is not immediately clear. Nonetheless, I have no doubt that the effects are potentially important for policy, especially in an African context. To illustrate, reforming governments have to move to systems that remove the incentive to shift resources abroad. This calls for broad-based liberalization, tax systems consistent with international norms, minimal controls on financial movements, and the avoidance of restrictions and distortions that work against the poor.

My perception is that capital flight is basically a sunk cost; not much can be done over the short term to encourage the reflow of resources held abroad by local residents. Therefore policies have to maximize the opportunities for growth based on the resources within the country. That is, the path forward has to rely on expanding the economy's current and future potential using policies that are devoid of the distortions that led to the past loss of wealth.

Perhaps I am wrong; it would be useful to know. We need detailed research on alternative paths of adjustment designed to promote equity and growth in a world characterized by a high degree of asymmetric capital mobility (i.e., capital will quickly flow out of developing economies but only slowly flow back in).

I am intrigued by the policy implications of the general result that there is no inverted U. Basic models of intersectoral resource reallocation (such as the Lewis model), which Bruno, Ravallion, and Squire mention in passing, suggest that inequality should worsen as developing countries are transformed from rural into urban-industrial societies. Since the evidence shows that inequality does not worsen as this reallocation occurs, what mechanism (or mechanisms) is counteracting the tendency for this distribution to worsen? Access to education might be a factor. But the urban-industrial population normally has better access to education than the rural population. On these grounds, resource reallocation and predominantly urban education should worsen inequality.

Clearly for the inverted U not to exist or to be blurred, other elements have to be at work. What are they? How do they relate to the economies in transition and the reforming economies in Africa, both of which are vigorously attempting to promote the intersectoral reallocation of resources as a means of eliminating distortions inherited from the past? Answers to these questions would deepen our appreciation of the economic reform process, and of the development process itself.

Conclusion

Bruno, Ravallion, and Squire have little to say about how the IFIs should address the issues of growth and inequality. One issue that concerns me is whether the IFIs fully take into account their own impact, both positive and negative, on growth and equity. Many of the policies that are now being undone in African countries—planning, tariff protection for local industry, state-sponsored industrialization—were once supported by IFIs. It is true that neither of the Bretton Woods institutions agreed with the extremes to which many governments pursued these policies. Nonetheless, IFIs and governments are now undoing a lot of what, in the past, was thought to be useful for promoting growth, improving equity, and reducing poverty. Time and experience have taught us otherwise.

I urge that we build on this lesson and begin to anticipate what problems may be generated by current programs of reform and adjustment. That none of us can grasp the full implications of our decisions does not mean we should not try. In this respect, it would be highly rewarding to think strategically about the policy prescriptions we are now implementing.

We all appreciate that economic development is a continual process of adjustment. We should avoid having to adjust in the future to problems that some structured forethought might have helped us avoid.

Comments

Dani Rodrik

Bruno, Ravallion, and Squire have summarized the state of our knowledge on the interrelationships among economic growth, income distribution, and poverty. They make a good statement of what we may call the emerging conventional wisdom on these issues:

1. The Kuznets curve is fiction. There is no systematic relationship between income levels and inequality.

2. Adjustment policies are not inherently detrimental to equity and are in fact good for poverty alleviation insofar as they enable economic growth to resume.

3. On theoretical and empirical grounds, there are reasons to believe that high levels of inequality in income and asset ownership are bad for subsequent economic growth.

4. There is no conflict between economic growth and poverty alleviation.

Policy Implications of the Analysis

I am in full agreement with the authors on these four points. In my comments, I amplify some of their discussion and raise some additional issues. I begin by stressing two other findings reported by the authors along the way, because these are of some significance for policy.

First, although inequality measures vary tremendously across countries (with Gini coefficients ranging from 0.20 to 0.65), such measures tend to remain quite stable over time in practically all countries for which time-series data exist. Hence, if South Korea and Taiwan have low Gini coefficients in the 1990s, this is primarily because they had low Ginis in the late 1950s; Brazil has high inequality now because it has had high inequality at least since the 1950s. One can attribute the differences in distributional outcomes in Latin America and East Asia to neither changes in the level of incomes in the intervening period nor differences in government policy. (I also take from this the conclusion that the World Bank has overdone the significance of shared growth in East Asia. The implied counterfactual in the shared-growth scenario seems to be one of growth with a significant deterioration in the distribution of income; but as the result just cited indicates, it is not clear why this is a reasonable counterfactual.)

Second, measured poverty rates appear to be sensitive to changes in income distribution. This implies that government policies that redistribute income to the poor (without adverse effects on incentives and accumulation) can have a big impact on poverty.

Two sorts of general policy conclusions follow from the empirical evidence taken together. The first one, and the one emphasized by the authors, is that the focus of the World Bank and the IMF on stabilization and adjustment policies that promote growth is not in need of serious rethinking insofar as the objectives of equity and poverty alleviation are concerned. I think that is basically right. Although I am perhaps more skeptical than the authors are about how much we actually know about the nature of the "correct" adjustment policies, it seems reasonably well established that countries that have grown fast have done so at little cost to equity and with many gains on the poverty front.

The second implication, mentioned more in passing, is that there may be something to be said in favor of a more frontal attack on income inequalities. This is a consequence of the findings that more equity helps with current poverty, and it is probably also good for long-run growth. But then how do we go about achieving more equity? The authors discuss some ideas—for example, the roles of education, land reform, access to credit, and trade strategy are mentioned—but they do not go as far as I would have liked to see. Consider some of the issues and difficulties.

First, is inequality susceptible to policy? Many of the countries listed in table 5.1 have gone through wild gyrations in policy, with apparently little effect on Gini coefficients. (The large increases in Gini coefficients observed in countries in transition have to be taken with a grain of salt. What is clearly going on is that previously nonmarketed or unmeasured sources of income are becoming marketized.) If cross-country differences in equality are due to structural reasons or historical accidents (e.g., land reforms imposed by outside powers), we are left with a rather fatalistic conclusion.

My own attempts at identifying the determinants of cross-country variation in inequality are summarized in table 5.3. I have regressed a measure

Table 5.3
Determinants of Inequality Across Countries

Independent variables	Dependent variables: Income share of top 20 percent of the population divided by that of bottom 40 percent	
	Ordinary least squares	Instrumental variables
Constant	4.58[a]	2.35
	(3.07)	(0.74)
Primary enrollment ratio	0.03[b]	0.05
	(1.71)	(1.65)
Secondary enrollment ratio	−0.08[a]	−0.13
	(−4.92)	(−3.28)
Mineral and fuel exports (percentage of GNP)	−10.65[a]	−15.70
	(−3.42)	(−2.94)
Agricultural land (percentage of total land)	−0.04[a]	−0.05
	(−3.05)	(−2.70)
Urban population (percentage of total population)	0.06[a]	0.12
	(3.53)	(2.73)
Number of countries	43	43
R-squared	0.47	0.22

Notes: All data are from World Bank, *World Tables* (at or around 1990). In the instrumental variables regression, agricultural land, GNP per capita, irrigated land (as a percentage of total land), population, population density, and mineral and fuel exports are used as instruments for school enrollment ratios and urbanization. T-statistics are in parentheses.
a. Significant at 1 percent level.
b. Significant at 10 percent.
c. Significant at 5 percent level.

of inequality (the income share of the top 20 percent of the population divided by the bottom 40 percent) on a number of explanatory variables. I show here only the equation with the best fit. The results support some of the points made by the authors but also contain some nuances and differences. The secondary school enrollment ratio is strongly and negatively associated with inequality, corroborating the importance of access to education. Note, however, that the sign on primary school enrollment is positive, and the opposite of what would be expected. There may be interesting questions regarding the level of education that one would want to target from an equity standpoint. Second, I find a negative association between inequality and the importance of mineral and fuel exports in national income. This, too, seems to contradict some of the results in the literature cited by the authors. Third, a preponderance of agricultural land is negatively correlated with inequality. Fourth, urbanization is positively associated with inequality. Since there may be reverse causality running from inequality to some of the right-hand-side variables, particularly the educational variables and urbanization, I have also run the same equation using instrumental variables (second column of table 5.3). The results remain broadly unchanged, even though the fit becomes worse. I have tried additional variables as well, including per capita income and openness to trade, and found them to be statistically insignificant.

A specification like this one suggests that both structural and policy variables are important in determining inequality. Hence, the apparent stability of Gini coefficients over time notwithstanding, appropriate policies may well contribute to improved equity. Before drawing policy conclusions, however, we clearly need to understand better the determinants of inequality.

If one handicap is inadequate knowledge about which policies, if any, are conducive to equity, another is that the observed statistical relationship between equity and subsequent economic growth may not be exploitable by policy. To see this most clearly, consider the Alesina-Rodrik or the Persson-Tabellini story about why inequality is bad for growth. In each case, the idea that inequality is bad is based on reasoning that in equilibrium, inequality generates more redistributive political activity, *and* such activity is harmful to growth. These models take for granted that attempts to redistribute income will act as a tax on investment. Consequently, we have a somewhat paradoxical situation: While equality is good for growth—if equality is inherited as a result of historical or exogenous factors—policies that aim at achieving more equality are bad for growth.

I do not suggest that these political economy stories are to be taken very seriously. The point, rather, is that the policy conclusions to be drawn from the empirical evidence are not so straightforward and depend heavily on the specific mechanism that links equality to subsequent growth. Unfortunately, we do not have reliable evidence on the mechanism at work.

Effects of Adjustment Policies

I agree with the authors' bottom line on the effects of adjustment policies; however, their case can be strengthened by bringing greater analytical clarity to the discussion. In particular, I would make some distinctions.

First, I would distinguish among three components of adjustment: macroeconomic stabilization, institutional reform, and relative-price reform. The first two do not necessarily entail large distributional consequences, while the third necessarily does so. It is, of course, true that the requisite changes in relative prices will often benefit the poor, but this does not always need to be so.

I would also distinguish between reform of unsustainable policies (such as an overvalued exchange rate) versus reform of damaging but otherwise sustainable policies (such as quantitative restrictions on imports). The consumption booms that are often experienced under the first class of policies cannot be maintained for long. Consequently, it will be misleading to undertake before- and after-type comparisons regarding consumption behavior.

Finally, I would distinguish between measures of welfare based on current consumption versus measures based on the present discounted value of current and future consumption. If we think of the adjustment costs incurred by individuals during the transition as an investment in future earning capabilities, current consumption will be a very poor measure of the true well-being of these individuals. Just as we do not think of an investment in a profitable activity as making us worse off because our current consumption has to be reduced by an equivalent amount, we should not think of a worker who has to learn new skills in, say, an export-oriented industry, as necessarily having lost out during the adjustment.

Bruno, Ravallion, and Squire present a balanced and judicious statement of the issues. Their policy conclusions are strong where the evidence is strong; they are cautious where the evidence is weak or open to diverse interpretations. There are two issues on which we need more information: We need a better understanding of the determinants of inequality across countries and more research on the channels through which equality influences subsequent growth.

6   Equitable Economic
Transformation

John Flemming

This chapter concentrates more directly on the equity matter than the transformations, but they are, of course, linked through the political process. Only if the transformations fulfill certain conditions of political acceptability will the momentum of the reform process be sustained and with it the growth it should eventually foster. A particularly simple model (Balcerowicz 1994) suggests that the electorate's critical faculties are suspended for a predetermined period after the fall of communism and that anything could be done during the opening of this window of opportunity.

It is certainly true that oppositionist forces take time to regroup, but the extent, and particularly the duration, of this opening must depend in part on the public's reaction to the measures being implemented and its assessment of their consequences. I focus on this as a potential rather than an actual problem whose operation has been observed and monitored. The potential problem can be summarized briefly.

Under communism, the transition economies were recorded (e.g., in World Bank tables) as delivering greater equality and better education, literacy, and health than other economies with comparable levels of per capita income. Moreover, although much of the old regime and its ideology were discredited and rejected, some validity was attributed to a greater concern with these matters than was believed to characterize market economies.

These (re)distributionist values confronted a postcommunist situation in which performance on many of the relevant indicators was almost bound to decline. The liberalization of trade and prices created opportunities for well-placed entrepreneurs, while threatening the continued employment of some categories of workers in particular sectors overexpanded under the previous regime.

In the former Soviet Union (FSU), where reform was typically relatively slow and partial, there were not only unequal responses to the opportunities of a market disequilibrium but also extensive opportunities for arbitrage between free and regulated markets for those with access to the necessary permits and licenses, whether acquired legally or not.

Unemployment typically rose from negligible levels to the mid-teens in Central and Eastern Europe, while it was kept low in the FSU, partly by retaining some people in nominal employment at a much lower wage (often the statutory minimum) than was being paid to nonredundant workers. Whether open or hidden in this way, de facto unemployment contributed to a deterioration in income distribution and reflected a fall in output and, generally, in average incomes.

One reason for the prevalence of the less open form of unemployment in the FSU was that only in this way could redundant workers and their families retain access to a wide range of social and other services and benefits supplied through enterprises. The equitable transfer of such services from the enterprise to some agency of government is a major challenge in itself. In the meantime, the quality of services offered varied to some extent with the diverse financial position of the enterprise.

Where the supply of social services has been shifted to the government, these services have been subject to acute budgetary pressures arising from the need to rectify inherited fiscal deficits and stabilize inflationary situations. Also, the process of legitimizing private economic activity while the opportunities for monitoring and taxing it were embryonic created widespread and large shadow economies, which did not contribute to the budget. In several cases, a key determinant of whether to stay in (or come in to) the light or to fade into the shadows depended on whether, in the former case, the activity would be a net contributor or a net recipient of tax money.

There are conflicting accounts as to the effect of these pressures on the quality, quantity, and distribution of health care, education, and similar services. Certainly academic staff, whether teaching or conducting research, in public institutions have typically felt hard done by. It is more difficult to identify the discontent of their "customers." Equally, the strongly negative UNICEF reports on health in transition economies may be influenced by discontented suppliers; nevertheless, the circumstantial and other evidence for a decline in both average quality and especially the distribution of services, with consequences for aggregate morbidity and mortality statistics, is strong, especially in the FSU.

The rest of this chapter discusses data and policy issues, and then provides conclusions. The recommendations and reconsiderations may be more relevant in several respects to the countries of the Commonwealth of Independent States (CIS) than to those of Eastern Europe, where the problems have already proved not to be insuperable.

6.1   Economic Development and Social Indicators

Social Indicators Under the Previous Regime

Table 6.1 draws on World Bank and United Nations sources but is taken from the European Bank for Reconstruction and Development's (EBRD) 1994 *Transition Report*. For reference, aggregate data are also supplied on low-, middle-, and high-income countries (as classified by the World Bank) and also on the Group of 7 (G-7) countries and six South American countries comparable in size, income, and other indicators.

Table 6.2 presents a very small sample of late communist income distributions with the same comparators. Among the comparators, equality is greatest in G-7 countries, followed by the high-income group, with South America next, and both middle- and low-income groups last, with much lower shares in the bottom quintile particularly.

Against this background of middle-income countries' lowest-quintile share being less than half that in the G-7, the few late communist countries listed had lowest-quintile shares on average three times those of middle-income countries (four times, if Yugoslavia is excluded), twice those of the South American sample, and 50 percent higher than the G-7 countries that were three times richer. Almost as striking a story relates to the top end of the distribution, with the highest-decile share of these late communist countries, excluding Yugoslavia, equal to half that in South America, at the bottom of the high-income range, and significantly lower than that of the G-7 countries.

The claim about the persistence of egalitarian values derives partly from anecdotes, partly from surveys (such as that done by Rose et al. 1994), and partly from political developments. These take the form of parliamentary resistance to acts on pensions (e.g., in Poland) or other benefits (e.g., in Hungary), even where on paper these benefits represent exceptionally high replacement rates. In practice, some such ratios are eroded by inflation (Micklewright and Nagy 1995). There is also the electoral success of reform communists in all the recent elections in, for example, Poland, Lithuania, Hungary, and Estonia.

Table 6.1
Estimated Real Incomes and Other Indicators of Development for Each Country in Transition

	PPP-Based GDP per capita (in international dollars), 1982	Share of agriculture (GDP per capita), 1992	Share of urban Population in total population (in percent), 1982	Infant mortality (per 1,000 live births) 1991	Life expectancy at birth (in years), 1982	Total fertility Rate, 1992	People per doctor, 1982	People per hospital bed (latest available observations), 1987–1992	Secondary school enrollment, 1991	Energy use (equivalent per capita, in kg), 1992
Albania	2,000	56	36	32	73	2.9		246	79	421
Tajikistan		33	32	49	69	5.1	350	96		
Georgia	2,470	48	56	19	72	2.2	170	90		
Armenia	2,500	41	68	21	70	2.8	260	120		1,092
Uzbekistan	2,600	39	41	42	69	4.1	290	83		
Azerbaijan	2,650	29	54	31	71	2.7	250	101		
Romania	2,750	20	55	23	70	1.5	560	113	80	1,958
Kyrgyz Republic	2,820	28	38	37	66	3.7	280	85		1,148
Lithuania	3,710	28	68	16	71	2.0	220	79		
Moldova	3,870	33	47	23	68	2.3	250	77		1,600
Turkmenistan	3,950	48		54	66	4.2	290	92		
Latvia	4,690	24	71	17	69	1.8	200	72		
Kazakhstan	4,780	38	57	31	68	2.7	250	75		4,722
Poland	4,880	8	63	15	70	1.9	490	153	83	2,407
Ukraine	5,010	23	67	18	70	1.9	230			3,885
Bulgaria	5,130	16	68	16	71	1.5	320	100	71	2,422
Estonia	5,250	13	72	13	70	1.8	210	82		
Slovak Republic	5,620	6		13	71	2.0	280		97	3,202

Hungary	5,740	7	66	15	69	1.8	340	99	81	2,392
Russia	6,220	13	74	20	69	1.7	210	73		5,665
Belarus	6,840	24	66	15	71	1.9	250			4,154
Czech Republic	7,160	6		10	72	1.9				3,873
Low income	1,300	30	27	73	62	3.4	6,000	1,050	40	335
Middle income	4,000	10	67	42	69	3.0	2,100	450	55	1,750
High income	17,800	3	78	7	77	1.7	420	144	93	5,100
G-7 countries	19,600	2.5	78	7	77	1.7	402	120		4,864
South America	5,500	12.3	73	39	68	3.3	1,186	540		780

Source: EBRD, *Transition Report* (October 1994), p. 7.

Table 6.2
Percentage Share of Income or Consumption

	Lowest 20 percent	Second 20 percent	Third 20 percent	Fourth 20 percent	Highest 20 percent	Highest 10 percent
Poland (1989)	9.2	13.8	17.9	23.0	36.0	21.6
Hungary (1989)	10.9	14.8	18.0	22.0	34.4	20.8
Yugoslavia (1989)	5.3	10.7	16.2	23.7	44.2	27.4
Bulgaria (1992)	10.4	13.9	17.3	22.2	36.2	21.9
Low income	2–9	6–13	10–16	19–22	40–60	25–45
Middle income	2–7	7–12	11–16	19–22	45–60	25–45
High income	4–8	10–13	16–18	22–25	40–45	20–30
G-7 countries (various years)	6.2	11.7	17.2	24.0	41.1	25.0
South America (various years)	4.1	8.0	12.4	19.7	55.9	40.1

Source: EBRD, *Transition Report* (October 1994), p. 8.

Per Capita Output, Income, and Consumption Since 1990

Table 6.3 shows the path of recorded output in twenty-five transition economies since 1990, as published in April 1995. Two-thirds of the economies are shown as resuming growth. Table 6.4 presents the data on the cumulative fall, the date of the turning point, the extent of the subsequent recovery, the 1995 output level, and the unemployment rate.

It is, of course, necessary to enter several caveats about the data reflected in these tables. Figures were distorted under the old regime, probably upward, and downward under the new regime as coverage ceased to be complete and enterprises saw merit in understating output and incomes. Poland's relatively small decline and large recovery reflect revised figures (earlier ones depicted a much greater decline); however, even here, unemployment is in the high teens and still rising.

Eastern Europe as a whole saw a decline in gross domestic product (GDP) of over 10 percent and has experienced a smaller recovery since 1993. There is little reason to doubt that the region has experienced a setback to output and a rise in unemployment larger than that experienced in the great slump of the 1930s. UNICEF is not the only agency to make comparisons between the current problems of the region and such earlier episodes.

The CIS has seen an even more serious decline not yet generally reversed and owing little to the devastations of war or civil war. Output was projected to decline a further 5 percent in 1996. Remarkably, how-

Table 6.3
Growth in Eastern Europe and the Former Soviet Union (percentage change)

Countries	Real GDP			1994 Estimate	1995 Projection
	1991	1992	1993		
Albania	−27	−10	11	7	5
Armenia	−11	−52	−15	0	
Azerbaijan	−1	−23	−13	−22	−10
Belarus	−1	−10	−12	−22	−10
Bulgaria	−12	−6	−4	0	4
Croatia	−14	−9	−3	1	4
Czech Republic	−14	−6	Neg	3	5
Estonia	−11	−14	−3	5	6
Macedonia, FYR	−12	−14	−14	−7	Neg
Georgia	−21	−43	−40	−35	
Hungary	−12	−4	−2	2	3
Kazakhstan	−13	−14	−12	−25	−12
Kyrgyz Republic	−5	−25	−16	−10	2
Latvia	−8	−34	−12	3	3
Lithuania	−13	−38	−16	2	4
Moldova	−12	−29	−9	−25	
Poland	−8	2	4	5	5
Romania	−13	−14	1	3	3
Russia	−13	−19	−12	−15	−7
Slovak Republic	−15	−7	−4	5	4
Slovenia	−8	−5	1	5	6
Tajikistan	−13	−34	−28	−25	
Turkmenistan	−5	−5	−10	−20	−5
Ukraine	−12	−17	−14	−23	2
Uzbekistan	−1	−11	−2	−3	−4
Aggregates					
Eastern Europe	−10	−4	1	3	4
Commonwealth of Independent States	−12	−19	−13	−17	4

Source: EBRD, *Transition Report Update* (April 1995), p. 24.
Note: Neg = negligible.

Table 6.4
Recorded Output: Cumulative Falls, Turning Points, Recovery, and Unemployment

Country	Fall (in percent)	Point	Recovery (in percent)	1995 Index	1994 Unemployment
Albania	35	1992–1993	25	80	
Armenia	65	1994	Neg	35	26 (1993)
Azerbaijan	55 so far	Not yet		45	
Belarus	45 so far	Not yet		55	2.5
Bulgaria	20	1994	4	83	13
Croatia	25	1994	5	80	18
Czech Republic	20	1993	8	86	3
Estonia	25	1993–1994	11	83	2
Macedonia, FYR	40	1995	Neg	60	19
Georgia	80 so far	Not yet		20	
Hungary	17	1993–1994	5	87	10
Kazakhstan	65 so far	Not yet		35	9
Kyrgyz Republic	45	1995	2	56	
Latvia	45	1994	6	58	7
Lithuania	55	1994	6	48	2
Moldova	55	1995	Neg	55	
Poland	8	1992	17	108	
Romania	25	1993	7	80	17
Russia	50 so far	Not yet		50	11
Slovak Republic	25	1993–1994	9	82	2
Slovenia	13	1993	12	97	15
Tajikistan	70 so far	Not yet		30	14
Turkmenistan	40 so far	Not yet		60	
Ukraine	50	1995	2	51	
Uzbekistan	20 so far	Not yet		80	0.5
Eastern Europe	14	1993	8	93	0.3
CIS	50	Not yet		50	

Source: Author's calculations.
Note: Neg = negligible.

ever, only Armenia reports a remotely commensurate level of unemployment. Before turning to that subject, however, I address the distributional issue. Data on distribution year by year are hard to obtain in most of the countries.

Income Distribution and Transfers

In Russia, the ratio of the income of the top decile to that of the bottom decile nearly doubled between the end of 1991 and the end of 1993 and rose further in 1994 (to 14 from 5.4 in 1991; *Financial Times*, April 19, 1995). According to *Russian Economic Trends*, the Gini coefficient of personal incomes in Russia rose from 0.28 in late 1991 to over 0.4 in late 1994, while according to the *Economist* (April 29, 1995), in the United Kingdom it rose from 0.23 in 1977 to 0.34 in 1991, and in the United States from 0.35 in 1969 to 0.4 in 1992. Thus, a trend to greater inequality is not restricted to transition economies, but the Russian experience is of a different order—doing in three years what took fifteen years of radical policy changes in the United Kingdom and twice as much as occurred more spontaneously in nearly twenty-five years in the United States.

Income distribution in Russia has thus deteriorated unprecedently to be less equal than most G-7 countries, from having been more equal five years before, and this relative decline among the poorer coincided with an apparently almost catastrophic 50 percent decline in the mean, implying a dramatic deterioration of conditions for the poor, as is shown in table 6.5, where poverty is defined in terms of a percentage of 1989 wages. On the 35–45 percent criterion, its incidence has quadrupled in Bulgaria, the Czech Republic, the Slovak Republic, and Russia but increased by 50 percent or less in Hungary, Poland, and Romania. Extreme poverty increased fivefold to tenfold in the former group and two to three times in the latter. The table also shows the incidence of poverty in different demographic groups. This reveals that the relative position of children deteriorated twice as much as that of the elderly. Indeed, the position of the elderly has hardly declined at all in the Czech Republic, Hungary, Poland, and Romania.

Figure 6.1 shows that the Gini coefficient has risen in all transition economies except Belarus and the Slovak Republic and that there is a weak relationship with cumulative GDP declines aggravating the implication of either change for the poor. On these data, there is little to choose between the CIS and the Eastern European economies as far as relative impoverishment is concerned.

Table 6.5
Eastern Europe: Incidence of Poverty and Extreme Poverty Among Households, Persons, Children, Adults, and Elderly, 1989–1993

	Poverty					Extreme Poverty				
	1989	1990	1991	1992	1993	1989	1990	1991	1992	1993
	Estimates of Poverty and Extreme Poverty (percentage of relevant population)									
Bulgaria (poverty line = 45 percent, 1989 average wage)										
Households		13.6	49.0	53.1	54.7		2.1	11.3	23.3	23.9
Children		17.7	61.7	59.9	64.4		2.0	16.8	26.6	32.2
Adults		11.0	49.2	48.7	53.7		1.3	12.0	20.1	24.9
Elderly		18.3	50.0	59.7	58.6		3.8	10.6	27.6	24.6
Population		13.8	52.1	53.6	57.0		2.0	12.7	23.4	26.2
Czech Republic (poverty line = 35 percent, 1989 average wage)										
Households	4.6	7.6	23.8	18.2		0.3	0.3	0.8	1.6	
Children	4.2	12.5	43.2	38.3		0.3	0.3	0.2	1.1	
Adults	4.4	7.6	26.8	22.6		0.2	0.1	0.5	1.8	
Elderly	5.7	3.2	12.9	9.6		0.4	0.1	0.3	0.4	
Population	4.2	8.6	29.8	25.3		0.2	0.2	0.2	1.3	
Hungary (poverty line = 40 percent, 1989 average wage)										
Households	12.3		13.9			0.5		1.5		
Children	20.6		27.0			1.1		3.7		
Adults	12.3		18.5			0.7		2.4		
Elderly	11.8		10.6			0.3		0.4		
Population	14.5		19.4			0.7		2.5		
Poland (poverty line = 40 percent, 1989 average wage)										
Households	22.9	38.3	33.9	35.7		5.1	11.3	8.1	10.4	
Children	32.3	60.2	58.7	61.8		8.3	23.6	21.3	25.9	
Adults	19.7	37.9	37.0	40.1		4.8	13.0	10.8	13.4	
Elderly	29.5	39.5	29.2	29.5 ·		5.2	7.8	3.8	5.2	
Population	24.7	43.1	41.2	43.7		5.8	15.0	12.3	15.1	
Romania (poverty line = 45 percent, 1989 average wage)										
Households	29.9	17.6	25.1	44.3		7.7	2.4	6.8	15.2	
Children	41.2	28.6	38.1	62.8		10.8	3.4	11.6	26.1	
Adults	29.8	18.2	25.7	47.2		7.1	2.4	6.9	16.4	
Elderly	43.9	21.0	32.1	45.9		14.4	3.6	8.4	15.3	
Population	33.9	21.4	29.7	51.5		8.6	2.8	8.4	19.1	
Slovak Republic (poverty line = 40 percent, 1989 average wage)										
Households	5.7	6.2	24.9	30.3	34.5	0.2	0.2	2.4	2.9	
Children	8.8	10.0	42.4	51.1	—	0.2	0.3	6.0	8.1	
Adults	4.2	4.5	21.2	27.0	—	0.1	0.1	2.1	2.8	
Elderly	6.2	6.7	25.4	29.0	—	0.2	0.2	2.5	2.4	
Population	5.8	6.4	27.7	34.1	—	0.1	0.1	3.2	3.9	

Table 6.5 (continued)

	Poverty					Extreme Poverty				
	1989	1990	1991	1992	1993	1989	1990	1991	1992	1993
Russia (poverty line = 40 percent, 1989 average wage)										
Households										
Children										
Adults										
Elderly										
Population	15.8	14.0	15.5	61.3		2.5	2.7	2.5	23.2	

Estimates of the Poverty Gap
(percentage of relevant poverty line)

	1989	1990	1991	1992	1993	1989	1990	1991	1992	1993
Bulgaria		21.9	27.2	36.4	36.6		21.7	18.8	25.9	26.6
Czech Republic	8.3	2.7	14.5	16.5		18.1	16.4	16.1	13.6	
Hungary	16.3		16.9			14.8		20.0		
Poland	25.9	30.4	27.9	30.5		22.3	25.5	25.8	27.1	
Romania	28.1	21.3	28.7	33.1		24.9	17.9	25.4	26.9	
Slovak Republic	12.4	13.2	16.5	19.3		11.3	17.9	17.4	17.7	

Source: MONEE database, International Child Development Center, Florence, Italy.

The real value of transfers has fallen largely as a result of lags in indexation relative to wages. The scope for this mechanism to operate is obviously proportional to inflation rates, which are presented in Table 6.6.

Nominal replacement rates have also been reduced in a number of cases. They were often much more generous under the old regime than would be thought wise in market economies. Transition has put budgets under strain for several reasons, and transfers have come under corresponding scrutiny, sometimes resulting in delayed indexation and sometimes in explicit nominal adjustment.

Unemployment

Rising unemployment will have contributed to inequality in income and consumption; however, it is considered here not only for that reason but as a socioeconomic indicator in its own right. Unemployment, traditionally reported as negligible throughout the region, has risen everywhere. As table 6.4 shows, it has reached double digits in Armenia (26 percent) and Eastern Europe (14 percent) but remains in single digits or lower in the CIS (2 percent), the Baltic countries (4 percent), and the Czech Republic (3 percent).

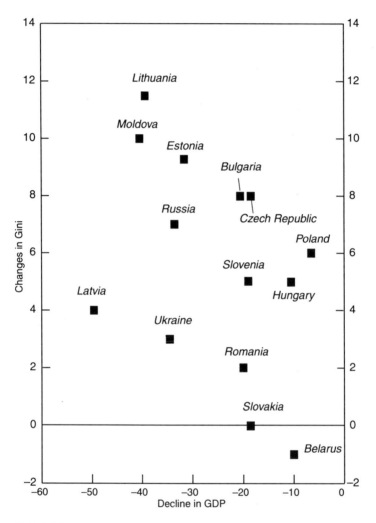

Figure 6.1
As GDP of transition economies declines, inequality increases, 1987–1993. Source: C. M. Davis, Wolfson College.

Table 6.6
Inflation in Eastern Europe and the Former Soviet Union (percentage change)

| | Retail and consumer prices (end year) | | | | |
	1991	1992	1993	1994 Estimate	1995 Projection
Albania	104	237	31	16	10
Armenia	N.A.	1,341	10,996	1,100	
Azerbaijan	126	1,395	810	1,800	150
Belarus	93	1,558	1,994	1,875	300
Bulgaria	339	79	64	122	70
Croatia	149	937	1,150	−3	3
Czech Republic	52	13	18	11	10
Estonia	304	954	36	42	20
Macedonia, FYR	115	1,691	244	54	18
Georgia	131	1,463	7,492	7,000	
Hungary	32	22	21	21	28
Kazakhstan	150	1,176	2,169	1,000	100
Kyrgyz Republic	170	1,771	1,366	87	45
Latvia	262	958	35	26	20
Lithuania	345	1,175	188	44	30
Moldova	162	2,198	837	111	25
Poland	60	44	38	30	23
Romania	223	199	296	62	40
Russia	144	2,318	841	205	100
Slovak Republic	58	9	25	12	10
Slovenia	247	93	23	18	10
Tajikistan	204	1,364	7,344	−45	
Turkmenistan	155	644	9,750	1,100	500
Ukraine	161	2,000	10,155	401	120
Uzbekistan	169	910	885	423	100

Source: EBRD, *Transition Report Update* (April 1995), p. 25.

Clearly, recorded output falls account for little of the variation of recorded unemployment rates either across or between groups. More important are the roles of enterprise in income support and welfare provision and in the level and control of benefit distributions.

Health

Table 6.7 reports the change in many indicators of health and welfare between 1989 and 1993 for nine countries (seven in Eastern Europe, Russia, and Ukraine). The picture is generally, but not uniformly, gloomy. It is particularly dismal for Russia, Ukraine, and Bulgaria and relatively good for Poland, the Czech Republic, and Hungary.

Not only has the crude birthrate fallen everywhere, but the incidence of low birthweight has risen everywhere except in Albania and Hungary, while life expectancy has also declined, except in Poland and the Czech Republic. Education indicators, mainly enrollment, have declined, except in Hungary.

Table 6.8 gives more detailed health sector figures for Russia for 1990 through 1993. These figures are almost uniformly bleak, with dramatic increases in the incidences of diphtheria (up 400 percent), measles (up 150 percent), and syphilis (up 400 percent).

Pressures on Budgets

Pressure on budgets derives from four forces:

1. The old regime was undermined by intensifying repressed inflation, as growing fiscal deficits were monetized and the natural consequences restrained by price controls.

2. Liberalization not only involved a once-and-for-all price jump but continuing inflation if deficits were not curtailed.

3. The diversion of resources into the shadow economy involved a narrowing of the tax base, as did recession, and the loss of revenue at a time when explicit taxation replaced proprietorial accrual of nearly all nonlabor income to the state.

4. Remaining state enterprises had their profitability squeezed by competition from more enterprising and less fiscally compliant private enterprises, further eroding the tax base—indeed, calling in many cases for cash or credit subventions.

These many pressures impinged on transfer payments as well as product subsidies and social expenditures, as illustrated in table 6.9.

Table 6.7
Summary of Welfare Changes in Nine Eastern European Countries, 1989–1993

Indicator	Albania	Bulgaria	Czech Republic	Slovak Republic	Hungary	Poland	Romania	Russia	Ukraine	Number of countries De-crease	In-crease	No data	Percentage deterioration	Bank	Average change in indicator
Income and expenditure-based indicators															
Real per capita income[a]		−39.2	−17.8	−30.3	−12.8	−38.3	−20.7	−38.3	−3.7	8	0	1	100	1	−22.3
Poverty rate[b]		−43.2	22.1	29.4	4.2	19.0	17.6	36.0		7	0	2	100	1	24.5
Food share[b]		4.1	0.1	1.0	0.3	−6.9	5.9	12.3	6.6	7	1	1	88	10	2.9
Calorie consumption per capita[a]		−18.0		−3.3	−5.7	−5.1	−9.2	−2.0	−18.7	7	0	2	100	1	−8.9
Demographic indicators															
Crude marriage rate[a]	−4.5	−33.8	−18.4	−19.1	−18.0	−19.8	−7.8	−27.8	−13.7	9	0	0	100	1	−19.8
Remarriage rate[a]		−49.1	−9.9	−38.5	−28.3	−29.2	−13.8			6	0	3	100	1	−28.1
Crude divorce rate[a]	−16.9	−22.0	−3.2	1.7	−13.5	−43.7	−17.1	11.1	11.6	3	6	0	33	27	−10.2
Crude birthrate[a]	−22.3	−21.4	−5.9	−9.8	−3.6	−14.5	−31.7	−34.2	−20.0	9	0	0	100	1	−18.2
Mortality indicators															
Life expectancy, males[c]		−0.9	0.4	−0.1	−0.9	0.6		−5.2	−2.0	5	2	2	71	17	−1.0
Life expectancy, females[c]		−0.7	0.7	−0.1	−0.1	0.5		−1.8	−1.0	5	2	2	71	17	−0.3
Infant mortality rate[a]	7.7	7.8	−14.8	−21.2	−15.5	−16.9	−13.4	12.9	15.6	4	5	0	44	26	−4.2
1–4 mortality rate[a]		−5.2		−12.5	−27.3	−18.3	−29.1	−3.8	−4.9	0	8	1	0	29	−12.6
5–19 mortality rate[a]		0.7	8.0	1.3	−1.5	−12.4	−14.6	19.2	6.9	5	3	1	63	19	1.0
20–39 mortality rate[a]		10.0	5.2	3.7	10.6	−8.1	−3.1	65.8	28.0	6	2	1	75	13	14.0
40–59 mortality rate[a]		4.1	−2.1	−9.2	8.7	−9.2	12.2	50.2	27.3	5	3	1	63	19	10.3

Table 6.7 (continued)

Indicator	Albania	Bulgaria	Czech Republic	Slovak Republic	Hungary	Poland	Romania	Russia	Ukraine	Number of countries — Decrease	Increase	No data	Percentage deterioration	Bank	Average change in indicator
60+ mortality rate[a]		-0.7	-4.5	-7.7	1.6	-1.3	1.5	17.0	16.6	4	4	1	50	24	2.8
Maternal mortality rate[a]	-46.9	-24.1	-9.7	-74.0	-36.0	10.3	-64.4	3.7	-20.1	2	7	0	22	28	-29.0
Health indicators															
Abortion rate[a]	60.1	7.7	-26.1	-8.3	-12.0	-84.5	488.7	10.3	0.8	5	4	0	56	23	48.5
Low birth weight rate[a]	-3.2	33.7	13.9	13.6	-5.7	3.9	48.8	7.1		6	2	1	75	13	14.0
New tuberculosis cases[a]		45.2	4.3	35.2	14.9	4.0	59.0	14.1	9.7	8	0	1	100	1	23.3
Social cohesion and protection indicators															
Percentage of births to mothers under 20[b]		4.0	1.9	2.4	0.2	1.0	2.2	5.5	4.8	8	0	1	100	1	2.4
Number of adoptions[a]		-12.5	-15.8	33.2	-6.0	-21.9		13.1	14.7	4	3	2	57	22	0.7
Crime rate[a]		194.6	87.0	50.4	82.9	53.6	87.5	67.9	24.6	8	0	1	100	1	81.1
Youths sentenced[a]		-68.8	-20.1	24.4	6.7	123.6	58.3	45.8	10.0	6	2	1	75	13	22.5
Homicide rate[a]		80.3	22.1	42.9	46.3	12.4	-51.5	141.1		6	1	2	86	12	
Child education indicators															
Crèche/parental leave coverage[b]		-2.1	-11.6	-3.5	4.3	-18.2	0.4	-10.4	-9.5	6	2	1	75	13	-6.3
Preprimary enrollment rate[b]		-13.0	-16.0	-13.4	0.9	-6.0	-9.7	-12.7	-3.7	7	1	1	88	10	-9.2
Primary enrollment rate[b]	-4.0	-6.6	1.2	1.6	0.1	-0.9	-3.4	-0.6		4	4	1	50	24	-1.6
Secondary enrollment rate[b]	-12.0	-7.5	-0.1	0.3	3.3	1.7	-19.8	-4.8	-5.6	5	3	1	63	19	-5.6

Total number of:										Total
Observations	9	29	28	29	29	29	26	28	23	230
Deteriorations	6	24	17	20	18	17	18	25	20	165
Improvements	3	5	11	9	11	12	8	3	3	65
Percentage of deteriorations	67	83	61	69	62	59	69	89	87	71.7

Source: MONEE database, International Child Development Center, Florence, Italy.
Note: 1992/1989; 1991/1989; 1990/1989; 1993/1990; 1992/1990: Estimate.

The reported cases dropped by 66 percent probably due to more frequent underreportings. The CPI used for this calculation is suspect. Other indicators, such as industrial production and food consumption, suggest a much sharper decline.

Aggregation of child population aged 0–2 in crèches and cared for by persons on parental leave. Only crèche enrollment rates included.

Per 1,000 population includes death due to homicides, purposely inflicted injuries, and other violence; although LEB data are available, they do not appear consistent with the mortality data and are therefore omitted.

a. Units are as a percentage.
b. Units are in percentage points.
c. Units are in years.

182 John Flemming

Table 6.8
Russia's Health Sector, 1990–1993

Indicator	1990	1991	1992	First half of 1993
Birthrate	13.4	12.1	10.8	9.6
Salmonellosis	70.4	74.2	80.1	82.0
Diphtheria	0.8	1.3	3.1	4.6
Whooping cough	16.9	20.8	25.0	29.0
Measles	12.4	13.8	15.2	30.0
Cancer	264.5	266.0	267.6	269.2
Tuberculosis	34.2	34.0	35.8	43.0
Syphilis	5.3	5.8	13.4	26.8
Hospital beds	137.5	134.7	130.9	124.3
Doctors	46.9	44.3	44.0	42.7
Invalids from childhood	43.1	61.6	62.0	62.0
Infant mortality	17.4	17.8	18.0	18.8
Maternal mortality	47.4	52.4	50.8	52.0
Male mortality (40–44 years)	7.6	8.0	8.8	10.9
Crude death rate	11.2	11.4	12.1	14.4
Life expectancy	69.2	69.0	68.6	67.2

Source: MONEE database, International Child Development Center, Florence, Italy.

6.2 Policy Issues

Policies Relating to Output and Employment
There has been an enormous amount of discussion on the causes of the fall in output in transition economies. Is, or was, it due to restrictive stabilization policies, or the breakdown of the old coordination (planning) mechanism without its replacement by the network of organic contacts crucial to a market economy? Was destocking important, or the collapse in trade with former Council for Economic Assistance (CMEA) partners? Was that collapse inevitable, or the result of partially uncoordinated reforms? Did liberalization of trade and prices lead to asymmetrical responses by winners and losers? Did the losers contract more rapidly than the winners could, or would, expand? Do the statistics impute high values to reduced activities, which subtract value at world prices?

There is an element of truth on all the suggested hypotheses, but few of them call for reconsideration of policy. Stabilization and liberalization could, and should, not be avoided. Up to a point, however, their speed may be a choice variable.

Table 6.9
Index of Real Public Health Expenditure in Eastern Europe, 1990–1993 (1989 = 100)

	1990	1991	1992	1993
Computed using the overall GDP deflator				
Albania	100.0	115.9	142.5	85.7
Bulgaria	111.1	100.0	120.0	102.1
Czech Republic	104.1	91.2	154.1	
Slovak Republic	109.6	104.9	96.9	81.1
Hungary	107.7	108.5	106.1	96.0
Poland	144.7	116.7	124.3	
Romania	107.6	96.7	77.8	
Russia	124.1	69.7	60.0	67.4
Ukraine	108.0	110.7	118.2	
Computed using the consumer price index for all services[a]				
Albania				
Bulgaria	93.4	70.2	68.9	52.5
Czech Republic	94.8	81.1	122.9	
Slovak Republic	68.1	70.5	72.9	70.0
Hungary	115.6	115.5	101.4	82.7
Poland	106.3	75.2	73.6	
Romania	104.8	93.4	86.7	
Russia	120.8	94.6	63.2	33.6
Ukraine				

Source: MONEE Database, International Child Development Center, Florence, Italy.
a. No reliable price index of medical services is available.

Stabilization is best done quickly, and so is liberalization in the sense of decriminalizing trading activities and abolishing the monopoly of state trading organizations.

Prices also should almost certainly be free from administrative control. It would even then be possible to intervene to affect the path of liberalized prices. This could most easily be done either by offering a transitional employment subsidy or transitional protection.

The argument for an employment subsidy is that with specific capital goods, liberalization of a very distorted economy will typically lead to a sharp fall in the market-clearing real wage even if labor is shifted out of value-subtracting activities into ones where it can make a modest positive contribution, so that real output at world prices actually rises.

The market-clearing real wage falls because labor shed by value-subtracting activities drives down the marginal physical product elsewhere very rapidly, given the fixed stock (in the short run) of specific (putty-clay) capital. The fall in the real wage would challenge political sustainability even if the market cleared. In practice, political, social, and benefit-induced constraints, such as minimum wages or unemployment compensation, tend to convert an incipient fall in real wages into actual unemployment.

If this is much above the 10 percent norm of Western Europe since 1980, and we have seen that it is in many cases, the shadow wage probably falls considerably below the market wage. In a competitive labor market, an employment subsidy might not raise real wages but might enable (low-) value-adding enterprises to pay the conventional wage. If the subsidy is less than the benefit due to the unemployed, it is quite possible for output, consumption, investment, and the net fiscal position all to improve. The danger lies in a noncompetitive response in which the subsidy raises wages rather than employment.

An alternative procedure, involving fewer risks with the budget, is to convert all the inherited distortions (except those requiring more than 100 percent effective protection) into transparent border taxes and to announce from the start that they will be phased out over, say, ten years (as advocated in a different context by, for instance, Little, Scitovsky, and Scott 1970).

Neither measure, if credible, should distort the allocation of either capital or labor. Investment in a sector should be more sensitive to future, undistorted prices than to current prices. Workers in enterprises kept going by the policies are on notice to raise efficiency or to get out. Even if their true current value-added is low, it is higher than in the more realistic short-term alternative of unemployment. How can the temporary nature of this transparent distortion be guaranteed and made credible?

The first point to make is that a policy of free trade is not credible if it generates unemployment and a political backlash. Indeed, protective distortions have increased since 1991 in most of Eastern Europe. A less provocative initial stance might have been easier to sustain.

The European Community/European Union might also have imposed declining ceilings on Eastern European tariffs in the European Agreements, even if they did not initially bind. A group of reforming countries eliminating similar distortions at the same time could lend each other credibility in a customs union that would reduce the misallocation cost of the policy for small, open economies. As it is, protectionist lobbies may believe that they have liberal governments on the run and will be able to extract ever greater concessions.

It is important not to respond to rising unemployment by offering a more generous safety net for job losers. In this analysis, such a measure not only has an immediate budgetary cost but almost certainly pushes up the reservation real wage, increasing unemployment.

Policies Relating to Liberalization, Quasi-Rents, and Rent Seeking
The recommended procedure, most obviously in the case of a protective structure's mimicking the old distortions, effectively takes away large, positive quasi-rents in previously controlled sectors, and converts, from negative to positive, quasi-rents in some other cases. This should not reduce total profits (rents) and resources for investment because it raises total resource utilization.

Unrestrained quasi-rents in disequilibrium would otherwise attract protection racketeers and contribute to income inequality, corruption, and criminality (see the homicide figures in table 6.8). Such racketeers would not plow back their profits, because to do so would erode the quasi-rents. Racketeers also thrive in a world of less transparent support to unprofitable, but value-adding, enterprises through partial control, direction of credit, discretionary granting of exemptions, and so forth.

Again, the distinction needs to be made between the urgency of dismantling administrative controls and the decade over which convergence on world prices is best achieved. These could be reconciled by market-conforming interventions, such as protective duties, although their enforcement in the CIS would not be easy.

If such measures reduced the proportion of loss-making enterprises to a low enough level, they would facilitate the more rapid application of bankruptcy laws and the implementation of privatization polices, which are delayed in many cases by policy compromises.

Policies Relating to the (Re)integration of the Shadow Economy
The budgetary problems already discussed are linked to the narrowing of the effective tax base relative even to diminished GDP. In Ukraine, for instance, a figure of 40 percent was widely quoted in 1994 for the share of GDP contributed by the shadow economy. Under these circumstances, the (re)integration of the shadow economy into the regular economy is vital.

One approach would be to send in shock troops in jackboots to enforce the letter of still-extant antienterprise regulations and taxes. This would be disastrous. It would lead to the closure of many valuable activities and set back private enterprise for a decade. It is also unnecessary because a 40 percent increase in income is more than is needed.

Clearly if one believed the base-broadening operations would be successful, one could afford a 25 percent reduction in nominal tax rates. Suppose they were to amount to 60 percent (see EBRD 1993, p. 49), then 60 percent of 60 percent of GDP would yield 36 percent. The tax rate could be cut to 40 percent, and if all liabilities were enforced, revenue would rise. The challenge is to come up with a credible enforcement program to allow the tax rates to be cut before enforcement begins, so as to ensure the survival of the egg-laying geese.

As important as explicit taxes in this context is the array of regulations with which the survival of private enterprises in particular can be challenged. Typically those operating in the shadows do not get away free but pay protection money and payoffs to induce officials to turn a blind eye. This means that a credible, clear, liberal regime would be attractive to them, even with a significant explicit tax rate. It would, however, have to provide adequate assurances that unofficial depredation would cease. Moreover, if the corrupt officials rely on the payments of the shadow economy to provide them with a living wage, it may be necessary to provide for larger salaries out of the additional revenue, diminishing the scale of tax cuts that can be considered.

Ukrainian experience suggests that there is scope for a package of reforms along these lines that would deregulate the economy, reduce regulatory and fiscal burdens on enterprise, and provide greater revenue. The trick by which it should be achieved, however, involves elements of confidence, which are not easy to construct. Several of the transition economies, especially in the CIS, present a tougher case than did the Israeli case of the 1970s (Bruno and Habib 1976).

Policies Relating to Social Safety Nets and the Delivery of Social Services

One reason for the low recorded unemployment in much of the CIS is that redundant workers are retained on enterprise payrolls, for several reasons. One is that the excess wage tax makes it attractive to reduce average wages by retaining or even hiring people at the statutory minimum wage, which, partly because of inflation, is even lower relative to the average wage than unemployment compensation typically would be in the West. Another, suggested by Blanchard, Commander, and Corricelli (1975), is that boosting nominal employment may improve access to bank

Table 6.10
Enterprise-Provided Social Benefits in Russia: Type and Availability by Firm Size, November 1992 (in percentage)

	Number of employees			
	80–350	351–700	701–900	901 and Up
(Sample size)	(10)	(11)	(10)	(10)
Housing (permanent)	20	50	80	50
Housing (temporary)	10	30	40	30
Kindergarten	40	50	80	80
Land for dachas	30	70	70	90
Canteens (subsidized)	40	60	80	90
Polyclinics (access)	20	20	50	70
Community houses	0	10	30	30
Fitness facilities	0	0	10	20
Sanatoriums	0	60	40	50
Food stores with subsidized prices	80	80	70	80
Sick pay	0	0	30	30
Housing rental assistance	0	0	0	10
Other forms of housing help	0	60	40	40
Transport allowances	30	30	10	50
Maternity allowances	100	100	100	90
Child care allowances	100	100	90	100
Paid vacations	40	70	70	30
Predismissal allowances	80	90	80	90
Sanatorium vouchers	80	90	90	90

Source: Commander et al. (1993).

credit and that this explains continued hiring, despite the 50 percent fall in output across many sectors. The rise in unemployment is smaller than would have occurred if many new entrants to the labor force failed to find jobs.

While these two factors might account for a supply of low-paid jobs, the supply of people to fill them requires that benefits elsewhere be very modest. This is true not only of cash benefits, which may be available in only relatively few places, but also of many other benefits. Table 6.10 sets out some relevant facts about enterprise-based welfare benefits (in Russia) from a World Bank survey. The survey identified nineteen benefits, which can be grouped under headings such as housing benefits, child benefits, food aid, health, and recreation. Although the inference is not strictly valid and the samples are small, it would appear that virtually every enterprise offers assistance to employees under every major heading. This underlines the extent to which social support has been enterprise based and the reluctance of people to allow enterprise links to lapse, especially if substantial cash income from a private enterprise is not available.

The enterprise basis of social provision is unacceptable in the medium term for three reasons:

1. It may be doubted whether those normally employed but on minimum wages perform the economic role of the unemployed in a market economy. Do they effectively restrain nominal wage increases? Do they constitute a pool of labor from which new enterprises can recruit? The excess wage tax probably serves to undermine the first role, and the insecurity of much full-time private employment would make even such people reluctant to accept private sector jobs while their attachment to old enterprises may reduce their search activity.

2. Existing enterprise-based systems are probably not spreading to new businesses whose employees will not be covered.

3. Privatization and subsidy reduction will make it increasingly difficult for old enterprises to offer uniform or equitable benefits.

Thus, a high priority should be attached to transferring responsibility for social provision from enterprises to some organ of the state, such as the municipalities. This is not simply to propose the transfer of a liability from one to the other. A suitable payroll tax would, in aggregate, replace enterprises' in-kind liabilities and finance the new state supply of a reduced list of standardized market-conforming benefits. In practice, such a program faces three difficulties:

1. Organizing state provision in replacement of provision sometimes integrated with enterprise operations.

2. Synchronizing the transfer over a suitable area so that the tax can be introduced and the transfer made on an essential revenue- and expenditure-neutral basis.

3. Dealing with the interenterprise distributional consequences of a uniform payroll tax, for example, in replacement of provision whose value in relation to payroll will have varied with many factors especially demographic ones. This is particularly true of China, where state-owned enterprises have a liability for pensions that do not feature in the World Bank survey.

6.3 Conclusion

The data I have surveyed suggest a serious problem of the equity of transition. Depending on how quickly the transition economies can catch up with richer market economies, some increased inequality was implicit in their transition and thus inevitable. However, the decline in output, speed of adverse redistribution, and decline in social provision and associated welfare indicators were not inevitable and have contributed to political trends inimical to the sustenance of the reform program, particularly in CIS countries.

The proposals for more coherent and radical reform programs reintegrating the gray economy and transferring social provision from enterprises to government are broadly conventional. Any originality in this discussion lies in an urging of caution in the advocacy of a bigger and better social safety net to compensate any "victims" of transition. This is because their number is largely due to the decline in recorded output, and consequent fiscal problems would almost certainly be aggravated by such a program of expenditure, which would raise effective reservation wages. A program of transitory protection or employment subsidy, particularly the former, would not strain the budget, would reduce demands on the safety net, and, by increasing the proportion of enterprises viable financially, would reduce their need for soft credits facilitating the hardening of budget constraints and early orderly privatization.

Note

I am grateful to my colleague, C. M. Davis of Wolfson College, Oxford, for directing me to most of the detailed data presented in this chapter.

References

Balcerowicz, Leszek. 1994. *Common Fallacies in the Debate on Economic Transition in Central and Eastern Europe*. European Bank for Reconstruction and Development. Working Paper no. 11.

Blanchard, O., S. Commander, and F. Corricelli. 1995. "Unemployment and Restructuring in Eastern Europe and Russia." In S. Commander and F. Corricelli, eds., *Unemployment Restructuring and the Labor Market in Eastern Europe and Russia*. Washington, D.C.: Economic Development Institute World Bank.

Bruno, M., and J. Habib. 1976. "Taxes, Family Grants, and Redistribution." *Journal of Public Economics* 5 (1–2) (January–February): 57–80.

Center for Economic Reform. *Russian Economic Trends*, various issues. Moscow.

Commander, S., L. Liberman, C. Ugaz, and R. Yemtsov. 1993. *The Behavior of Russian Firms in 1992: Evidence from a Survey.* Working Paper no. 1166. Washington, D.C.: World Bank. European Bank for Reconstruction and Development. 1994. *Transition Report.* London.

European Bank for Reconstruction and Development. 1983. *Annual Economic Outlook.* London.

European Bank for Reconstruction and Development. 1995. *Transition Report Update.* London.

Little, I. M. D., T. Scitovsky, and M. F. Scott. 1970. *Industry and Trade in Some Developing Countries.* London: Oxford University Press.

Micklewright, John, and Gyula Nagy. 1995. "Unemployment Insurance and Incentives in Hungary." In David M. G. Newbery, ed., *Tax and Benefit Reform in Central and Eastern Europe.* London: Centre for Economic Policy Research.

Rose, Richard, and Christian Haerpfer. 1994. *Studies in Public Policy.* Glasgow: Center for the Study of Public Policy, University of Strathclyde.

Comments

Danuta Gotz-Kozierkiewicz

In any discussion of equitable economic transformation, due attention should be paid not only to quantitative changes in economies, in terms of their stabilization targets, but also to qualitative ones, which are indispensable in structural and systemic reforms. The size of the quantitative changes in transition economies so greatly exceeds that of similar efforts in market economies—even those with extreme distortions—that they add another dimension to the quantitative changes. Therefore, what deserves careful retrospective analysis are the fundamental imbalances that existed in transition economies at the very beginning of the stabilization and transition process. These imbalances provide the background for Flemming's chapter, but are not clearly explained.

Initial Imbalances

I will provide a brief description of these imbalances, thus contributing to a buildup of a more complicated and controversial concept of equity in economic transformation. Although this approach does not adequately clarify the concept, it may help put the transition process in the proper perspective.

All of the economies Flemming referred to were, at the beginning, in relatively large internal and external disequilibria. These economies were severely distorted, as they were masked by, for example, nonmarket distributive processes. Furthermore, these economies had relatively low wages and nonwage incomes, supplemented by high levels of social protection. This social protection was fairly equally distributed and of much broader scope than in most market economies. Consumption and production subsidies played an enormous role in supporting real incomes, especially in urban areas. (According to estimates by B. Milanovic of the World Bank, in Poland during the mid-1980s, the subsidies' share in consumption amounted to about 40 percent.)

The price of labor, as well as the prices for goods, other services, domestic money, and foreign currencies, was far from a market-clearing level (with hidden unemployment). The distorted price system resulted in, inter alia, tremendous discrepancies in people's incomes measured by the purchasing power parity and the official exchange rate.

The reduction in people's real incomes was a fundamental, if not the only, contributing factor to the stabilization of the economies in transition. In the case of Poland, which is not unique among postsocialist countries but is more dramatic because adjustment was completed in a short period (in terms of the price paid for larger disequilibria at the beginning point, the so-called shock therapy used to overcome this, and probably its relative success), the reduction in incomes accounted for a large portion of money savings. The so-called corrective inflation was absorbed by closing the gap between the initial supply, which was much too low, then reduced further by a decrease of about 20 percent in GDP in 1990–1991, the unexpectedly large trade surplus in 1990, the reduction in demand that reflected a 30 percent decrease in the population's real income, and a threefold real-term reduction in money savings.

Winners and Losers

The first stage of Poland's adjustment created one big winner: a state budget with a surplus, which resulted from an increase in state-owned enterprises and the banking sector. This financial improvement was short-lived—it existed only in the second half of 1991—and it contributed to the crisis in public finance, which worsened with the economic recovery that followed.

The state budget surplus at the beginning of Poland's transition resulted in an unrealistic assessment of state budget constraint. This assessment led to an insufficient reduction in people's incomes derived from the budgetary sector, whereas in 1991 a misassessment had contributed, for example, to a relative improvement for pensioners compared with average income earners.

It appears that an economic recovery makes it difficult to achieve a more equal distribution of the results of accelerated economic growth. This should be the time to offer social groups the opportunity to rebuild the incomes they lost at the earlier stage of stabilization. At the same time, the increase in wages and other incomes in the medium term should be very moderate, to preserve sustainable economic growth and strengthen stabilization.

The average wage in Poland ($3,000–4,000 per year, depending on whether the official exchange rate or a purchasing power parity is used) places it among countries with a very moderate per capita income. The difficult issue of equitable income distribution could be approached by taking into consideration three income groups that are particularly controversial in terms of their relationship to wages in the enterprise sector: pensioners, wage earners in the budgetary sector (e.g., teachers, professors, physicians, white-collar workers), and workers in rural areas (e.g., farmers).

The ratio of more than 70 percent of the average pension to the average income earned in the Polish economy is relatively high by international standards, but low considering the low reference level (average income) and the large portion of money savings lost. The ratio of the average wage in the budgetary sector to that in the enterprise sector has been reduced to about 82 percent, from more than 100 percent at the beginning of stabilization. The ratio of the average farmer's income to that of the average urban worker fell even more over 1990–1993 because agricultural product prices increased more slowly than prices for other goods and services and because of low efficiency and productivity.

Problems with these three income groups deserve careful attention due to their impact on macroeconomic stabilization. Another issue is, of course, intragroup income distribution.

At the end of Flemming's chapter, one asks the question that should have been raised at the beginning: What does equitable economic transformation actually mean? This question was never asked. How to measure equity remains unanswered.

Comments

Grzegorz W. Kolodko

Official statistics, as Flemming rightly points out, do not provide a satisfactory record of the social costs of transition. Distortions, however, are not as simple. For instance, after the transition, the level of private sector output and employment may have been still underrecorded, but not as much as previously when the private sector was illegal or harassed. The growth of the private sector has probably been overestimated.

Distortions of Economic Trends

A major distortion of economic trends in the transformation is introduced by Flemming himself, for he measures cumulative decline by taking 1990 as the base year (tables 6.1 and 6.2), thus totally neglecting the fall that took place in that year. For most countries, including Poland, this is the source of a gross underestimate of the cost of transition. At the same time, in terms of employment, the Polish economy has been doing better than Flemming suggested; in 1995, unemployment was stabilizing, and it is now falling. Having said this, nobody can argue with Flemming's main proposition that "the region has experienced a setback to output and a rise in unemployment larger than that experienced in ... the 1930s."

Inflation and Income Distribution

Inflation at fast, variable, and unanticipated rates obviously had adverse effects on income distribution, as the weaker groups naturally lost out with respect to those able to assert their relative strength. However, Flemming states that "the real value of transfers has fallen largely as a result of lags in indexation relative to wage." The only evidence he offers is high inflation rates, to which this effect should be "obviously proportional." While pensioners everywhere lost out in absolute terms, a deterioration in their relative position did not follow automatically. The ratio between average pension and average wage remained fairly stable in the Slovak Republic from 1989 to 1992, at around 60 percent, rising in between; it fell only slightly in Hungary, from 63 percent to 61 percent, over the same period. Poland is the most spectacular counterexample to Flemming's contention. Since May 1990, the share of pensions in total income has grown considerably as a result of the introduction of a more favorable method of pension calculation, the anchoring of minimum pensions to 35 percent of the average wage, the mandatory quarterly indexation of old-age and disability pensions and the generous increase granted in December 1990 to pensioners aged 80 and over (UNICEF 1993, p. 39, table 5). At first nominal wages lagged drastically with respect to prices, while pensions were indexed to prices; as money wages started rising faster than prices recovering in real terms, pensions were linked to money wages. The net effect was a steady rise of the ratio of average pension to average wage, from 53.3 percent in 1989 to 65 percent in 1990, 76.2 percent in 1991, and 86.3 percent in 1992. (Another Polish peculiarity was the worsening of pension distribution. The top two pensioner deciles, which received about 22 percent of total pensions in 1989, received 29 percent of total pensions in 1992.) If we are looking for the heaviest losers in the transition—in Poland, as anywhere else in the area—these are children, not pensioners. From 1989 to 1992, the percentage of children under age sixteen living in households below the poverty line (45 percent of the average wage) rose from 28 percent to 57.6 percent in Poland, 14.1 percent to 29.1 percent in Hungary, 38.1 percent to 70.1 percent in Romania, and 10.9 percent to 41.3 percent in the Slovak Republic, where poverty is defined as 40 percent of the average wage (UNICEF 1993).

The aging of the European population in the next few decades will place a heavy burden on national economies (Federal Trust 1995). The age-dependency ratio (the number of people aged sixty-five and over, as a percentage of persons aged fifteen to sixty-four) is expected to rise in the European Union from 21.4 percent in 1990 to 41.5 percent in 2040. But there is no doubt that in some Central Eastern European economies, especially Poland, this is a time bomb with a much shorter fuse. In Poland, the switch of pension indexation from money wages to prices—still a generous link by international standards—is an essential, and overdue, step of economic policy, delayed by electoral concerns that threaten the hard-won financial stability. Flemming's strong words of caution about pensions and safety nets are well taken.

Avoiding Complacency

There may not be much point today in performing a postmortem on the true causes of the drastic recession of the first three years of stabilization and liberalization; bygones are bygones. But Flemming attempts one and suggests that there is little room for reconsideration of policy. This is somewhat complacent. Even without using the benefit of hindsight, surely the cost of stabilization could have been reduced without unintended credit shocks, without the additional shocks of initial inflationary over-devaluations followed by excessive revaluations or instant trade liberalization followed by later protectionism, or without the subjection of state enterprises to excessive and discriminatory taxation—to name but a few of the mistakes that could have been avoided. It is significant that today even Flemming should end up supporting the idea of "transitory protection."

In the short run, the transformation can be made more equitable by standard instruments of economic policy for containing unemployment, such as employment subsidies (which Flemming rightly recommends) and other instruments of active labor policies, and public works. These are precisely the progressive policies that have been shrewdly implemented to contain unemployment in the Czech Republic.

Looking ahead, the best way to make postcommunist transformation more equitable is through the resumption and acceleration of economic growth—hence the particular emphasis on growth and investment in the Polish government's Strategy for Poland program, implemented at the beginning of 1994—for instance, the provisions for switching budgetary expenditure to greater investment, encouraging household investment in housing, granting access to credit by small enterprises and farmers, and reducing the fiscal burden on productive investment by accelerated depreciation allowances. In due course, international capital inflows can be relied on to lower interest rates, regardless of the domestic monetary policy stance, thus relaunching investment and growth.

References

Taverne, Dick, rapporteur 1995. *The Pension Time Bomb in Europe.* A Federal Trust Report. London: Federal Trust for Education and Research.

UNICEF. 1993. *Central and Eastern Europe in Transition: Public Policy and Social Conditions.* Regional Monitoring Report no. 1. Florence: UNICEF, November.

Comments

Nicholas Stern

John Flemming provides a description of the fall and rise of output in Eastern Europe and the former Soviet Union since 1989, together with some data on the rise in inequality and poverty and the change in demographic indicators, particularly life expectancy. In most countries of the region, output has started to rise after strong falls. In all countries for which data are available, inequality and relative poverty have risen, and in some, particularly Russia, life expectancy has fallen sharply. Flemming's analysis of the causes of change in inequality is largely in terms of unemployment. His suggested policy is to provide, through employment subsidies or protective tariffs (which would decline over roughly a decade), for the maintenance of employment in otherwise bankrupt firms. Further, he issues a warning on the dangers of an overly ambitious approach to the design of social safety nets in relation to fiscal burdens and potential effects on reservation wages, and thus future employment.

Comments on Two Recommended Policy Measures

My commentary begins with a brief discussion of the recommended policy and then raises some broader issues about the underlying analysis of equity and poverty. The suggested employment subsidy is, in my view, a nonstarter. In theory, it should be used to keep employment going in otherwise bankrupt firms (thus saving the output and exchequer costs of their closure). In practice, it would be very difficult to target these firms by trying to design an administrative procedure to identify them. The results would be likely to be gross error, bureaucracy, manipulation, and corruption. Thus, the effect would probably be a further drain on the public accounts and an erosion of public confidence in the transition process, with little effect on employment. If the employment subsidy were made universal, it could be crippling on the budget, with only moderate savings through reduced employment benefit or subsidies elsewhere. Attempts to "tax it back" from profitable firms would be unlikely to work well enough to recover the revenue.

The version of employment maintenance involving protective tariffs would not run into the same revenue problems. If implemented, it would also have the merit of avoiding the reversals of tariff policy that have occurred in some countries where an overly enthusiastic reduction of tariffs in the first instance has been followed by a rise. It is much better for sensible expectations if policy is seen to be predictable (and monotonicity over time in tax or tariff policy probably helps in this regard). On the other hand, it would be a mistake to expect huge employment response (or dramatically successful employment defence) from tariffs of the magnitude of 10 percent or 20 percent. Real wages, for example, are already a tiny fraction of Western competitors in most of the countries. As economists, however, we recognize that there is always a margin where some effect arises. But there is also a margin of disadvantage for the nontradable sector, which is discouraged by such protection. On balance, I would not expect to see a huge impact on employment or inequality.

Analytical Points

There are two specific but important analytical points arising from the chapter, which I note here before passing to broader issues. First, there must be reservations about the analogy between a distorted market economy (as seen in many developing countries) and the old command economy. The change from command to market economy is much more basic than the more standard structural adjustment involved in recasting prices and the fiscal system. The second is well recognized but sufficiently important to be emphasized here; this concerns data quality. Incomes are hard to measure in mature market economies. In the former command economies, with so much rationing and direct provision, the problems of measurement were severe. They are perhaps still more so (although in different ways) in the disorder of the transition and where there are now disincentives to report income. Thus it is not easy to construct a broad comparative picture of inequality from the cross-country income comparisons reported. I would place special emphasis on the mortality figures as more indicative of social conditions in this context. What has happened to mortality in Russia (particularly of males) must be seen as among the major calamities of modern times. It surely reflects the stress of the upheavals as they have developed in Russia, particularly among the losers. As evidence in the *Transition Report* (1995) shows, there are systematic differences in social indicators across countries of the region, and there is a strong association between more favorable movements in social indicators and firmness in economic policies for liberalization and stabilization.

Broader Issues

The most fundamental question to ask in any analysis of poverty or income distribution is, Who are the poor? or What are the characteristics of those in the lower fractiles of the distribution? This is true of an Indian village, an advanced economy, or an economy in transition. Thus, Flemming skips over a basic question. If the poor are the old or the infirm, or in families with numerous children (perhaps with only one parent present), then a focus on employment per se may miss the crucial aspects of poverty and inequality. The force of this argument is moderated if the support for these categories of individuals exposed to poverty operates entirely through the firm, but that is unlikely to be the case even in Russia. The paucity of data implies that a detailed and comprehensive description of the characteristics of the poor in transition economies is not easy; that is where I would recommend starting an investigation of this issue, from the perspective of both analysis and policy.

A second, and related, set of questions concerns the unit of analysis—the individual or household—and the concept of income, earnings, consumption, or wealth to be used. In practice, the most disaggregated level available for the measurement of consumption is likely to be the household (although income and earnings may be available by individual). Within the income category, it is important to distinguish incomes that are pretax and transfer from those that are posttax and transfer. We should also ask about the period of analysis. If those in the lower-income deciles are constantly changing, a given income distribution may be regarded as less problematic from an ethical perspective than one where the current poor are the future poor. Liquidity considerations apart, this would lead us toward a focus on wealth. However, reliable data on wealth are hard to come by. It was not always clear how the data Flemming reports had treated these important empirical issues.

We know that in most countries, at least among members of the Organization for Economic Cooperation and Development, transfers have a much stronger effect on distribution than taxes. Redistribution occurs largely through the expenditure side of the budget. Thus having identified the poor, the next question is how to reach them through expenditures. This puts to one side, however, the very important question of how to generate the economic growth that will allow rising incomes.

For those who are poor and able to work, the right strategy is surely to look for ways of finding them employment. Economic growth is central in this context. In some developing (and increasingly in developed) countries, cash for work (or "workfare") programs may be feasible. For those who cannot work, direct support is likely to be necessary, at least in the short and medium terms. In the longer term, private pensions or insurance may make important contributions.

While poverty involves a focus on the lower end of distributions, equity involves looking across the spectrum. Here we may ask about the sources of wealth in the transition economies. Central among these are housing, small businesses, and the natural resource endowments. There is little wealth in the ownership of an obsolete or bankrupt company. From this perspective, the transition has been inequitable in a number of respects. Housing has largely gone, or will go, to sitting tenants. These may be people who were well placed to manipulate the old regime. The rewards for such manipulation in housing may be large, but in many cases concerning natural resources, they have been astronomical. Such inequity can raise (understandable) resentments that damage the political acceptability of the new economic system.

There is no doubt that the political resentments against the inequities seen in the transition process so far are serious. These arise partly from those who find their economic position severely damaged for reasons they see as no fault of their own. There is no doubt that transition has moved the goalposts, and we might reflect on the fact that radical changes in the rules (e.g., concerning taxation) are sometimes seen as inequitable in capitalist societies. We might put this reflection to one side by recognizing that the rules of the game have been altered—because the earlier ones were repugnant and had disastrous consequences—and in the process inevitably there must be changed expectations and losers. We should acknowledge, however, that these feelings of inequity are strengthened by the perception that there are gainers who owe their positions to, putting it cautiously, haphazardness. At worst, the gains arise from recent manipulation, rewards for past manipulation, or criminality. Some action on poverty and inequity in transition economies is not only of importance in its own right but may be basic to the further progress of the transition itself.

Reference

European Bank for Reconstruction and Development. 1995. *Transition Report*. London.

7 Monetary and Fiscal Policy for Equitable Economic Growth

Arnold C. Harberger

The key word in the chapter title is *equitable*, and the obvious question is, How do monetary and fiscal policies for *equitable* economic growth differ from monetary and fiscal policies for economic growth (with no qualifying adjective)?

My considered answer to this question is "not very much," for several reasons. In the first place, let us define as "good" economic policies those that promote the efficient operation of the economy and at the same time intelligently support the process of growth. I believe that good policies thus defined typically produce long-term benefits for all (or nearly all) segments of society. In particular, nothing in our experience suggests that the real level of welfare of, say, the bottom quintile in a society does not improve as economic growth takes place. More important, it is, on the whole, true that the poor as well as other segments of society fare worse under policies that work against the efficient operation of the economy and that put sand in the wheels of the growth process than they do under what I have called "good" policies. My conclusion is that adding the qualifying adjective *equitable* does not alter the general shape of the overall economic policy that is appropriate. In other words, equity considerations, at least up to a certain point, do not conflict with the growth objective.

Second, and quite in harmony with the first point, most of the policies that aim in the direction of making a society and polity more equitable can be equally well, if not better, pursued in a growing economy than in a stagnant one. I have in mind policies oriented toward helping the poorest segments of society fulfill their basic needs: nutrition, education, medical care, and perhaps housing. Some of these policies, particularly in the fields of public health and education, can be thought of as directly supporting the process of economic growth, but even those that are not directly supportive do nothing to get in the way of economic growth. The only point of potential conflict that I see is the general competition among different types of government programs for the fiscal resources available at any given moment. I do not emphasize this, or even place much weight on it, because I believe that most countries (most developing countries, at least) can do a considerably better job than they are now doing with respect to helping the poor meet their basic needs, without seriously impinging on the growth rates or growth potential of their economies.

The optimism I have expressed concerning the compatibility between the objectives of equity and growth stems in considerable measure from a view of what it is possible for governments to do. A government that tried, for example, to squeeze a society's income distribution to the point where the richest had no more than five times the per capita command over resources of the poorest would end up dooming its economy to stagnation, if not extinction. On that definition of equity, there is enormous conflict between equity and growth.

For the efficient operation of an economy, its resources should be, in the main, allocated so as to maximize their contribution to meeting economic demand. This will lead to different types of labor having different rewards, depending on the capacities with which they are endowed and the demand for those capacities. The land resources of society will gravitate to their most productive uses, and the reproducible capital will seek the best return. All of these forces together will generate a distribution of before-tax income. At some point the government must decide what tasks it will attempt to do, and it must then extract, from the before-tax distribution of income, the resources necessary to finance its operations. In this view of the world, equity considerations enter in two ways: on the expenditure side and the tax side. In a well-functioning modern economy, the public sector budget will end up with the lower-income groups receiving in government services (or grants) more than they pay in taxes, and with the upper-income groups paying more in taxes than they receive in government services.

In such an economy, healthy political debate will focus on exactly what to include among the tasks of government and exactly how to raise the necessary funds. But healthy debate will not take it as the responsibility of government to determine the final after-tax distribution. The responsibility of government is to set its own tasks and raise the money for them. Issues of equity arise on both sides of the tax-expenditure equation, but I shall argue that the challenges and opportunities are considerably greater on the expenditure than on the tax side of the ledger. In particular, if we consider the income distribution of a typical developing country and apply to it a tax system that is sensible in terms of its impact on efficiency and growth and reasonably progressive in the sense of concentrating relative sacrifice on the upper-income groups, we will find that the relative distribution of after-tax income is not greatly different from that of before-tax income. On the other hand, if we consider a plausible pattern of distribution of government services among income groups, we will find here a much greater potential impact on the relative economic status of rich and poor. For many countries, the tax system remains in urgent need of reform in order to make it more conducive to efficiency and growth. In the process, it is likely also to become more equitable, but it is unlikely to generate a big difference between the before-tax and the after-tax distribution of income. Expenditure systems are also in urgent need of reform. Here we find fertile ground for the intelligent pursuit of equity objectives. Good policies on the expenditure side can significantly improve the level of living of the poor, as well as the prospects for their children.

7.1 Macroeconomic Policy: Some Mistakes of the Past

Important mistakes have been made in three major areas in the past: inflation, the boom-and-bust syndrome, and populism.

Inflation

At this stage of history, little need be said about inflation as a useful instrument for bringing about good results in economic policy. The historical record shows that serious inflations have resulted basically from the "bankruptcy" of governments—that is, unable (or unwilling) to meet their expenditures from any more appropriate source—so they have turned to the printing presses, thus creating inflation.

In the major inflations of recent decades, almost invariably gross domestic product (GDP) per capita goes down as the inflation moves to its peak, and it recovers as the inflation is brought under control. Table 7.1 records a number of important recent episodes in Latin America, chosen for having had peak inflation rates of around 100 percent or more, followed by a substantial reduction of the inflation rate. Note that in spite of the known problems of effectuating a program of stabilization, all of these countries experienced significantly better growth of per capita GDP during the years of falling inflation than during the years of rising inflation.

One key factor that helps explain this result is that, on the whole, these countries had significantly better economic policies during their stabilization periods than during their periods of accelerating inflation. Here I

Table 7.1
Economic Growth Rates in Major Inflation Episodes

Country	Episode Years	Annual Inflation Rates (in percent)			Average Annual Growth Rate of per Capita GDP	
		Start	Peak	End	Rising Inflation	Falling Inflation
Argentina	1970, 1976, 1980	14	444	101	.004	.031
	1981, 1985, 1986	105	672	90	−.025	.011
	1986, 1989, 1993	90	3,080	11	−.013	.030
Bolivia	1981, 1985, 1989	32	11,750	15	−.055	−.013
Chile	1971, 1974, 1979	20	505	33	−.035	.012
Mexico	1981, 1987, 1992	25	132	16	−.022	.011
Peru	1977, 1985, 1987	38	163	85	−.012	.065
	1987, 1990, 1993	85	7,482	49	−.104	.016
Uruguay	1964, 1968, 1970	42	125	16	.003	.050
	1970, 1973, 1978	16	97	45	−.011	.030

Sources: International Monetary Fund, *International Financial Statistics*, various issues (Washington, D.C.).

would like to emphasize the ways in which inflation per se works to hamper economic efficiency and the process of growth.

The key to the most adverse effects of inflation lies in the way that it affects the signals emerging from an economy's price system. In a stable economy, rising prices are signals that a good or service has become scarcer or more desired, or both. Price rises should act to attract more resources to an activity, and price falls to deter them. With a stable price level, the bulk of price movements are signals of this nature. More generally, movements in relative prices provide these kinds of resource allocation signals. But when an inflation process is under way, particularly a major one, the different prices of the economy do not all move up in lockstep; some rise in steps, others in big jumps, still others in irregular patterns. The vision that people have of relative prices changes day by day. In this kaleidoscope of changing relative prices, it is much harder to discern the true signals of greater or lesser scarcity or desirability. Hence, economic agents are slower to respond, and the efficient operation of the economy is impaired.

Inflation affects the growth process in a similar way. For nearly fifty years we have known that an important part of economic growth stems from improvements in total factor productivity. Such improvements can also be called by another name: real cost reductions. I prefer this designation because it reminds one immediately that this is a goal that every businessperson, every manager, every engineer is seeking, day by day, week by week, year by year. It reminds us that the nature of growth is multifarious, coming out of all the different ways that economic agents find for reducing real costs. The problem with inflation is that it blurs relative price signals, thus making it harder for businesspeople to recognize opportunities to reduce real costs. With a stable general price level, relative price signals can be seen as in bright sunlight; with moderate inflation, it is more like in a hazy mist; with rampant inflation, one gropes as in a dense fog to perceive relative prices. So when a significant inflation is under way, businesspeople become more tentative about testing new ideas, and when they do test them, they fail more often because price relationships are often misperceived. The end result is a smaller contribution of real cost reduction (total factor productivity improvement) to the growth process.

This is not the end of the story of the relation between inflation and growth. Another important contributor to growth is investment, and there are at least two ways in which inflation tends to crowd out productive investments. On the one hand, fiscally induced inflations usually reflect situations in which the government is seeking resources everywhere it can find them. This includes the capital market, whether it is primitive and rudimentary, or sophisticated and modern. More pressure from the side of the government crowds out productive investments and thus reduces the contribution of investment to growth.

There is a related connection between inflation and growth that operates through the monetary system. I like to work with the vision of the monetary system that *International Financial Statistics* initiated nearly fifty years ago. This focuses on the balance sheet of the consolidated banking system of a country (central bank plus deposit money banks). The liabilities of this consolidated system are mainly money plus quasi-money, and its assets are mainly net foreign assets plus credit to the public sector plus credit to the private sector. The important point is that inflation causes people to reduce their real balances of money plus quasi-money. This reduction in banking system liabilities squeezes the asset side of the consolidated balance sheet, tending to squeeze total bank credit in real terms. Moreover, if the inflation is being fueled by expanded government borrowing from the banking system, then the government's share in total bank credit is likely to increase, thus compressing private sector credit even more, and through it, of course, the rate of investment in productive capital assets.

There is thus a whole host of ways in which inflationary policies impinge on economic growth. The lessons of history in this regard should not be forgotten.

Boom-and-Bust Syndrome

There are analogies between the problems that policymakers face in their task of guiding a nation through good times and bad and the problems that ordinary households face as they confront the vicissitudes of daily life. The perils of wishful thinking, the temptations that lure one, the moral dilemmas that never cease to arise, the difficulties of maintaining discipline in the face of adversity, one's terrible reluctance to cut back: All these fit as easily in the world of the policymaker as in the world of the householder.

Nowhere is the analogy more poignant than in what I call the boom-and-bust syndrome: the tendency to live beyond one's means when times and prospects are good and then to be forced to tighten one's belt when times turn bad. Consider two oil-exporting countries in the Western Hemisphere: Ecuador and Mexico. Between 1978 and 1980, the dollar value of Ecuador's merchandise exports rose by two-thirds, and that of Mexico's went up by 250 percent. One would think that such a bonanza would signal the wisdom of special efforts to build up their productive capital stock and perhaps to pay off some foreign debt. But such was not the case. Gross fixed capital formation was 14.8 percent of GDP in Ecuador in 1977 and 13.8 percent in 1978. With the oil bonanza, it went to 12.8 percent in 1979, 14.7 percent in 1980, and 14.3 percent in 1981. In spite of the oil boom, Ecuador ran a larger average current account deficit over 1979–1981 than it did in 1977–1978. In Mexico, fixed capital formation went up by some 5 percentage points of GDP, but the current account deficit went up by even more. The sad truth is that by 1983, Ecuador's GDP per capita was no higher in real terms than it had been in 1978 (in spite of the fact that real oil prices were well above their 1978 levels), while Mexico's was barely 7 percent higher (in spite of 1983's exports being more than triple 1978's in nominal dollar terms and more than double in real dollar terms).

The oil-exporting countries were the lucky ones, for they were in a position to benefit from the oil bonanza. But in a curious twist of fate, it seemed that some nonoil countries gained more from the oil boom than the oil countries themselves. The mechanism was the huge expansion of international lending, as the great international banks recycled their "petrodollars" (deposited predominantly by Saudi Arabia and the Persian

Gulf States). During the years 1979–1982, the current account of Brazil had deficits totaling more than $50 billion (over $400 per capita); Argentina's ran over $12 billion (also over $400 per capita), Chile's over $10 billion (around $900 per capita), Peru's over $3 billion (around $200 per capita), and Uruguay's over $1.5 billion (around $500 per capita).

Stimulated in part by the borrowing binge, GDP per capita peaked in Argentina and Brazil in 1980, in Chile and Uruguay in 1981, and in Peru in 1982. There ensued the great international debt crisis during which real GDP fell absolutely in every one of these countries. The balance of trade in goods and nonfinancial services turned positive in Argentina from 1982 through 1991; in Chile, from 1983 to 1993; in Peru, from 1983 to 1986; and in Brazil and Uruguay, from 1983 to the present. This meant that the large net resource transfer into these countries that occurred in their period of boom was reversed and turned into an outward net resource transfer in their period of bust. Real GDP per capita did not return to its early 1980s peak until 1989 in Chile and 1992 in Argentina and Uruguay. In Brazil and Peru, it was still below 1981 levels in 1992 and 1993.

This is not the place to try to analyze in detail how all these countries could quite plausibly have managed their affairs more prudently, keeping a closer rein on their borrowing and spending in the boom years and thus leaving themselves less saddled with debt, and in a better position to continue to resume healthy growth after the flow of petrodollars was cut off. Perhaps the key variable in this story is the country's real exchange rate, which, though not itself an instrument of policy, can certainly be considered a variable of legitimate (and sometimes serious) policy concern. All of the countries discussed underwent dramatic currency appreciations in the boom years and had to pay a huge price in terms of major real depreciations of their currencies later. Countries that have attempted to use the policy instruments at their disposal to keep real exchange rates within range of what are thought to be their medium-term equilibrium levels have had little reason to regret these policies. Particular instances of this type of policy include Brazil (1968–1979), Chile (1965–1970 and 1985 to the present), and Colombia, in a broad characterization of its policy (since the late 1960s).

Populism

It is not easy to define what I (let alone others) mean by the word *populism*, but its broad connotation is clear: politicians promising much more than they can deliver and then trying to carry through on their impossible promises anyway. It includes having cheap bread and buses and rents when their true economic costs are much higher; imposing arbitrary sharp wage increases independent of movements of productivity and other conditions in the labor market; keeping failing enterprises alive in order to avoid laying off their workers; building huge government bureaucracies that have little or no (or even negative) economic yield or function; making credit cheap and easily available to preferred groups (and sometimes quite broadly); and failing to cover government expenditures by taxes, and when taxes are imposed, choosing them in terms of their political resonance rather than their economic impact. This list could easily be made longer.

Bouts of populism have been witnessed in Latin America (the area of the developing world with which I am most familiar) for a long time. In recent decades we have had Presidents Goulart and Sarney in Brazil, President Allende in Chile, President and Mrs. Perón in Argentina, and Presidents Echeverría and López Portillo in Mexico. In all these cases, the economy was left in critical condition, in urgent need of major surgery as far as economic policy was concerned. The important lesson to be learned from these and other experiences with populism is that it does not achieve the objectives that were proclaimed for it. Inflation is almost always its consort, as are widespread economic distortions, ill-functioning markets, and counterproductive foreign trade incentives. Except when populist regimes are very short-lived, they typically end up with real incomes and real wages lower than at their start.

No one should ever make the mistake of confusing populism and democracy. To my knowledge, the oldest extant democracy in the world is Switzerland, which has proved itself quite resistant to the populist virus over the centuries. Nor are so-called left-wing governments predestined to be populist. Some link of that kind may once have existed, but recent history has shown that parties of left, right and center can all embrace good economics and implement good economic policies.

7.2   Key Features of Good Economic Policy

Experience has taught us a great deal about the types of policies and policy packages that allow an economy to perform up to (or, better, close to) its potential. It is probably fair to say that a reasonably wide consensus has emerged concerning things a country definitely should try to do and other things it should definitely avoid doing. There is no single place where this emerging consensus is fully codified, so I shall content myself with drawing on two sources familiar to me.

In April 1983, a conference was held in Mexico City under the auspices of the Institute for Contemporary Studies (ICS). The topic was world economic growth, and the bulk of the papers were country studies of developed and developing economies. The focus of the papers was to try to distinguish in each case what the country's policymakers had done that was right and also what had been their principal errors (both of commission and of omission) in economic policy.

It fell to me to summarize the results. I ventured to draw thirteen lessons of economic policy (Harberger 1984):

1. Avoid false technicism in economic policymaking.

2. Keep budgets under adequate control.

3. Keep inflationary pressures under reasonable control.

4. Take advantage of international trade.

5. Recognize that some types and patterns of trade restrictions are far worse than others, and work to liberalize and rationalize them.

6. If import restrictions are excessive and reducing them is politically impossible, mount an indirect attack on the problem by increasing incentives to export.

7. Make tax systems simple, easy to administer, and (as much as possible) neutral and nondistorting with respect to resource allocation.

8. Avoid excessive income tax rates (50 percent was selected as representing a plausible marginal rate that should not be exceeded).

9. Avoid excessive use of tax incentives to achieve particular objectives.

10. Use price and wage controls sparingly, if at all.

11. Rarely can a cogent economic justification be found for quotas, licenses, and similar quantitative restrictions on output, imports, exports, and so forth.

12. Policy professionals tend to take a rather technical view of the problems associated with public sector enterprises, emphasizing the many extra constraints and demands that are typically placed on their operations.

13. However it is determined, the borderline of public sector and private sector activity should be clear and well defined. When the two compete in a given area, the same rules should govern their operations.

It would be easy to augment this list, but I prefer to leave it as a rough reflection of where a group of experienced policy professionals (the bulk of the conference participants) stood some dozen years ago.

Some six and a half years after the ICS Conference in Mexico City, another conference was held in Washington, D.C., this one under the auspices of the Institute for International Economics. The focus of this conference was what John Williamson, its organizer, initially labeled the "Washington consensus," but at the conference's end he felt that the term "universal convergence" might have been more accurate. Williamson's (1990) summary description of the content of the Washington consensus is "macroeconomic prudence, outward orientation, and domestic liberalization." The great compatibility between Williamson's "consensus" and my "lessons" should already be apparent. (Neither of us claims to be the author, only the scribe of what we set down.) Following is my attempt to put ten main points of the Washington consensus into a form similar to the thirteen lessons:

1. Countries should maintain fiscal discipline, though not necessarily strictly balanced budgets.

2. Education and health are high-priority expenditures; indiscriminate subsidies are to be condemned; many infrastructure investments will pass the cost-benefit test.

3. Taxes should ideally be levied on a very broad base, and with moderate marginal tax rates.

4. Interest rates should be market determined; negative real interest rates, which often tend to emerge in inflationary episodes, should particularly be avoided.

5. A competitive real exchange rate is the first essential element of an outward-oriented economic policy.

6. The second element of such a policy is import liberalization. Tariffs are far better than licenses and quotas, and distortions should be kept to a minimum by limiting tariff dispersion.

7. Foreign direct investment is viewed with considerable favor, while the consensus is more neutral with respect to controls on financial flows into developing countries.

8. Privatization of public enterprises has been viewed with favor by Washington institutions, but many experts prefer to view it on a case-by-case basis.

9. Deregulation is an important step in the modernization of economies that carry heavy burdens of detailed state control over economic activities. One should aim for simple rules of wide applicability: the rules of the game.

10. Advanced economies often take property rights for granted; many developing countries have yet to recognize their fundamental importance for the operation of a modern market economy.

Between the "lessons" and the "consensus" one can get a good sense of the directions in which thinking about economic policy has evolved over the past couple of decades. There is not even a wisp of approval for many elements of policy that were accepted by many almost as dogma during the 1950s and 1960s: the detailed planning of the economy through the use of planning models; the strategy of import substitution behind very strong barriers to trade; the use of subsidized interest rates and allocated credit as important policy measures guiding resource allocation; the wide-spread reliance on public sector enterprises, almost always including electricity, telecommunications, and transport, and typically going far beyond them; and the use of inflation in many countries as the standard device for covering fiscal deficits.

Although there are many areas of economic policy not explicitly mentioned in the twenty-three points listed, I believe that these points are extremely useful in setting the stage for the discussion that follows.

7.3   Tax Policy in Developing Countries

In this section, I summarize what I believe to be the contemporary (or at least the emerging) consensus on tax policy for developing countries.

Value-Added Tax

Perhaps the most important innovation in the tax field in the past half-century is the value-added tax. This tax first emerged in France in the early 1950s and has experienced a phenomenal spread to all parts of the globe. It has gained most ground in places where it has replaced an old-type sales tax, levied in cascade fashion on every successive stage of production. It has made least headway where (as in the United States) it would compete with a retail sales tax, which has a quite similar ultimate base. In some cases, it has succeeded in supplanting a whole host of tiny nuisance taxes, many of them initially levied in earmarked fashion, with their revenues reserved for financing particular classes of outlay.

Tax professionals recognize that in spite of its typically broad base, the value-added tax never comes very close to being a fully general tax. Educational and medical expenses are usually outside its net, as are expenditures for casual labor and household servants in most countries, plus the imputed rent on owner-occupied housing. On the whole, these reductions of its base lead to a situation where, with very good administration, a uniform value-added tax of 10 percent, designed as a consumption-type tax, will have a yield of no more than 5 to 7 percent of aggregate consumption, as measured by the national income accounts. In spite of this, which some may consider a limitation, the value-added tax is the principal single source of revenue in a considerable number of developing and developed countries. Rates in such countries have ranged all the way from 5 to 6 percent at the bottom to 18 to 20 percent at the top.

In the context of this chapter, the issue arises of the potential progressivity of a value-added tax. It is relatively easy to implement a value-added tax with varying rates, particularly if it is administered using the credit method. With that method, every selling entity pays the full tax on the value of its sales but can then claim a credit for the tax embodied in its purchases (as evidenced by receipts or other documentation). Thus, if a maker of yachts buys wood, glass, paint, and other materials embodying a value-added tax paid at the rate of 20 percent, and if the yachts themselves carry a tax rate of 30 percent, the yacht maker simply pays at 30 percent on the full value of the yachts, then proceeds to receive a credit for the 20 percent tax paid on the embodied materials. In the end, 30 percent has been paid on the value-added at all stages, adding up to the final sales value of the yachts.

There is a considerable history of value-added taxation at different rates for different products, though more so in advanced than in developing countries. The consensus is that having different rates makes administration more difficult, mainly because of the tendency of taxpaying firms to try to falsify the composition of their output, exaggerating their sales of low-rate products and understating those to which higher rates apply. Perhaps for this reason, developing countries have tended to avoid multiple rates of value-added tax.

The most significant situation of multiple rates that one still finds in developing countries is the practice of zero-rating certain products. This says that a zero rate is applied to the sales of certain products of a firm, although the standard rate may still be applied to others of its products. Zero rating usually is applied to items viewed as basic necessities, such as bread, rice, and canned and powdered milk. Sometimes it is extended to all or most food items.

The difficulties of administration that emerge with different rates also carry through to cases of zero rating side by side with a single standard rate. Once again the problem is one of exaggerating the sales of zero-rated items and understating those of taxed items. Tax professionals, on the whole, seem to favor eliminating zero rating, or at least keeping it to a minimum, concentrated on easily tracked items whose sales records cannot readily be inflated.

The one area where tax professionals look with some equanimity on differentiated treatment under a value-added tax is in leaving certain classes of sellers entirely out of the system. For example, in a country with thousands or millions of small farmers, many perhaps illiterate, and most unaccustomed to the twists and turns of double-entry accounting, it is probably wise for the authorities simply to leave agriculture out of the value-added tax net. When this is done, the government may even end up collecting more revenue than by including the farmers in the network. The reason is that when farmers sell to food processors, and the food processors then pay value-added tax on their sales, they in effect pay tax on the farmer's sales (to them) plus their own value-added. In this case, the government gets more revenue than it would by including the farmers in the network, because nobody gets to take a credit for the value-added tax embodied in the farmers' purchases of fertilizer, seeds, tools, and other inputs.

That is only one side of the story, however. In addition, there are the sales that farmers might make directly to consumers (as in the Sunday markets and fairs common in developing countries). In principle, these sales would be taxable if farmers were included in the network; the tax on them is unequivocally lost when the farmers are left out. Thus, by leaving the farmers out, the government receives additionally the value-added tax embodied in their inputs but loses the potential value-added tax on their direct sales to consumers. Many tax professionals believe that direct sales to consumers are very hard to tax successfully in any case, so the government actually gains revenue while saving significant administrative costs by leaving the farmers out.

Some tax professionals modify this story slightly. Instead of recommending that all farmers be left out of the value-added tax net, they urge that large, modern farms be included and farms below a certain size excluded.

The value-added tax is important as a revenue source, and although a certain degree of progression can be built into it, such progression comes at a significant cost in terms of greater administrative effort as well as of evasion itself. I am trying here to lay the groundwork for my later conclusion that, come what may, no developing country is likely to be able to have a tax system that is very powerfully progressive.

Taxation of Imports: The Uniform Tariff

In the past decade or so, there has been a huge movement, across many developing countries, toward lowering the rates of import tariffs that they impose and, equally important, bringing them much closer to uniformity. Chile was a leader in this area, imposing a 10 percent uniform tariff in 1979. The rate of that tariff has been modified several times since, but it has never ceased to be uniform. It stands today at 11 percent. Many other developing countries have moved in the direction of uniformity, without going all the way. Whereas twenty years ago tariffs commonly ranged up to 100 percent or more, with many exempt items, today in many countries the tariff rates all lie between, say, 10 and 20 percent or between 5 and 15 percent.

The merits of a uniform tariff are not that it is optimum from any technical point of view. It is better defended as a very big step in the right direction, compared with where one was before. Differentiated tariffs have the serious flaw of providing rates of effective protection that are typically some multiple of the rate of nominal protection—a multiple that varies arbitrarily with the world market prices of final products and imported inputs, and with productive techniques (how much of importable inputs is used, and to what tariff rates are they subject?)

With a uniform tariff rate of, say, 10 percent, all issues of effective protection are clarified. All import-substitute activities are given effective protection at the rate of 10 percent, and all export activities (so long as they are rebated the amount of import tariffs embodied in their cost structure, as permitted by the rules of the General Agreement on Tariffs and Trade) are given zero effective protection. This may not be a tax professional's nirvana, but it is a lot better than the world as we saw it not too long ago, with effective protection rates that reached as high as 500 percent or more and went for certain activities as low as −20 or −30 percent.

An important added advantage of a uniform tariff lies in the field of political economy. Once there exist high and low rates of tariffs, producers will make great efforts to obtain high rates for their products and low rates for their important inputs. That is, each producing entity will be striving to make its rate of effective protection as high as possible. Political life being what it is, it is very hard for a tax authority or a tariff commission to resist this type of pressure from every side, and once a concession is made to one or a few, the rest will predictably line up again to get their share.

How much easier it is for the authorities to resist such pressures when the plaintiffs simply have no high and low rates to point to. The authorities can then maintain quite correctly that "you are being treated just like everybody else," and this blunts, or even forestalls, most of the pressures that would otherwise emerge.

Taxation of Income from Capital
One of the important insights that has come to be widely accepted as the world capital market becomes ever more open is that the incidence of the corporation income tax, or its twin, the enterprise income tax, tends to fall mainly on labor. Indeed, it is easy to construct examples in which this tax is more than fully borne by labor.

The key to understanding this apparently counterintuitive result is the recognition that capital has always been relatively highly mobile, and it is becoming ever more so. It is not so much that foreign capital is ready to move into developing country capital markets with great ease. Rather, it is that the families and groups that own the bulk of the enterprises there can easily move their capital to London, New York, Zurich, Hong Kong, or anywhere else. In these centers, the families can earn the market rates of return of the world capital market. In many developing countries, even their own nationals require a significant risk premium in their own market, vis-à-vis London and New York, but that is something they would likely demand in the presence of a corporation income tax or in its absence. If such investors are willing to accept a 5 percent real return in New York, they may very well insist on the expectation of a 10 percent net-of-tax return on their industrial and similar investments at home. This means that if there is no tax, investment projects will face a likely cutoff rate of expected return of around 10 percent. If now a 33 percent corporation tax is imposed, this cutoff rate of return will be 15 percent, and many investments will now be rejected, though they would have been accepted at a 10 percent cutoff rate. The capital that would have gone into these investments will likely flow abroad (or fail to flow in from abroad). Less capital will thus be working with the labor force in the developing country in question, and the equilibrium real wage accordingly will be lower. This is the mechanism by which labor comes to bear part, or all, or more than all of the burden of the tax.

In the simplest models of corporation tax incidence in an open economy, the assumption is made that the product of the corporate tradable sector has its price determined in the world market, so the price cannot rise when the tax is imposed, nor can the equilibrium net-of-tax return to capital fall, for the reason stated. So if neither product price nor capital's net return can move to absorb the tax, the burden has to fall on labor, which is assumed to be substantially immobile, internationally. It could happen that wages would not adjust at all, or would adjust but not enough to absorb, in the corporate tradable sector, the full burden of the tax. In either of these circumstances, the developing country that imposed the tax would abandon the production of the good in question. In order for it to continue to produce the good on a continuing equilibrium basis, the wage of labor has to fall by enough to absorb the tax. But if wages fall in the corporate tradable sector, they must also fall in the rest of the labor market. It is here that the burden on labor can become significantly greater than the total yield of the tax. The fall of wages in the rest of the economy can cause the prices of services to fall, benefiting their demanders. They can also cause land rents to rise as agriculture, producing a tradable product, sees its labor costs fall while its product price is maintained. Thus, labor's burden is reflected not only in tax revenue to the government but also in benefits to buyers of services and owners of land.

I have but barely sketched the line of analysis of corporation tax incidence in the open economy. The key features of the argument have been published in several places over the past decade or more. More recently, I have revisited this topic and attempted to loosen some of the more rigid assumptions, allowing the prices of developing country corporate sector products to have some flexibility rather than be fully fixed in world markets. I also allowed, more for the U.S. case than for that of a developing country, for the world rate of return to capital to fall as one of the consequences of the imposition of the tax (in this case in the United States). These various attempts to bring more flexibility and realism into the analysis leave basically untouched the principal conclusion that labor is very likely to bear all or more than all of the burden of the corporation income tax (except when the major countries of the world move their rates up and down together). For independent policy actions by developing countries, it is very hard to escape the conclusions that labor will bear the burden (Harberger 1995, chap. 2).

I have provided extensive technical detail because I felt it necessary to support rather than simply assert the likelihood that the corporation income tax falls largely on labor. This is another pillar of the final conclusion that it is extremely difficult to find sensible tax policies that have strong redistributive consequences.

Given this analysis, I believe that the trend among developing countries to integrate their corporation income taxes with their personal

income taxes should be welcomed. One can say, with numerous qualifications, that absolutely full integration of the corporation income tax
with the personal income tax almost amounts to the abolition of the corporation tax. One reason for keeping the corporation income tax, at least
as a shell, concerns multinational companies, whose income would likely
be taxed by Washington or London if it were left free of tax in Brazil or
Mexico. Another reason has to do with monopoly profits, more common
in the small markets of developing countries than in the highly competitive arenas of the United States and perhaps the European Union.
Monopoly profits are not, in an analytical sense, fully accounted for as
part of the marginal product of capital, but they are commingled with the
return for capital for tax purposes, and the corporation income tax thus
helps the government take its bite out of them.

    Most efforts at integrating the corporation income tax with the per-
sonal income tax are only partial. If we have, per share, 300 of profits and
100 of corporation income tax, with 60 paid in dividends and 140 re-
invested within the corporation, there are four ways in which integration
can take place:

1. Full integration. Each domestic shareholder declares the full 300 of
profits per share and claims the 100 of corporation income tax as "withholding."

2. Integration with gross-up of dividends. Since the corporation tax rate
is one-third, 90 would be imputed as income to the shareholder and 30 of
what had been paid at the corporate level would be considered as withholding.

3. Integration based on dividends but without gross-up. The shareholder
declares 60 as dividend income and counts one-third of this amount as
withholding.

4. Dividends free of tax at the personal level. This is equivalent to the
second way if the shareholder has a marginal tax rate equal to the corporate rate. (Where this fourth way is employed, the top marginal rate of the
personal income tax is often made equal to the corporate rate.)

    The developing countries that have moved toward integration have, to
the best of my knowledge, settled on either the third or fourth method.
Thus, by design, they yield only partial integration, and the incidence
analysis given above would still apply to the "unintegrated" portion of
the corporation income tax.

Indexing the Tax System for Inflation

Inflation wreaks havoc with the implementation and administration of any tax system that has not been inoculated against it. Businesspeople suffer from having depreciation allowances, based on historic cost, that bear no relation to the true economic depreciation, at current prices, of the assets in question. Lenders complain about having to declare as income the full amount of interest they receive, even though a good part of it merely compensates for the loss in value of the loan through inflation, and thus might more appropriately be considered amortization. Investors complain that they are being taxed on capital gains, even when the asset they have sold has produced a loss in real terms. Tax administrators, budget directors, and finance ministers all complain of the so-called Tanzi effect, encompassing a variety of mechanisms by which an ongoing inflation erodes the real value of tax revenues.

It is possible to modify a tax system by a series of patches, each addressing one of the above problems or a similar one. One can permit the revaluation of assets for depreciation purposes; one can legislate that the cost basis of assets can be adjusted for inflation before computing capital gains that will be subject to tax; the tax authorities can apply an inflation factor, or even an interest rate somewhat above the inflation rate, to update tax liabilities between the time the taxes accrue and the time they are paid. All of these patches have been tried in one or another country, but in the end they remain just that—patches.

Anyone who looks closely at the problems that inflation creates for a tax system will quickly realize that each patch is designed to deal with a particular problem but calls attention to another, somewhat similar, problem that has not yet been dealt with.

The obvious answer is to index the entire tax system. This sounds like an enormous task, enmeshed with complications at every step. But closer examination reveals that it is actually easier to index the whole tax system than it is to implement a series of individual partial patches.

This is not the place to go into a full discussion of tax indexing. But readers should realize that a few simple rules are sufficient to cover the vast majority of cases. For the taxation of business income, all real or indexed assets are written up by the annual (or other periodic) inflation factor, and the amount of the write-up is added to taxable profits. Similarly, all real or indexed liabilities (including, in this case, capital and surplus) are written up by the inflation factor, with the amount of this write-up being subtracted from taxable profits. And finally, depreciation is taken on the written-up value of depreciable assets. These three rules deal, almost as if by magic, with the whole panoply of the inequities induced by inflation. They do not cope, of course, with indirect taxation; here the inflation issue is met by sticking to ad valorem rates. And on the side of administration, tax liabilities should always be translated into fully indexed "tax units," thus dealing for all taxes with the burdensome issue of the Tanzi effect.

Unfortunately, a mythology has grown up among some tax authorities and many public figures, according to which the indexing of a tax system is thought to signal a weakening of the government's resolve to maintain price stability. This is sad, particularly in a world where general price levels rarely go down—where the issue is not whether there will be inflation but only how much. The time to index a tax system is when the rate of inflation is low, when taxpayers and administrators alike find the changes relatively modest and often welcome. They would quickly learn that the costs of compliance are no greater than under a nonindexed system and would easily accommodate themselves to the new procedures. Then, when trouble strikes and the inflation rate spurts up for whatever reason, the economy and the society will be in a far better position to deal with it. Moreover, because an indexed system can deal with the Tanzi effect, while a nonindexed system cannot, it is very likely that if an inflationary process starts, it will go less far under an indexed system, because real tax revenues will be better maintained, fiscal deficits will be smaller, with a consequently smaller gap to be financed through inflation.

I find it difficult to fathom why countries have not been willing to move to full indexation in a timely way. We do not say that fastening a seat belt means we intend to have an accident or that buying fire or health insurance means that we are courting disasters of these types. Why can our societies not view tax indexing in the same light?

On Taxes and Income Distribution
The bulk of this section has been devoted to discussing important aspects of the design and administration of tax systems. The underlying purpose was to convince readers that the tax system is unlikely to be a major determinant of the income distribution of a country. Rather than enter into a lengthy disquisition on this point, I shall content myself with presenting what I believe to be a decisive example.

In setting up column 2 of table 7.2a, I have tried to mirror the type of income distribution actually found in many developing countries. It is a highly unequal distribution, but that is what one actually finds.

Table 7.2
Income Distributions Before and After Tax

Quintile of families (1)	Income before tax (2)	Tax (3)	Income after tax (4)	After-tax distribution $[(4) \div k^a]$ (5)	Relative "transfer" $[(5) - (2)]$ (6)
a. With sharply progressive taxation					
First	4	0	4	5.56	+1.56
Second	6	1	5	6.94	+0.94
Third	10	2	8	11.11	+1.11
Fourth	20	5	15	20.83	+0.83
Fifth	60	20	40	55.56	−4.44
Total	100	28	72	100.00	0.00
b. With moderately progressive taxation					
First	4	.3	3.7	4.47	+.47
Second	6	.6	5.4	6.52	+.52
Third	10	1.3	8.7	10.51	+.51
Fourth	20	3.0	17.0	20.53	+.53
Fifth	60	12.0	48.0	57.97	−2.03
Total	100	17.2	82.8	100.00	0.00

Source: Author's calculations.
a. The value of k is 0.72 for table 7.2a and 0.828 for table 7.2b.

The tax system I have assumed is highly progressive—much more progressive than one is likely to find in reality. This was made intentionally unrealistic in order to reinforce my main point: that it makes no sense to think of the tax system as a vehicle for making major changes in the income distribution. The total tax burden shown in table 7.2a is much higher than the tax burdens usually found in developing countries. Given that the assumed system is so progressive, this again has the effect of giving greater scope to the redistributive potential of the tax system. Yet when all is said and done, the relative after-tax distribution is not very different from the before-tax distribution.

Now we should ask, Given the constraints discussed in the earlier parts of this section, how could one expect to get a tax system as progressive as this one, in a typical developing country? Table 7.2b moves in the direction of greater realism while still maintaining a significant degree of progressivity in the tax system. It raises less revenue than the example of table 7.2a, and the tax system is moderately less progressive. Here the conclusion comes through even more strongly: The relative income distribution is not greatly altered by this tax system.

It is extremely important, as we think seriously about tax systems, to internalize the lesson of this section. We are on the wrong track if we think that equity considerations should lead us to think of the tax system as a redistributing vehicle. We are on the right track if we apply equity considerations to find a distribution of the tax burden that accords reasonably well with a society's sense of what is fair, just, and appropriate.

7.4   Equity on the Expenditure Side

Expenditures and Income Distribution

The expenditure side of the budget offers greater scope than does the tax side for differential relative impact on different income groups. This is clearly illustrated in table 7.3. The two parts of the table are built to mirror the two parts of table 7.2, adding reasonable (i.e., not excessively extreme) assumptions about the expenditure side.

I do not believe it ever makes a great deal of sense to try to allocate the whole of government expenditures as benefits to particular income groups. When we undertake this kind of exercise, we are not trying to allocate the generalized benefit of "having a government" versus "living in anarchy." Rather, we are trying to allocate the benefits that people can reasonably be thought to recognize, to perceive. In real-world cases we should limit ourselves largely to items like education, medical care, nutrition, housing, plus, perhaps, the costs of the highway network. To these should be added other direct transfers plus the subsidies implicit in artificially low prices for such items as food, water, and electricity.

This is not the place to pursue in detail the issues of coverage and measurement of benefits. Suffice it to say that we explicitly do not want to try to allocate such items as general government administration, the defense budget, the costs of police, the courts, and the penal system. And since these costs have to be paid, our preferred method works out to yield a net tax burden. It is the remaining expenditures, which are more readily assigned to specific beneficiary groups, that we would deal with directly in an expenditure allocation. (My approach here is the best one to apply in any serious attempts to work with the notion of expenditure incidence. It does no good, and in fact clouds the basic issues, to impose arbitrary allocations for defense, justice, and administration, and thus because of the size of the expenditures, to end up imposing on the resulting estimated

Table 7.3
Income Distributions After Taxes and Expenditures

Quintile of families (1)	Income before taxes (2)	Minus tax plus benefits (3)	Dist. of perceived income [(2) + (3)] (4)	Absolute perceived income [(4) ÷ k^a] (5)	Net tax (−) transfer (+) [= (3)] (6)	Relative "transfer" [(5) − (2)] (7)
a. With sharply progressive taxation						
First	4	−0 + 2.8	6.8	7.91	+2.8	+3.91
Second	6	−1 + 2.8	7.8	9.07	+1.8	+3.07
Third	10	−2 + 2.8	10.8	12.56	+0.8	+2.56
Fourth	20	−5 + 2.8	17.8	20.70	−2.2	+0.70
Fifth	60	−20 + 2.8	42.8	49.76	−17.2	−10.24
Total	100	−28 + 14	86.0	100.00	−14.0	
b. With moderately progressive taxation						
First	4	−.3 + 1.7	5.4	5.91	+1.4	+1.91
Second	6	−.6 + 1.7	7.1	7.78	+1.1	+1.78
Third	10	−1.3 + 1.7	10.4	11.39	+0.4	+1.39
Fourth	20	−3.0 + 1.7	18.7	20.48	−1.3	+0.78
Fifth	60	−12.0 + 1.7	49.7	54.44	−10.3	−5.56
Total	100	−17.2 + 8.5	91.3	100.	−8.7	0

Source: Author's calculations.
Note: Assumes that perceived benefits equal half of total taxes and perceived benefits are equally distributed among quintiles.
a. The value of k is 0.86 for table 7.3a and 0.913 for table 7.3b.

distribution of benefits a particular coloration that largely stems from the arbitrary allocations themselves).

In the exercises of table 7.3, half of the burden goes to general, unallocated purposes, and the remaining half produces perceived benefits that are equally distributed across the quintiles. Some may think this is not a generous assumption, but I believe it is when viewed in the light of the world's realities. More important, I want to show that with this assumption, expenditures exert a lot more influence on the relative distribution of income than we found for the taxes analyzed in table 7.2.

The tax scenario employed in table 7.3a is the same as that for table 7.2a, and the same is true for tables 7.3b and 7.2b. Thus, one can quickly pass to the final columns of both tables. With expenditures taken into account as I have described, the top quintile loses about two and a half times as much in each panel of table 7.3 as in the corresponding panel of table 7.2 (compare −10.24 with −4.44, and −5.56 with −2.03). In a similar way, the gains of the bottom quintile are about two and a half times as large in the top panel (+3.91 versus +1.56) and about four times as large in the bottom panel (compare +1.91 with +0.47). This latter case is important because the tax assumptions of the top panel were intentionally biased toward progressivity, while those of the bottom panel are likely to be closer to the truth in most cases.

Political Economy of Public Expenditures

I believe that it makes sense to use an equal distribution of perceived benefits from government expenditures as something like a yardstick against which to judge real-world cases. Obviously it would not be a sensible yardstick if all or most countries routinely did better than that. But in fact, at least for the great bulk of developing countries, the assumption of a flat (per capita or per family) distribution of perceived benefits is quite optimistic. As a yardstick, it is simply a reference point, but I am betting that careful study will show that for many, if not most, developing countries, it could be turned into a sensible, intelligent, humane, yet plausibly realistic goal.

Let me start from some of the unpleasant facts. In many of the poorest countries, the children of the poorest quintile get virtually no education, their families receive virtually no medical care, and even the simplest public health amenities (like potable water and minimal sewerage facilities) are often lacking. Such countries are far below the standard implied by a flat distribution of perceived benefits.

Now consider the middle-income countries (like Argentina, Brazil, Chile, Colombia, and Mexico), with which I am more familiar. Even here, it is hard to argue that the poorest families receive their proportionate share of perceived benefits. Consider the quantity and quality of public schooling in poor urban neighborhoods versus those that are not so poor, or in poor rural villages versus the median rural village. Now proceed to ask similar questions about medical care, sanitation, and other public health benefits; I find it hard to believe that the bottom quintile receives 20 percent of the total perceived benefit for any of these major classes of public expenditures.

The reason for these unpleasant facts is not hard to find: Everywhere in the world, the poor lack not only economic but also political power. In many societies, these two types of power are concentrated in a numerically small elite. But even where this is not true, those who share political power with the top economic group are more likely to be at the next rungs down the economic ladder, not at the very bottom. According to this view, reality would likely differ from table 7.3b by having more of the relative transfer go to the third and fourth quintiles, and perhaps less to the second, but certainly less to the bottom quintile.

In those places where the bottom quintile is not left so far behind, it is interesting to ask why this is so. Is it because in those (I believe relatively few) countries the poor wield a significant amount of political power? Or is it because of a sense of decency, altruism, and empathy for the poor, arising within those strata of society where the political power actually rests?

Perhaps it is better if it is the latter, because I think it is easier to reach people by moral suasion if they are in any event inclined to want to alleviate the suffering and to raise the sights and the opportunities of the poor than it is to reach the poorest people (from a vantage point elsewhere in the world like Washington, Tokyo, Paris, London, or Berlin) by persuading (or otherwise helping?) them to obtain a greater piece of that elusive quantity called political power.

Policies Targeting the Very Poor

By now there is a widespread recognition of the "scandalous" distributive outcome of some expenditure-side policies. For decades it has been noted that most Latin American countries allocate a huge portion of their education budgets to their universities, that attendance at these institutions is heavily subsidized, often almost free, and that those who enter these subsidized universities come disproportionately from well-to-do families; indeed, they are often the products of expensive private primary and secondary schools. (Something similar happens in many advanced countries, where, at the very least, the beneficiaries of subsidized university education come much more from the upper than from the lower half of the income distribution.)

This is a problem whose technical solution is readily at hand: Simply charge competitive tuition to cover the costs of higher education and deal with the special needs of the poor through scholarships and special loans. But this technical solution does not face up to the political economy problems of the interest groups that support the status quo. If university tuition is zero, the middle classes do not want to give that up; if it is merely subsidized, they want the subsidies to continue. Actually there has been some movement in several Latin American countries, and in most state universities in the United States, in the direction of increased tuition and reduced subsidies for higher education, but this movement has on the whole been quite slow, and largely impelled by budgetary crises rather than any fundamental reappraisal of the problem.

Clearly an educational policy that concentrated its subsidies on students from lower-income families would be more egalitarian than the system described above, but it still might find few qualified clients, owing to the deficiencies of the primary and secondary education available to the poor. In short, it takes great effort to keep the educational system from being a regressive transfer mechanism.

The shantytowns of Latin America are famous under many different labels (*favelas, villas miserias, barriadas, poblaciones callampas*, etc.), and government after government has mounted programs to deal with them. In the past, many of these programs probably aimed too high, attempting to provide a quality of housing that was out of phase with the income and tastes of the people concerned. The consequences were overcrowding (compared with the plan) of the new, more spacious dwellings, as the recipients augmented their incomes by sharing the space with numerous "cousins" (genuine or not), and an incapacity of the programs to reach more than a small fraction of the subject population, in part because of their high cost per dwelling unit.

The current wisdom on this problem is inclined toward more modest contributions from the state, combined with substantial self-help from the recipients. One model is for the government to provide clear title to a small lot, plus a concrete slab with sanitary facilities attached, and let the recipients build around it. This combination has been found to produce self-built houses of surprisingly solid construction and good durability.

Medical services for the poor always pose problems. Medical doctors do not want to live in poor communities; indeed, it is often difficult to get them to locate their practices there, even when the population-to-physician ratio is five or ten times that found in the richer neighborhoods and towns. Again, this problem extends to advanced countries as well as developing ones. One line of solution is to put medical stations in poor neighborhoods, staffed perhaps by nurses and nurses' aides. These stations then serve to give quick treatment in emergencies and for minor ailments, while filtering patients up the ladder to group practice medical clinics or central hospitals, depending on the severity of the case.

On quite another plane, small farms and other very small enterprises in developing countries have often suffered from the sheer inaccessibility of credit. Some recent programs have achieved significant success by target-ing these tiny businesses. In contrast to earlier programs, most of which failed in their purpose, these recent programs do not try to give sub-sidized credit but rather make credit available at an interest rate high enough to cover all costs. Some of these programs have managed the issue of creditworthiness by extending credit to groups of mini-enterprise owners, who jointly cosign each loan and thus in effect internalize what would otherwise fall as a burden of default risk on the lender. The experi-ence of programs of this type suggests that small enterprises can make very productive use of even quite modest amounts of credit. One sum-mary version of their story says that they suffered in the past from the lack of availability of credit rather than too high a price for it. Thus, sen-sible programs providing such availability can succeed, without requiring a subsidy element.

Other Targeting Issues

There are no panaceas in the policy areas we are exploring, so we can be sure that targeting the very poor also has its problems and limitations. I shall mention two cases: where the poor are too numerous and where the very poor are a separate category, almost disjointed from the rest of society.

In very poor countries, it may make little sense to draw a line at the twentieth or thirtieth percentile of families arrayed according to their economic status. In such countries, the economic hardships suffered by even the fiftieth and sixtieth percentiles may be hard to distinguish from those facing the bottom two quintiles. In such countries, the importance of attacking poverty at its roots, helping to educate the children of the poor, improving public health and medical care, and so forth is likely to be even greater than in middle-income countries with an identifiable, hence targetable, lower stratum.

I see an issue here but feel it is mainly semantic. If one thinks of the primary motivation as arising from a concern for basic human needs, this concern leads naturally to targeting the lower deciles of the population in most countries, and it leads to policies of wider coverage in countries where the vast majority suffers from extreme poverty. The problem is more difficult in these latter countries, but the basic policy instruments for handling it are much the same.

Special cases arise in countries with poor minorities that are somehow separated or otherwise distinct from the rest of the population. It was only on my third extended stay in India that I finally learned that the bottom stratum in that country was not occupied by landless laborers (as I had always thought) but by millions of "forest people" living in primitive tribal conditions in forests and jungles all over India. In a similar vein, the whole Amazon basin is dotted with tribes of natives, many of whose life-styles differ little from what they were five centuries ago. Whatever one can say about these cases, one surely does not want simply to amalgamate these groups with, say, the bottom quintile of bulk of the population of the country. At the very least they deserve to be thought of, and very likely treated, in different ways that recognize their unique characteristics.

7.5 Aiding the Escape from Poverty

I am particularly grateful for the opportunity to write this chapter, for it gives me a chance to express in an important forum some ideas that have been brewing in my mind for several years. These ideas were sparked, in part, by my experience in 1987–1989 as a member of the International commission on Central American Reconstruction and Recovery. At one point in the deliberations of that commission, we were examining a very pessimistic document, which lamented that in spite of the experience of eighteen years (1960–1978) of almost uninterrupted growth and prosperity throughout the region, the absolute number of people living in poverty had remained about constant from 1960 to 1985.

Escape from Poverty

I was troubled by this document because it seemed to overlook the fact that the population of the region had doubled in the interim. What then had happened, I asked, to the children of the families who were living in poverty in 1960? Obviously, they could not all have still been in poverty in the early to mid-1980s. A simple demographic projection would suggest that over a quarter-century, something like half the children of the poor had managed to raise themselves out of poverty status. This important "fact" has stuck in my mind ever since, for we are not talking simply about a few lucky individuals who made their way up the economic ladder, but literally millions of people who somehow crossed that invisible line dividing the truly poverty stricken from the rest of society.

Here we have an important phenomenon that we do not fully understand: vast numbers of people who have in fact escaped from poverty. We need to know more. Who are they? What are the main routes they took to effectuate their escape? What policies and institutions aided, and what others may have tended to frustrate, the process?

On a somewhat different plane, I was quite convinced, on the basis of what I already knew about Central America, that, except possibly for Costa Rica, there had not been any substantial policy support for this observed massive "escape from poverty." Hence, I wanted to learn more about how it had been accomplished, with a view to possible new policies that might be designed to grease the wheels of the escape mechanisms and thus make them still more effective.

On the Central American Commission, we were not in a position to initiate a major (and necessarily expensive) study of the phenomenon. But I was able later to engage in a brief experiment, whose whimsical title was "Ask Any Grandmother." The idea was to try to start assembling oral histories of poor families. One would ask a grandmother when and where she was born, the occupations of her parents, the type of house she lived in as a girl (What kind of roof, floor, windows, plumbing? How many people in how many rooms?). One would also ask how many siblings she had, how many died in infancy or childhood, and other similar questions. One would inquire, too, about schooling levels—of her parents, her siblings, herself. Then one would turn to her own marriage, her own children, the house she and her family lived in as the children were growing up. And finally one would ask questions about her children's marriages, their children (her grandchildren), and all their conditions of life.

The idea was to build up a family saga, covering three, or maybe even four, generations, with information that could help us piece together a vision of what life was like at each stage. How much progress had there been overall? How many siblings and how many children had made their way out of poverty? How had this been accomplished?

I still feel that one or more major studies of this type should receive high priority from some source of funding, so as to help us break the cycle of our own lack of knowledge. The brief experiment to which I referred took place in El Salvador around 1990. It was far too hasty, far too rough, and far too small a sample to support any strong conclusions. But the basic facts that came through were as follows. First, the poor, even those who stayed poor, had experienced significant advances with respect to housing, life expectancy, infant mortality, and other areas, moving from one generation to the next. Second, there were many cases of family members (brothers, sisters, children and grandchildren of the interviewees) who had indeed effectuated the escape from poverty. The two most common routes were through building up a small business and receiving an education sufficient to surmount poverty, usually by becoming nurses, accountants, secretaries, engineers, and similar other occupations, and rarely through becoming medical doctors or lawyers.

Another tantalizing tidbit of information that came out of the survey had to do with emigration. There were two effects, both easily verifiable through macroeconomic data. First, some of the children and grand-children of the interviewees had emigrated, mainly to the United States. That simple fact automatically lifted them out of poverty status, as far as the Salvadoran grandmothers were concerned, regardless of what kind of job they had in the United States. Second, remittances from these emi-grants turned out, in several cases, to be important supplements to family income. This is not an isolated phenomenon, for even when U.S. foreign aid to El Salvador was at its peak of around $400 million, it was rivaled in size by emigrant remittances. Since then, U.S. aid has plummeted while the remittances have grown (even doubled, by some estimates).

Socioeconomic Mobility
Closely related to the escape from poverty is the general question of socioeconomic mobility, which deserves much closer study than it has received. It has important implications for the way in which a society might appropriately deal with poverty. Countries clearly differ from one another with respect to such mobility. At the one extreme, we have the ancient (perhaps not-so-ancient) Indian caste system, whereby economic status was simply inherited, generation after generation. At the other extreme, we have the vision we call the "American dream," which may be more reality than dream, given the high incidence our professions, execu-tive boards, and governments of people whose origins were below or near the median of our population. Obviously, the underlying reality with respect to socioeconomic mobility should have an important bearing, for example, on educational policy: People should be trained for the jobs they are likely to get. That reality also has a bearing on the ease with which the poverty problem can be "solved."

Just as in the case of the escape from poverty, we need much more information than we have about socioeconomic mobility in general. What are the backgrounds of a country's nurses, accountants, engineers, law-yers, and doctors? How many of them came from the same social stratum? How many rose from below? How receptive are the society's organisms (professional societies, clubs, other social groupings) to penetration from below? All of these phenomena are natural objects of study by social sci-entists. And such study, in some depth, will help us talk more sensibly about matters such as income distribution.

My own fear is that the process of upward social mobility is much slower in most developing countries than it is in the United States, or even in Western Europe (post–World War II). One gets the sense that the elites in developing countries, apart from being on the whole modern and well educated, tend to be highly prolific and are also pretty good parents. This means that their children are likely to be given the best of preparation for life in the upper stratum. This preparation, together with the sheer numbers in the upper stratum, poses a significant barrier to new entrants trying to break into that upper stratum from below.

In the end, it is relatively easy for me to envision the children of the poor in developing countries making a rather impressive escape from poverty. But I see them mainly becoming the secretaries, the draftsmen, the nurses and nurses' aides, rather than the leaders of business, finance, and government. It is easier for me to see, in Latin America, children of European grandparents (who may have arrived penniless a generation ago) rising to the very top than the children of the native poor.

For these things I have no clear answers, no obvious solutions. I think I see progress in most contemporary societies, in terms of socioeconomic mobility as well as in terms of more mundane measures like GDP per capita. But this progress is limited and often painfully slow. Outsiders can do virtually nothing, and even insiders relatively little, to speed it up. But perhaps with greater understanding of the phenomenon and its mechanisms, and with the general opening of economies around the world, old sources of resistance will begin to crumble, and societies will experience opening in contexts that go beyond just financial markets and international trade.

7.6 World Market Forces Affecting National Income Distributions

The fundamental proposition of this chapter is that, within any modern market economy, the distribution of before-tax income is substantially determined by the relative scarcity and abundance of different factors of production, in relation to the demand for their services. One of its main themes has been that at any given moment in time, policymakers can adjust this distribution, but they cannot change its basic shape. On the expenditure side, government can act to make society more humane and civilized; on the tax side, it can distribute the burden of its expenditure according to reasonable canons of fairness. But when all is said and done, the distribution of income will still be fundamentally determined by the powerful forces of supply and demand.

This story can apply equally well in a relatively closed or a relatively open economy, but the latter can introduce special features, which I explore in this section. Economics has long lived with the so-called factor-price-equalization theorem. This theorem points out that under certain quite plausible circumstances, the mere fact of international trade in final products can lead to the equalization of the prices of productive factors across countries—something that one might expect to happen if the productive factors were able to migrate freely, but perhaps not otherwise.

Volumes have been written first pointing out and then trying to explain the fact that the tendency pointed out by the factor-price-equalization theorem did not seem to be revealed in the real world. In my judgment, the deepest answer to the riddle is that, historically, backward countries have used backward productive processes, and advanced countries have used advanced productive processes. Because of this, it may have taken twenty workers combining with $20,000 of capital to produce in Bangladesh or Haiti the same output produced by one worker combining with $20,000 of capital in Canada or Japan. Once this fact is recognized, it is easy to see how Canadian and Japanese workers can earn twenty times the wages of their Haitian or Bangladeshi counterparts. This sort of differentiation, based on differential efficiency of productive processes, has been one of the most profound explanations of international differences in the real wage rates of equivalently skilled (or unskilled) workers.

The problem—if we want to call it a problem—is that times are changing, and there are very strong tendencies for the productive processes of backward countries to be upgraded. When today we see Manhattan shirts from Thailand, Florsheim shoes from Brazil, and Hamilton-Beach mixers from Mexico, we can be quite sure that they were made under the close supervision of those companies' managers, using the most efficient techniques at their disposal. That is, the productive processes of many once-backward nations have been modernized. They have moved closer to the efficiency levels of the advanced countries.

I believe this is the main reason that real wages have been so stagnant in many of the advanced economies over the past ten to twenty-five years. Table 7.4 records some outstanding instances. The table data are certainly compatible with the idea of intensified competition from new sources of supply like Taiwan, Korea, Malaysia, Thailand, and now China and India, plus the modern assembly plants in Mexico and Central America.

It is important to note that the stagnation of real wages in the countries shown in table 7.4 did not mean at all that GDP was stagnating. In the

Table 7.4
Recent Cases of Real Wage Stagnation

Country	Beginning	Ending	Beginning[a]	Ending[a]	Length of period (in years)
Australia	1975	1990	99	100	25
Canada	1977	1993	100	101	16
Denmark	1976	1992	94	102	16
Netherlands	1976	1992	97	100	16
New Zealand	1964	1992	98	100	28
Sweden	1975	1993	100	97	18
United Kingdom	1975	1990	95	100	15
United States	1965	1993	100	98	28

Source: International Monetary Fund, *International Finance Statistics Yearbook, 1994* (Washington, D.C.). For each country, the real wage datum is the IFS wage series divided by the IFS consumer price series for the given year.
[a] 1990 = 100.

United States, for example, GDP more than doubled between 1965 and 1993, and population rose by about a third. Real income per capita rose at nearly 1.5 percent per annum. So it was not the U.S. economy that was stagnating, just the real wages of factory workers. Those with newly prized skills of computer programming and financial analysis fared much better over the same period. This situation helps to support my main point: that competition through international trade has narrowed real wage differentials in routine manufacturing-type jobs and is likely to continue to do so, thus affecting the income distributions we will see.

This heightened international competition will, I predict, keep real manufacturing wages from rising much in countries like the United States and Canada over the coming decades. It will also make it much harder for this type of real wage to rise in countries like Japan, Taiwan, and Korea and also in countries like Argentina, Chile, and Mexico.

These forces will inevitably have an impact on income distributions. I believe the most likely outcome is a further trend away from equality. If the capital factor becomes relatively scarce worldwide, so that real rates of return rise further, this trend toward increasing inequality will be strengthened. If real interest rates stay constant or fall, the trend will be somewhat weakened. But I believe the trend will continue to be present virtually worldwide, as an open world economy plus vastly increased mobility of capital-cum-technology give us a further demonstration of factor price equalization in action.

This pressure toward factor price equalization will clearly benefit people in countries like China, India, Indonesia, and Bangladesh, as modern factory methods vastly improve their productivity. These forces will also benefit consumers worldwide, who will continue to be able to find good shirts for ten to fifteen dollars, good shoes for less than forty dollars, good dresses for less than thirty dollars, and so forth (all at today's real value of the dollar). The same forces will also make it harder for the equilibrium real wage to rise in middle-income countries. I do not believe we will see many repeat performances of the type of happy miracle we saw in Taiwan or Spain or Brazil, where huge spurts of GDP growth led to notable rises in the wages of ordinary workers. Life in the early twenty-first century is going to be much tougher. It is not going to be easy for average Argentine or Chilean or Mexican factory workers to increase the relative advantage they now hold over, say, Thai, Chinese, and Indian workers. A lot of their benefit will come instead from their role as consumers of all the products whose real international prices are kept low, thanks to the efforts of those Thai, Chinese, and Indian laborers.

7.7 Summing Up

This is the place to try to put in perspective the various themes that I have treated. In my view, there is vast scope for policy improvement in most countries regardless of whether one's principal goal is economic growth or greater equity. Plenty can be done in both directions. Moreover, there is no substantial conflict between the two objectives, so long as one maintains a certain degree of realism about what are plausible, potentially feasible policy alternatives.

I have not emphasized—but only because I thought it so obvious—the degree to which improvements in education, public health, and medical care in general play genuinely positive roles in the process of economic growth. In most developing countries at least, there is great scope for policy actions in these fields, which will end up simultaneously promoting the causes of economic growth and social equity.

It is possible to consider improvement in education and health policies taking place and, in my view, improving equity, even if the overall Lorenz curve showing the income distribution of society remains substantially unchanged. It is also possible to consider expenditures that are focused on the very poor and have an impact on the overall distribution of benefits in the society. Such policies of targeting the lowest-income groups are one of the main vehicles for promoting greater equity and should be high on the list of intelligent, feasible ways of moving toward a more just and humane society.

But what does (or can) it mean to implement policies that focus on the very poor? It is easy to define and describe individual policies like medical clinics in poor neighborhoods or self-help housing programs to replace existing slums, but will that change the overall distributional picture in a society? The answer I have already suggested is that the expenditure side has a potentially greater impact on a society's distribution of income or benefits or measured welfare, but even this impact may be regarded by some as scant.

In the discussion of the expenditure side, I bring into consideration issues of political economy. In every society with which I am familiar, the poor lack political as well as economic power. For better or worse, I believe that policies that improve the status of the poor are more likely to come out of the decisions of those who have more political power than out of the poor themselves "taking command." Thinking along these basically evolutionary lines, I set up examples in which the perceived benefits of government outlays are equally distributed across the five quintiles of the income distribution. Some may respond "And you call this targeting?" To this, my retort is, quite definitely, yes, compared with where things stand today in just about every developing country in the world. The fact is that in most countries, the poor now receive much less than their per capita share of government outlays. It would be a major step to move even half the distance from where most countries are to a simple level of parity for the very poor. This is a sensible way for us, trying to look at realistic alternatives, to frame the problem.

I have emphasized that the tax system is not an appropriate vehicle for effectuating major shifts in the Lorenz curve. I show in table 7.2a that even a tax system that takes more than two-thirds of all taxes from the top quintile, with this amounting to 20 percent of total national income before tax, creates a distribution of after-tax income that is only moderately different from that of before-tax income. In my view, and thinking of relatively poor countries, we cannot classify the tax systems of table 7.2 as inequitable, even though their impact on the distribution of income is relatively modest.

This brings us to another important point. It does not make sense to think of the income distribution of a country as something the government can determine. Nor, what is much the same thing, should it be viewed as something for which the government should be held responsible. The income distribution at any moment is the product of the distribution of resource endowments at that moment (together with the existing pattern of demand) and is thus largely the product of history. A policy that today gives good educational opportunities to the children of the poor, aids them in their "escape from poverty," and fosters upward socioeconomic mobility in general may very well have a significant impact on the distribution of income twenty-five years hence, but not on the distribution of income today.

Once one manages to set aside the idea of government's "determining" the income distribution, one can look to other ways of conceptualizing its role. I like to think of society's deciding what tasks it assigns to government. These tasks may be larger or smaller; they may be more or less oriented to growth or equity. But in the end, there will be a series of tasks that society through its government takes on. The good society, in today's world, would include in these tasks the sort of targeted policies I have mentioned, as well as policies to improve mobility and aid in the escape from poverty. They would also include policies that directly promote economic growth, preserve ancient cultures, and safeguard the environment, among others.

When, through its decision-making processes, a society settles on a range of governmental tasks, there inevitably arises the question of paying the bill. In my view, the right way to think about taxes is to ask, How can this bill be fairly divided among us? It is in these terms that distributions of taxes like those of table 7.2a, and even of table 7.2b, can quite readily be thought of as meeting sensible standards of equity.

An incredible force has been already exerted by the spread of modern technology and management to countries with very low levels of real wages. This tendency has kept the real prices of manufactured products low, but it has had many other consequences, chief among them putting a powerful brake on the advance of real wages of typical factory workers, particularly in advanced countries. Table 7.4 gives eight significant cases of the outcome of this process (together with other forces that may have been at work). I see this wage pressure as continuing into the foreseeable future, with new factories in China, India, and Indonesia bringing unrelenting new competition into the markets for tradable goods. I believe that this will hold back the advance of real wages in the advanced countries, though not at all (necessarily) their growth processes. This represents an important exogenous force leading toward less equal income distributions in the advanced countries. The same pressures out of, say, China, India, and Indonesia will make it less easy for middle-income countries to gain market share in the world markets for tradable goods and, perhaps even more so, to enjoy rapid advances in real wages while doing so. Among the many exogenous forces operating to determine income distributions worldwide, the prospect of ever greater new supplies, coming from now-poor countries, is a relatively new and very important one.

Out of all of this there emerges a sort of existential view that governments cannot determine the fate of their societies, or their rate of growth, or their income distribution. But this does not mean that governments are powerless, nor does it free them from heavy moral responsibilities.

We know that governments possess almost unlimited potential to do harm. The great Latin American inflations are case studies in which bad monetary and fiscal policies brought misery to their countries. Table 7.1 records a little-known fact concerning these (and many other) great inflations: The economy grew more while disinflating than while inflating. I do not attribute this to any simplistic, mechanical connection, because I recognize that in all those cases the countries in question had bad economic policies "on the way up" (as the rate of inflation was rising), and significantly better policies "on the way down." Still, inflation by itself tends to inhibit economic efficiency and growth, predominantly through blurring people's perception of relative prices. When inflation is induced by government deficits financed at the banking system, it also crowds out productive investment, thus further deterring growth.

Other instances in which nations suffered disasters brought about in whole or in part by ill-conceived policies include numerous cases of what I have called the boom-and-bust syndrome. This is represented by major export booms on the one hand, or huge international borrowing sprees on the other, followed by vast suffering when adjustment eventually had to take place. Prudence in managing and containing the boom or the spree could have greatly reduced the degree of suffering that followed.

Finally, I mention populism as a portmanteau term for much of what is bad in economic policy. Populism is not to be equated with democracy, or with serving the people, or, at least now, with left-wing governments. Rather, it should be seen as thinking only of the present—of today's or tomorrow's benefits and not of next week's or next year's costs. It should be seen as doing what comes easily and avoiding hard decisions and choices. It should be seen as caving in to the demands of pressure groups rather than trying to mold and channel them productively, when not outright resisting them. One can find many real-world examples of populism thus defined, and to my knowledge, all of them have led to economic disaster.

If it avoids the temptations of populism, boom-and-bust, and inflation, what should a government do to carry out its responsibility? I reviewed two attempts (by John Williamson and myself) to summarize the converging views of policy professionals as to certain key norms appropriate for economic policy in developing countries. In this summary I can do no better than use Williamson's (1990) terse distillation: "macroeconomic prudence, outward orientation, and domestic liberalization" (p. 1).

I brought up four important innovations of tax policy of the past forty years or so: the value-added tax, the notion of a uniform (or more nearly uniform) structure of import tariffs, the idea of integrating corporation and personal income taxes, and the indexation of tax systems for inflation. My motive in introducing these topics was partly to bring my readers down to ground level in thinking about what are sensible and relevant options on the tax side of the fiscal policy equation. But this also provided the opportunity to comment on a number of specific matters that have special import for income distribution:

• It is possible to introduce a degree of progression in a value-added tax system, but its benefits have to be weighed against significant extra vulnerability to evasion, even if one fights back with higher-cost administrative efforts.

• Significant differentiation among rates of import tariffs can lead to huge economic inefficiencies by giving vastly different degrees of effective protection to different activities.

• Personal income tax rates above 50 percent are very hard to justify in the light of their efficiency and incentive costs.

• Labor is likely to bear the burden of any unilateral rise in the rate of tax on the income of corporations (or businesses in general) once an open economy setting is posited (this means that moves toward integration of the corporate and personal income taxes are likely to benefit labor).

• It is much easier to index a tax system than people think. By its nature, full indexation promotes both equity and efficiency; far from "inviting" more inflation, indexing—by reducing or eliminating the so-called Tanzi effect, by which inflation erodes real tax revenues and thus brings about even larger real deficits—actually helps to keep incipient inflations from exploding.

But when all is said and done, and even with what one might call quite heroic efforts to create an equitable tax system, one does not greatly modify the shape of the income distribution as one moves from before-tax to after-tax concepts. This is the point of table 7.2 and is a key pillar supporting the main line of thinking in this chapter.

Once one comes down to earth in a discussion of these topics, there are a great many things that governments can do to make their societies more just and equitable. Great challenges exist all through the developing world, to overcome the handicaps against which the poor must struggle. The great priorities for our time are these:

• Bringing to the poor the benefits of simple preventive public health programs, such as potable water, sewerage, insect control, and basic immunizations.

• Bringing the level of outlays per child on education for the poorest segments of the population much closer to the standard for the rest of society.

• In most countries, raising the level of educational effort in general and paying lots of attention to its quality as well as its quantity.

• Bringing at least elementary medical care to within close reach in poor towns and neighborhoods and providing ready access to more sophisticated medical treatment for the cases that warrant it.

• Dealing with problems of inadequate housing by offering programs with a substantial self-help component, thus providing modest housing to a broad client population—in contrast to many past programs that gave highly subsidized housing to a lucky few.

• Seeking ways to reinforce the mechanisms of on escape from poverty that have worked in the past. In each country this would start with efforts to ascertain what those mechanisms have been.

• Seeking ways to promote the opening of the upper strata of society to freer entry from below. Few modern visions of the good society will stand up if the doors to upward socioeconomic mobility are closed (or open only a crack).

This agenda is important, because it entails vast efforts, huge challenges, and overcoming enormous obstacles. Yet its budgetary costs are not so great that they could not readily be financed in many countries by diverting money from lower-priority uses. Where this is not likely to be the source of enough funds to do the job, it will probably be in countries like Guatemala and El Salvador, where taxes now take up less than 10 percent of GDP. In these cases, the tax take could be significantly raised without impinging seriously on economic growth or other objectives.

This is the basis on which I assert that if we stick with what is realistic and plausible, and if we attack sensibly and intelligently the problems of achieving greater equity while promoting economic growth, we will find no serious conflict between these objectives.

References

Harberger, Arnold. 1984. "Economic Policy and Economic Growth." In Arnold C. Harberger, ed., *World Economic Growth*, pp. 427–466. San Francisco: ICS Press.

Harberger, Arnold. 1995. "The ABCs of Corporation Tax Incidence: Insights into the Open-Economy Case." In *Tax Policy and Economic Growth*, pp. 51–73. Washington, D.C.: American Council for Capital Formation; Center for Policy Research.

Williamson, John. 1990. *Latin American Adjustment*. Washington, D.C.: Institute for International Economics.

Comments

Christian Morrisson

Economies, Fluctuations, Growth, and Equity

I agree with Harberger's analysis of the negative impact of inflation on growth and add a comment: Inflation also has a negative impact on income distribution or, more precisely, wealth distribution. The majority of urban poor have only cash assets; rich households possess mainly real assets and often invest part of their liquidity in foreign currency or abroad. As a result, poor households are proportionally much more affected by the erosion of the value of currencies through inflation. In this respect, a restrictive monetary policy reduces tax inflation and has a positive impact on wealth distribution. This process was demonstrated by the studies made by the OECD Development Centre's Adjustment and Equity project, which was completed in 1992.

On the other hand, even if "equity considerations do not conflict with the growth objective," we must qualify the assertion. Everybody knows examples of equitable growth, such as Taiwan in the 1960s and the 1970s. But contrary examples exist too. In some countries, growth performance coincided with high inequality or increasing inequality in the past (e.g., France or the United Kingdom from 1800 to 1870) and more recently (Brazil in the 1960s and the 1970s; Chile in the 1970s and the 1980s). So to ask if fiscal policy can have an impact on equity is a pertinent question. For example, enrollment rates in primary and secondary schools and education expenditures (as a percentage of GDP) were lower in Brazil and Thailand than in Taiwan (comparing these countries not for the same year but for the same per capita GDP).

Concerning the boom-and-bust syndrome, the nontradable sector benefits during a boom period from an improvement of the terms of trade between the tradable and nontradable sectors. The evolution of the internal terms of trade may increase inequality to the extent that average income in the nontradable sector is usually higher than income in the tradable sector. For example, in six of the seven countries in this sample (Cameroon, Hong Kong, Iran, Madagascar, Malaysia, Mexico, and Zambia), the average income is higher in the nontradable sector than in the tradable sector. We can also assume that part of the bonus that was not invested, as Harberger showed, was spent on public sector salaries or lavish public expenditure, benefiting the top quintile.

I agree with the picture of populism but propose to differentiate two stages in the process. During the first stage, politicians give subsidies (for bread or buses) and the wage increases they have promised. We can then observe a popular decrease in inequality between households. In the second stage, however, all the negative consequences of the populist strategy emerge. Finally, real incomes and real wages fall to a lower level than at the beginning, which explains the ensuing unpopularity of this policy package. Depending on whether priority is given to subsidies for poor households or to advantages for large bureaucracies, levels of inequality may rise or fall during this second stage.

An additional argument in favor of lower taxation of imports is that the trade protection worsens income distribution in developing countries. According to regression on a sample of twenty countries (Bourguignon and Morrison 1989), the income share of the bottom 40 percent of the population is on average three points lower in a highly protected economy, while the top 20 percent gains by the same amount. Because our objective is equitable economic growth, this income effect is an important advantage of trade liberalization, which must be taken into account.

Taxes, Public Expenditure, and Equitable Growth

Harberger's analysis of taxation is careful but nonetheless arouses comment. The conclusions on the relative impact of public expenditure and taxation are correct. My analysis of a sample of forty-three developing countries some time ago leads to the same conclusions. But two points require clarification. First, since government cannot tax income from capital (and as income tax in developing countries concerns only the top decile), value-added tax must be progressive. Two rates are needed: very low or zero for necessities and a standard rate for other items. Naturally, two rates involve additional costs, but these must be balanced against the disadvantage of regressive taxation, as the consumption-income ratio decreases with income. Second, a figure higher than twelve for taxes supported by the top quintile (table 7.2) is consistent with reality. For example, with a value-added tax of 20 percent on consumption equal to 50 and a 10 percent income tax, we can reach sixteen instead of only twelve.

Perhaps we could be less pessimistic concerning the targeting of public expenditures. One example will suffice as a demonstration. In Tunisia, the enrollment rate in primary schools is nearly 90 percent in both urban and rural zones, and grants to university students are given only to poor households; consultations for poor people in medical stations or public hospitals are free, whereas private physicians and clinics are for people who are less poor. Such a policy ensures benefits to the lowest quintiles equal to or higher than benefits to the top one.

Finally, two expenditure items seem decisive to obtain growth with equity. The first is expenditure on primary and secondary education. Enrollment rates in these schools always have a significant and positive coefficient for the income share of the poorest 40 or 60 percent. The second expenditure item is public expenditures in rural zones (mainly on infrastructure, technical assistance, and credits), to increase the labor productivity of agriculture. In regressions explaining the income share of the poorest 40 or 60 percent, the ratio of labor productivity in agriculture to labor productivity in the rest of the economy has a positive and significant coefficient.

Promoting Socioeconomic Mobility

The considerations Harberger expressed on socioeconomic mobility are very important. Nearly all controversies on inequality concern income distribution in one year, whereas there are very few studies on socioeconomic mobility in developing countries. I agree that this mobility can solve poverty problems in some respects. For this reason, it is necessary to scrutinize fiscal policy carefully in order to distinguish measures that promote mobility. Of course, primary and secondary education are an efficient factor of mobility, but there are other expenditures, like technical assistance and credits to craftsmen or infrastructure and assistance in rural zones. This means that if a government's fiscal policy is directed toward equity, it must be designed not in a yearly range but in a long-run perspective. Also, we must aim at equity (equal opportunities for everyone) more than equality.

Implications of Openness

Finally, I think that Harberger's conclusions on the world market affecting internal income distribution are correct. As the factor price equalization benefits factory workers, developing countries might be able to combine growth with decreasing inequality. Advanced countries, however, are likely to face more and more difficulties as the same process results in increasing inequality. In the future, this increase in inequality could be a real threat for the political and social stability in those countries.

Reference

Bourguignon, F., and C. Morrisson. 1989. *External Trade and Income Distribution.* Paris: OECD.

Comments

Lawrence Summers

Arnold Harberger's chapter is filled with insight and wisdom. The most important insight concerns maintaining an appropriate degree of humility regarding what governments and international organizations can and cannot accomplish with respect to the natural forces that shape economic life. Now that the cold war is over, it is worth noting just how many lives have been lost in efforts that had as their fundamental raison d'être the idea that governments can shape or ignore the power of natural economic forces. Such efforts have cost tens, if not hundreds, of millions of lives in this century. As people in international organizations mention "our countries" and as academic advisers use the term "we" to describe policies that are undertaken in places where they have spent only a week or two, it is well worth maintaining that sort of humility as we go forward.

Conceptions of Equity and the Equity Implications of Rent Seeking, Trade, and Targeting

My first observation is about conceptions of equity, a complicated notion to which traditional economists' conceptions do not always do full justice. Economists tend to view equity in terms of ultimate outcome. That sometimes contrasts with most other people's perceptions of equity, which have much more to do with notions of just and unjust acquisition. For example, most people feel very differently about billionaires who have built businesses by selling products successfully than they do about corporate raiders who buy privatized companies, only to flip them for enormous gains two years later. Similarly, a 1995 *New York Times* article that refers to Mexico's privatization efforts as a Mexican "garage sale" reminds us how important it is to keep most people's conception of equity considerations in mind as we design economic development programs. I am unsure how, as economists, we can address these issues more satisfactorily. Nonetheless, it is essential for such equity concerns to become a more central part of our thinking.

I also argue that this goal supports the worldview Harberger urged, one favoring less extensive government involvement in distributional issues. That is the case because it is fair to presume that explicit distributional choices made by government can often be perceived as unfair.

My second observation involves the question of rent seeking, latent in Harberger's chapter and stressed in all of Anne Krueger's work, as well as in chapter 9, by Alberto Alesina. In the classic model, one had the triangle and the rectangle, and the rectangle was dissipated seeking itself. If that were really true, rent seeking would have no inequitable consequences. The result would be simply resource dissipation.

The real world is more complicated. Large parts of rents are not in fact dissipated. They are transferred, and then they become the source of substantial inequity. We must therefore constantly consider this process of rent creation and the inequities that it engenders.

We must also bear in mind the difficulty of implementing reforms once rents have been created. My favorite example involves the proposals in the United States to repeal tax deductions for the three-martini lunch. The people who consume the three-martini lunch are not the chief lobbyists against such provisions; rather, the chief lobbyists are the restaurateurs who provide these lunches. In a sense, they have a point. Restaurants are not an especially profitable industry. Once the rent is introduced, it is then necessarily inequitable to remove that rent. That is why we must be extremely cautious about creating such entitlements.

My third observation involves trade, and the link between trade and wages. I used to marvel over the willingness of policymakers with no knowledge of the relevant analytical models to speak about complicated subjects. I am about to do so, so my remarks on this subject are prejudices rather than analysis. I believe that Harberger is right when he asserts that the important point about the changing trade relations between developing and industrialized countries is neither that there has been a reduction in trade barriers, nor that there is all that much physical capital going from the industrialized countries to the developing countries. The significant change, rather, is that the production function in developing countries is evolving and catching up with the production function in developed countries.

On the other hand, I suspect that Harberger is wrong in asserting that this is a major factor shaping income distributions in industrialized countries, despite the a priori appeal of that argument. I disagree because I think that such a change in the developing world is just too small a tail to wag too big a dog. If one looks at the fraction of imports into the United States that come from developing countries, it is not that large—on the order of 3 percent of GDP, depending on how one measures it. True, a certain amount of economic activity competes very directly with that. Nonetheless, the proportion is small. Moreover, the fraction of U.S. imports that come from countries in which wages are less than 50 percent of U.S. wages has increased remarkably little over the past twenty-five years. In 1970, Japan was such a country. For all of these reasons, I find it difficult to see how so small a move could account for the kinds of seismic changes in income distribution that we have seen.

One of Harberger's points may have verged on error. In his discussion of what has happened to factory workers as distinct from the rest of the population, he may have ignored the point he made with respect to the corporate income tax: that wages in one sector must equalize with wages in another, because people are not born as factory workers. If there are some natural processes of wage equalization, then the tremendous improvements in service sector productivity should benefit workers in all sectors.

Harberger's idea regarding factory workers is very tricky. It is exceedingly politically incorrect for economists to think what he is asserting because the next question is, If trade really is shaping the income distribution the way Harberger suggests, then why not have protection?

I suspect that more intellectual energy goes into debunking these arguments than may be warranted. There is almost certainly an effect that works in the direction that Harberger talks about. However, I suspect it is not nearly as important as the changing technology of production, which is difficult to measure, and the fact that we have an increasingly competitive, efficient world that probably means that a whole set of mechanisms now exist to drive wages equal to widely dispersed marginal productivities. I think, for example, about the fact that the wages of academic economists are now much more dispersed than they were a generation ago. That is almost certainly due to the fact that academic economists are more willing to move and that more entrepreneurial universities are more prepared to pay for the professors they want. I suspect that kind of mechanism is more pervasive as an explanation for widening inequality than the change in international trade.

My fourth observation concerns targeting. Any discussion of targeting must take into account the need to maintain political support. I have heard it said that programs for poor people are poor programs. I am all for targeting, but I am humbled by the knowledge that one of the United States's most successful social achievements has been the elimination of poverty among the aged. That task has been accomplished through our principal nontargeted program. One must therefore question how successfully programs that are too well targeted can be maintained and whether there is not some case to be made for adopting principles of universality. That may be the most politically viable way to benefit the poor. Perhaps Harberger's emphasis on universal primary education and setting a goal of getting the bottom fifth—a fifth of the resources—is actually consistent with that notion.

Possible Fragility of a Consensus View

In reading this book, I am struck by the degree of consensus: We all seem to agree on what the right model is for going forward. I hope that we are right, and believe that we are, but there have been similar consensuses in the past, all based on careful evaluation of evidence. And yet just at the moment when everybody thought the consensus model correct, events typically proved the consensus view wrong. So I do have some nagging doubts. Recall that there was a time when there was an equal degree of agreement on the wisdom of import substitution strategies or the importance of national industrial development banks. It is worth remembering these former consensus views as we proceed confidently forth. Nonetheless, I cannot think of anything else that I have read that offers as much insight, and as much wisdom for further progress, as Harberger's chapter.

External Sector and Income Distribution

Jagdish Bhagwati

The question of income distribution has never been distant from the concerns of economists preoccupied by the problems of development from the earliest postwar years. Indeed, there is nothing to the fashionable assertion that poverty and income distribution are novel concerns.

I had personal experience of this ignorance and the moral arrogance based thereon when I was the keynote speaker at the twenty-fifth anniversary of the Institute for Development Economics in Antwerp. When I had finished, a Dutch Social Democrat economist-cum-politician sarcastically remarked from the floor that it was "good to see Professor Bhagwati, long the champion of growth, finally talking about poverty." I could not help shooting back, "As it happens, I was looking at my 1966 paperback, *The Economics of Underdeveloped Countries* (London: Weidenfeld and Nicolson) last week, in view of my speech today, thinking back on how Professor John Chipman had written to me that an economist colleague of his at Minnesota had remarked with astonishment to him that I had just published a book with the photograph of a starving child in it. Having heard the complaints of people like you, I feared nonetheless that my chapter 1 would be entitled 'Growth.' Imagine my surprise when I found the title to be: 'Poverty and Income Distribution!'"

I retell this story not merely to show the lack of connectedness to facts that some economists on the left exhibit in this policy area, but also because of the sweeping charge made that anyone who talks about efficiency and growth must somehow be soulless in his or her disregard for poverty.[1] In fact, our thinking in the policy circles in India during the early 1960s was precisely focused on the amelioration of poverty and built after much reflection on the view that (given the enormity of the problem and the inability of redistribution to solve it, even on a one-shot basis) growth, by providing gainful employment to the rural poor, was the only way to make a sustained long-run attack on poverty. Indeed, we felt that far from being a passive trickle-down strategy, growth was an activist "pull-up" strategy. It was thus an indirect antipoverty strategy. The so-called antipoverty programs could be regarded as constituting a direct antipoverty strategy (whose governmental financing, in fact, could not even be sustained if growth of income, and hence of tax revenues, were to stagnate).[2] The optimal strategy for attacking poverty must then consist of exploiting these two alternative strategies in a suitable mix.

Although this optimal mix is hard to determine since the answer must reflect knowledge of several elusive relationships, one ought to be able to assert that *within* each of the two component strategies, the policymaker must try to achieve the maximum rate of return. The policy reforms that have now swept across the developing countries can be seen in that light as replacing the old, unproductive, even counterproductive, policy framework with a new policy framework that is likely to produce improved efficiency, growth, and hence the precondition for a sustained improvement in living standards and the amelioration of poverty.

A critical component of that new framework (naturally called, in Washington, the "Washington consensus") is a more dramatic integration of one's economy into the world economy.[3] There is also a considerable conversion to this view by policymakers in the developing countries. In this chapter I address this external component of the consensus, probing its rationale, keeping centrally in view the questions of poverty and income distribution as areas of concern. I focus mainly on trade and direct investment, while touching briefly on other aspects of the external sector, such as migration questions.

8.1   Attitudes to Integration in the World Economy: An Ironic Reversal

Since I propose to consider the efficiency implications of the integration of the world's nations into the world economy and set the distributional questions within that context, I begin with the observation that the phenomenon of increased trade and investment flows, as countries increasingly exploit the external sector, presents opportunities for gains, while simultaneously creating fears that present obstacles to the exploitation of these opportunities.

Economists are generally likely to see the increasingly interdependent world, with its growing exchange of goods and services and flows of funds to where the returns are expected to be higher, as one that is gaining in prosperity as it is exploiting the opportunities to trade and to invest that have been provided by the postwar dismantling of trade barriers and obstacles to investment flows. This is the conventional mutual-gain or non-zero-sum-game view of the situation. It is also the appropriate one. And indeed many developing countries that were skeptical about, and even hostile to, this *benign-impact* view of the interaction between themselves and the world economy at the beginning of the postwar period, and through much of it, have now embraced it.

But there is an irony.[4] Where the developing countries (the South) were skeptical of the benign-impact view and the developed countries (the North) were confident of it, today the situation is reversed. Indeed, our concerns today are with the skepticism, even hostility, that is found in influential groups within the developed countries regarding the notion of integration into the world economy through trade, investment, and migration; the developing countries, on the other hand, are relatively free from such skepticism and hostility.

In the 1950s and 1960s, the South generally subscribed not to the liberal, mutual-gain, benign-impact view but to *malign-neglect* and even *malign-intent* views of trade and investment interactions with the world economy.[5] It was feared that integration into the world economy would lead to disintegration of the domestic economy. The malign-neglect view is manifest most clearly in the famous *dependencia* theory that President Cardoso of Brazil formulated in his radical youth as Latin America's foremost sociologist; the malign-impact view was most vividly embodied in the concept and theory of neocolonialism.

Trade thus had to be protected. The inward-oriented, import-substituting (IS) strategy was the order of the day almost everywhere. Only the Far Eastern economies, starting mainly in the early 1960s, shifted dramatically to an outward-oriented policy posture. The results, attributable principally to this contrast in orientation to the world economy but partly also to initial advantages such as inherited land reforms and high literacy rates, were to produce the most remarkable growth experiences of this century. At the time, however, the developing countries were certainly in an inward, cautious mode about embracing the world economy. By contrast, the developed countries, the North, moved steadily forward with dismantling trade barriers through the General Agreement on Tariffs and Trade (GATT) Rounds and with firm commitment to multilateralism as well, subscribing essentially to the principles of multilateral free trade and freer investment flows as the central guiding principles for a liberal international economic order that would ensure economic prosperity for all participating nations.[6]

Today the situation is almost reversed. The fears of integration into the world economy are being heard, but not from the developing countries, which see great good from it as they have extensively undertaken what the GATT has called "autonomous" reductions in their trade barriers, that is, unilateral reductions outside the GATT context of reciprocal reductions. Of course, not all of these reductions, and increased openness to inward direct foreign investment (DFI), have resulted from changed convictions in favor of the liberal international economic order and its benefits to oneself, though the failure of policies based on the old pro-inward-orientation views and the contrasting success of the Far Eastern countries following the pro-outward-orientation views have certainly played an important role, especially in Latin America and Asia. But some measure of the shift must also be ascribed to necessity resulting from the conditionality imposed by the World Bank and, at times, by the IMF as several debt-crisis-afflicted countries flocked to these institutions for support in the 1980s, and equally from their own perceived need to restore their external viability by liberal domestic and international policies designed to reassure and attract DFI.

If the South has moved to regard integration into the world economy as an opportunity rather than a peril, it is the North that is now fearful. In particular, the fear has grown, after the experience with the decline in the real wages of the unskilled in the United States and with their employment in Europe in the late 1970s and through the 1980s and beyond, that by trading with the South, with its abundance of unskilled labor, the North will find its own unskilled at risk.[7] The demand for protection that follows is then not the old and defunct "pauper-labor" argument, which asserted falsely that trade between the South and the North could not be beneficial. Rather, it is the theoretically more defensible income distributional argument that trade with countries with paupers will produce paupers in our midst, that trade with the poor countries will produce more poor at home.

If trade clearly exhibits the ironic reversal that I have observed, this is the case also with DFI. In the 1950s and 1960s, the developing countries were as fearful of inward DFI as they were of free trade. The fears were of predation, both political and economic. Regulation of DFI—both its volume and certainly its sectoral composition—was the order of the day.[8]

The viewpoint of the developed countries was ideologically at the other end of the spectrum, with a few notable exceptions: Canada, which viewed itself as a Southern country to the North of its neighbor, the colossal United States, and France, where Servan-Schreiber got a whole generation to worry about the "American challenge," that is, the influx of U.S. multinationals and their threat to the future of what we now call "national champions."

Today the role is reversed again. The developing countries are in fierce competition to attract DFI, indulging in what can only be described as a race to the bottom in offering giveaway advantages to the multinationals and reaching inferior Nash equilibria. The many developing countries that have belatedly become participants in this game can be found at the annual World Economic Forum in Davos, where second-tier politicians and CEOs from the developed countries gather together with top-tier politicians and business executives of these latecomers in the shared hope of making contacts and striking deals. Few influential voices can be heard against inward DFI in these countries today.

But voices against outward DFI, as against trade, can be heard from the unions and from the likes of Ross Perot in the developed countries today. "Our jobs will go abroad" is the refrain, and the fear. There is also a fear that the threat to take factories abroad weakens the bargaining position of labor and depresses wages, compounding the adverse effect of globalization on workers and on income distribution.

A similar role reversal can be found on issues of international migration. In the 1950s and 1960s, the developing countries were seized with the issue of the brain drain. Indeed, there developed a massive theoretical literature on the phenomenon and on policy solutions to the problems it was feared to pose.[9] Today the developing countries see the out-migration of their skilled workers as an opportunity to be sought for their nationals, using in effect a diaspora model rather than the brain drain models to think about the phenomenon. For the unskilled, out-migration is seen even more directly as an opportunity.

By contrast, the developed countries are now in ferment over the "threat" of immigrant inflows, especially as borders are increasingly becoming more porous to unskilled illegal immigrants. This fear, common to both the European Union (EU) and the United States, contrasts with the general shortage of unskilled labor that led to the extensive reliance on guest workers until the mid-1970s in the EU and the generally relaxed attitude of the United States toward illegal immigration until the 1980s.

Again, despite the rhetoric of trade in services and the sentiments built into the General Agreement on Trade and Services (GATS) agreement at the World Trade Organization (WTO), the developed countries are not about to open their borders to significant inflows of temporary suppliers of medical and other "skilled-labor" services.[10] Entry-restricting devices, such as qualifying examinations by the professional associations before entry is allowed by immigration authorities, can be counted on to restrict the trade in such skilled services in the foreseeable future.[11]

8.2   Trade, DFI, and Income Distribution: The Developing Countries

Against this background, I now consider in depth the question of the effect of trade and DFI on developing countries, as discussed fearfully in the 1950s and 1960s, and the optimistic thinking that has developed on these matters in the light of subsequent experience. Then I will consider the fearful concerns that have arisen now in the developed countries in regard to trade and DFI on wages and jobs, suggesting that these fears are misplaced and need to be surmounted if current theoretical and empirical analysis is a guide.

The Indirect Effect: Trade

Did the export-promoting (EP) regime, relative to the IS regime, create a superior growth performance, thus aiding in the pull-up effect on poverty and income distribution? A backward glance at the earliest analyses of this question is invaluable.

In particular, the static efficiency effects of the two regimes were the focus of the famous Organization for Economic Cooperation and Development (OECD) Development Center project directed by Little, Scitovsky, and Scott (LSS) in the late 1960s, of which the Bhagwati and Desai (1970) volume on India was a major case study.

When Bhagwati and Desai (1970) came out, documenting the allocative inefficiency of India's IS regime in various ways, including the painstaking and detailed institutional documentation and analysis of the senseless "criteria" used by the Indian Tariff Commission to give tariff protection and used by the import and industrial licensing authorities to allocate scarce licenses to activities targeted for capacity creation and utilization, the IS proponents attacked it on the same ground as the LSS synthesis study was faulted: It was "static" and did not address "dynamic" factors, such as the effect of these alternative regimes on growth rates, and, indeed, on the components of growth, such as savings rates, investment rates, X-efficiency and technical innovation, and entrepreneurship.

A principal objective of the Bhagwati and Krueger National Bureau of Economic Research (NBER) project that followed—with some countries (such as India, on which I collaborated with T. N. Srinivasan) overlapping with the LSS project—was, therefore, to address these growth issues, and indeed Bhagwati and Srinivasan (1975) on India, and my own synthesis volume (Bhagwati 1978), did address all of these questions. Thus, part 4 (with five chapters) of Bhagwati and Srinivasan was entirely devoted to growth effects, with chapter 15 devoted to investment, innovation, and growth and chapter 16 to savings and the foreign trade regime. So were many chapters in Bhagwati (1978).

The main substance of the detailed arguments, both theoretical and empirical, in these growth-related analyses was twofold. First, the argument that the IS strategy possessed some key dynamic advantages over the EP strategy that would outweigh the static losses documented in the LSS project was implausible, to say the least, and, second, the relationships between trade strategy and the gray-area subjects like savings, entrepreneurship, and technical change were theoretically tenuous in any event.

Of course, the opposite argument that the EP strategy is necessarily Pareto superior to the IS strategy on each of these different dynamic dimensions is equally difficult to sustain as a general proposition. I did worry therefore (Bhagwati 1978) as to why, despite this lack of strong theory and evidence of linkage between EP strategy and each component of growth, the association of the EP strategy, when credibly sustained, with faster growth rates of both exports and income in the countries being studied in Bhagwati and Krueger project seemed to emerge nonetheless.

Before I discuss this further, let me note that in their excellent review of the existing empirical knowledge about the effects of alternative trade strategies on growth, Ann Harrison and Ana Revenga (1995) cite a number of conflicting cross-sectional studies across many countries, suggesting that the overall benefits of the EP strategy for growth may also be unwarranted. This does not surprise me. These types of regressions across numerous countries, which have come into general usage at the World Bank and by some developmental economists, do not make much sense; there are many differences among countries that cannot be understood and accounted for in such exercises. That the results of these exercises go in different directions is hardly a matter for surprise. I would expect virtually anything to come out of this type of analysis, cynically approving results that go my way and rejecting those that do not.[12]

I favor the approach underlying the LSS and Bhagwati and Krueger projects, where detailed analytical studies of the experience of selected countries over time are undertaken in great depth. When this is done, the

relevance of specific and critical factors becomes clear, such as whether the
EP strategy was sustained and credible, whether the other strategic decisions implied different intertemporal choices so that growth rates could
not be compared as if they were exponential,[13] and so on, and then one
can adjust for these complexities to make inferences. This does not rule
out regressions across countries, but these regressions are the tip of
the iceberg where there is much sophisticated analysis of the economy
of each country in the regression prior to formulating an appropriate
regression. When this was done in the Bhagwati and Krueger project, the
results did seem to suggest that the EP strategy was more productive of a
stronger growth of exports and income. Why?

I thought that the observed EP strategy, for many endemic reasons
spelled out in Bhagwati (1978), had fewer distortions in terms of the difference between the effective exchange rates for exports and imports (respectively, EERx and EERm) and in terms of the variance among different
EERm's as well. Thus, the EP strategy seemed to imply a modest bias
in favor of exports, while typically the IS strategy seemed to carry the
bias against exports to excessive degrees, whereas the variance of EERs
among different activities was generally higher in the IS regimes than in
the EP regimes. These two phenomena would imply allocative inefficiency
in the use of resources. If one then had no mitigating offset in the matters
of, say, savings rates—as in the second-best Galenson-Leibenstein-Bator-
Dobb-Sen analyses of choice of techniques where static efficiency is sacrificed to increase the savings rate that cannot be adjusted as desired by
using fiscal policy—or innovation, then growth rates would also increase.
In terms of the Harrod-Domar model, any permanent change of efficiency
that reduces the marginal capital-output ratio, v, will increase the growth
rate (s/v) as well, given the choice of the average savings ratio, s.[14]

I speculated also about various ways in which the enhanced export
performance, more readily explained under the EP strategy, itself might
be directly associated with, indeed lead to, improved growth performance
(Bhagwati 1978, chap. 8). Here I considered the question of increased
X-efficiency and exploitation of scale economies, on both of which I
argued that there was little empirical evidence that increased exports
were associated with greater X-efficiency or greater exploitation of scale
economies.[15]

I also advanced the hypothesis that since EP regimes must be effectively built on macrostability, the increased exports went with moderate
inflation and the absence of the serious overvaluation of the exchange rate

that created the bias against exports. But this macrostability itself is conducive to greater growth. Hence, the association of exports with growth may reflect the underlying macrostability that produces both, rather than a causal relationship between the two phenomena.

Subsequent reflection, especially on the contrasting performance of India, which remained long wedded to IS, and of the Far Eastern "Little Japans," the original "Four Tigers," (Hong Kong, Taiwan, South Korea, and Singapore—also known as East Asia) has convinced me that an important ingredient of the latter countries' success was the fact that the EP strategy, by integrating these countries more effectively and profitably into the expanding world economy, enabled these countries to raise the marginal efficiency of capital and, hence, increased the inducement to invest and, therefore, private investment rates, to the phenomenal levels that everyone has commented on, with private savings then raised as well to take advantage of these investment opportunities. Equally, the expanded export earnings enabled these countries to increase imports of capital goods embodying new technologies, which became the physical counterpart of the increased investment rates. But the cost of these capital goods was well below their social marginal product to the Four Tigers because their prices are determined in world markets and just-less-than-the-latest vintage machines can be obtained, like secondhand goods, internationally at bargain prices. Besides, given their lack of intellectual property protection, the cost in many cases must have been the cost simply of learning to reverse-engineer and use the technology.[16]

Thus, both India and the Far Eastern countries began in the 1950s with an IS strategy, with governmental expenditures on infrastructure providing the necessary infrastructure for private investment and the assurance and spur to move toward a "superior" Rosenstein-Rodan equilibrium. This creation of the inducement to invest, which all shared, could not be a continuing inducement. The Far Eastern economies shifted to the external sector for maintaining and strengthening the inducement to invest. By contrast, India parted ways and turned to an IS strategy, which then constrained its investment incentives to the domestic markets at the margin. Thus, the Indian economists were talking about the investment in industry being constrained by the growth of agriculture and the resulting growth of demand, whereas the Far Eastern economies with their EP strategy never looked back. Equally, the Indian IS strategy meant a reduced, greatly diminished, absorption of foreign technology. India's inward-looking IS strategy then cost it both accumulation and technology, the two sources of rapid growth.[17]

The Direct Effect: Trade

Leaving aside the issue of the effect of the EP strategy on growth and, hence, indirectly on reducing poverty over time, we may ask whether the EP strategy would not also improve the real wages of the poor directly.

If the EP strategy shifts the allocative structure to labor-intensive goods, then we know from the Stolper-Samuelson argument that this would improve the real wages of labor under well-defined conditions.[18] The question then posed by the opponents of the IS strategy, after the LSS and Bhagwati and Krueger projects had examined the static and dynamic efficiency aspects of the IS and EP strategies, was whether the factor endowments, production, and trade structures of the developing countries were likely to be such as to support the contention that the IS strategy, even if inferior on these grounds, had immediate income distributional advantages. To analyze this in the mammoth-project fashion, Anne Krueger developed yet another ten-country NBER project, which focused on two questions: What were the relative factor intensities of their exportables and importables, and Would protection encourage a shift toward capital-intensive production? The answers given were that EP strategy should shift the trade and production structure toward labor-intensive goods, establishing a presumption in favor of, rather than against, the EP's favorable effects on income distribution. Harrison and Revenga (1995) have complained, however, that the project did not actually go on to establish empirically that such a shift did occur in the countries as they made the transition from IS to EP strategies. Nonetheless, given the findings of Krueger and her colleagues, it seems fair to conclude, at minimum, that a strong case that IS would improve income distribution toward labor seems hardly supportable.[19]

DFI

The view taken in my analysis of the different trade strategies was that DFI was as good or bad as a country's own policies. If the EP strategy was being followed, it would get more out of the incoming export-oriented DFI than if the DFI was coming in simply to exploit the protected IS-strategy home market.[20] I further hypothesized that, ceteris paribus, the inflow would be limited by the size of the home market in IS-strategy countries, whereas it would be greater in EP-strategy countries where it aimed at world markets.

Both of these so-called Bhagwati hypotheses have been run through cross-country regressions (Balasubramanyam and Salisu 1991; Balasubramanyam, Salisu, and Sapsford 1996), with encouraging results. Harrison and Revenga (1995) also report tentative support for this type of finding in their ongoing research. The results are what one would expect from the theoretical arguments, so they may be taken as consonant with the theory rather than as proof of it in view of the caveats I have already expressed concerning such cross-country regressions.

8.3 Trade, DFI, Real Wages of Unskilled Labor, and Unemployment: Developed Countries

It is no secret that the developed countries are now preoccupied with the question of the impact of trade and (outward) DFI on the real wages and employment of their unskilled. Indeed, the haunting fear of the unions and many policymakers is that international trade is a principal source of the pressures that translate into wage decline or unemployment of the unskilled.[21] As Bhagwati and Dehejia (1994) put it: "Is Marx Striking Again?" Perhaps we should have added: "With the Aid of Samuelson," since the principal reason to think that trade may be harming real wages of the unskilled is the early postwar work of Paul Samuelson on factor price equalization and, more directly, on the Stolper-Samuelson theorem that bears immediately on the issue at hand.[22]

I have examined the question of trade explanations at great length (Bhagwati and Dehejia 1994), and the issue has been extensively treated in Bhagwati and Kosters (1994). My conclusion is that the trade explanation is exceptionally weak for the 1980s, that there are good theoretical and empirical reasons that trade did not cause the adverse impact one might fear, and that the case for the overwhelming role of technical change (biased against the use of unskilled labor) in explaining the misfortune of the unskilled is very strong, indirectly and directly.

Here I recapitulate, elaborate, and evaluate the main linkages that have now been advanced between trade and real wages, extending the argumentation well beyond that in Bhagwati and Dehejia (1994), finished in mid-1993, in the light of further empirical research and theoretical reflections that have emerged since then.[23]

Clarifications and Caveats
As Deardorff and Hakura (1994) have pointed out, it is necessary to be clear about the theoretical question that one is asking. In particular, I note two different questions, of which the first is the one that I address in this chapter.

Question 1: Will the freeing of trade, or an exogenous change abroad (resulting in a shift in the foreign offer curve), adversely affect the real wages of our unskilled? The empirical counterpart of this question is whether this happened during the 1980s and through the 1990s to date.

Question 2: If domestic technical change is driving down the real wages of our unskilled, would the adverse effect on real wages be dampened or amplified if the economy were characterized by free trade rather than by protection?

It is clear that the former is the policy question that we are asking today. The question during the debate over the North American Free Trade Agreement was whether freer trade with Mexico would adversely affect the wages of the unskilled in the United States. When we look at the 1980s experience, again we seek to know whether the endogenous factors affecting the emergence of developing countries in world trade, with or without rich-country liberalization, have done damage to the real wages of the unskilled in these rich countries. In both cases, the intermediating mechanism has to be a decline in the relative prices of the unskilled-labor-intensive importables, which would lead to the decline in the real wages of the unskilled that was observed in the 1980s.

We would thus have an explicit or implicit model that gives what we must look for, exactly as we must get the reduced form we test from a model if it is to have any plausibility or even economic meaningfulness. Without this, we will see that we may be drawing unwarranted (even if objectively correct) conclusions.

This appears to me to be especially the case with arguments in the United States such as that the trade deficit in the 1980s had an impact on real wages because of a good correlation between its size and the real wage decline. But this tells us nothing convincing, because it is possible for an inward or outward transfer (a trade deficit or surplus) to have no impact at all on the terms of trade and, hence, no impact on real wages.[24] (Figure 8.1 shows this straightforward argument in the conventional, static, general equilibrium framework.)[25] A key part of the argument would have to be an intermediating effect on goods prices in the required direction.

Indeed, as Deardorff and Hakura (1994) point out, the problem with many of the empirical studies of the relationship between trade and wages, including the most cited ones, is that the relationships estimated have not been grounded in well-specified models whose validity is tested as it should be. Thus, the factor-content calculations for the United States,

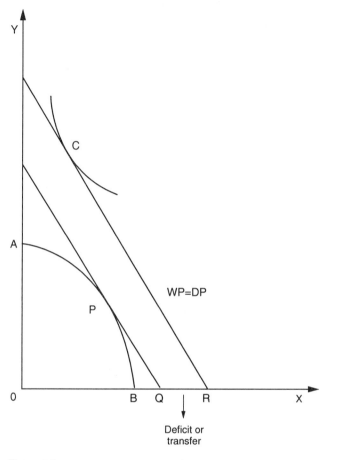

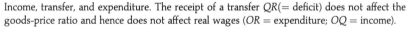

Figure 8.1
Income, transfer, and expenditure. The receipt of a transfer $QR(=$ deficit) does not affect the goods-price ratio and hence does not affect real wages (OR = expenditure; OQ = income).

which were held to show the adverse impact, were not undertaken in the context of an analysis that would have enabled the investigators to see immediately that they should also test to see whether the goods prices behaved in the manner required by their inference. Hence, I agree with these authors that the empirical studies are often tantalizing but lead to no compelling conclusions.[26]

I now distinguish among several theoretical approaches that can be taken to the problem, several to be found in the literature to date, probing them in some depth from the analytical viewpoint and in regard to their consonance with the facts as I see them.

The Stolper-Samuelson Explanation In this section, I consider the principal approach that *the prices of unskilled-labor-intensive goods have fallen and caused the real wages of unskilled labor to fall in turn—an economy-wide, North-South (Stolper-Samuelson) explanation.* A favorite explanation has been that trade with the South (poor countries), as a result of their enlarged presence in world markets and their freeing of trade barriers, has led to the fall in the real wages of unskilled labor in the North.

Goods Prices and Factor Prices This argument requires, at the outset, that the prices of the goods using unskilled labor should have fallen too, as I first noted in 1990 when encountering Borjas, Freeman, Katz (1992). These authors argued that trade was the cause of the decline in real wages, but did not examine the behavior of goods prices (see the detailed critique in Bhagwati 1991b, 1991c, 1994b; Bhagwati and Dehejia 1994).

Thus, in general equilibrium we have, in figure 8.2, the familiar Samuelson relationship between goods prices (P_x/P_y) and factor prices or the wage differential (W_u/W_s) in the right quadrant, and the Stolper-Samuelson relationship between the good prices and the real wage of unskilled labor in the left quadrant (assuming, as explained below, that the economy is incompletely specialized in production). Evidently, then, the real wage of the unskilled cannot fall unless the relative price of good Y, which is intensively using unskilled labor, has fallen. This analytical necessity has nothing to do with what happens to quantities (of, for example, imports, production, and consumption).

Having then examined the terms of trade data for U.S. exports and imports of manufactures and finding that they showed a slight rise in the relative prices of imports, I conjectured that the goods prices had actually gone the other way from that required by their conclusion (Bhagwati 1991a). Evidently the much-cited Borjas, Freeman, and Katz study was flawed, not merely in its methodology but, I feared, also in its conclusion linking real wage decline to trade (in the Stolper-Samuelson fashion).

The detailed empirical investigation by Lawrence and Slaughter (1993) (which followed Bhagwati 1991a, 1991b) did confirm my conjecture for the United States. Subsequently Sachs and Schatz (1994) appeared to overturn the Lawrence-Slaughter findings. But they rely on removing from the data set the prices of computers whose prices have fallen substantially. And even then the regression based on the new data set yields a coefficient of the required sign that is both very small and statistically insignificant.[27] The Sachs-Schatz regression cannot be accepted by serious scholars and the Bhagwati-Lawrence-Slaughter empirical findings remain unscathed.

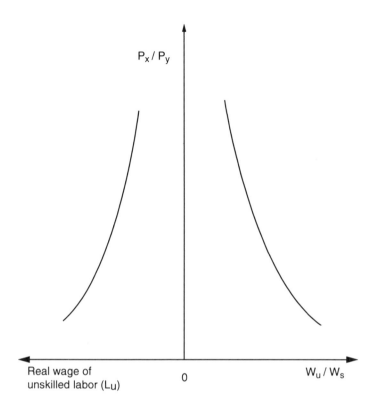

Figure 8.2
Goods prices and wage differential. The figure assumes that good X is skilled-labor intensive, while good Y is unskilled-labor intensive. The real wage of unskilled labor is drawn on the Stolper-Samuelson assumption of incomplete specialization in production. $W_u W_s$ is the ratio of unskilled to skilled labor wages.

Lawrence (1994) notes this and also reports that the goods price be-havior in Germany and Japan, with and without computers, does not sup-port the trade explanation either. Nor do the shifts in factor ratios support the explanation for the U.S. data, according to Lawrence and others.

In short, the necessary empirical evidence on price behavior during the 1980s for the absolutely critical element in this particular trade explana-tion is exceptionally weak at best. Perhaps this conclusion will be over-turned by further work, but as of now it seems to have survived scrutiny. Even the further empirical work on estimating goods prices for the United States by Leamer (1995) confirms that the 1980s were not characterized by the required behavior to get the Stolper-Samuelson argument off the ground.

Goods Prices and Real Wages As noted in Bhagwati and Dehejia (1994), even if the goods prices were behaving as required, the conclusion that the result would be a decline in the real wages of unskilled labor requires added assumptions familiar to the students of the Stolper-Samuelson theorem, many of which can be violated in the real world. I recount some of the main arguments that are pertinent here, recalling that the core Stolper-Samuelson theorem, in its simplest 2×2 version, says that the real wage of the factor employed intensively in the good whose price has fallen will also fall unequivocally, while the other factor's real wage will rise unequivocally.

This core proposition (as also the factor-price-equalization theorem, which requires a unique relationship between goods and factor prices to deduce factor price equalization from goods price equalization) fails as soon as you get complete specialization (nondiversification); both factors will improve their real wages as goods prices change further, lifting both boats instead of sinking one as the other symmetrically rises. The goods prices may change sufficiently so as to have the "lifting-all-boats" effect outweigh the redistributive effect embodied in the Stolper-Samuelson argument, leaving both factors better off than before, that is, even when the price of unskilled-labor-intensive imports has declined (as it appears not to have during the 1980s), the real wage of unskilled labor could have improved (if the goods price change was substantial enough to produce the nondiversification and a large enough lifting-all-boats effect).

To see this, consider figures 8.3 and 8.4, the real wage of L_u, the unskilled labor (in terms of a mix of both goods, apparel and machinery), is mapped out in these matching figures for different goods-price ratios P_m/P_a, given the supply of unskilled and skilled labor as follows.

First, under autarky, vary P_m/P_a from D to C, for incomplete specialization. The real wage of L_u then falls unambiguously from D to C as P_m/P_a rises. Q is the equilibrium production point, given the demand, as depicted.

Since, under autarky, production must equal consumption, the range DC defines all the real-wage variations that are possible under autarky. So as depicted in figure 8.4, $EDQCR$ is the dotted curve linking real wage of L_u to goods-price ratios under autarky. The real wage does not change as you vary P_m/P_a at C and D.

Under free trade, production is no longer equal to consumption. Therefore, it is possible to specialize in production at D and C and to trade from there at P_m/P_a below DS and above CV, respectively. Correspondingly, the real wage will now improve for (both factors and therefore) L_u at both

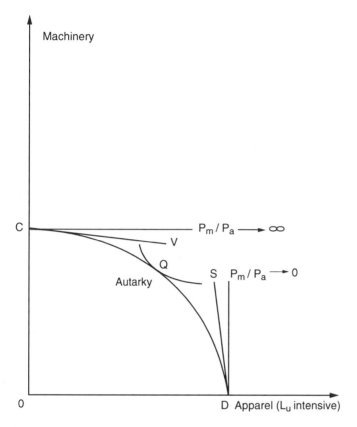

Figure 8.3
Goods-price ratio and specialization

D and C as P_m/P_a varies further. The free trade curve in figure 8.4 therefore is $ZDCH$.

If follows then that:

• DC is the range over which the conventional Stolper-Samuelson re-distributive effect operates.

• The real wage of L_u will fall (in figure 8.4) from autarky at Q when free trade improves P_m/P_a (the price of apparel using L_u intensively falls), down to when specialization in manufacturing emerges at C. But:

• For P_m/P_a improving beyond that, the real wage of L_u will bounce back, improving up to $G(= Q)$ and then beyond to improvement over autarky and even to $F(= D)$ and beyond to levels that exceed the best real wage achievable under autarky.

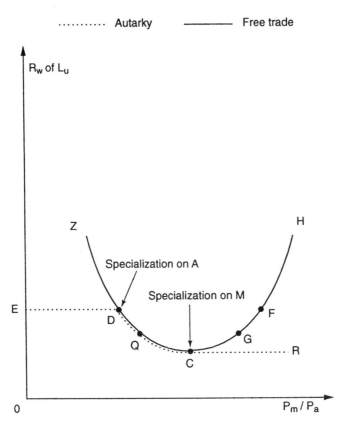

Figure 8.4
Trade, goods prices, and real wage

If we are indeed in this ballpark, then it becomes critical to know what the consumption patterns are. For example, as terms of trade continue to improve beyond what brings about specialization on a good in the 2×2 model, both factors will benefit, but their benefit will depend on how much of the other good they consume (with no benefit in the extreme case where nothing of the other good is consumed by a factor). In this regard, it is important to note that several studies, such as Cline's (1990) on textiles, show that the lower-income groups are quite intensive in their consumption of imported, unskilled-labor-intensive goods, so that the adverse Stolper-Samuelson effect is that much more likely to be swamped by the "lifting-all-boats" effect at issue.

Equally, scale economies can overturn the redistributive effect, improving the real wages of both factors. Panagariya (1980) demonstrated this first, using the conventional model where perfect competition is allowed to continue. Helpman and Krugman (1985) redemonstrated the result when scale economies lead to imperfect competition. As Brown, Deardorff, and Stern (1993) have reminded us, the Helpman-Krugman result was under the special case where the output per firm did not change with trade, and they have extended the analysis to the more general case where this is not so.[28]

I am known for my skepticism about the empirical importance of scale economies and could be properly chided if I show warmth toward them when they produce results that I would like to see. But the Panagariya and the Helpman and Krugman reminders are important for those who think scale economies are truly significant in thinking about the real world.

Then again, there could be lifting-all-boats effects from more competition and discipline resulting from the freeing of trade, causing X-efficiency effects, which may be formally modeled as Hicks-neutral technical change. If we do this and assume that the effect operates throughout the economy in both traded sectors in a 2×2 model, then clearly both factors see their real wages improving from this cause, countervailing and possibly reversing the fall in the real wage of the Stolper-Samuelson-effect-impacted factor. Evidently the argument can be extended to the case where the Hicks-neutral technical change is differentially greater in the import-competing sector and, with suitable assumptions, to biased technical change as well.

The empirical evidence on this hypothesis is hard to find. However, Levinsohn's (1993) ingenious work on the imports-as-competition hypothesis, while not quite in the form suggested here, is successful in testing that hypothesis with the use of Turkish industry data under ideal, near-controlled-experiment conditions. More work needs to be done to make this argument empirically more compelling.

Five further comments are in order.

First, although the goods prices do not conform to the Stolper-Samuelson thesis, the quantity-of-imports studies, such as the fine work of Adrian Wood (1994), suggest otherwise. Imports of unskilled-labor-intensive goods have certainly increased, and such increases have been associated with the fall in real wages. However, the intermediation via price fall cannot be avoided. This is readily seen in figure 8.5, where apparel imports, increasing due to increased domestic demand, leave both the price and domestic production unchanged and, hence, could not affect the wage of the unskilled in apparel manufacture.

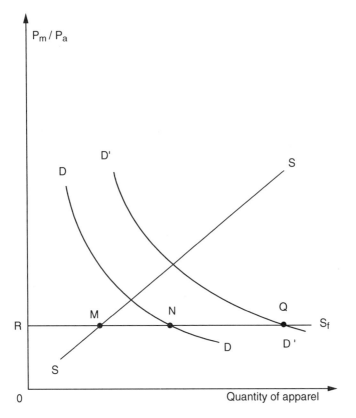

Figure 8.5
Increase in imports at fixed import price. As demand increases from DD to $D'D'$, this economy raised its imports from MN to MR, S_f being the foreign supply curve. The price
remains unchanged at OR, and therefore there is no effect on factor rewards either.

This argument becomes critical in entertaining skepticism concerning,
if not rejecting, the Borjas-Ramey (1994) argument that the growth of
imports has led to the decline in the wages of the unskilled. They show
that there is a tight time-series relationship between imports as a share
of GDP and the skilled-wage differential (rather than the real wage of the
unskilled); note that there are no data here on relative goods prices. But in
general equilibrium analysis, it is easy to show that both the correlated
phenomena may be a result of, say, technical change (the explanation that
seems much the more likely to many).[29]

To see this, consider figure 8.6. If the technical change is in the skilled-
labor-intensive good, machinery, it will lead to a disproportionate increase in the output of machinery, indeed, even to a decline in output of

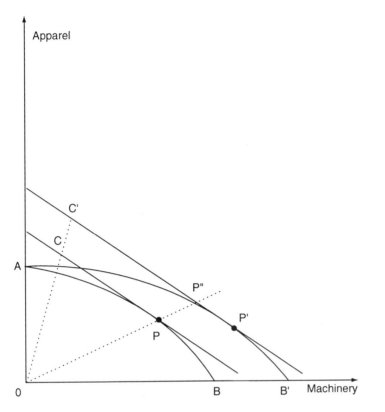

Figure 8.6
Technical change, production, consumption, and trade under constant goods-price ratio. The economy grows from AB to AB' because of Hicks-neutral technical change in machinery. With goods prices unchanged (at $CP = C'P'$), the production of machinery rises and of apparel actually falls (the so-called Rybczynski effect). If consumption shifts proportionately from C to C', then trade as a proportion of national income will rise; it would be constant only if P shifted to P'' proportionately.

apparel (this is the well-known Rybczynski effect). The net effect will, ceteris paribus, be to increase imports (and trade) as a proportion of gross national product as the economy grows due to technical change.[30]

Equally, one can show that the Hicks-neutral technical change in machinery will increase the relative wage of skilled labor since it will disproportionately increase the demand for skilled labor in which it is intensive. Figure 8.7 shows this using the well-known Findlay-Grubert (1959) diagram. Given the goods-price ratio exchanging A for M, we can take the tangent QR to these two isoquants, and that yields the associated factor-price ratio. When Hicks-neutral technical change occurs in machinery, the

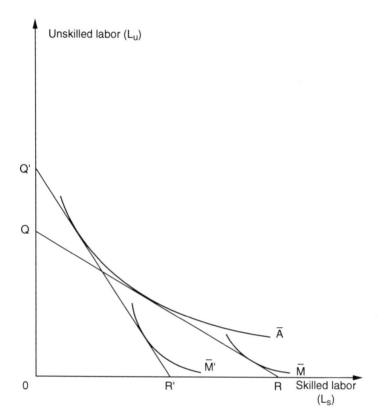

Figure 8.7
Technical change, factors-price ratio, and real wage of skilled workers. The factors-price ratio
shifts from QR to $Q'R'$, with machinery experiencing Hicks-neutral technical change, so that
M is produced now by M' isoquant. The L_u/L_s ratios in both apparel and machinery
increase in consequence alongside the increased real wage of labor.

same M can be produced by fewer factors, shifting M down to M'. The
new factor-price ratio $Q'R'$, consistent with the same goods price ratio
(A/M), is then yielded by the tangent to A and M'. $Q'R'$ relative to QR
then shows a rise in the relative wage of skilled labor. Thus, both variables, the skilled wage differential and imports as a share of GDP, will
move up with (relatively greater) technical change in the skilled-labor-
intensive industries, and this will happen at unchanging relative goods
prices.

Second, let me then turn to the question: Why did the domestic prices
of labor-intensive goods not fall during the 1980s? I offer three alternative
explanations and then draw implications for the issue at hand.

Explanation 1   One explanation is that even though the prices of unskilled-labor-intensive goods would fall as the pessimists feared, the voluntary export restrictions (VERs) on textiles, shoes, and other items, and the antidumping actions against several other products that broke out in the early 1980s, implied export restraints that translated into an effective (countervailing) rise in c.i.f. landed prices and, hence, in U.S. domestic prices as well.

Textile trade experts note that the Asian competition in textiles and apparel became heated during the latter half of the 1970s but that its effects on domestic adjustment were substantially mitigated by the swift response of the industry in tightening the Multi-Fibre Agreement's restrictiveness. Indeed, it is well known that administered protection (consisting of antidumping actions, VERs, and a variety of export-restraining arrangements between governments) began in the first half of the 1980s in the United States and Europe. The restrictiveness of trade barriers may therefore have generally increased, offsetting the Stolper-Samuelson effect by selectively moderating the goods-price effect, as necessary, in the first place (as the price data of Lawrence and Slaughter 1993 indicate). Such elasticity and selectivity are, in fact, a characteristic of the "administered" protection as embodied in antidumping actions, VERs, and so forth, and make them both a preferred instrument of protection by industry and a more serious hazard to free trade than conventional protection.[31]

Explanation 2   There may be something to explanation 1, and it is certainly worth exploring in depth to see what weight it carries empirically, but the truly compelling explanation (explanation 2) may well be that the OECD countries were not facing a huge shift in the foreign offer curve as far as unskilled-labor-intensive manufactures were concerned. Countries are on a continuum of factor endowments, and it is conceivable that much of the expansion of such exports from newly exporting countries such as China has been absorbed by the more mature developing countries, such as those in East Asia, leaving few net exports to the OECD countries.

That is exactly what appears to have happened in the 1980s. As the Australian economist Ross Garnaut (1996) has noted recently, if you measure the ratio of net exports of labor-intensive manufactures to world trade in such manufactures, China takes off from a broadly flat ratio of around 2 percent through the 1970s to a dramatic rise in the 1980s that reaches almost 14 percent by 1994, whereas the East Asian ratio goes almost inversely in the opposite direction, falling to virtually zero by 1994. If one reverses the normal flow from casual empiricism to informed statistical analysis, the Garnaut finding will be plausible to those who parented during the 1980s and found their children's toys from East Asia being replaced by ones made in China!

The paradox of price behavior in the 1980s, with the prices of labor-intensive goods failing to fall and trigger the Stolper-Samuelson explanation may then be resolved simply: it is a mistake to assume that endogenous factors such as growth and liberalization in the developing countries must result in a massive shift of net supplies to the OECD countries, including the United States.[32]

Explanation 3   The preceding two explanations relate to how the foreign supplies of labor-intensive manufactures have shifted for OECD countries, that is, to the shift in the foreign offer curve facing these countries. But a third explanation of why the observed goods prices of labor-intensive goods did not fall in the 1980s may relate to the OECD countries' own offer curve, that is, to the changes in their demands for such goods. Such a demand shift could have outweighed whatever supply shift may have occurred from the non-OECD, poor countries, so that the observed international terms of trade shifted in favor of labor-intensive goods.

Such a demand shift would have occurred due to both technical change and capital accumulation in the OECD countries. Technical change does, with some empirically unimportant exceptions, draw resources away from the nonprogressive industries, which would generally include labor-intensive manufactures. Equally, the accumulation of human and physical capital tends to do so.

Two further observations may be made in regard to technical change in the United States as an explanation of the adverse effect on real wages of the unskilled. First, technical change also extends to qualify improvements in products and, hence, generally to underestimate the fall in the price of these products. Since U.S. exports disproportionately contain such products relative to its imports, a fact noted by Irving Kravis (1956) long ago, an adjustment for quality change would make the observed "true" related prices of labor-intensive manufactures rise even more than the unadjusted data for the 1980s. Second, although capital accumulation will generally tend to leave real wages unaffected, technical change will not, and technical change biased against the use of unskilled labor can be the principal cause of its real wage decline.

Finally, what does all this say about future prospects? The typical worry often voiced is that when large, poor countries such as China and India come on board with their trade expansion due to domestic growth or trade liberalization, all hell will break loose, pushing the prices of labor-intensive goods down to low levels and crushing the real wages of the unskilled in consequence.

If the reason that the domestic prices of unskilled-labor-intensive goods here did not fall during the 1980s was the compensating growth of administered protection, a possibility that I have already suggested for investigation, this would not be reassuring, for it would mean that trade did not hurt real wages because protection prevented it from doing so by offsetting the fall in goods prices that trade would have induced. That is surely no argument for being free from worry on the income distributional effects of trade if protectionist responses are to be ruled out.

However, we can easily exaggerate the pressure on the prices of unskilled-labor-intensive goods from poor countries' trade liberalization, or from the expansion of their trade at any given level of their trade barriers, and the adverse effect on real wages of the unskilled in the rich countries.

Thus, in regard to effects on goods prices, the focus on the expansion (in formal terms) of the offer curve from the poor countries is misleading. It forgets that the offer curve of the rich countries will also be expanding. Given the fact that the poor countries' national incomes add up to only a small fraction of the national incomes of the rich countries and that the averages of the trade-to-GNP ratios between the two groups are not much apart, the net demand for the unskilled-labor-intensive exports of the poor countries may well rise instead of fall.

But even if prices were to fall for imported unskilled-labor-intensive goods in the next decade, it is by no means inevitable that this will translate into a fall, rather than a rise, in the real wages of the unskilled in the OECD countries. I have already recounted several reasons, implicit and explicit, in Stolper-Samuelson (1941) that all factors of production can gain from the fall in import prices and the associated trade expansion that trade with the South may bring. These reasons are not at all unrealistic. It is then simply a fallacy to think that the hand of Stolper-Samuelson theorem is an iron fist aimed at the real wages of our unskilled workers.

Next, it is perhaps worth noting also that the adverse effect on the real wages of the unskilled, if any, will increase with the decline in the prices of the unskilled-labor-intensive goods, but so will the gains from trade increase as the improvement in the terms of trade becomes greater. The latter would increase our income further yet and thus, ceteris paribus, lead to more revenue at any given tax rates. This should ease the constraints on spending to relieve the increased trade-determined distress to the unskilled. Thus, we have a built-in stabilizer, in terms of reduced revenue constraints, as the impact on real wages of the unskilled rises (if at all) if trade with the South drives down the real wages of the unskilled.

Again, whether one is a pessimist or an optimist (as I am) on the issue at hand, agreement on one policy option seems possible. Both could unite in support of policy programs to limit the growth of population (and, hence, of unskilled workers) in the large, poor countries. The optimists will support such programs because they are desirable for large, poor countries, such as India and China, and this is also the considered view of these countries' policymakers, as evident from the 1994 Cairo Conference on Population.

But the pessimists should support population control programs, in our own interest. If immigration, which directly brings the unskilled aliens from the poor countries into our midst, cannot be totally controlled by us and borders often tend to get beyond control, *and* if trade is also viewed by the pessimists as simply an indirect way of letting in such alien labor, both phenomena amounting to pressure on the real wages of the un- skilled, then the situation is fairly grim. It is especially grim if the decline of the political ability to redistribute prevents us from compensating for the decline in real wages of the unskilled.[34] In that case, the pessimists can only hope for lower pressures from the unskilled abroad, which implies our assistance in acceleration of their capital accumulation and technical progress on the one hand, and in ensuring the effective control of their population growth, on the other.

The shift from the Bush administration's more complacent attitudes on population control, prompted largely by the religious right, to the Clinton administration's energetic support of effective population policies at the Cairo Conference, prompted partly by liberal views concerning women's rights, can then be explained also as a response (among several) to the fears of the adverse effect of trade with the South on the real wages of our unskilled.

Kaleidoscopic Comparative Advantage and Higher Labor Turnover: An Alternative Trade Explanation

My view of the Stolper-Samuelson North-South trade explanation of the decline in the real wage of unskilled labor during and since the 1980s is, thus, profoundly skeptical, on current evidence and on theoretical grounds as well.[35]

But that is not all that one can say about the possible effect of trade on real wages. I have suggested ((Bhagwati, 1991c), Dehejia (1992a, 1992b) has explored analytically, and Bhagwati and Dehejia (1994) have elaborated an alternative trade explanation for real wage decline. The explanation, which has nothing to do with the Stolper-Samuelson analytical framework and looks at trade more generally than in a North-South framework, has essentially four elements:

1. Greater internationalization of markets (that is, rising trade-to-GNP ratios, greater role of transnational corporations in globalizing production), the diffusion of production know-how within OECD countries (as documented by Baumol, Blackman, and Wolff 1989), and the increased integration of world capital markets (as discussed in Frankel 1994) have narrowed the margin of comparative advantage enjoyed by many industries in all major OECD countries. There are more footloose industries now than ever before leading to greater volatility in comparative advantage, that is, more "knife-edge" and, hence, kaleidoscopic comparative advantage between countries.

2. This will lead to higher labor turnover between industries and, hence, to more frictional unemployment.

3. Increased labor turnover could flatten the growth profile of earnings due to less skill accumulation.

4. The previous three elements could explain an increasing wage differential, ceteris paribus, if skilled workers have greater transferability of workplace-acquired skills than do unskilled workers.[36]

This theory has yet to be investigated. In particular, whether comparative advantage has indeed become thin, resulting in the kaleidoscope effect (element 1), has not been documented empirically.[37] There is some suggestive evidence on elements 3 and 4 in labor studies, as noted in Bhagwati and Dehejia (1994) and also in Lisa Lynch's (1995) recent work.

The evidence on element 2, concerning higher labor turnover, has undergone a flip-flop; but fortunately for the Bhagwati and Dehejia argument, the evidence presently favors the hypothesis that labor turnover rates increased in the 1980s. Whereas the early thinking was that such turnover indeed increased (see, in particular, The Economist 1993 and OECD 1994), later studies suggested otherwise. Thus, as Bill Dickens has reminded me, recent U.S. data from the population survey show that the percentage of men with their current employer for less than a year did not change in the 1980s. Similarly, he argues that the U.S. Department of Labor data on the reallocation of employment between industries seem to show no upward trend (though the Bhagwati-Dehejia thesis would survive if there was increased turnover within industries as well). Similar conclusions seem to have been drawn by Diebold, Neumark, and Polsky (1994) and Farber (1995).

On the other hand, the recent findings of Stephen Rose (1993) and the related findings of the National Commission for Employment Policy (Rose 1994, 1995), an independent commission set up under the Job Training Partnership Act as an independent advisory body reporting to both the president and the Congress, have utilized more pertinent longitudinal data to argue the opposite. Yet further research by Idson and Valletta (1996) has demonstrated for the United States a higher rate of permanent displacements in the 1980s.[38] In short, the Bhagwati-Dehejia thesis is back in the picture as far as the turnover hypothesis is concerned.

Rents and Unionization
The above arguments are *economy-wide* trade explanations, but there are *industry-specific* trade explanations of what happens to industries affected by import competition.

Where these are competitive industries, clearly the earnings of the productive factors within them will be reduced at the outset. When the industry is wiped out, these earnings will go to zero, of course. The overall final effect on real wages of these factors, including the unskilled, however, cannot be determined without finding out the general equilibrium implications of the parametric change, which will take into account, for instance, the absorption of the displaced factors elsewhere in the economy, which means going back to the economy-wide explanation.

What does the presence of unions, and, hence, of rents to the unskilled in the unionized sectors, do for the argument? There are models of several kinds of imperfect competition in factor markets in the general equilibrium analysis of international trade that could be extended to address the question of the overall impact of changing goods prices on real wages. But the answers could be quite unexpected. For example, if unions maintained a wage differential between homogeneous insiders and outsiders, the conventional inferences, such as that a fall in the relative price of the unionized sector's good would lead to a fall in its relative production and presumably a fall in the unionized factor intensively used in it, would not necessarily hold, undermining the Stolper-Samuelson-type argument (inferring factor reward changes from goods price changes).[39] To my knowledge, there is no analysis of the effects of price declines in unionized industries, such as the automobile industry, that satisfactorily addresses these deeper analytical issues that arise when the effects of unions are considered.

We know that during the 1980s, the big unionized sectors in the United States, especially autos and steel, were politically powerful enough to shield themselves significantly through antidumping actions and VERs, OMAs (organized marketing arrangements), and so forth from the effects of foreign competition (which was overwhelmingly from the North, not the South). Given both the small percentage of the U.S. unskilled labor force in unionized manufacturing sectors even at that time, and the substantial cushioning of competition through trade restraints in any event, it is highly unlikely that the analysts can demonstrate (through this route) a significant overall role for trade in affecting real wages in the United States during the 1980s.[40]

International Capital Mobility: Globalization and Real Wages

So far I have considered only the question of a direct link between trade and real wages. But there are fears of an adverse impact on real wages of the unskilled that follow from fears arising from international capital mobility. Thus, a major worry of the unions is that the outflow of capital drives down real wages of unskilled labor. However, during the 1980s, in the United States, more DFI came in than went out, both during the period and relative to the 1950s and 1960s. Moreover, the United States ran a current account deficit so that foreign savings came in, if that is the measure one wants to work with instead. The facts are therefore against that hypothesis.

But if one uses a bargaining-type framework, it might be said that the bargaining power of employers has increased relative to that of employees because employers increasingly can say in a global economy that they will pack up and leave and, therefore, for any given output, its distribution between L_u income and other income including profits may have shifted against L_u.

To my knowledge, systematic empirical evidence for such a bargaining model as a determinant of relative rewards between factors within any U.S. industry is not available. Nor do we know whether, for any of these industries, there is evidence of an international relocation elsewhere of part of its local production having altered distribution against L_u income.[41]

At a time when total union membership is down to roughly 12 percent of U.S. private employment, however, I doubt if this explanation is likely to be important in any event—unless, of course, the longstanding decline in unionism is itself attributed in a significant measure (as it probably cannot be) to the loss of bargaining power due to the threat of exit by firms to other countries.

Static versus Dynamic Effects

My analysis of different approaches to the question of the link between trade and wages would not be complete without reference to the growth or dynamic effects that trade can have on wages by affecting several different fundamentals, such as the rate of accumulation and technical change.

If technical change or accumulation is agreeably affected, even as the initial static effect on real wages is adverse, the overall effect in the long run could swamp the static effect. The effect of trade on X-efficiency through competition, as discussed earlier (in reference to Levinsohn 1993), suggests, for example, that if this effect operates continuously and is not a one-time effect, it would certainly help to improve growth rates and, hence, pull up real wages over time.

This is a matter of importance since we will have to make up our minds as to how trade, in specific parametric cases, interacts with growth and affects real wages of the unskilled. Evidently the Far Eastern countries, whose rapid growth rates of capital and income since the 1950s cannot be delinked from their outward orientation in trade, did well in regard to their real wages, outweighing any static adverse effect that the importation of unskilled-labor-saving technology may have had on real wages in the short run.

Our problem today may then well be that with growth rates rather low (whether exogenously or endogenously to trade), we are unable to outweigh the drag on real wages that is being provided by either trade (which I strongly doubt) or technology (which I suspect is the true and overwhelming cause of the problem).

8.4   Conclusion

My analysis leads me to an optimistic conclusion about the effect of freer trade on the real wages of the unskilled in the rich countries. The evidence for the North-South (Stolper-Samuelson) argument is thin at best. The evidence for the North-North (Bhagwati-Dehejia) argument is equally thin. To date, there is no compelling evidence for the capital-mobility-cum-bargaining model either. The big-ticket weapons in the war chest of the pessimists are therefore without firepower.

Yet the issue remains politically salient because the linkage seems overwhelmingly intuitive. It will continue to affect policy in several areas, and not to our advantage. To cite one compelling example, it certainly fuels the push for including labor standards in the WTO since the objective of the unions that provide the main political force for such inclusion in a social clause is precisely to raise in any way they can the cost of production of their rivals in the poor countries. This issue is dividing the rich and the poor countries. It is also an issue where I fear that the current U.S. position lacks probity and statesmanship and instead appears to be a prisoner of lobby-led special-interest politics.[42]

In turn, I have no doubt that it is a principal reason for the infatuation of the United States with preferential trading arrangements (PTAs), such as free trade areas, even though the WTO has been jump-started and we would expect the United States to return to multilateralism. These PTAs between a hegemon and nonhegemons enable the hegemon and its lobbies pushing for trade-unrelated issues, such as intellectual property protection, environmental demands, and labor standards demands, to extract significant concessions from nonhegemons when the latter are bargained with one on one rather than in their greater numbers and strength directly in Geneva. The concessions that President Salinas made on these nontrade issues to the United States were far greater than those available from the poor countries en bloc at Geneva. And now Chile will have to accept them to get into NAFTA.

The sequential bargaining with nonhegemons, made possible by choosing the PTA route selectively with economically and politically vulnerable nonhegemons rather than exclusively the multilateral mode of trade negotiations with all nonhegemons, enables the hegemon to extract much more on nontrade issues—what John Whalley has called "side payments" —than what the hegemon can extract in the multilateral context directly. The desire to raise the poor countries' costs of production to "manageable" levels by imposing expensive environmental and labor standards on them is more readily fulfilled if the PTAs are embraced as a strategic bargaining strategy alongside the multilateral negotiations.[43] This desire has political salience, precisely because of the fear that free trade imperils our real wages (and jobs).[44]

Notes

My thanks are due to Nancy Birdsall, Susan Collins, Don Davis, Vivek Dehejia, Arnold Harberger, Anne Krueger, Robert Lawrence, Assar Lindbeck, Jacob Mincer, Lalith Munasinghe,

Dani Rodrik, T. N. Srinivasan, Larry Summers, Martin Wolf, Adrian Wood, and Naohiro Yashiro for helpful comments on the subjects discussed in this chapter.

1. Whether the Bretton Woods institutions, the IMF, and the International Bank for Reconstruction and Development, explicitly focused on poverty and income distributional problems at the time is a different issue. I agree with the view that they have generally been the followers, not the leaders, in this area. On the other hand, it is equally important to give them their due by noting that their focus on efficiency and growth can be seen quite properly as an indirect, instrumental focus on the amelioration of poverty, although a clear and forceful expression of that view is probably hard to find.

2. For an extended analytical treatment of this approach to growth and poverty issues, see Bhagwati (1988a) and also the analysis in Bhagwati (1993, chap. 2).

3. To those of us who have argued since the mid-1960s for the chief elements of that "Washington consensus," when Washington's policy czars acquired a coherent conception of them and grasp of their importance only about two decades later, the suggestion that these ideas are somehow their creative gift in the last few years is rather quaint. The only major change in thinking that has come about in the past two decades has to do with whether democracy is conducive to or hinders development. The early pessimism in this regard, prompted by the notion that democracy would handicap taxation and hence resource accumulation by the state, has now given way. I have written on this theme (Bhagwati 1995a).

4. I made this irony the principal theme in Bhagwati (1996a).

5. These different economic-philosophical positions are discussed in depth in Bhagwati (1977, chap. 1).

6. See, for example, Bhagwati (1988b, chap. 2) on the question of free trade, and Bhagwati (1991, chap. 2) on the issue of multilateralism.

7. The evidence in support of this phenomenon in the 1980s, for both the United States and several other countries, is reviewed and synthesized nicely by Kosters (1994).

8. For a theoretical analysis of these concerns, see Bhagwati (1983, chap. 42).

9. The issue attracted attention from such leading international economists as Harry Johnson, Tony Scott, Herb Grubel, Ron Soligo, and Al Berry. I too worked a great deal on the problem, writing several theoretical articles and exploring new questions, approaches, and ideas, such as the second-best nature of the optimal income tax problem of James Mirrlees in the presence of international personal mobility. See, in particular, Bhagwati (1983, 1986), Bhagwati and Partington (1976), and Bhagwati and Wilson (1989).

10. I have considered the issue of temporary inflow of skilled migrants, as part of trade in services, in several writings. In particular, see Bhagwati (1986; 1987a; 1987b, chap. 14–16). I have also written on exporting patients and importing doctors as part of trade in medical services (Bhagwati 1993).

11. The role of qualifying examinations in varying the inflow of foreign medical graduates into the United States, as required by the domestic market conditions, which I advanced as part of the analysis of the brain drain (Bhagwati 1976), has now been established in a careful econometric analysis by Debojyoti Sarkar (1995).

12. This approach is further marred by the arbitrary specification of proxies for preferred policies, a procedure that yields the desired results but has no scientific basis at all. Thus, economists Sachs and Warner (1995) use arbitrary cutoffs, such as 40 percent tariffs and 20

percent black market premiums, to classify countries into open and unopen trade groups and to arrive at pro-openness conclusions in regard to growth rates across the world. Such work, even when it yields conclusions that I and others find agreeable, is best rejected as unacceptable argumentation in scholarly discourse.

13. For instance, compare the exponential growth rate in the basic "one-good" Harrod-Domar model with the nonexponential growth paths under the "putty-clay" Feldman-Mahalanobis models (nicely reviewed in Chakravarty 1959). Thus, as every well-schooled developmental economist knew by the early 1960s, the Soviet growth experience could be explained as rationally exhibiting a J-curve, with lower growth rates when the capital goods base was being built up and with accelerated growth rates later. The eventual decline in growth rates much later was, however, arguably due to the altogether different reason of declining technical change, as Sovietologists such as Joe Berliner and Padma Desai began writing about in the late 1970s and early 1980s, the former with detailed institutional-cum-analytical analysis and the latter using econometric estimation of production functions. See Berliner (1976) and several of her own and others' econometric analyses synthesized in Desai (1987, chap. 1). The near disintegration of the Soviet economy under Gorbachev, and the difficulties afflicting the Russian economy under Yeltsin, can be attributed on the other hand, to the difficult problems of transition, which are yet another story. How, then, can the growth rates of the Soviet Union be simply put into a cross-country regression without understanding these deep processes?

14. I am using the basic Harrod-Domar model here, not its later variants inspired by Solow's Nobel Prize–winning work.

15. Thus, for example, greater exports may come from more small-scale firms rather than from the expansion of given firms to larger scale. I am afraid that in many CGE studies calculating the gains from trade from, say, CUFTA and NAFTA, it is simply assumed that scale economies will emerge as trade expands with the proposed trade arrangement.

16. I expanded on this theme in my keynote speech to the Cornell University Conference on East Asian Growth in honor of Professors Lin and Tsiang (see Bhagwati 1996b). I also integrated there the role of literacy and education in the explanation of the East Asian miracle.

17. My analysis parts company altogether with Krugman's (1994), which simply assigns the Far Eastern growth to increased investment without asking the key and pertinent question: What led to this investment explosion? It also parts company with Rodrik's (1994) explanation of the Far Eastern miracle, which assigns only an accommodating role to foreign trade and grossly exaggerates the ability of bureaucrats in the Far East to figure out the superior Rosenstein-Rodan equilibrium and the ability of this factor, in any event, to provide an ongoing spur to private investment. Also see Little (1996).

18. In discussing below the reverse effect of trade on the real wages of the unskilled in the developed countries, I note several caveats to the Stolper-Samuelson theorem to make inferences about adverse effects on the real wages of specific factors of production. The inferences about the beneficial effects, however, are easier to make.

19. I have considered alternative ways of looking at the effect of the IS and the EP strategies on income distributional questions (Bhagwati 1978, pp. 197–204), and the findings were generally skeptical again of IS proponents' claims.

20. I had argued, following Harry Johnson's (1967) demonstration of immiserizing growth, that capital inflow induced by tariff-jumping, IS-variety policies could be immiserizing. However, Brecher and Alejandro (1977) showed that such immiserization would necessarily

follow if the inflow occurred when the imported good was capital intensive. See Bhagwati (1978, pp. 211–214) for further discussion.

21. The commonly accepted view is that any pressure on unskilled labor translates into real wage declines in the flexible labor markets of the United States and in unemployment in the inflexible labor markets of Europe.

22. The Stolper-Samuelson argument relates the decline in real wages of the unskilled to decline in the relative price of unskilled-labor-intensive products. The factor-price-equalization argument, centrally related to the Heckscher-Ohlin theory, links the decline in the relative price of unskilled-labor-intensive goods to free trade with unskilled-labor-abundant countries.

23. I draw here on Bhagwati (1996d).

24. Of course, there are numerous ways in which transfers can affect goods prices (e.g., the terms of trade); see any graduate-level textbook, such as Bhagwati and Srinivasan (1983, chap. 12). The point in the textbook is that they need not, and any analysis that implicitly assumes that they must have (and that, too, in a particular direction) because real wages fell, is not acceptable.

25. The legend for figure 8.1 explains the proposition.

26. My critique of Borjas and Ramey (1994), which follows, is similar in spirit.

27. Thus, Sachs and Schatz (1994) estimate the following equation, dummying out for computers (p. 38):

Change in price = 0.04   − 0.02 low   − 0.02 computer $R^2 = -0.03$.
                  (1.47)   (−0.62) skill intensity (−1.04) dummy

The parentheses under the coefficients represent t-statistics. Note that none of the variables is significant. The authors admit that these results are "less than robust" (p. 36), though they argue that they are in the "right" direction. Actually, the estimates are unacceptable.

28. These authors have a fuller analysis of the effects of scale economies on factor rewards than the single point that I have highlighted. They have also used the Michigan Computable General Equilibrium (CGE) model, as applied to U.S.-Mexico trade, incorporating the scale effects, and argued that the real wages in the United States will in fact rise, not fall, as a result of freeing trade with Mexico.

29. Indeed, for the specific configuration of technical change and factor-intensity conditions modeled below, such correlation is inevitable, not just a possibility.

30. The increased demand is not being arbitrarily introduced into the analysis; it is intrinsic to the analysis of technical change, because such change increases income.

31. The fact that world, not just domestic, prices of unskilled-labor-intensive goods have increased instead of falling suggests that the VER explanation may be relevant; VERs may be expected to raise the export prices by the amount of the rents.

32. See Garnaut (1996, fig. 6). North American imports have risen but not as much as the "fallacy of aggregation" would have us believe. Added to the increased demand for labor-intensive goods imports in the OECD countries, the mild rise in the average prices of these goods is easy to understand. See my analysis in Bhagwati (1997), which examines the impact of changes in different fundamentals on the offer curves of the rich and poor countries in explaining the observed, stylized facts on world trade and prices of traded goods.

33. This is what international economists call the Rybczynski theorem.

34. The parallel between trade and immigration as indirect and direct ways of affecting real wages in the same direction was at the heart of the political debate on the first national immigration legislation, enacted in the United Kingdom in 1905. At the time, free traders were free immigrationists, whereas the protectionists were anti-immigrationists, and free immigration was described as "free trade in paupers." See Bhagwati (1991b) for details and an analysis.

35. I have concentrated here on several reasons why the Stolper-Samuelson theorem may not obtain. These would generally undermine the factor-price-equalization theorem as well. Of course, the Stolper-Samuelson effect could obtain in the rich countries even if the factor-price-equalization theorem did not obtain.

36. As for increased differential in favor of the skilled workers, increased turnover could explain that if we were to argue that the search period between jobs is more likely to be used by the skilled to add to their skills through study than by the unskilled. Once you have been trained and "socialized" to train, it is easier to find the motivation to retool and retrain; if you have never been socialized to train in the first place, you may turn more readily into a couch potato, watching TV during fallow periods.

37. Don Davis, of Harvard University, plans to explore this question, using some of the existing literature on changes in "product-line" specialization of firms. The theoretical exploration of the concept of knife-edge, kaleidoscopic comparative advantage, especially the conditions under which it is accentuated by globalization, is also necessary.

38. Farber (1996) shows that the incidence of the displacements is more evident for senior, educated workers. I have dealt with these questions, and the evidence, in Bhagwati (1996c).

39. There is, in fact, a considerable literature on this subject, with contributions by Steve Magee, Murray Kemp, Jagdish Bhagwati, T. N. Srinivasan, Ronald Findlay, Ronald Jones, and others in the 1970s. See the literature review in Bhagwati and Srinivasan (1983), which explains why the responses of outputs, for example, to goods price changes, may not be "normal" in the presence of such factor-market imperfections.

40. For a complementary discussion of rents, citing the broader literature on the subject, which includes efficiency-wage arguments, see Bhagwati and Dehejia (1994).

41. The threat of exit may exist, of course, even if no exit has actually occurred in the industry.

42. I have discussed the nuanced objections to a social clause in the WTO and outlined a set of alternative, better ways to promote one's ideas about labor standards, in several recent writings and in TV, radio, and other debates with the protagonists of a social clause. In particular, consult Bhagwati (1995c).

43. I have developed the idea of sequential bargaining and the associated idea of a "selfish hegemon" that pursues an agenda serving its national interest (defined with or without lobbies) in several recent writings (see, in particular, Bhagwati 1994b).

44. As I argue in Bhagwati (1996c), the attempts at imposing a variety of standards on the poor countries as a precondition of their market access to the rich countries can be judged to be an attempt at moderating the competition at source, as a form of "export protectionism" and "intrusionism" as contrasted with the import protectionism and "isolationism" that we are conventionally used to as a response to competitive pressures.

References

Balasubramanyam, V. N., and M. Salisu. 1991. "EP, IS and Direct Foreign Investment in LDC's." In A. Koekkoek and L. B. M. Mennes, eds., *International Trade and Global Development: Essays in Honor of Jagdish Bhagwati*, pp. 191–207. London: Routledge.

Balasubramanyam, V. N., M. Salisu, and D. Sapsford. 1996. "Foreign Direct Investment and Growth in EP and IS Countries." *Economic Journal* 106 (434) (January): 92–105.

Baumol, William, Sue Blackman, and Edward Wolff. 1989. *Productivity and American Leadership: The Long View*. Cambridge, Mass.: MIT Press.

Berliner, Joseph. 1976. *The Innovation Decision in Soviet Industry*. Cambridge, Mass.: MIT Press.

Bhagwati, Jagdish. 1964. "The Pure Theory of International Trade: A Survey." *Economic Journal* 174 (293) (March): 1–84.

Bhagwati, Jagdish. 1966. *The Economics of Underdeveloped Countries*. London: Weidenfeld and Nicholson.

Bhagwati, Jagdish. 1976. *The Brain Drain and Taxation: Theory and Empirical Analysis*. Amsterdam: North-Holland.

Bhagwati, Jagdish. ed. 1977. *The New International Economic Order: The North-South Debate*. Cambridge, Mass.: MIT Press.

Bhagwati, Jagdish. 1978. *Anatomy and Consequences of Exchange Control Regimes*. Cambridge, Mass.: Ballinger.

Bhagwati, Jagdish. 1983. "International Factor Movements and National Advantage." In Robert Feenstra, ed., *Essays in International Economic Theory*, vol. 2. Cambridge, Mass.: MIT Press.

Bhagwati, Jagdish. 1986. "Economic Perspectives on Trade in Professional Services." *University of Chicago Legal Forum* 45:45–56.

Bhagwati, Jagdish. 1987a. "International Trade in Services and Its Relevance for Economic Development." Annual Lecture of the Geneva Association. In Douglas Irwin, ed., *Political Economy and International Economics*, pp. 235–269. Cambridge, Mass.: MIT Press.

Bhagwati, Jagdish. 1987b. "Trade in Services and the Multilateral Trade Negotiation." *World Bank Review* 1(4):549–609.

Bhagwati, Jagdish. 1988a. "Poverty and Public Policy." Vikram Sarabhai Memorial Lecture. In *World Development* 16(5) (May): 539–556.

Bhagwati, Jagdish. 1988b. *Protectionism*. Cambridge, Mass.: MIT Press.

Bhagwati, Jagdish. 1991a. *The World Trading System at Risk*. Harry Johnson Memorial Lecture. Princeton: Princeton University Press.

Bhagwati, Jagdish. 1991b. *Free Traders and Free Immigrationists: Strangers or Friends?* Working Paper no. 20. New York: Russell Sage Foundation.

Bhagwati, Jagdish. 1991c. "Trade and Income Distribution." Paper presented at the Columbia University Conference on De-Industrialization, New York, November 15–16.

Bhagwati, Jagdish. 1993. *India in Transition: Freeing the Economy.* Radhkrishnan Lectures at Oxford University. Oxford: Clarendon Press.

Bhagwati, Jagdish. 1994a. "Free Trade: Old and New Challenges." *Economic Journal* 10 (423) (March): 231–246.

Bhagwati, Jagdish. 1994b. "Threats to the World Trading System: Income Distribution and the Selfish Hegemon." *Journal of International Affairs* (Spring).

Bhagwati, Jagdish. 1995a. "Trade and Wages: Choosing Among Alternative Explanations." Federal Reserve Bank of New York *Economic Policy Review* 1(1) (January): 42–47.

Bhagwati, Jagdish. 1995b. *Free Trade. "Fairness" and the New Protectionism: Reflections on an Agenda for the World Trade Organization,* Wincott Memorial Lecture. London: Institute for Economic Affairs.

Bhagwati, Jagdish. 1995c. "Trade Liberalization and 'Fair Trade' Demands: Addressing the Environmental and Labor Standards Issues." *World Economy* 18(6) (November): 745–760.

Bhagwati, Jagdish. 1995d. "Democracy and Development: New Thinking on an Old Question," Rajiv Gandhi Golden Jubilee Memorial Lecture. *Journal of Democracy* 6(4) (October): 50–64.

Bhagwati, Jagdish. 1996a. "The Global Age: From a Skeptical South to a Fearful North." Raul Prebisch Lecture delivered to the UNCTAD IX Conference, Johannesburg, South Africa, April 29.

Bhagwati, Jagdish. 1996b. "The 'Miracle' That Did Happen: Understanding East Asia in Comparative Perspective." Speech at Cornell University Conference on East Asian Growth, May 3.

Bhagwati, Jagdish. 1996c. "A New Epoch?" *New Republic.* Forthcoming.

Bhagwati, Jagdish. 1996d. "Trade and Wages: A Malign Relationship?" In Susan M. Collins, ed., *Imports, Export and the American Worker.* Washington, D.C.: Brookings Institution.

Bhagwati, Jagdish. 1997. "Play it Again, Sam: A New Look at Trade and Wages." Mimeo. Columbia University, Department of Economics.

Bhagwati, Jagdish, and Vivek Dehejia. 1994. "Freer Trade and Wages of the Unskilled—Is Marx Striking Again?" In Jagdish Bhagwati and Marvin Kosters, eds., *Trade and Wages: Levelling Wages Down,* pp. 36–75. Washington, D.C.: American Enterprise Institute.

Bhagwati, J., and Padma Desai. 1970. *India: Planning for Industrialization: Industrialization and Trade Policies Since 1951.* London: Oxford University Press.

Bhagwati, J., and Marvin Kosters, eds. 1994. *Trade and Wages: Levelling Wages Down?* Washington, D.C.: American Enterprise Institute.

Bhagwati, J., and Martin Partington, eds. 1994. *Taxing the Brain Drain I: A Proposal.* Washington, D.C.: American Enterprise Institute.

Bhagwati, J., and T. N. Srinivasan. 1975. *India.* New York: Columbia University Press.

Bhagwati, J., and T. N. Srinnvasan. 1983. *Lectures on International Trade.* Cambridge, Mass.: MIT Press.

Bhagwati, J., and John Wilson, eds. 1989. *Income Taxation and International Mobility.* Cambridge, Mass.: MIT Press.

Borjas, George, and Valerie Ramey. 1994. "Time-Series Evidence on the Sources of Wage Inequality." *American Economic Review, Paper and Proceedings* 84 (May): 10–16.

Borjas, George, Richard Freeman, and Lawrence Katz. 1992. "On the Labor Market Effects of Immigration and Trade." In G. B. Borjas and R. B. Freeman, eds., *Immigration and the Work Force: Economic Consequences for the United States and Source Areas*, chap. 7. Chicago: Chicago University Press.

Brecher, Richard, and Carlos Diaz Alejandro. 1977. "Tariffs, Foreign Capital and Immiserizing Growth." *Journal of International Economics* 7(4) (November): 317–322.

Brown, Drusilla, Alan Deardorff, and Robert Stern. 1993. "Protection and Real Wages: Old and New Trade Theories and Their Empirical Counterparts." Paper presented at the Bocconi University Conference, Milan, May 27–28.

Chakravarty, Sukhamoy. 1959. *The Logic of Investment Planning*. Amsterdam: North-Holland.

Cline, William. 1990. *The Future of World Trade in Textiles and Apparel*. Washington, D.C.: Institute for International Economics.

Collins, Susan, ed. Forthcoming. *Imports, Exports and the American Worker*. Washington, D.C.: Brookings Institution.

Deardorff, Alan, and Dalia Hakura. 1994. "Trade and Wages—What Are the Questions?" In Jagdish Bhagwati and Marvin Kosters, eds., *Trade and Wages: Levelling Wages Down?* pp. 76–107. Washington, D.C.: American Enterprise Institute.

Dehejia, Vivek. 1992a. "Capital-Skill Complementarity and Endogenous Wage Structure." Mimeo. New York: Columbia University.

Dehejia, Vivek. 1992b. "Kaleidoscopic Comparative Advantage and the Rising Skill Differential." Mimeo. New York: Columbia University.

Dehejia, Vivek. 1995. "Three Essays on International Trade," Ph.D. dissertation, Columbia University.

Desai, Pradma. 1987. *The Soviet Economy: Problems and Prospects*. Oxford: Blackwell.

Diebold, Francis, D. Neumark, and D. Polsky. 1994. *Job Stability in the United States*. Working Paper no. 4859. Cambridge, Mass.: National Bureau of Economic Research.

Economist. 1993. "Musical Chairs." July 17, p. 67.

Economist. 1994. "A Survey of the Global Economy." October 1, pp. 70ff.

Farber, Henry. 1995. "Are Lifetime Jobs Disappearing? Job Duration in the United States: 1973–1993." Mimeo. Princeton: Princeton University Economics Department.

Farber, Henry. 1996. *The Changing Face of Job-Loss in the United States*. Working Paper no. 5596. Cambridge, Mass.: National Bureau of Economic Research.

Findlay, Ronald, and Harry Grubert. 1959. "Factor Intensity, Technological Progress, and the Terms of Trade." *Oxford Economic Papers* 11(1) (February): 111–121.

Frankel, Jeffrey, ed. 1994. *The Internationalization of Equity Markets*. Chicago: University of Chicago Press.

Garnaut, Ross, 1996. *Open Regionalism and Trade Liberalization*. Singapore: Institute of Southeast Asian Studies and Sydney: Allen and Unwin.

Harrison, Ann, and Ana Revenga. 1995. *The Effects of Trade Policy Reform: What Do We Really Know?* Working Paper Series 5225. Cambridge, Mass.: National Bureau of Economic Research.

Helpman, Elhanan, and Paul Krugman. 1985. *Market Structure and Foreign Trade.* Cambridge, Mass.: MIT Press.

Idson, Todd, and Roy Valletta. 1996. "Seniority, Sectoral Decline and Employee Retention: An Analysis of Lay-Off Unemployment Spells." *Journal of Labor Economics* 14(4) (October): 654–676.

Johnson, Harry G., 1967. "The Possibility of Income Losses from Increased Efficiency of Factor Accumulation in the Presence of Tariffs." *Economic Journal* (March): 151–154.

Kosters, Marvin. 1994. "An Overview of Changing Wage Patterns in the Labor Markets." In Jagdish Bhagwati and Marvin Kosters, eds., *Trade and Wages: Levelling Wages Down?* pp. 1–35. Washington, D.C.: American Enterprise Institute.

Kravis, Irving. 1956. "Availability and Other Influences on the Commodity Composition of Trade." *Journal of Political Economy* 64(2) (April): 143–155.

Krugman, Paul. 1994. "The Myth of Asia's Miracle." *Foreign Affairs* 73(6) (November–December): 62–78.

Lawrence, Robert. 1994. *Trade, Multinationals, and Labor.* Working Paper no. 4838. Cambridge, Mass.: National Bureau of Economic Research.

Lawrence, Robert, and Matthew Slaughter. 1993. "Trade and US Wages in the 1980s: Giant Sucking Sound or Small Hiccup?" *Brookings Papers on Economic Activity: Microeconomics,* no. 2:161–210

Leamer, Ed. 1995. "A Trade Economist's View of U.S. Wages and 'Globalization'." Paper presented at the Conference on Imports, Exports and the American Worker, Washington, D.C., February 2–3.

Levinsohn, James. 1993. "Testing the Imports-as-Market-Discipline Hypothesis." *Journal of International Economics* 35 (August): 1–22.

Little, Ian. 1994. *Picking Winners: The East Asian Experience.* Occasional Paper. London: Social Market Foundation.

Little, Jane Sneddon. 1996. "U.S. Regional Trade with Canada During the Transition to Free Trade." *New England Economic Review* (January–Feburary): 3–21.

Lynch, Lisa. 1995. "Growing Wage Gap: Is Training the Answer?" *Economic Policy Review, Federal Reserve Bank of New York* 1 (January): 54–58.

Organization of Economic Cooperation and Development. 1994. *The OECD Jobs Study: Facts, Analysis, Strategies.* Paris: OECD.

Panagariya, Arvind. 1980. "Variable Returns to Scale in General Equilibrium Theory Once Again." *Journal of International Economics* 10(4) (November): 499–526.

Rodrik, Dani. 1994. "Getting Intervention Right: How South Korea and Taiwan Grew Rich." *Economic Policy: A European Forum* (United Kingdom), no. 20 (April): 55–107.

Rose, Stephen J. 1993. "Declining Family Incomes in the 1980s: New Evidence from Longitudinal Data." *Challenge* (November–December): 29–35.

Rose, Stephen. 1994. *On Shaky Ground: Rising Fears about Incomes and Earnings*. Research Report 94-02. Washington, D.C.: National Commission for Employment Policy.

Rose, Stephen J. 1995. *Declining Job Security and the Professionalization of Opportunity*. Research Report 95-04. Washington, D.C.: National Commission for Employment Policy.

Sachs, Jeffrey, and Howard Schatz. 1994. "Trade and Jobs in US Manufacturing." *Brookings Papers on Economic Activity* 1:1–84.

Sachs, Jeffrey, and Andrew Warner. 1995. "Economic Reform and the Process of Global Integration." *Brookings Papers on Economic Activity* 1:1–118.

Samuelson, Paul A. 1948. "International Trade and the Equalization of Factor Prices." *Economic Journal*, 58(2):163–184.

Samuelson, Paul A. 1949. "International Factor-Price Equalization Once Again." *Economic Journal* 59:181–197.

Sarkar, Debojyoti. 1995. "Organized Medicine and International Medical Graduates." Ph.D. dissertation, Columbia University.

Stolper, Wolfgang, and Paul A. Samuelson. 1941. "Protection and Real Wages." *Review of Economic Studies* 9(1):58–73.

Wood, Adrian. 1994. *North-South Trade, Employment and Inequality*. Oxford: Clarendon Press.

Comments

Nancy Birdsall

Bhagwati presents a fine exposition of the analytical models underlying economists' views on the benefits for a country's economic growth of trade and other forms of integration into the world economy. But it says too little about the effects of trade policy on income distribution in the developing countries, and too little about the political economy of trade policy and income distribution in general. These are controversial issues, but also critical issues for policy.

Trade, Growth, and Poverty

Bhagwati reminds us that, lamentably, we have little empirical evidence for some central and attractive conclusions of our analytical models. He argues there is virtually no empirical evidence for the now widely accepted view that in developing countries the export promotion strategy has been a cause of growth. And for lack of evidence, he worries over the view that technological change, and not trade, is responsible for the relative decline in the wages of the unskilled in the OECD countries.

Bhagwati also suggests that the fundamental mechanism by which trade causes growth in developing countries is the higher investment rates induced by greater openness as the marginal return to capital increases. More openness brings an embodied technology transfer and therefore increases productivity. Capital accumulation and technologically induced productivity change were the framework of the study in which John Page and I, and others at the World Bank, tried to understand the success of East Asia.

Bhagwati expresses annoyance at what he calls the "moral arrogance" of the left in claiming to have a monopoly on soft-heartedness and in claiming that hard-nosed advocates of free trade have no concern for the poor. Arnold Harberger's presentation in chapter 7 brings to mind the example of Chile, which illustrates Bhagwati's point. In Chile, with the democratic government that came to power several years ago, we have witnessed a happy marriage of a clear market orientation, including openness to global competition, with a firm commitment to social justice. Bhagwati is right that a preference for the market is no sign of lack of heart.

Openness and Income Distribution in Developing Countries

But what really matters is what Bhagwati has left out. For the developing countries, what are the income distribution effects of more openness and greater integration of economies into global markets? For developing and developed countries, what are the implications for economic policy of the political economy of income distribution, as affected by trade policy and the global integration of economies? If we take as given that an outward orientation and more open trade regimes are good for growth, indeed are international public goods, then what is needed to ensure that more openness does not undermine efforts to reduce poverty and improve income distribution, and does not become the lightning rod for opposition to adjustment reforms in developing countries in general? In developed countries, what policies, guided by what economic analysis, can ensure that the benefits of more open trade are not sacrificed because of legitimate worries about poverty and income distribution effects?

The effects of global integration on poverty and income distribution warrant consideration for both the developing and the OECD countries. For developing countries, Bhagwati argues that growth reduces poverty, export promotion is probably better for growth than import substitution (if only because the latter cannot be shown to have encouraged growth), and over and above the benign growth effect of open trade regimes on poverty, an export promotion strategy probably shifts the allocative structure toward labor-intensive exports, which probably improves income distribution.

Examining the situation confronting policymakers in Latin America illustrates what is left out of this exposition. In Latin America, there is already virtual consensus on the benefits for growth of integration into the world economy. But there is no consensus and in fact no evidence on the effects of such integration for reducing poverty and inequity. Indeed, concerns about the effects of open trade regimes on poverty seem justified in Latin America, especially in the short run (which Bhagwati wisely acknowledges).

Where the starting point is a high level of income inequality and the associated large numbers of poor, the short-run effects of opening the economy are likely to exacerbate the problems of poverty and inequality. The rich can insulate themselves from the costs of the adjustment, using the same economic and political tools that in many countries helped them resist adjustment in the first place. The rich are educated, have financial and physical assets, and have access to capital markets; they are thus able to exploit the new opportunities that liberalization of trade and investment brings. The poor in Latin America are increasingly concentrated in urban areas in low-wage and unskilled jobs in construction and other nontradables. They benefit little, at least in the short run, from the opening of economies. Indeed, recent research in Mexico, Chile, and Colombia suggests that the relative wages of the unskilled have declined in recent years in those countries, just as they appear to have declined in the United States (Robbins 1996). (Declines in wages of the unskilled in Mexico seem to belie Ross Perot's assumption that, with a great sucking sound, low-wage jobs would move south.) Thus, initial conditions and structural factors in Latin America mitigate against short-run benefits of trade opening for the poor, in contrast to at least some countries of Africa, where the rural poor are in agriculture and other tradable sectors that can benefit from trade liberalization.

The policy problem is not only, or primarily, the effects of more open trade regimes on poverty. Other components of adjustment, which necessarily complement and accompany the trade opening, such as cuts in public expenditures and high interest rates, induce the recession that in some countries has pushed the working class into poverty and the poor into destitution. But trade policy can, and has become itself, a visible and controversial aspect of adjustment reforms as they affect the poor and affect income distribution.

Trade and Income Distribution in OECD Countries

For the OECD countries, Bhagwati goes straight to the fundamental question of external sector and income distribution. His central point is that if there is no decline in the relative price of unskilled-labor-intensive goods, then there is no evidence that trade is the cause of the decline in the relative wage of the unskilled.

But Bhagwati the trade optimist is really struggling. He notes that administered prices may well have suppressed an otherwise negative effect on goods prices, disguising the true effects of trade in reducing the relative wages of the unskilled. He points out that positive general equilibrium effects of more open trade could offset the negative effects on relative wages, improving the welfare of low-wage workers by reducing the consumer prices of goods they favor. But what if people care about job security and their relative wages, and not only their absolute real income? He argues there is no evidence that mobile industries actually do move jobs out of industrial countries. But the analytic question is whether their ability to threaten such moves in itself can affect wages.

Surely these easy assumptions and worrisome counterhypotheses would benefit from creative empirical work and should be on the research agenda.

Finally, Bhagwati argues that increased growth has a stabilizing effect because increased revenues can be used to compensate the loser. True— but is it politically likely and politically feasible? Perhaps economists need to cope more analytically with an underlying problem: that people may care not only about equality of consumption but about equality of pay and equality of opportunities. Perhaps that should become a central starting point for new work on the external sector and income distribution.

Reference

Robbins, Donald. 1996. "Trade Liberalization and Inequality in Latin America and East Asia: Synthesis of Seven Country Studies." Paper presented at the American Economics Association meeting, San Francisco, January.

Comments

Naohiro Yashiro

Bhagwati has presented an excellent survey of the effect of an increased integration of one's economy into the world economy and income distribution. His conclusion is optimistic in the sense that the adverse effect of freer trade on the real wages of the rich countries is slight. Thus, he refutes the argument for raising the poor countries' costs of production to a "manageable" level by imposing expensive labor standards on them.

I am impressed by Bhagwati's ironic reversal of views on one's integration into the world economy between developing and developed countries. That is, in the 1960s, it was the South that was unwillingly integrated into the world economy for fear of being exploited or dominated by neocolonialism. Today the North is worrying about lower wages or higher unemployment, or both, due to the increasing imports of labor-intensive products from the South. Which views are correct, or are both incorrect?

According to textbook economics, an increased international division of labor through increased world trade and investment flows is desirable, because it implies the larger market and efficiency gains through pursuing economies of scale. In reality, however, the situation would not be that simple, mainly because factor price equalization, through increased trade flows, would push the wage level of the low skilled in the North toward the level of the South. Thus, although the country as a whole might benefit from an increasing international division of labor, the low-skilled sector might well lose the "rent" originally held in the less-integrated world economy. How large this cost would be is the major issue in Bhagwati's chapter.

Adverse Impact of Trade

Bhagwati has surveyed various empirical works that estimate the extent to which real wages decline with an integration into the world economy and found no concrete evidence. This leads to his "optimistic" conclusion. I have the following three comments on his proposition. First, the fact that real wages do not decline does not necessarily indicate that the low-skilled sector in the North is not affected by the South. The adverse impact of increased imports from the South can only be measured by a deviation from the "standard case" without the impact. As Harberger indicates in chapter 7, real wage stagnation or slower wage increases than the standard case may already reflect the factor-price-equalization process in a growing world economy. Second, the process of being integrated into the world economy is inherently of a general equilibrium nature. Bhagwati mentions the "overwhelming role of technical change," which may have offset the adverse impact from the South. My comment is that this technical change is by no means an accident but is induced by increased imports from the South. A major impact of imports is not only the increased availability of inexpensive products from abroad but also the stimulation of competition in the domestic market. This eliminates firms with lower productivity in the economy and shifts resources toward the higher-productivity sector, thereby improving the overall efficiency of the economy without any major scientific inventions. In this sense, even though wages in the low-skilled sector are adversely affected, the declining share in the economy, being absorbed by other growing industrial sectors, is not necessarily undesirable. Third, the role of government intervention against lowering wages in the low-skilled sector may also be important in explaining their relative wage stability. Bhagwati indicates trade policies such as antidumping actions, but why aren't the more direct income distribution measures for the low-skilled sector accounted for? Such subsidies to the low-skilled sector, which is adversely affected by increased imports, may be rationalized on the grounds that the benefits to the economy as a whole from freer trade should exceed the losses in a particular industry.

Trade and Immigration

Bhagwati suggests that freer trade and immigration have similar effects on real wages, based on the factor-price-equalization theorem. In fact, however, there is a marked difference in the effects on industrial structure and increased manufactured imports and immigration, because unskilled foreign workers tend to be concentrated in the low-skilled sector of the economy, thus deterring structural adjustment of industries. On the contrary, the increased imports of labor-intensive products would induce a more rapid shift of labor from the low-productivity to the high-productivity sector. Thus, although the wages in the low-skilled sector would be affected by being integrated into the world economy, increased trade should have a more favorable impact on leveling the average productivity and wage of the economy than on increased immigration. In the former case, the low-skilled sector of the developed countries would shrink, being replaced by imports; in the latter case, it would remain as it is, thus widening wage differentials between workers.

Conclusion

The pros and cons of free trade depend on whether the labor and capital in developed countries are smoothly shifted to the higher-productivity sector to absorb the shock of an increase in labor-intensive products from the South. If not, there will be higher unemployment, or lower wages, or both, in the North. Bhagwati, however, says not to worry about factor price equalization, because it does not yet affect real wages much.

I would extend his argument by saying that we should use the factor-price-equalization process to stimulate structural changes in the North. The workers in the North cannot maintain their wages higher than those of their counterparts in the South unless they produce more sophisticated or higher-value-added products. The increasing integration of developing countries into the world economy means more imports for developed countries, but also potentially more exports from the developed to the rapidly growing markets in developing countries.

It has long been said that developing countries need more trade than foreign aid. Since developing countries are rapidly catching up in technology and capital accumulation, the product quality gap between developed and developing countries has narrowed considerably. Our challenge is to stimulate structural adjustment in domestic industries in the North by allowing free trade. There is no alternative.

9

The Political Economy of Macroeconomic Stabilizations and Income Inequality: Myths and Reality

Alberto Alesina

Conventional wisdom holds that stabilization programs and policy reforms, particularly IMF-supported ones, hurt the poor in the short and medium run by forcing budget cuts, price liberalization, and an increase in unemployment. Income inequality increases, threatening the political sustainability of these programs. Thus, various forms of safety nets have to be created, and social spending has to be safeguarded or even increased. Sometimes associated with this conventional wisdom is a critical view of the IMF that this institution is callous to the social sufferings caused by stabilization programs. In fact, according to this view, the IMF has been agnostic on how the burden of the adjustment, particularly budget cuts, has to be allocated, since the IMF views the allocation of these costs as a domestic policy problem.

I believe that this conventional wisdom, and its policy implications are somewhat misleading and off the mark and may lead to substantial policy mistakes. Policy reforms involve a variety of issues: from budget cuts to removal of price controls; from trade liberalization to privatization; from tax reforms to transition from socialism to the market. I shall primarily focus on the topic of fiscal consolidation and elimination of budget deficits in less developed countries (LDCs), a choice dictated by my comparative advantage and my attempt at being concrete by focusing on a specific, and critical, component of stabilization programs. However, several general themes of this chapter apply to other issues of policy reform as well.[1]

My view is rather different from the conventional wisdom. Extreme income inequality fosters social instability and demands for redistribution. However, since the very poor have relatively little political voice, the redistributive process is captured by various vocal interest groups, such as urban trade unions, civic servants, and university students, depending on the country. So-called redistributive policies, including social spending on health, education, social security, and public employment, favor parts of the upper and middle classes, part of the lower middle class, and several powerful interest groups, but almost never the very poor. Furthermore, these redistributive policies often carry with them substantial deadweight losses, are often highly inefficient, and contribute to macroeconomic imbalances. The very poor often suffer not because of the stabilization policies but to some extent because of the so-called social policies that created the macroeconomic imbalances in the first place. Maintaining or expanding traditional channels of social spending during stabilization programs often amounts to preserving patronage, interest group entitlements, and corruption, but without reaching the very poor.

I see a serious danger that so-called politically sustainable stabilizations are those that do not challenge established and vocal interest groups who are not the neediest. The rhetoric of the "adjustment with a human face" can often become confused with preservation of established rents, at the expense of those who never had a voice. The role of the international community and the IMF is to support stabilization programs that break away from the inefficiency and inequity of traditional social policies. Concerns for reduction in income inequality and in poverty rates are not necessarily inconsistent with even severe budget cuts. On the contrary, cuts in benefits for vocal interest groups and reallocation of government spending can improve the welfare of the neediest and achieve macroeconomic stability.

The difficulty lies in creating a political coalition strong enough to implement this approach. Political sustainability and the role of international organizations should be viewed in this context. A successful stabilization program will have to be followed by bureaucratic and institutional reforms that break with traditional interest group politics and entrenched bureaucracies. I shall try to articulate this view by highlighting statistical supporting evidence and examples from various countries.

The paper is organized as follows. Section II discusses the relationship between initial income inequality and its effect on macroeconomic policies and outcomes. Section III argues that fiscal deficits and expansionary fiscal policies have generally not benefitted the very poor and have done very little to reduce income inequality. Section IV shows how different fiscal adjustments may or may not have regressive effects. Section V discusses whether fiscal adjustments can safeguard the poor. The final section discusses the role of the international community and of international organizations.

9.1   Income Distribution, Economic Policy, and Growth

Excessive income inequality leads to social pressure for redistributive fiscal policies, sociopolitical instability, unsustainable policy choices, and, possibly, low growth. The linkage running from income distribution to policy choices and economic outcomes is "highly complex and variable across time and countries" (Sachs 1989, p. 7). However, recent research sheds new light on different aspects of this chain of causation.[2]

Several channels imply an inverse relationship running from initial income inequality to growth. A fiscal channel suggests that income inequality creates a demand for redistributive fiscal policy. In a median voter model, the key measure of inequality is the level of income or wealth of the median voter relative to the average.[3] The poorer the median voter, relative to the average, the larger the amount of redistribution that a majority of voters will favor. More generally, a large, impoverished fraction of the population creates political pressure for redistributive policies. This pressure may take different forms in different institutional contexts but is generally felt in both democracies and dictatorships. In fact, in order to survive, even dictators cannot totally ignore popular demands. Redistributive fiscal policies lead to high levels of taxation, which negatively affect growth. Thus, the chain of causation goes from high initial income inequality to high taxes, and from large redistributions to low growth. An alternative argument is that the rich in very unequal societies have the political and economic resources to escape taxation by exiting the economy with capital flight or by tax evasion. Thus, demand for redistributive policies coupled with a vanishing tax base may lead to large budget deficits.

A second channel linking inequality and macroeconomic performance goes through political instability. Income inequality fosters social discontent and unrest. The associated threats to property rights, policy volatility, and government fragility depress productive investment, promote capital flight, and ultimately reduce growth.[4]

A recent strand of empirical research suggests that income inequality in the 1950s and the 1960s negatively affected economic growth in the following decades. Alesina and Rodrik (1994), Birdsall, Ross, and Sabot (1995), Clarke (1993), Perotti (1995), and Persson and Tabellini (1994), among others, provide supporting evidence on this link. Alesina and Perotti (1996b) and Perotti (1995) show that sociopolitical instability, measured by a composite index, increases with income inequality, and

Alberto Alesina

sociopolitical instability reduces private investment. An inverse relationship between political instability and growth is also documented by Barro (1991) and Alesina et al. (1996) among others. Berg and Sachs (1988) find that "countries with high income inequality had a significant greater likelihood, *ceteris paribus*, of having rescheduled their debts than did countries with low income inequality" (p. 271). Cukierman, Edwards, and Tabellini (1992), and Haggard and Kaufman (1990), for instance, document effects from government fragility to inflation. Since income inequality fosters sociopolitical instability, these results on inflation (and thus indirectly on budget deficits) suggest a linkage running from initial income inequality to macroeconomic imbalances. Rodrik (1994) suggests that different levels of initial income inequality may help in explaining the more successful experience of East Asian countries relative to Latin America in terms of growth and macroeconomic stability in the past three decades. Table 9.1

Table 9.1
Distributional Indicators for East Asian and Comparator Countries, circa 1960

Country	Gini coefficient for income	Gini coefficient for landownership
East Asian countries		
Hong Kong	0.49	
Indonesia	0.33	
Japan	0.40	0.47
Korea	0.34	0.39
Malaysia	0.42	0.47
Taiwan	0.31	0.46
Singapore	0.40	
Thailand	0.41	0.46
Unweighted average	0.39	0.45
Other countries		
Argentina	0.44	0.87
Brazil	0.53	0.85
Egypt	0.42	0.67
India	0.42	0.52
Kenya	0.64	0.69
Mexico	0.53	0.69
Philippines	0.45	0.53
Turkey	0.56	0.59
Unweighted average	0.50	0.68

Source: Rodrik (1994).

highlights the extent of the difference in income and land distribution in these two regions.

In summary, the point is, in Sachs's (1989) words, that "high income inequality ... contributes to intense political pressure for macroeconomic policies to raise the incomes of lower income groups, which in turn contributes to bad policy choices and weak economic performance" (p. 7). Latin American populism is a perfect example of this argument.[5]

One of my crucial arguments is that so-called redistributive policies and the associated growth of government and various policies of price controls, trade protection, and so forth rarely improve the welfare of the very poor in the bottom quintile of the income distribution. On the contrary, these policies become the battleground for various interest groups and rent seekers, so that these redistributive flows often end up in the hands of the more vocal rather than the more needy. Thus, the macroeconomic imbalances that eventually lead to IMF-supported adjustments are rarely the results of successful attempts at reducing poverty and inequality.

9.2 Redistribution to the Vocal

Macroeconomic imbalances leading to the need for policy reforms and stabilization policies can largely be explained by distributional struggles among vocal interest groups.[6] In most cases of major fiscal imbalances, with the associated high inflation, various market-distorting policies have not really increased the relative income level of the very poor.

After analyzing several cases of Latin American populism, for instance, Cardoso and Helwege (1991) conclude that "the history of populism makes conspicuous the paucity of genuine redistributive programs in Latin America" (p.59). On the contrary, Colombia, a macroeconomically stable and "populist-free" country by Latin American standards, shows some sizable improvements in income equality in the past two decades (Londaño 1989).

Several reasons for this failure of genuine redistributive policies in countries that have experienced macroeconomic imbalances are well known. One is that high inflation and hyperinflation are probably regressive, since the rich and the upper middle class can more easily shield themselves from inflation.[7] A second reason concerns tax evasion. Although data on tax evasion are, for obvious reasons, imprecise, various indirect methods of estimation and multicountry studies suggest that tax evasion is rampant in several LDCs and very high in some member countries of the Organization for Economic Cooperation and Development (OECD) as well.[8]

These arguments concerning the revenue side (tax evasion and the inflation tax) are relatively well known, thanks to the work of the authors already cited, among others. With specific reference to Latin America, Tanzi wrote as early as 1974 that "much of the empirical evidence available ... supports the conclusion that the tax systems of Latin America have done little to modify the existing income distribution" (p. 73). What is relatively less stressed in the literature is that even the so-called social spending programs do not really benefit the very poor in many developing countries. It goes beyond my scope here to provide consistent original empirical evidence on this point for every developing country; nevertheless, my review of a series of scattered sources suggests that the argument generally holds. To my knowledge, Tanzi (1974) was the first to address the issue of the distributional effects of public expenditures in a multicountry study. His conclusions, based on the scattered empirical evidence on Latin America available at the time, are very similar to my own point of view and are supported by the empirical evidence of the 1970s and the 1980s. With reference to social spending in general and education in particular, Tanzi (1974), after reviewing several studies, concludes that "first, it appears that even the supposedly pro-poor social type expenditure has little effect on income distribution. Second, the group that seems to be getting the greatest advantage from public spending is the urban middle class" (p. 81). Tanzi then analyzes the assumptions made in the empirical literature to reach these conclusions and argues that these already pessimistic calculations on education spending may actually be based on overly optimistic assumptions. Tanzi then proceeds to analyze other types of expenditures (not directly social) and reaches similarly pessimistic conclusions. His observations anticipate by a full two decades a discussion that is remarkably important today.

In an informative study, Pradhan (1996) collects, from a variety of sources, estimates of the benefit incidence of health and education subsidies for several developing countries. These two items, health and education, represent about 60 percent of total social services in developing countries. Social services are about 30 to 40 percent of the budget, so health and education are about 20 percent of the budget. Tables 9.2 and 9.3 suggest that, in very few cases, more than 50 percent of the benefits are received by the bottom 40 percent of the income distribution. A breakdown between the bottom 20 percent and the next 20 percent is not available, but my guess is that the bottom 20 percent receive fewer benefits than the next 20 percent. In the case of both health and education, the

Table 9.2
Benefit Incidence of Health Subsidies: Percentage of Government Subsidy Received by Income Group

Country and sector	Year of survey	Lower 40 percent	Middle 40 percent	Upper 20 percent
Public health				
Argentina	1980	69	27	4
Chile	1983	51	47	11
Colombia	1974	42	40	20
Costa Rica	1983	49	38	13
Dominican Republic	1984	57	44	9
Uruguay	1983	64	25	12
Indonesia	1978	19	36[a]	45[b]
Iran	1977	51	37	13
Malaysia	1974	47	37	17
Philippines	1975	27	33	40
Sri Lanka	1978	46	39	14
Hospitals				
Indonesia	1974	23	53	23
Malaysia	1974	36	34	20
Average		44	38	19

Source: Pradhan (1996); original source: Jiménez (1995).
a. These figures are for the middle 30 percent.
b. These figures are for the upper 30 percent.

middle 40 percent of the income distribution receives a sizable share of the benefits, very close to the share of the bottom 40 percent.

Thus, these data suggest that social spending in health and education has little, if any, redistributive effect in favor of the poor. For education, the reason is that subsidies to higher education are clearly regressive, since they disproportionately benefit the upper middle class (see table 9.3). These subsidies are generally not a trivial part of the budget of education expenses. For instance, between 1985 and 1989, spending on education programs other than primary and secondary education was about 30 percent of total spending on education in the sample of countries in tables 9.2 and 9.3.

In a careful study, Mingat and Tan (1986) conclude that public spending in education is very regressive in developing countries: "The share [of publicly provided education] received by farmers is much smaller than their representation on the population.... Manual workers and traders as

Table 9.3
Benefit Incidence of Education Subsidies: Percentage of Government Subsidy Received by
Income Group

Country and Sector	Year of survey	Lower 40 percent	Middle 40 percent	Upper 20 percent
All education				
Argentina	1983	48	35	17
Chile	1983	48	34	17
Colombia	1974	40	39	21
Costa Rica	1983	42	38	20
Dominican Republic	1976–1977	24	43	14
Uruguay	1983	52	34	14
Indonesia	1978	46	25[a]	29[a]
Malaysia	1974	41	41	18
Average		43	36	21
Higher education				
Argentina	1983	17	45	38
Chile	1983	12	34	54
Colombia	1974	6	35	60
Costa Rica	1983	17	41	42
Dominican Republic	1976–1977	2	22	76
Uruguay	1980	14	52	34
Indonesia	1978	7	10[b]	83[a]
Malaysia	1974	10	38	52
Average		11	32	57

Source: Pradhan (1996, p. 72); original source: Jiménez (1995).
a. These figures are for the middle 30 percent.
b. These figures are for the upper 30 percent.

a group receive a share roughly comparable to their representation in the population ... the white-collar group is the most successful in appropriating public education resources for themselves" (p. 269). These authors identify the worst problem as being in francophone Africa, where primary enrollment ratios are particularly low. According to their calculation, in this region, the ratio of public education resources appropriated by the farmers, relative to their share in the population, was about 0.6 in 1980. The same ratio for white-collar workers was almost 6, or ten times larger. For comparison, the same ratios in OECD countries were 0.95 and 1.2, respectively. Other regions in the developing world show ratios much more skewed in favor of the white-collar groups than in the OECD group, although not as skewed as those in francophone Africa.[9]

Specific examples of the regressivity of higher education spending are striking. Graham (1994) documents that all university students in Senegal have free tuition and a variety of expensive benefits. This is a country where, in the *bidonvilles*, the level of poverty is extreme. The lobby of university students in Senegal has been very effective at protecting its members from any reduction in benefits. In fact, Graham identifies civil servants and university students as two of the most powerful interest groups in Senegal and concludes that programs of poverty alleviation often "targeted politically vocal groups ... certainly not the poor.... [These vocal groups] had already cost the state a great deal of money in terms of defrayed university costs" (p. 132).

Clearly education has positive externalities, which justify government intervention. However, subsidizing higher-level public education at the expense of primary education, particularly in countries with high levels of illiteracy, is clearly the wrong policy from both an efficiency and a distributive point of view.

In a comparative study on public employment, Nunberg (1989) identifies several problems in a sample of LDCs, mostly in Africa and Latin America. She describes the basic problem as one of overexpanded public sector employment, with a very large wage bill that stems not so much from high salaries (which are typically eroded by inflation) but from job security provisions and various benefits and, especially, a large surplus of public servants. Large bureaucracies, with job security and low basic salaries, create the most favorable conditions for inefficiency, waste, patronage, corruption, and bureaucratic capture by various interest groups, not to mention fiscal imbalances. It is difficult to assess exactly the effect of overexpanded public employment on redistributive flows. It is hard to imagine, however, that public employment with these characteristics is the most efficient way of redistributing income toward the very poor as a group.

Several country-specific studies are good illustrations of the lack of true redistribution in social policies. In Brazil, social spending (equal to 25 percent of gross domestic product) on social security, education, housing, health, water and sanitation, and food and urban transportation, is generally viewed as regressive.[10] Social security, which in 1986 was about half of total social spending in Brazil, is considered regressive for a variety of reasons: Skilled urban workers are more likely to be enrolled than unskilled rural workers; deficits of social security systems are often paid out of the general budget, at the expense of other social spending programs; the system has allowed for all sorts of privileged positions with very generous conditions; the poorest unskilled workers drift in and out of the informal sector and often are cut out from the more generous provisions of the pension system. Angell and Graham (1995), for instance, report that in Brazil less than 20 percent of the poorest 40 percent of the population are covered by social security and receive about 3 percent of the total benefits.

Spending on education in Brazil reveals the same pattern: excessive spending on higher-level education at the expense of primary education. In the health sector, almost 80 percent (in 1986) of spending was of the curative type (hospitals, doctors, etc.) and concentrated in urban areas. Only about 20 percent was for preventive care, which is considered much more pro-poor and pro-rural, and actually is more cost-effective.

World Bank studies for Venezuela display similar results (Hausmann 1994). In evaluating this evidence, Angell and Graham (1995) conclude that "the problems in Venezuela's social sectors stem from decades of resource misallocation rather than from the fiscal constraints related to the adjustment" (p. 212). In the education sector, for instance, personnel costs absorb more than 90 percent of the education budget, and because of the rigidity of public employment, these costs are politically difficult to cut (Angell and Graham 1995). Although teachers may not be universally well paid, they benefit from job security, and certain teachers groups have certainly managed to obtain extremely generous arrangements. Hausmann (1994) notes that in Venezuela, "University Professors retire after 25 years of service with full pensions.... Most Professors ... retire before the age of 50" (p. 180). Although spending on higher education in Venezuela is more than 50 percent of the education budget (Angell and Graham 1995), "secondary school enrollment is amazingly low and entry to the free university system is unusually liberal" (Hausmann 1994, p. 178). Angell and Graham (1995) argue that the health system in Venezuela is extremely expensive and inefficient, provides poor services, and has regressive effects. Partly as a result of the poor state of social services in Venezuela, poverty increased in the 1980s.[11]

Aspe (1993) and, especially, Aspe and Sigmud (1984) show that in Mexico, between 1940 and 1980, and specifically from 1960 to 1980 (the two decades that preceded the debt crisis), income distribution worsened. The poor became poorer (in relative terms) because of government welfare policies, *not* despite them. In fact, most of the welfare and benefit programs have improved the conditions not of the very poor but of groups that had already been the main beneficiaries of economic growth:

the upper and middle urban classes. Three examples for Mexico highlight this observation: public policies for education, health, and housing.

In education, the ratio of spending for primary education over total spending in education showed a steadily declining trend from about .53 in 1960 to about .27 in 1979. The ratio of spending in primary education over spending in higher education reached a maximum of about 3.5 in 1962 and was about 1.0 in 1979. The spending per student in higher education was seventy-six times larger than spending per student in primary education in 1976.

Public spending for health was extremely skewed in favor of the urban population, particularly in Mexico City. In 1970, the ratio of inhabitants for paramedical personnel was 231 in the Federal District and 3,432 in the state of Oaxaca. Several other statistics on health service provisions confirm an extremely skewed regional distribution, with rural regions receiving less.

The process of urbanization and internal migration created an immense housing problem, with a large fraction of the population unable to afford buying or renting decent housing in big cities, particularly in Mexico City. The government reacted in a variety of ways, which resulted in sizable windfalls for the middle class but not much benefit for the poor. For instance, a new agency was created to provide subsidized loans to help finance housing, but the initial down payments and monthly payments necessary to qualify for this subsidy were way too high for the bottom quintile of the income distribution.[12] In the 1970s, a constitutional provision established that employers had to provide housing to workers. A fund targeted to workers in the formal sector was created that put together withholdings from workers' pay, employers' contributions, and state subsidies for housing construction. But because it was limited to the formal sector, the fund did not reach the poorest in the population, who are typically employed in the informal sector.

A cross-country study of the redistributive effects of social security is a paper in itself.[13] In his assessment of the evidence for Latin America, Mackenzie (1988) argues that "certain occupational groups participated in social security programs early on, and other groups were gradually included, not in the original plans but in entirely different and separately administered schemes. Substantial inequalities existed across plans" (p. 499). Coverage rates greatly varied across countries, but, according to Mackenzie, those covered were "privileged groups" (p. 512). The redistributive effects would be negligible if social security systems were completely funded by contributions of the beneficiaries, but typically this is not the case; social security systems, which cover privileged groups, are largely financed by the general budget, and the effect is regressive. In fact, Mackenzie's review of the available evidence leads him to conclude that where coverage of social security systems is broad, the redistributive effects are fairly neutral, and where coverage is more limited, social security systems have regressive effects (p. 512).

A particularly well-studied case of an unfair prereform social security system is that of Chile. Mesa-Lago (1985) describes how the preprivatization social security system favored white-collar workers and certain privileged unionized and politically active groups—for instance, government employees, mining sector workers, and financial sector workers. Mesa-Lago concludes that "the segment of the labor force with the most protection is made up of salaried personnel, working in strategic trades, with a high degree of unionization, and with a medium to high income; ... The segment of the population with the least protection is made up mainly of self-employed, unpaid family workers, working in agricultural and personal services and with a low income" (cited by Moufflet 1995, p. 55).

It should be clear that a strong case can be made that traditional social policies have not primarily benefited the very poor. This does not imply that all social policies are intrinsically flawed, but that a remarkably large part of those policies actually followed in the developing world have not reached the very poor.

9.3   Fiscal Adjustment and Budget Composition

When fiscal stabilization finally occurs, how are the expenditure cuts distributed? Which parts of the budget bear the brunt of the adjustment, and which parts are spared? Obviously the answer to this question varies from country to country, but it may be useful to consider a broad overview. In ongoing research, I have been looking at the composition of fiscal adjustment in OECD countries and a broad sample of countries including both OECD and developing countries.[14] In this approach, we isolate episodes of fiscal adjustment, defined as periods where the deficits fall significantly, of, say, a certain fraction of GDP.[15] We then look at what components of spending are cut and which types of taxes are increased; we find that, on average, the component of spending that receives the largest cut is public investment, with social spending and transfers typically untouched or receiving much smaller cuts. Particularly in developing countries, this evidence is clearly suggestive rather than conclusive, and caution is urged not to overinterpret these results because of the notoriously low quality of macrodata on public investment. However, it is comforting to note that this broad picture is confirmed by several more specific and disaggregate studies. For instance, Hicks and Kubisch (1984), looking at thirty-two cases of fiscal adjustment in the 1970s, show that infrastructure expenditure fell by 1.7 percentage points for every 1 percentage point cut in total public expenditure, and social spending had the lowest index of vulnerability: For every percentage point cut in total public expenditure, social spending was cut by 0.4 percentage points. Hicks (1989) argues that this pattern continued in fiscal adjustments of the 1980s. Analogous results are reported by Seeme (1984), particularly on the low vulnerability of social spending. Meyers (1986) finds that cutbacks in transportation and communication infrastructure exceeded average cutbacks in 70 percent of the episodes that he examined. For his sample of thirty-five cases of fiscal adjustments, central government investments were cut in half, and spending on health and education were cut 10 and 5 percent, respectively. The average cut in total expenditure was 16 percent in his sample.[16]

The cuts in public investments were not a reaction to their disproportionate increase before the adjustment. During the period of high deficit before the adjustment, public investment did not increase more than average. By examining the years that preceded fiscal adjustments, I found that the budget composition was relatively constant.[17] If anything, one could detect a tendency for transfers and subsidies to increase. In fact, Heller and Diamond (1990), who studied the evolution of budget composition in developing countries around the world for the period 1975 through 1986, found that relative to a baseline model, social expenditures appeared to have increased more than predicted, and capital expenditures increased less than the baseline prediction, particularly in Africa.

The picture that emerges from this evidence is rather clear: Public investment and infrastructure bear the largest share of fiscal adjustment, even though they are not the main source of the original fiscal imbalance. Social spending, transfers, and subsidies suffer much smaller cuts than public investments during fiscal adjustments, even though they generally increase during the period of imbalance.[18]

I find much to be worried about from this evidence. Public investment and spending on infrastructure are politically the easiest part of the budget to cut, relative to, say, public employment and transfers to powerful interest groups. They also imply a possibly quite large reduction in future growth—a high price to pay to safeguard the income level of interest groups today.[19] On the one hand, not all public investments are efficient. Thus, in principle, some of the cuts on public projects may not be of much consequence from the point of view of economic efficiency. On the other hand, it is not obvious that the less efficient projects would always be the first to go. Political patronage, lobbying, and corruption may actually preserve from budget cuts the least economically efficient, but more politically sensitive, projects.

From a macroeconomic perspective, there is indeed a good chance that in the next two decades, the public capital of infrastructures will be seriously affected in several developing countries that have experienced major fiscal adjustments. It is probably too early to detect significant differences in the infrastructure stock of adjusting and nonadjusting countries because capital stocks are slow moving. However, crumbling infrastructure in developing countries may be a serious problem in the next couple of decades.

The reduction in public investment may be considered a reasonable price to pay for the maintenance of social spending and transfer to the poor during the adjustment. However, the traditional social welfare program and social spending channel rarely reach the really poor but instead redistribute among the upper and lower middle classes (not always in favor of the latter!) and among various interest groups. Thus, the worry is that cuts in public investment serve the purpose of maintaining current income levels not of the very poor but of the very vocal.

9.4   Can Fiscal Adjustment Safeguard the Poor?

The somewhat scattered evidence reviewed so far suggests that fiscal adjustments, which typically accompany broad policy reforms, do not have to hurt the poor. The reason is simple: The pattern of spending that leads to the fiscal imbalances in the first place generally does *not* favor the poor, so even cutting traditional welfare spending programs typically hurts entrenched interest groups and parts of the middle class but not necessarily the very poor.

I am not arguing that fiscal adjustments never hurt the poor but that given the pattern of spending and taxation in the prestabilization period, it is *possible* to achieve fiscal consolidation *and* improve living conditions of the very poor. The achievement of this goal requires a rather drastic change in the composition of spending and a reform of traditional social welfare programs. For example, even a cut in overall education spending accompanied by a sharp redirection of funds from higher education to primary education may help fiscal consolidation and improve the conditions of the poor in both relative and absolute terms. On the revenue side, a reduction in the fiscal evasion of specific groups may significantly improve revenues without the need for a broad-based increase in tax rates. In summary, since the vocal, more than the poor, had benefited from fiscal imbalances, it is feasible not to reduce the welfare of the poor during adjustment.

Obviously economic feasibility does not imply political feasibility. Precisely because the vocal have more political leverage, they can oppose fiscal reforms they do not like. This is the biggest political dilemma that needs to be resolved. Fortunately, there are some indications that the goal of safeguarding the poor through fiscal adjustment and policy reform is attainable. For instance, Cardoso and Helwege (1993) argue that the post-1982 Mexican fiscal adjustment was accompanied by shifts in spending priorities, which in fact improved the welfare of the rural poor. Among others, the Solidarity Program was a successful initiative for switching welfare benefits to the rural poor.

According to a recent, well-documented study (Graham 1994), Bolivia's emergency social fund (ESF) is a success story of fiscal adjustment that not only safeguarded the poor but improved their welfare. Graham concludes that "Bolivian experience demonstrates the contributions that safety nets can make to the political sustainability of reform and to poverty reduction when they ... incorporate the demands and participation of the poor" (p. 1). The ESF, established in 1985 as part of structural reforms and economic adjustment, responded to projects proposed by local governments and other nongovernmental organizations and applied market-oriented principles to assistance programs. Graham writes that "the administrative unit of the ESF consisted of a small group of well-paid and highly qualified personnel.... At full capacity the program generated 20,000 man/months of employment per month" (p. 60). The ESF also promoted a variety of infrastructure projects, which reached the rural poor for the first time in Bolivian history. It remains to be seen whether the ESF really reached the poorest of the poor in rural areas. Clearly the temptation to use these funds for political patronage is very high, but, by and large, according to Graham, the history of the ESF is one of relative independence, efficiency, and the corruption-free use of funds. One reason for the ESF's success was that it was established outside the normal bureaucracy and the usual allocation channels of social spending.

On the taxation side, the recent fiscal adjustment in Argentina was helped by significant improvements in reducing widespread fiscal evasion. Part of this success is due to the establishment of new bodies of fiscal inspectors, with a clear mandate to reduce evasion and strong incentives to achieve this goal.

Even the Chilean adjustment under the Pinochet regime managed to implement fiscal reforms that safeguarded the very poor. Graham (1994) writes that "social spending on the poorest sector increased in both relative and absolute terms" (p. 28). Coverage for various poverty-alleviating programs was redirected to favor the very poor at the expense of the not so poor. On health services, this author concludes that "under the military regime the quality of public services declines.... At the same time the poorest groups were able to gain access [to health services]" (p. 32). Stewart (1991) reaches similar conclusions and underlines how several policies safeguarded the most vulnerable "even during the recessionary phase of the adjustment" (p. 1856). She also notes that various social spending programs were reformed and made less regressive. The privatization of the social security system in Chile eliminated various privileged positions. Overall, income distribution became more unequal as a result of the post-1974 Chilean adjustment. However, because of successful targeting and reforms in the social sectors, the very poor were safeguarded and improved their relative and absolute position.[20]

Thorbecke (1991) and Ravallion and Huppi (1991a, 1991b) document that throughout Indonesia's adjustment in the 1980s, the relative and absolute position of the poor, particularly the rural poor, actually improved. Thornbecke cites the composition of budget cuts in the fiscal adjustment as the reason for this success but notes that budget cuts fell disproportionally on capital investment and infrastructure, an example of the trend already documented for a large sample of countries. Thus, future growth and future further reduction in poverty may be threatened. Ribe et al. (1990) document that in Korea during the swift and successful adjustment in 1980, "subsidized medical programs aimed at the poor were expanded" (p. 7). As a result, health statistics improved during the adjustment.

More generally, the scattered and scarce evidence is that fiscal adjustments in particular, and stabilizing policy reforms in general, have or have not hurt the poor depending on initial conditions and on how they have been implemented. This conclusion emerges from both Bourguignon, de Melo, and Morrison (1991) and Lipton and Ravallion (1993), who survey the available evidence. After reviewing the results from computable general equilibrium exercises on several countries that experienced fiscal adjustments, Bourguignon, de Melo, and Morrison conclude that these countries "show considerable diversity in the evolution of income distribution during *adjustment*" (p. 1505).[21] Lipton and Ravallion, in particular, emphasize that the welfare impact of fiscal adjustment depends on how spending is cut and conclude that one "should be wary of simple theoretical arguments about the welfare impact of adjustment.... Evidence will be typically needed to solve the issue" (p. 55). The scattered evidence on this point is inconclusive.[22] The distributional effects of adjustments depend on initial conditions and the composition of budget cuts.

The final issue to tackle more directly is that of the temporary increase in unemployment that allegedly accompanies fiscal adjustments. The argument is that the aggregate demand contraction caused by the fiscal consolidation causes a major recession, which worsens income inequality and threatens political sustainability. In other words, there is a J curve effect: Reform makes things worse before making them better. I agree with Rodrik (1996) when he notes that "for a proposition that is startlingly lacking in empirical support, [this] piece of conventional wisdom is surprisingly strongly held" (p. 29). The contractionary effects of fiscal adjustments are questionable. From a theoretical standpoint, the aggregate demand effects can easily be compensated by gains in credibility, which may reduce real interest rates. This credibility effect may kick in rather quickly. The empirical evidence is, in fact, mixed. In OECD countries, Giavazzi and Pagano (1990) and Alesina and Perotti (1995) note that several major fiscal contractions have not been accompanied by recessions; in fact, some of them have been expansionary. Rodrik (1994) notes that several recent fiscal adjustments in LDCs have been accompanied by consumption booms and also correctly points out that often fiscal adjustments occur in stagnant economies. It is not obvious at all that growth would not have been even lower without the fiscal adjustment.

In summary, the answer to the question posed in the title of this section is that economically it is quite feasible (perhaps even easy) to restructure the budget so as to achieve fiscal stabilization and improve the welfare of the very poor. The stumbling block is political: obtaining the necessary political support to implement this type of fiscal adjustment and reform.

One plausible answer is that reformers have to take advantage of moments of exceptional politics, proceed quickly, and, if possible, seek new alliances for political support. This is an argument in favor of shock therapy. Reforms have to signal a significant break with past failed policies. Moreover, there is probably no point in trying to compensate the vocal interest groups who will have to see their privileges cut. On the contrary, much has to be gained by reaching out to groups who have not benefited from the prereform policies.[23] Two difficulties arise. First, those who have not benefited from prereform politics are, almost by definition, the less vocal and less politically organized—often the very poor. Second, government bureaucracies that have to manage adjustments and reforms are often a primary conservative force, that is, an antireform interest group, since they were often a significant part of the beneficiaries of the pre-reform status quo.

Understanding how different countries cope with these difficulties would go a long way in exploring different degrees of success in policy reforms. The next section provides some suggestions on how international organizations in general, and the IMF in particular, can help in this respect.

9.5 The Role of International Organizations

Attention to Budget Composition

In order to understand the distributional effects of public spending and budget cuts, one needs to disaggregate the budget in detail. Traditional levels of disaggregation—say, in spending on health, education, social security, and investment—are not sufficient to evaluate how different programs affect income groups. The importance of budget composition should be clear by now: Only fairly radical shifts in the direction of spending can achieve the goals of consolidating the budget without hurting the poor.

My sense is that there is too much of a gap between the macroeconomic adjustment programs, typically drafted by the IMF, and the detailed country studies, often outside a specific macroeconomic context, drafted by the World Bank. A closer interplay between these two approaches may be very productive.

Specifically, I do not think that IMF policy advice can ignore the issue of the composition of fiscal adjustments, as a couple of examples will show. First, suppose that a country's fiscal imbalance is due primarily to underfunded pension systems.[24] If a fiscal adjustment relies on tax increases without tackling the unsustainable dynamic of the pension system, it cannot lead to a permanent fiscal consolidation, and the short-run successes are purely illusory. Second, suppose that a fiscal adjustment is not accompanied by the above-sketched kind of reform of the social spending delivery system and leads to an even more unequal distribution of benefits. In the medium term this may lead to political backlash. Thus, both purely economic reasons (the pension example) and political reasons (the backlash argument) suggest that the probability of success of a fiscal adjustment is not independent of its composition.[25] For this reason, the IMF cannot shy away from discussing composition.

The counterargument is that the composition of the budget is a domestic political problem, which the IMF should be agnostic about. I certainly see the logic and the importance of this point, and I appreciate how sensitive this issue is. However, the intricacy of the relationship between budget composition, income distribution, and the economic and political sustainability of fiscal reforms is too important for the IMF to ignore. In fact, World Bank–IMF technical assistance on spending reallocation and implementation of truly equitable social safety nets (as opposed to buyouts) could be quite valuable. Unfortunately, the problem of "techniques" needing "technical" assistance is only part of the problem. Most of the difficulties are political.

Circumventing Traditional, Entrenched, and Captured Bureaucracies

Various interest groups and entrenched bureaucracies often form alliances, which are much of the problem that created the budget imbalance. Traditional bureaucracies and traditional social service delivery channels have often been one of the sources of fiscal imbalance and mistargeting of spending, and they can be a powerful obstacle to budget adjustment and reform. In the short run, it may be necessary to establish new bureaucratic bodies that break from traditional channels. Successful new programs developed outside traditional bureaucratic channels in the context of exceptional politics and shock therapy may have beneficial demonstrative effects and may create powerful incentives for the traditional bureaucracies. A successful new program may also generate political support for broader bureaucratic reforms. The most difficult problem is how to incorporate new bureaucratic entities into the main body of public bureaucracy, avoiding the problems of rejections and conflicts between old and new.

Safety Nets

The use of safety nets to relieve short-run costs of policy reforms is often advocated as a crucial ingredient for the political sustainability of reforms; however, safety nets may or may not work depending on how they are implemented, as Graham (1994) as convincingly demonstrated.

Since the benefits of safety nets are widely praised, it may be useful to raise a few red flags. First, the administration of safety net programs during adjustments may suffer the same problems of misdirection of social spending. Graham (1994) documents several examples of this problem. For instance, she examines the effect of a safety net program in Senegal created to alleviate the problems of newly unemployed civil servants, but this very expensive program "produced only a small improvement in permanent employment.... It was ... a 'sweet deal' to various groups who were opposed to adjustment, particularly ... civil servants" (p. 131). Second, the "new" unemployed, particularly former public employees displaced by the fiscal adjustment, are typically much more vocal than the "old" unemployed, who were not part of the active labor force in the first place. One should be careful not to overcompensate the new unemployed—for instance, laid-off union members—at the expense of those who were never union members and never worked in the protected sector. Third, it is important that public programs that support employment not interfere excessively with market forces and not slow the speed of reforms. In my view, the World Bank and the IMF should not provide a blanket support for any safety net program but carefully select those that do not represent the continuation of failed social policies of the past.

The Role of Foreign Aid
Can foreign aid accelerate and help stabilization programs? The interest group politics approach that underlies this chapter implies that vocal groups manage to attract spending in their favor and shield themselves from taxation. The same approach can also explain why stabilizations and reforms are often delayed, even when it is increasingly obvious that a stabilization sooner or later will have to be implemented and the longer one waits, the more costly the stabilization will be.

Several arguments may explain delays, including irrationality and policy mistakes. However, for several reasons (see Alesina and Perotti 1995, in particular), a war-of-attrition model is one of the most promising ways to rationalize delays in the adoption of fiscal stabilizations. The idea, as developed in Alesina and Drazen (1991), is that different groups are strong enough to "veto" stabilization programs they do not like, but no group, at least at the beginning, is strong enough to impose on all the others the burden of the stabilization. Fiscal adjustment is delayed until this impasse is resolved, even though delays are inefficient for the economy as a whole.

The crucial ingredients in the model are uncertainty and distributional conflicts. Each group must be uncertain about how costly it is for the opponents to delay reforms and hold on to the status quo. A stabilization occurs when a group succumbs, and it is willing to accept being a "loser," that is, bearing a disproportionate cost of the stabilization. Delays occur because it is in the interest of every group not to give in until it is clear which is the weakest group. The passage of time and the accumulation of prestabilization costs reveal which group can no longer wait. Stabilizations occur with no delay in only two cases: if it is clear from the start which of the groups is politically weaker, so that no political conflict takes place, or if the conflicting groups agree on an equitable division of the burden of stabilization so that there is no losing group, and stabilization is reached by consensus. The latter solution is more difficult in politically polarized societies with a history of harsh political conflict.

Foreign aid can speed up or delay the resolution of this war of attrition, depending on how it is disbursed.[26] Intuitively, aid that is disbursed unconditionally and makes life easier for everybody in the prestabilization economy actually may delay the stabilization and be counterproductive.[27] In fact, it makes various factions less willing to give in, since standards of living before the stabilization are increased. However, aid can be beneficial if it helps resolve the war of attrition. This may occur if aid is disbursed promptly as soon as a political opening appears, that is, as soon as one can detect the sign of a possible resolution of the political impasse, which can occur because of the political consolidation of one side or as a result of a political compromise. Well-timed and prompt aid can have a substantial effect by helping the more promising political coalition formulate reforms. Aid that arrives at the wrong time may simply prolong the war of attrition and be counterproductive.

An important element is conditionality and monitoring. Aid that is channeled through traditional bureaucracies may not reach the truly needy, for the arguments already put forth. On the contrary, incentive schemes for aid recipients may help reformers in their efforts since they can offer a prize, contingent on their success. In order to ensure the long-term sustainability of fiscal reforms, the incentive schemes must go beyond the achievement of macrogoals, such as a budget balance in one particular year. They must include the incentives for reform of unfair and bankrupt social security systems, retargeting of social spending programs, bureaucratic reforms, and improvement in the tax collection system to reduce fiscal evasion.

Institutional Reforms

Successful and sustained policy reforms need to pay much attention to the institutional level. It is not enough for the policy adviser to tell policymakers what policy to follow in a particular situation. It is crucial that institutions be set up to create incentives for politicians to follow— adequate policies, possibly at all times; World Bank and IMF involvement in institutional building and reform is crucial. It is not enough to advise countries that they should cut spending and redefine spending priorities. Countries should also be advised about bureaucratic reforms and changes in fiscal rules and institutions.

Unfortunately, reforms of the bureaucracy and the delivery system for social services are much more complex, less understood, longer to implement, and less visible than shock therapy macroeconomic stabilization policies.[28] However, they are necessary for the long-run sustainability of reforms. A particularly important issue for policy reform is that of budget institutions, defined as all the rules and regulations according to which budgets are prepared, approved, and implemented. For high-debt and deficit countries struggling for policy reforms, certain budget institutions can be more conducive than others to fiscal restraint. Space constraints do not allow for an extensive discussion of this point.[29] However, three critical points have to be stressed. First, budget institutions must limit the possibility for various interest groups to use the budget process as a battleground for special interests. For instance, limits on the type of amendments permissible in the legislative process are one example among many.[30] So are rules that limit the powers of spending ministers in regard to the individual (treasury minister, prime minister, head of state) who is ultimately responsible for the overall budget balance. Spending ministers are more likely to be responsive to various sector-specific special interests; the treasury minister may be more responsive to the interests of the taxpayers. Second, concerning the transparency of the budget and the constraints on creative budgeting procedures, even tough rules meant to enforce fiscal discipline can be circumvented by creative budgeting. Typical examples of untransparent procedures are off-budget items; creativity in the relationship between the central government budget and the budget of the public sector as a whole, including local governments; and public enterprises. Third, the implementation of the budget has the potential for overspending in favor of special interests if the appropriate checks and balances on the bureaucracy are not in place.

Institutions alone cannot enforce sustained budget discipline if there is no political will to sustain it. However, appropriate institutions can help reform-oriented leaders to push through credible budget consolidations. A lively debate in academic and policy circles recently has highlighted the benefits and costs of alternative monetary institutions, particularly different degrees of central bank independence. A similar discussion on budget institutions could be equally productive.

Notes

I thank James Buchanan and Anne Krueger and several participants for their useful and stimulating comments. I also thank for comments, conversations, and bibliographic suggestions Robert Bates, Jorge Dominguez, Carol Graham, Cheik Kane, Roberto Perotti, Sanjay Pradhan, Dani Rodrik, Jeffrey Sachs, Vito Tanzi, Aaron Tornell, Andres Velasco, and especially Marianne Fay. Francesco Caselli provided excellent research assistance.

1. For instance, issues similar to those discussed below apply to subsidized or price-controlled allocation of goods by the public sector. I am grateful to Robert Bates for this observation.

2. A large body of literature in the 1960s and 1970s addressed the link from economic growth to income distribution. A large portion of this literature was inspired by the Kuznets curve hypothesis of an inverted U curve linking inequality and growth. For a survey of this literature, see Adelman and Robinson (1988).

3. For formal models in this spirit, see Meltzer and Richards (1981), Alesina and Rodrik (1994), Persson and Tabellini (1994), Bertola (1993), and Perotti (1993).

4. On the other hand, the traditional Kaldorian argument (Kaldor 1956) suggests that income inequality promotes growth, because the rich have a higher propensity to save and invest than the poor.

5. For a discussion of populism see, in particular, Dornbusch and Edwards (1991).

6. See Krueger (1974) for a pathbreaking contribution on interest group politics.

7. Probably one of the first arguments concerning the distributive effects of hyperinflation goes back to Bresciani-Turroni (1937). For a recent discussion of the evidence, see Cardoso and Helwege (1991).

8. See, for instance, Tanzi (1982) and especially Tanzi and Shome (1993).

9. These data come from table 5 of Mingat and Tan (1986).

10. See, for instance, Angell and Graham (1995) and several World Bank reports cited in it.

11. World Bank (1991), as reported by Angell and Graham (1995, p. 212), documents that the income of the poorest 10 percent of the population fell by almost 20 percent in the 1980s. In 1982, 10 percent of the population was classified "extremely poor" and 22 percent "critically poor." In 1989 these figures had increased to 22 percent and 31 percent, respectively.

12. For example, if in 1977 a family in Mexico City wanted a "social-interest house" it had to pay between 14,000 and 28,000 pesos as a down payment and monthly payments of 1,128 pesos. The bottom two quintiles of the income distribution had a monthly income below 1,163 pesos.

13. For an excellent study of social security around the world, see World Bank (1994).

14. For results on OECD countries, see Alesina and Perotti (1996a).

15. Results are fairly insensitive to the choice of the fraction of GDP chosen as a threshold for defining a fiscal adjustment.

16. I am particularly grateful to Marianne Fay for pointing out these findings to me.

17. In the case of OECD countries, however, the share of transfer programs significantly increased.

18. For a more detailed analysis of OECD countries that reaches similar conclusion, see Alesina and Perotti (1996a).

19. For instance Barro (1991) documents the positive effects of public investment on long-run growth and the negative effect of government consumption.

20. See Graham (1994), Angell and Graham (1995), Bourguignon, de Melo, and Morrison (1991), and Ribe et al. (1990) on this point.

21. The countries in the studies were Chile, Cote d'Ivoire, Ecuador, Malaysia, Morocco, and Indonesia.

22. In an almost book-length article, these authors can devote only two pages to a review of the available evidence.

23. On this point, see Graham (1994) and Williamson (1994).

24. This is certainly the case in many OECD countries and LDCs.

25. For empirical evidence on this point for OECD countries, see Alesina and Perotti (1996a).

26. See Casella and Eichengreen (1994) for a formal discussion of this point.

27. A related theoretical argument is put forward by Drazen and Grilli (1993). They show that in a war of attrition, an economic "crisis" can have beneficial effects because it speeds up adjustment. The argument about unconditional aid is a similar one, in the opposite direction.

28. See Naim (1994) for a discussion of this point.

29. For original work on fiscal constitutions and rules, see Buchanan and Wagner (1977) and Brennan and Buchanan (1980). For a recent critical survey, see Alesina and Perotti (1996c).

30. For further discussion, see Alesina and Perotti (1996c) and the references cited there.

References

Adelman, Irma, and Sherman Robinson. 1988. "Income Distribution and Development." In Hollis Chenery and T. N. Srinivasan, eds., *Handbook of Development Economics*. Amsterdam: North-Holland.

Alesina, Alberto, and Allan Drazen. 1991. "Why Are Stabilizations Delayed?" *American Economic Review* 81:1170–1188.

Alesina, Alberto, and Roberto Perotti. 1995. *The Political Economy of Budget Deficits*. Staff Papers no. 42. Washington, D.C.: IMF.

Alesina, Alberto, and Roberto Perotti. 1996a. "Fiscal Expansions and Fiscal Contractions in OECD Economies." *Economic Policy* 21:205–248.

Alesina, Alberto, and Roberto Perotti. 1996b. "Income Distribution, Political Instability, and Investment." *European Economic Review* 40:1203–1228.

Alesina, Alberto, and Roberto Perotti. 1996c. *Budget Deficits and Budget Institutions*. Working Paper no. 5556. Cambridge, Mass.: National Bureau of Economic Research.

Alesina, Alberto, Sule Ozler, Nouriel Roubini, and Phill Swagel. 1996. "Political Instability and Economic Growth." *Journal of Economic Growth* 1:189–212.

Alesina, Alberto, and Dani Rodrik. 1994. "Distributive Politics and Economic Growth." *Quarterly Journal of Economics* 109:465–490.

Angell, Alan, and Carol Graham. 1995. "Can Social Sector Reforms Make Adjustment Sustainable and Equitable? Lessons from Chile and Venezuela." *Journal of Latin American Studies*, forthcoming.

Aspe, Pedro. 1993. *Economic Transformation: The Mexican Way*. Cambridge, Mass.: MIT Press.

Aspe, Pedro, and Paul Sigmud. 1984. *The Political Economy of Income Distribution in Mexico*. New York: Holmes and Meier.

Barro, Robert J. 1991. "Economic Growth in a Cross-Section of Countries." *Quarterly Journal of Economics* 106:407–444.

Berg, Andrew, and Jeffrey Sachs. 1988. "The Debt Crisis: Structural Explanations of Country Performance." *Journal of Development Economics* 23:271–306.

Bertola, Guiseppe. 1993. "Factor Shares and Savings in Endogenous Growth." *American Economic Review* 83:1184–1199.

Birdsall, Nancy, David Ross, and Richard Sabot. 1995. "Inequality as a Constraint on Growth in Latin America." In David Turnham, Colon Foy, and Guillermo Larráin, eds., *Social Tensions, Job Creation and Economic Policy in Latin America*, pp. 175–207. Washington, D.C.: OECD and Inter-American Development Bank.

Bourguignon, François, Jaimie de Melo, and Christian Morrison. 1991. "Poverty and Income Distribution During Adjustment: Issues and Evidence from the OECD Project." *World Development* 19:1485–1508.

Brennan, Geoffrey, and James Buchanan. 1980. *The Power to Tax*. Cambridge: Cambridge University Press.

Brescian-Turroni, Costantino. 1937. *The Economics of Inflation*. London: Allen and Unwin.

Buchanan, James, and Richard Wagner. 1977. *Democracy in Deficit*. New York: Academic Press.

Cardoso, Eliana, and Ann Helwege. 1991. "Populism, Profligacy and Redistribution." In Rudiger Dornbusch and Sebastian Edwards, eds., *The Macroeconomics of Populism in Latin America*. Chicago: University of Chicago Press and National Bureau of Economic Research.

Cardoso, Eliana, and Ann Helwege. 1993. *Latin America's Economy*. Cambridge, Mass.: MIT Press.

Casella, Alessandra, and Barry Eichengreen. 1994. *Can Foreign Aid Accelerate Stabilizations?* Working Paper no. 4694. Cambridge, Mass.: National Bureau of Economic Research.

Clarke, George. 1993. "More Evidence on Income Distribution and Growth." Mimeo. Rochester, N.Y.: University of Rochester, Department of Economics.

Cukierman, Alex, Sebastian Edwards, and Guido Tabellini. 1992. "Seignorage and Political Instability." *American Economic Review* 82:537–555.

Dornbusch, Rudiger, and Sebastian Edwards, eds. 1991. *The Macroeconomics of Populism in Latin America*. Chicago: University of Chicago Press and National Bureau of Economic Research.

Drazen, Allan, and Vittorio Grilli. 1993. "The Benefits of Crises for Economic Reform." *American Economic Review*, no. 83:598–607.

Giavazzi, Francesco, and Mario Pagano. 1990. *Can Severe Fiscal Contractions Be Expansionary? Tales of Two Small European States*. Working Paper no. 3372. Cambridge, Mass.: National Bureau of Economic Research.

Graham, Carol. 1994. *Safety Nets, Politics and the Poor*. Washington, D.C.: Brookings Institution.

Haggard, Stephan, and Richard Kaufman. 1990. *The Political Economy of Inflation and Stabilization in Middle-Income Countries*. Policy Research Dept. Working Paper no. 444. Washington, D.C.: World Bank.

Hausmann, Ricardo. 1994. "Sustaining Reform: What Role for Social Policy?" In Colin I. Bradford, Jr., ed., *Redefining the State in Latin America*. Paris: OECD.

Heller, Peter, and Jack Diamond. 1990. *International Comparisons of Government Expenditures Revisited*. Occasional Paper no. 69. Washington, D.C.: International Monetary Fund.

Hicks, Norman. 1989. "Expenditure Reduction in High Debt Countries." *Finance and Development* 26 (March): 35–37.

Hicks, Norman, and Anne Kubisch. 1984. "Cutting Government Expenditure in LDC's." *Finance and Development* 21:37–39.

Jiménez, Emmanuel. 1995. "Human and Physical Infrastructure: Public Invenstment and Pricing Policies in Developing Countries." In Hollis Chenery and T. N. Srinivasan, eds., *Handbook of Development Economics*, vol. 3, chap. 43. New York: North-Holland.

Kaldor, N. 1956. "Alternative Theories of Distribution." *Review of Economic Studies*, no. 23:83–100.

Krueger, Anne. 1974. "The Political Economy of the Rent-Seeking Society," *American Economic Review* 64:291–303.

Lipton, Michael, and Martin Ravallion. 1993. *Poverty and Policy*. Working Paper no. 1130. Washington, D.C.: World Bank.

Londaño, J. C. 1989. "Income Distribution in Colombia: Turning Points, Catching Up and Other Kuznetsian Ideas." Mimeo. Cambridge, Mass.: Harvard University.

Mackenzie, G. A. 1988. *Social Security Issues in Developing Countries*. Staff Papers. Washington, D.C.: International Monetary Fund.

Meltzer, Allan H., and Scott F. Richards. 1981. "A Rational Theory of the Size of Government." *Journal of Political Economy* 89(5):914–927.

Mesa-Lago, Carmelo. 1983. "Social Security and Extreme Poverty in Latin America." *Journal of Development Economics* 12:83–110.

Mesa-Lago, Carmelo. 1985. *Social Security in Latin America*. Pittsburgh, Penn.: University of Pittsburgh Press.

Meyers, Kenneth. 1986. *A Reappraisal of the Sectoral Incidence of Government Expenditure Cutbacks*. CPD Discussion Paper no. 1986-14. Washington, D.C.: World Bank.

Mingat, Alain, and Jee-Peng Tan. 1986. "Who Profits from the Public Funding of Education: A Comparison of World Regions." *Comparative Education Review* 30:260–270.

Moufflet, François. 1995. "The Chilean Social Security Reform." Senior thesis, Harvard University.

Naim, M. 1994. "Latin America: The Second Stage of Reform." *Journal of Democracy* 5:33–48.

Nunberg, Barbara. 1989. *Public Sector Pay and Employment Reform*. Discussion Paper no. 68. Washington, D.C.: World Bank.

Perotti, Roberto. 1992. "Income Distribution, Politics and Growth." *American Economic Review* 82:311–317.

Perotti, Roberto. 1993. "Political Equilibrium, Income Distribution, and Growth." *Review of Economic Studies* 60 (October):755–776.

Perotti, Roberto. 1995. "Income Distribution, Democracy and Growth." Unpublished.

Persson, Torsten, and Guido Tabellini. 1994. "Is Inequality Harmful for Growth? Theory and Evidence." *American Economic Review* 84:600–621.

Pradham, Sanjay. 1996. *Evaluating Public Spending: A Framework for Public Expenditure Reviews*. Discussion Paper no. 323. Washington, D.C.: World Bank.

Ravallion, Martin, and Monika Huppi. 1991a. "Measuring Changes in Poverty: A Methodological Case Study of Indonesia During the Adjustment Period." *World Bank Economic Review* 5:52–82.

Ravallion, Martin, and Monika Huppi. 1991b. "The Sectoral Structure of Poverty During an Adjustment Period: Evidence for Indonesia in the Mid 1980s." *World Development* 19:1653–1678.

Ribe, H., S. Carvalho, R. Liebenthal, P. Nicholas, and E. Zuckerman. 1990. *How Adjustment Programs Can Help the Poor*. Discussion Paper no. 71. Washington, D.C.: World Bank.

Rodrik, Dani. 1994. "Understanding Economic Policy Reforms." *Journal of Economic Literature* 34:9–41.

Sachs, Jeffrey. 1989. "Social Conflict and Populist Policies in Latin America." *Labour Relations and Economic Performance*. Working Paper no. 2897 Cambridge, Mass.: National Bureau of Economic Research.

Seeme, Hafeez. 1984. *Patterns of Reduction in Sectoral Government Expenditure in LDCs: A Preliminary Investigation*. Country Policy Dept. Discussion Paper. Washington, D.C.: World Bank.

Stewart, Frances. 1991. "The Many Faces of Adjustment." *World Development* 19:1847–1864.

Tanzi, Vito. 1974. "Redistributing Income Through the Budget in Latin America." *Banca Nazionale del Lavoro Quarterly Review* 108:65–87.

Tanzi, Vito, ed. 1982. *The Underground Economy in the United States and Abroad*. Lexington, Mass.: Lexington Books.

Tanzi, Vito, and Parthasarathi Shome. 1993. *A Primer on Tax Evasion*. Staff Papers no. 40. Washington, D.C.: International Monetary Fund.

Thorbecke, Erik. 1991. "Adjustment Growth and Income Distribution in Indonesia." *World Development* 19:1595–1614.

Williamson, John, ed. 1994. *The Political Economy of Policy Reform*. Washington, D.C.: Institute for International Economics.

World Bank. 1994. *Averting the Old Age Crisis*. Oxford: Oxford University Press.

Comments

James M. Buchanan

Alberto Alesina's argument is addressed to fellow economists in the international establishment whose evaluative standards give pride of place to distributional norms. From this perspective, Alesina deserves high marks. He shows that there need be no necessary conflict between helping the poor and achieving macrostabilization and growth objectives. The discussion exhibits a sophisticated understanding of institutional realities; there is almost none of the romantic imaging of enlightened political leadership that might have described a comparable enterprise two decades past.

Under this interpretation, Alesina's argument is presumably aimed to persuade the economists and the decision makers in the international agencies and donor governments to ignore pleas from those who would propose holding back on tough policy reforms, allegedly for distributional equity reasons. But to what ultimate purpose? If the basic institutional-constitutional structures remain in place, will not any reforms be dissipated in their effects, distributional or otherwise? Although Alesina does recognize the point, there is not enough emphasis on the straightforward Wicksellian linkage between changes in policy and changes in the rules under which policy options are chosen. This linkage is surely a worthy object for positive inquiry, the results of which are necessarily preliminary to any evaluation of within-rule policy options.

If we enter the realm of normative political philosophy (an area into which Alesina does not venture), we may try, as best we can, to place ourselves behind some carefully defined veil of ignorance or uncertainty in order to derive Rawlsian-like principles of justice, as among persons and social classes, both intra- and intergenerationally. When we do so, the conventional distributive norms applied only to existing members of a polity may become either unimportant or even seem to become perverse.

But to what extent is any such exercise culture and history dependent? I consider the liberal enterprise, exemplified in the Rawlsian effort, to be more universalizable than many modern critics, whether from the left or the right. But as economists, we should not cavalierly put aside either the communitarian or the conservative critique, despite the implied threat to our raison d'être.

Comments

Anne Krueger

Policy Reforms and the Poor

Alberto Alesina confronts a widely held belief: that "stabilization programs and policy reforms, particularly the IMF-supported ones, hurt the poor in the short and medium run by forcing budget cuts, price liberalization and by increasing unemployment." He suggests instead that the redistributive process is captured by various interest groups (such as urban labor unions and civil servants) who are politically far more vocal, visible, and influential than the truly poor. It is these groups, he says, who are the beneficiaries of redistributive programs, are most hurt by policy reform efforts, and are politically influential in opposing reforms. Many others have come to believe this, but the view has not been linked to the political influence, and therefore "capture," of redistributive measures, and it is in that linkage that Alesina makes a significant contribution.

That the poor may not suffer in reform programs has been asserted for years. In the early 1980s, the World Bank documented that significantly more than half the value of the free rice distributed by Sri Lanka benefited the upper half of the income distribution. Later in the 1980s, a major project on the political economy of agricultural pricing, also sponsored by the World Bank, documented that the poor were losers from those policies because the exchange rate overvaluation that normally accompanies the earlier regime feeds through into lower real prices for agricultural exports, which in turn affects the wages of rural landless laborers (the truly poor) and encourages investments in capital-intensive industries, thus providing fewer employment opportunities for unskilled workers than does a more outer-oriented set of trade policies. Another World Bank study, on trade liberalization, documented the absence even of noticeable unemployment effects in urban areas resulting from trade liberalization.

Prereform Conditions, Counterfactuals, and Revealed Preferences

There is even more systematic evidence about the income distribution impact of policy reform than that presented by Alesina. But there are other compelling considerations. Quite aside from redistributive mechanisms, the policies in prereform periods tend to benefit the upper-income groups. I have in mind import-substitution policies that benefit, at least in the short run, local owners of capital, trade union members, and those able to use influence to receive import licenses; parastatal enterprises, which benefit upper-level civil servants; and interest rate ceilings and credit rationing, which benefit those who qualify for bank credits. All of these policies are undertaken in the name of economic growth and yet clearly benefit those at the upper end of the income distribution (or those who are rich after these policies have been in place) while in fact constraining growth. Dismantling these policies can affect the income distribution as much as, if not more than, redistributive policies.

A second major reason that examination of only the beneficiaries of redistributive policies is not the only compelling line of evidence has to do with the counterfactual question: What would happen in countries having the economic difficulties of Turkey in 1980, Brazil in 1993, or Chile in 1973–1974 if they did not undertake political reform programs? Quite clearly the economic costs of the preexisting programs were substantial and would have increased in the absence of policy changes.

Yet a third major consideration is the revealed preference of voters. Judging by popular reactions (as seen through elections, most recently in Argentina and Brazil), reducing inflation is one of the most popular acts a politician can do. And past reform programs (such as that in Turkey in 1980–1981) have won elections for the reformers. Even in Chile, when elections were finally held, all parties committed themselves to perpetuate the economic reforms that had been undertaken.

Suggested Studies

There is ample evidence that inflation hurts the poor, who have few means of protecting themselves against it. But the evidence from the polls strongly suggests that whatever dislocations do occur in a reform program are small contrasted with the relief the voters feel when the rate of inflation is sharply reduced.

Thus, I strongly concur with Alesina's thesis as to the income distributional effects of policy reform. I would hope that he will delve further into the political mechanisms that give rise to the capture of growth policy, as well as redistributive policy, by the middle- and upper-income groups.

10

Equity Implications of IMF Policy Advice

I

Monetary Policy: Equity Issues in IMF Policy Advice

Manuel Guitián

A key aim of IMF monetary policy advice, particularly in its surveillance activities, is to foster measures that will promote stability in the value of the currency, particularly price stability in the medium term. This objective is critical because of the adverse impact that high and variable levels of inflation have on economic activity and well-being in general. It relates also to the IMF's traditional concern in its surveillance, program design, and lending activities with safeguarding the external position of a country, that is, with exchange rate and balance of payments viability, since weakness in the balance of payments and unrealistic exchange rates are typically associated with an excessive (inflation-generating) rate of monetary expansion.[1]

Equity is often interpreted as requiring that policies do not increase the degree of inequality in income distribution or maybe that they serve to decrease this inequality. Since the objective of IMF advice is to create a noninflationary economic environment and since in any case monetary policy ultimately affects only the rate of inflation, an examination of equity issues in IMF policy advice can best be conducted by means of a comparison of the differences in income distribution in a high-inflation and a low-inflation economy. The focus of this analysis therefore will be on monetary management. Exchange policy aspects, which bear an intimate relationship with monetary policy and developments, will not be addressed in detail here because I have examined them at length elsewhere.[2]

My approach will be not to look at particular monetary policy measures that might be adopted in the context of an IMF-supported stabilization program. Such measures may have temporary consequences for income distribution in the short run insofar as they may have real effects (although the direction of such effects is not unambiguous); in any case, these effects are best seen as the result of the initial inflation that is being combated, that is, as the consequence of the factors that contributed to and sustained the inflation, rather than being attributable to the adoption of appropriate monetary measures themselves. Instead, I will argue that IMF monetary policy advice can best be judged in terms of assessing the efficiency of monetary policy implementation for price level performance and the distributional effect of inflation. First, I look at the modalities of how IMF policy advice serves to bring down inflation. In this regard, I recall that IMF advice entails not only the setting of macroeconomic targets but also the formulation of structural reforms to help achieve these targets. In particular, it aims at improving the workings of the instruments of monetary policy. Advice in this regard is frequently supported by technical assistance from the IMF. Second, I present new evidence on the existence of a measurable link between income distribution and the rate of inflation.

10I.1   IMF Monetary Policy Advice

Basic Principles

IMF monetary policy advice can be summarized in three principal recommendations: (1) It is intended to stabilize the price level, in order to provide the basis for a sustainable balance of payments and noninflationary growth; (2) it should not be used for additional (or alternative) purposes, such as financing of the government or of selected economic sectors; and (3) it should be conducted in a way that gives market forces their proper role in the pricing and allocation of credit.[3]

The rationale for the first policy prescription is that an inflationary environment hampers economic activity by distorting the signals that guide the efficient allocation of resources. It is also centered on the principle of monetary neutrality; that is, in the long run, monetary policy is unable to change real output. In other words, monetary policy influences nominal variables (such as the price level), but it cannot alter real variables (such as output, employment, growth, or the terms of trade) on a sustained basis. It can, though, have important effects on these variables in the short run.[4] In this regard, these views, which now are accepted widely, reflect the hard-learned lesson in many countries that any attempts to realize short-term gains on the economic activity front by relaxing antiinflationary discipline will tend to do more harm than good. Under flexible exchange rates, short-term gains in output are likely to lead to a persistent increase in the rate of inflation, and maybe financial instability, which, in turn, will lead to a need to undertake costly economic adjustment. Under fixed exchange rates, such expansionary monetary policy will lead to an increasing current account deficit, loss of reserves, and, later, the need for possibly painful adjustment measures, including a reduction in domestic absorption, import compression, and exchange devaluation.

The second recommendation—that monetary policy should focus primarily, if not solely, on the medium-term objective of price stability—reflects a broad experience that when multiple objectives are specified, conflicts often arise among them and, consequently, those on the inflation front can be jeopardized.[5] Furthermore, the recommendation may be viewed as an attempt to promote "first-best" policy assignments throughout the spectrum of macroeconomic policy, since any attempts to direct monetary policy toward additional goals, even if these are legitimate public policy objectives, will distract from the need to implement appropriate policies through other instruments (for instance, fiscal policy or public sector structural reform) and will compromise the principal task of monetary policy.

The third recommendation—favoring the role of market forces in the conduct of monetary policy—translates the general view on the efficiency of market-based resource allocation to the financial sphere. Prices in financial markets, that is, interest rates, should be given their appropriate role to ensure an efficient allocation of savings and credit. For this to work best, a number of sectoral and institutional prerequisites, on which I touch later, should be in place. Prior to this stage, policymakers may not be able to rely fully on market forces and may have to operate policy through credit allocation if insufficient basis exists for using money markets for this purpose. In such cases, however, IMF advice is aimed at assisting a country to undertake structural reforms so that a market-based operation of monetary policy can be established.

Market-Based Implementation of Monetary Policy

An increasingly important aspect of IMF policy advice is the adoption of monetary policy instruments that will enable countries to operate monetary policy more efficiently and effectively. This has an important bearing on the overall topic being discussed, as use of such instruments will assist in the achievement of countries' anti-inflationary targets.

I first examine the links between the nature of monetary instruments and the effectiveness of the operation of monetary policy. I show that a transition to indirect instruments of monetary policy assists the operation of monetary policy. I then summarize the experience of countries that have made this transition. Insofar as the transition helps the achievement of the country's anti-inflationary objectives, it is clear that advice regarding this transition reinforces the general advice regarding the reduction of inflation and will thus also serve to reinforce the equity implications of this advice.

Concept   Direct instruments of monetary control, such as credit ceilings and interest rate controls, have been used in the past by most countries. They have a superficial attraction in that they are easy to implement and seem able to achieve given quantitative targets.[6] Yet they are likely to have serious drawbacks from an efficiency perspective and for equity reasons. Credit ceilings, the most common direct instrument, tend to ossify the role of large lenders and large borrowers, thereby limiting possible inroads that new participants—frequently the (small) private sector—can make. In addition, there is a tendency for controls to multiply and costs of intermediation to increase, as the authorities attempt to thwart attempts to circumvent the initial controls. This leads to disintermediation out of the formal financial sector, so that the targets that are apparently achieved in fact relate only to a declining share of overall activity within the economy. Finally, direct instruments are often associated with attempts to micromanage monetary conditions, thus subverting the objective of using monetary policy solely to bring down inflation.

In recent years, there has been a growing trend to abandon such direct instruments and to move to indirect instruments of monetary management. Often with IMF support, countries have eliminated credit and interest rate controls, introduced uniform reserve requirements on bank deposits, and begun managing liquidity conditions through the purchase and sale of government or central bank securities on primary or secondary markets. This approach can depoliticize the allocation of credit and reduce the protection of existing large institutions by fostering competition in the financial sector. Greater competition tends to decrease the cost of financial intermediation and fosters the reintegration of the informal with the formal financial sector. Thus, it enables the monetary authorities to manage monetary conditions in the economy as a whole, thereby rendering monetary policy more effective and facilitating the achievement of inflation targets on a sustained basis.

Experience   Table 10I.1 summarizes the experience of a sample of countries with the introduction of indirect instruments of monetary control. The empirical results provide firm support for the view that indirect monetary instruments enable the authorities to manage monetary conditions more effectively. Experience from the sample group of countries shows

Table 10I.1
Results of Introducing Indirect Methods of Monetary Control

Result	Measured by	Percentage of Countries
Financial stability increased after transition period	Decline in standard deviation of M2/M0	83 percent
Financial deepening	Decrease in ratio of M1/M2	58 percent
Financial efficiency	Decline in interest rate spread	82 percent
Extension of formal financial sector	Increase in deposit market share of banks	55 percent
Extension of formal financial sector	Increase in loan market share of banks	83 percent
Increased access by private sector to credit	Share of private sector	82 percent
Lower inflation	Decline in inflation rate	70 percent

Source: Alexander, Baliño, and Enoch (1995, tables 7, 8).

that after a transition period, the volatility of most monetary aggregates declines. Similarly, interest rate spreads typically narrow, banks take a larger role in financial intermediation, and the private sector's share in total credit increases. Finally—and most important from the perspective of the subject of this chapter—it appears that the authorities can increase their ability to contain inflation. Indeed, it is worth noting that of the twenty countries examined in the study, fourteen showed lower inflation following their introduction of indirect instruments than in the previous period.

10I.2   Relationship Between Inflation and Income Distribution

Inflation not only distorts resource allocation, but it may also alter income distribution, and often in an unpredictable manner. Thus, in calling for policies to ensure low inflation and a sustainable balance of payments, the IMF's monetary policy advice does imply equity considerations; it favors an environment in which the distributional outcome is safe from the non-neutralities of adjustment and inflation-related costs.[7]

Theoretical Linkages Between Monetary Policy and Income Distribution

Here I briefly examine the major transmission channels through which monetary policy can influence income distribution, as well as present empirical evidence of such a link.

Anticipated Inflation   Rational expectations literature indicates that in a frictionless world, anticipated inflation is costless. Yet in the imperfect world in which we live, even anticipated inflation is likely to have costs and distributional effects. Among these, first, the well-known inflation tax will fall only on holders of money and other financial assets whose yield is fixed in nominal terms. To the extent that certain segments of society —most likely the less affluent—rely on cash holdings or have no access to indexed assets, they will have to bear a disproportionate share of such a tax. Second, in many progressive tax systems bracket creep will increase the real tax burden of certain affected segments. Third, the costs of price adjustments may contribute to the misallocation of resources and eventually increase prices to both consumers and producers.

Unanticipated Inflation   Unanticipated inflation, as the term suggests, takes the economy by surprise. Hence, in addition to effects identified for anticipated inflation, important real effects will emerge. By its surprise nature, this type of inflation will not be cushioned by indexation schemes and will reduce both the real value of nominal assets and nominal debt. Thus, it favors the holders of nominal debt and real equity at the expense of holders of nominal assets. The distributional consequences depend on the relative size of holdings of these assets and liabilities across the population. In addition, unanticipated inflation is costly to those locked into nominal contracts. In the most discussed case, this reduces real wages but favors the owners of capital; however, it applies equally to all other types of nominal contracts.

Inflation Uncertainty   After the notion of a predictable and stable financial environment has been lost, the resulting uncertainty will generate additional costs. First, it imposes a hedging cost on savers and investors as they try to insure themselves against the inflation surprises and the associated distortions in asset allocation. Second, uncertainty imposes a risk premium on all transactions of longer maturity (including nominal contracts) or, in the limiting case, prevent longer-term nonindexed transactions. Finally, inflation uncertainty distorts relative price signals and causes a general economy-wide increase in transaction costs. In addition to their direct effects on income distribution, such distortions reduce the overall quantity of resources to be distributed by forcing the economy to operate inside the frontier of production possibilities.

Empirical Evidence on the Relationship Between Inflation and Income Distribution

Despite compelling arguments linking monetary policy and inflation to income distribution, only a few empirical tests have been conducted. To a large extent, this is due to the lack of both a suitable theoretical framework and consistent data—the latter leading to mostly small samples and, hence, inconclusive results. The discussion here seeks to answer the questions of whether inflation leads to a change in the degree of inequality in income distribution and whether there is a systematic measurable change in the relative position of different income segments due to inflation.

Results from Pooled Time-Series and Cross-Section Data   The classic starting point for discussions of overall income distribution is Kuznets's (1955) model, which links the distributive outcome to the level of economic development.[8] While refuting Pareto's earlier notion of a stable income distribution across countries, it ascribes but a minimal role to discrete effects of policy. In this model, a change in macroeconomic policy would affect income inequality only to the extent that it led to an accelerated rate of economic growth.

Subsequently, other researchers have found troubling the notion of policy invariance of income distribution.[9] Thus, "extended Kuznets" models were developed in which additional explanatory variables related to policies are included. These researchers have presented models introducing an array of additional variables into the basic Kuznets model, but to date little attention has been paid to those of a financial nature.[10]

This omission has now been addressed in a study by Bulir and Gulde (1995), who tested an extended Kuznets model of income distribution in which inflation, inflation uncertainty, and financial instability were added as supplementary explanatory variables. In addition, the model included a proxy for government redistribution efforts.[11] To avoid the problems that small samples usually entail, a comprehensive pooled cross-section time-series database was constructed. It contains more than 120 observations for eighteen countries with a wide range of inflation experiences and is thus more comprehensive than previous studies.[12]

The stylized results of the empirical work, summarized in table 10I.2, prove to be suggestive with respect to the link between inflation and income inequality as well as that between the more traditional growth and fiscal spending variables.[13] To start with the financial variables, the most important focus here, the results indicate clearly that both increases in

Table 10I.2
Empirical Determinants of Income Distribution

Explanatory variable	Direction of impact
Level of inflation	Increases inequality
Variability of inflation	Increases inequality; effect is stronger than the level of inflation
Variability in nominal rate	Increases inequality; effect is less than the exchange of the inflation variability but more than the level of inflation
Per capita income	At very low-income levels, leads to more inequality, but in more developed countries countributes to equality
Level of fiscal spending	Has equalizing effect on income distribution
Country-specific effects	Are important in all cases; direction varies

Source: Table 10IA.1.

inflation and its variability lead to an increase in the inequality of the overall income distribution.[14] It seems also that although inflation itself increases income inequality, inflation uncertainty has an even stronger effect in this regard.[15] In addition, the variability of the nominal exchange rate was included as a proxy for overall instability in nominal asset prices. It too appears to exert a statistically significant effect on increasing income inequality, albeit with a much lower quantitative effect than does inflation variability. The critical result, however, is that for all the financial variables tested, the high level of statistical significance instills confidence in the validity of the relationship between higher inflation, inflation variability, or exchange rate variability, and increasing income inequality.

For completeness, I also briefly summarize the results on the non-financial variables included. As to the level of income, some limited support is found for the Kuznets hypothesis, in all cases and for both specifications of the variable, the expected signs are obtained. In five cases, the estimated coefficients are significant at the 10 percent confidence level. In addition, the role of public expenditures as an equalizing factor receives support. In all cases, the expected negative sign is found at levels of significance at the 10 percent level (two cases) or 5 percent level (four cases).

Results from Individual Country Studies   The cross-country findings support the view that inflation increases overall income inequality. Two further questions emerge: To what extent does this finding hold for an individual country over time, and within a country, who (which income bracket) exactly wins and who loses from inflation? To anticipate one of

Table 10I.3
Impact of Inflation on Overall Income Distribution (country-specific results)

Country	Change in income distribution[a]
United States	Less unequal
United Kingdom	No impact
Canada	More unequal
Italy	Less unequal
Greece	More unequal
Sweden	N.A.
Finland	Less unequal
Israel	More unequal
Russia	More unequal

a. Country sample chosen by data availability. Measured by change in Gini coefficients. For detailed results, see Table 10IA.2.

the most interesting findings, it appears that stronger effects of inflation on increasing income inequality seem to occur in poorer countries.

The empirical tests in this section are based on models developed by Schultz (1969), which include an examination of the effects of inflation on overall income distribution in individual countries, and by Blinder and Esaki (1978), which test the effect of inflation on the relative shares of income quintiles. Table 10IA.2 in the chapter appendix lists new estimation results for Finland, Israel, and Russia. The countries were chosen largely on the basis of data availability. To put the results in perspective, table 10I.3 (and table 10IA2) also present those from major previous studies in the field.[16]

In discussing these results, I focus primarily on the impact of inflation on income distribution.[17] To start with the effect on overall distribution in individual countries (table 10I.3 and Appendix table 10IA.2), a striking result is that in four cases—for Canada, Greece, Israel, and Russia— higher inflation increases inequality, consistent with the findings of the cross-country study. Equally noteworthy, the estimations indicate that the direction of the effect is not uniform. In three countries (the Unites States, Finland, and Italy), it appears that the overall distribution of income is in fact equalized through inflation. However, not too much should be read into these results, as it is only for the United States, Italy, Greece, and Israel that the coefficients on inflation are statistically significant at the 10 percent confidence level.

As to the issue of how the aggregate results come about—that is, which segments of society win or lose from inflation—table 10I.4

Table 10I.4

Impact of Inflation on the Income Distribution in Selected Countries: Effects on Different Income Groups

Country	Income share of lowest quintile	Income share of second quintile	Income share of third quintile	Income share of fourth quintile	Income share of top quintile
Higher income					
United States	+	+	−	−	−
United Kingdom	+	−	+	−	−
Canada	−	+	−	+	+
Italy	+	+	+	+	−
Sweden	+	+	−	−	−
Finland	−	+	+	−	+
Lower income					
Greece	−	−	−	−	+
Israel	−	−	−	−	+
Russia	−	−	+	−	+

Source: Appendix table 10IA.2.

Note: Income quintiles group population in successive 20 percent groups and measure the share accruing to these groups. A plus sign means that the respective group increased its share due to inflation; a minus sign means its share was eroded.

presents the stylized results obtained in desegregated estimations. The most notable result here is the apparent diversity of outcomes. For the newly estimated countries (Finland, Israel, and Russia), the first quintiles lose, and the top quintile wins, from inflation. For Israel, but not for the others, the intermediate three quintiles also all lose, and in Finland and Russia, the sign patterns are mixed. A comparison of results with those of previous studies reveals a similar dispersion, consistent with the notion that idiosyncratic factors may tend to explain the bulk of differences in income distribution. The diversity of outcomes notwithstanding, a second look at table 10I.4 (and table 10IA.2 in the chapter appendix) supports a number of inferences:

• Judging from the size of coefficients, the share of the bottom and the top income quintiles is more affected by inflation than is that of the middle groups.

• The poorest quintile loses share more often than do the other quintiles. Similarly, the richest quintile is the most likely to gain from inflation. However, in the United States, the United Kingdom, Italy, and Sweden, all countries in which low-income groups tend to hold nominal debt, the relation is reversed, with the poorest gaining shares with inflation and the richest losing.

• Looking at the countries with the lowest per capita incomes in the sample—Greece, Israel, and Russia—inflation emerges as an unambiguously regressive tax, which reduces the income share of the lowest and raises the share of the highest quintiles.

10I.3   Conclusion

The philosophy underlying this chapter conforms to the so-called Washington consensus that stresses the importance of macroeconomic stability, outward economic orientation, and domestic liberalization. It is also in line with the new development paradigm, which, besides redefining the role of government in this area, focuses on how critical a stable macroeconomy is for the development process. And it confirms what I would call the central bank consensus, which emphasizes how essential an ingredient for a proper macroeconomic performance price level stability is.[18]

In this spirit, I have argued that since IMF monetary policy advice is designed to lower a country's inflation, an assessment of the equity implications of such monetary policy advice is best gauged through the examination of the income distributional implications of inflation. To this end, I have drawn on studies undertaken recently in the IMF's Monetary and Exchange Affairs Department that show that IMF policy advice helps improve the ability of monetary authorities to implement monetary policy, and thus to bring down inflation. In addition, these empirical studies show that, very broadly, lower inflation and lower inflation volatility tend to decrease income inequalities. With the appropriate caveats, it therefore can be said that a country that decides to follow the IMF's advice in the monetary policy area should have a lower and more predictable level of inflation and, ceteris paribus, more equitable income distribution than would otherwise be the case.

Finally, my arguments support a widely held view: There may be some transitory income distributional implications of monetary policy that are related to its short-run effects on the real economy, but such temporary effects do not indicate that distributional objectives should themselves be an aim of monetary policy. Monetary policy should be addressed to the attainment and maintenance of stability in the value of the currency, in both its internal (domestic price level) and external (exchange rate) dimensions. Direct income distributional objectives would be best achieved by use of other instruments of policy.

Appendix

Table 10IA.1
Effects of Inflation on Income Distribution: Cross-Country Evidence

Equation number	N	Constant	RGDP	RGDP²	Y	Y²	Exp/GDP	Inflation 1 (level)	Inflation 2 (standard deviation)	Exchange rate (standard deviation)	R^2	SEE
10A.1	121	0.445** (0.031)	-0.0005* (0.003)	-0.0005* (0.0003)			-0.0005* (0.0003)	0.00001** (0.000001)			0.88	0.019
10A.2	114	0.398** (0.015)	0.0008 (0.0017)	-0.00002 (0.00017)			-0.0009** (0.00027)		0.0021** (0.0008)		0.94	0.014
10A.3	123	0.447** (0.032)	0.0052* (0.0030)	-0.00051* (0.00028)			-0.0005* (0.0003)			0.0004** (0.00008)	0.88	0.019
10A.4	118	0.310** (0.116)			0.0011 (0.0018)	-0.00000 (0.00003)	-0.0009** (0.0003)	0.00001** (0.000002)			0.88	0.020
10A.5	111	0.420** (0.054)			0.0002* (0.0011)	-0.00002 (0.000014)	0.0008** (0.00024)		0.0023** (0.0008)		0.94	0.014
10A.6	120	0.323** (0.117)			0.0008 (0.0016)	-0.00000 (0.00002)	-0.0009** (0.0004)			0.0004** (00.00008)	0.87	0.020

Notes: Ordinary least squares results for pooled cross-section time series. The Gini coefficient is the dependent variable. Standard errors, parentheses, are heteroskeclastic-consistent estimates.

N, number of observations; RGDP, PPP-based per capita income, with data from Summers and Heston (1991); Y, PPP-based per capita income relative to the United States, with data from Summers and Heston (1991); Exp/GDP, percentage share of government expenditure in GDP; Inflation 1, average annual inflation; Inflation 2, standard deviation of monthly inflation over the year; Exchange rate, standard deviation of monthly nominal exchange rate changes. *,** denotes significance at the 10 and 5 percent level of confidence, respectively.

Table 101A.2
Impact of Inflation on Income Distribution in Blinder-Esaki Model (|t| in parentheses)

Dependent variable	United States[a]	United Kingdom[b]	Canada[c]	Japan expected inflation[d]	Japan unexpected inflation[d]	Italy[e]	Greece[f]	Sweden[g]	Finland[h]	Israel[i]	Russia[i]
Gini coefficient	-0.005 (3.69)	0.3E-5 (0.01)	0.0003 (0.65)			-0.00137 (2.50)	0.023 (4.00)		-0.0003 (0.42)	0.00003 (1.57)	0.000007 (0.19)
Bottom quintile	0.031 (2.82)	0.02 (1.80)	-0.0111 (0.78)	-0.008 (0.67)	-0.038 (3.05)	0.0297 (2.32)	-0.036 (2.40)	0.0005 (1.66)	-0.0200 (0.60)	-0.00079 (1.85)	-0.00049 (0.38)
Second quintile	0.010 (0.77)	-0.03 (1.80)	0.0022 (0.08)	-0.035 (2.33)	-0.061 (3.90)	0.0317 (1.95)	-0.027 (4.10)	0.0007 (3.50)	0.0438 (1.26)	-0.00073 (1.53)	-0.00022 (0.24)
Third quintile	-0.007 (0.50)	0.01 (0.64)	-0.0176 (1.33)			0.0402 (2.25)	-0.009 (3.03)	-0.0003 (1.50)	0.0084 (0.32)	-0.00038 (0.64)	0.00134 (1.88)
Fourth quintile	-0.023 (1.64)	-0.01 (1.46)	0.0107 (0.94)	-0.073 (3.75)	0.004 (0.20)	0.0135 (1.09)	-0.001 (0.27)	-0.0004 (4.00)	-0.0101 (0.21)	-0.00050 (0.58)	-0.00140 (1.23)
Fifth quintile	-0.005 (0.16)	-0.01 (0.34)	0.0158 (0.37)	0.075 (2.36)	0.127 (3.87)	-0.1150 (2.42)	0.013 (3.30)	-0.0011 (2.75)	0.0015 (0.03)	0.00263 (1.46)	0.00077 (0.28)
Top 5 percent	-0.008 (0.24)	-0.01 (0.32)		0.071 (2.90)	0.081 (3.35)		-0.050 (1.00)				
Top 10 percent			0.0231 (0.62)						0.0062 (0.18)	0.00213 (1.25)	

[a] Blinder and Esaki (1978), 1947–1974 (annual data), GNP deflator. Pretax family income. Estimates for Gini coefficients (own computations) are for 1978–1988.
[b] Nolan (1987), 1961–1975 (annual data), GDP deflator. Pretax income of tax units. Estimates for Gini coefficients (own computations) are for 1965–1982.
[c] Buse (1982), 1947–1978 (annual data), GNP deflator. Pretax income data, including taxable and nontaxable incomes.

d Yoshino (1993). 1964–1988 (annual data). GNP deflator. Unexpected inflation is computed as $\pi_t^e = \pi_{t-1}^e + 0.2(\pi_{t-1} + \pi_{t-1}^e)$. The shares of the income among families are bottom 20 percent, 21–50 percent, 51–80 percent, and top 20 percent. Household pretax monetary income (without in-kind transfers).

e Brandolini and Sestito (1994), 1977–1991 (annual data), consumer price index. Household income adjusted to make equivalent net of taxes and social contributions and excluding income from final assets.

f Livada (1992). 1963–1986 (annual data), consumer price index. The type of income distribution data is not known.

g Björklund (1991), 1975–1988 (annual data), consumer price index, without time ttrend. Pretax income data, including taxable social and unemployment benefits.

h Own computations, 1977–1984 (annual data), consumer price index, without time trend. Pretax household income shares.

i Own computations, 1986–1992 (annual data), consumer price index, without time trend. Disposable individual equivalized income.

j Own computations, December 1991–September 1994 (quarterly data), consumer price index. Pretax individual monetary incomes.

Notes

I thank my colleagues Bill Alexander, Charles Enoch, Ales Bulir, and Anne-Marie Gulde for their help in the preparation of this chapter.

1. For an early discussion of these points, see Guitián (1973, 1981). A recent discussion of conditionality is found in Guitián (1995a).

2. See, in particular, Guitián (1994a) for a detailed analysis of the considerations behind the choice of an exchange rate regime and its monetary policy implications.

3. The rationale and implementation of these basic principles are examined in detail in Guitián (1994b, 1994c).

4. This view implies that the long-run Phillips curve describing the relationship between inflation and unemployment is vertical at the level of unemployment determined by the fundamental factors in the economy (the natural rate of unemployment). For a classical statement of these propositions, see Friedman (1968). For a recent elaboration, see Guitián (1995b).

5. Focus on price stability as the primary objective of monetary policy is an increasingly common feature of modern central bank legislation.

6. For a general discussion of these issues, see Alexander, Baliño, and Enoch (1995).

7. An early discussion of distributional issues in the context of IMF-supported programs from the fiscal standpoint can be found in International Monetary Fund (1986).

8. Over the process, growth first leads to increasing income inequalities, but in the later stages of development it will have an equalizing effect. In a graph, this will show up as the famous U-shaped Kuznets curve. See Kuznets (1955, 1963) and Campano and Salvatore (1988).

9. See, e.g., Thurow (1970) and Atkinson (1975).

10. Examples of extended Kuznets models include Adelman and Fuwa (1992) and Milanovic (1994).

11. See Bulir and Gulde (1995) for detailed results.

12. The countries included are the United States, Austria, Switzerland, the Netherlands, Norway, the United Kingdom, Italy, Peru, Chile, Brazil, Bangladesh, Indonesia, South Korea, Thailand, Malaysia, Pakistan, Greece, and Israel. The Gini observations fall in the period from 1960 to 1992. Using more than one observation per country allows filtering out country-specific effects.

13. For the detailed statistical results, see table 10A.1 in the chapter appendix. The overall fit of the equation is quite satisfactory. Although only a smaller proportion of the overall level is explained by the array of proposed explanatory variables, this is in line with the standard result of the income distribution literature, stating that the largest part of income distribution is due to country-specific idiosyncratic factors.

14. The Gini coefficient is the most commonly used measure of income distribution. It is defined as double the area enclosed by the 45-degree line and the Lorenz curve, that is, the cumulative income accruing to particular shares of population. If everybody's income is

equal, the Gini coefficient will be zero; if all income is concentrated with one income earner, it is equal to one. For a survey of different income distribution measures, see, e.g., Bulir and Gulde (1995).

15. As indicated by a somewhat better statistical fit of the model when the standard deviation of inflation is substituted for the rate of inflation.

16. The standard model for single-country Gini studies is Schultz (1969), and for single-country studies of income shares, it is Blinder and Esaki (1978). The major empirical work in the area includes studies for the United States, 1947–1974 (Blinder and Esaki 1978); Canada 1947–1978 (Buse 1982); the United Kingdom, 1961–1975 (Nolan 1987); Japan, 1964–1988, (Yoshino 1993); Italy, 1977–1991 (Brandolini and Sestito 1994); Greece, 1963–1986 (Livada 1992); and Sweden, 1975–1988 (Björklund 1991).

17. The models by Schultz (1969) and Blinder and Esaki (1978) also include unemployment and other explanatory variables.

18. For a description of the Washington consensus, see Williamson (1990); for an examination of the new development paradigm, see Summers and Thomas (1993); and for an extensive study of what I have called the central bank consensus, see Deane and Pringle (1995).

References

Adelman, Irma, and Nobuhiko Fuwa. 1992. "Income Inequality and Development During the 1980s." *Indian Economic Review*, special issue: 329–345.

Alexander, William E., Tomás Baliño, and Charles Enoch, eds. 1995. *The Adoption of Indirect Instruments of Monetary Policy*. Occasional Paper. Washington, D.C.: IMF.

Atkinson, Anthony B. 1975. *The Economics of Inequality*. Oxford: Clarendon Press.

Björklund, Anders. 1991. "Unemployment and Income Distribution: Time Series Evidence from Sweden." *Scandinavian Journal of Economics* 93(3): 457–465.

Blinder, Alan S., and Howard Y. Esaki. 1978. "Macroeconomic Activity and Income Distribution in the Postwar United States." *Review of Economics and Statistics* 60 (November): 604–609.

Brandolini, Andrea, and Paolo Sestito. 1994. *Cyclical and Trend Changes in Inequality in Italy, 1977–1991*. Servizio Studi. Rome: Banca d'Italia, July.

Bulir, Ales, and Anne-Marie Gulde. 1995. *Inflation and Income Distribution: Further Evidence on Empirical Links*. Working Paper WP/95/86. Washington, D.C.: IMF.

Buse, Adolf. 1982. "The Cyclical Behavior of the Size Distribution of Income in Canada: 1947–78." *Canadian Journal of Economics* 15 (May): 189–203.

Campano, Fred, and Dominick Salvatore. 1988. "Economic Development, Income Inequality and Kuznets' U-Shaped Hypothesis." *Journal of Policy Modeling* 10(2): 265–280.

Deane, Marjorie, and Robert Pringle. 1995. *The Central Banks*. London: Viking, 1995.

Friedman, Milton. 1968. "The Role of Monetary Policy." *American Economic Review* 58 (March): 1–17.

Guitián, Manuel. 1973. *Credit Versus Money as an Instrument of Control.* Staff Papers, vol. 20, no. 3. Washington D.C.: IMF, November.

Guitián, Manuel. 1981. *Fund Conditionality: Evolution of Principles and Practices.* Pamphlet Series no. 38. Washington, D.C.: IMF.

Guitián, Manuel. 1994a. "The Choice of an Exchange Rate Regime." In Richard C. Barth and Chorng-Huey Wong, eds., *Approaches to Exchange Rate Policy: Choices for Developing and Transition Economies,* pp. 13–36. Washington, D.C.: IMF.

Guitián, Manuel. 1994b. "Rules or Discretion in Monetary Policy: National and International Perspectives." In Tomás Baliño and Carlo Cottarelli, eds., *Frameworks for Monetary Stability: Policy Issues and Country Experiences,* pp. 19–41. Washington, D.C.: IMF.

Guitián, Manuel. 1994c. "The Role of Monetary Policy in IMF Programs." In J. A. H. de Beaufort Wijnholds, S. C. W. Eiffinger, and L. H. Hoogduin, eds., *Framework for Monetary Stability,* pp. 185–209. Dordrect: Kluwer.

Guitián, Manuel. 1995a. *Conditionality: Past, Present, Future.* Staff Papers, vol. 42, no. 4. Washington, D.C.: IMF, December.

Guitián, Manuel. 1995b. "Inflation and Growth: Is There a Trade-Off?" Paper presented at the Conference on China in the World Economy: Inflation and Growth, Beijing, May 10–12.

International Monetary Fund. 1986. *Fund-Supported Programs, Fiscal Policy, and Income Distribution.* Occasional Paper no. 46. Washington, D.C.: IMF, September.

Kuznets, Simon. 1955. "Economic Growth and Income Inequality." *American Economic Review* 45 (March): 1–28.

Kuznets, Simon. 1963. "Quantitative Aspects of the Economic Growth of Nations: VIII. Distribution of Income by Size." *Economic Development and Cultural Change* (January): 1–80.

Livada, Alexandra. 1992. "Macroeconomic Effects on Income Distribution." Mimeo. Athens: Athens University of Economics and Business.

Milanovic, Branko. 1994. *Determinants of Cross-Country Income Inequality: An "Augmented" Kuznets' Hypothesis.* Policy Research Working Paper no. 1246. Washington, D.C.: World Bank, Policy Research Department, Transition Economies Division, January.

Nolan, Brian. 1987. *Income Distribution and the Macroeconomy.* Cambridge: Cambridge University Press.

Schultz, T. Paul. 1969. "Secular Trends and Cyclical Behavior of Income Distribution in the United States: 1944–1965." In *Six Papers on the Size Distribution of Wealth and Income,* pp. 75–106. National Bureau of Economic Research Studies in Income and Wealth, vol. 33. New York and London: Columbia University.

Summers, Lawrence H., and Vinod Thomas. 1993. "Recent Lessons in Development." *World Bank Research Observer* 8 (July).

Summers, Robert, and Alan W. Heston. 1991. "The Penn World Table (Mark 5): An Expanded Set of International Comparisons, 1950–1988." *Quarterly Journal of Economics* 106 (May): 327–368.

Thurow, Lester C. 1970. "Analyzing the American Income Distribution." *American Economic Review* 60 (May): 263–264.

Williamson, John, ed. 1990. *Latin American Adjustment: How Much Has Happened?* Washington, D.C.: Institute for International Economics.

Yoshino, Osamu. 1993. "Size Distribution of Workers' Household Income and Macroeconomic Activities in Japan: 1963–88." *Review of Income and Wealth* 39 (December): 393–400.

II

Macroeconomic Adjustment with Major Structural Reforms: Implications for Employment and Income Distribution

Vito Tanzi

Economists' and policymakers' perceptions of the role of macroeconomic policy in achieving stabilization and economic growth have undergone profound changes in recent decades. Thirty years ago, stabilization policy was synonymous with demand-management policy. As epitomized by the Phillips curve, policymakers were assumed to face a trade-off between growth (low unemployment) and inflation. Policymakers could choose, from the curve, the desired combination of unemployment and inflation.

Starting with the seminal works of Phelps (1967) and Friedman (1968), the existence of a long-run trade-off between inflation and unemployment began to be questioned. This questioning brought to the forefront the notion of a "natural" rate of unemployment. This natural rate, at least in the United States, was typically higher than the full employment estimates of the 1960s and served to temper any thoughts that demand-management policy could be used as a tool to increase economic growth and employment permanently.

An important implication of these developments is that the economy tends to return to the natural rate of unemployment and its potential rate of growth, over the long run, without any assistance from demand-management policies. This implies that close attention should be paid to supply-side factors in policy attempts to promote growth. Needless to say, not all economists accepted the notion that short-run macroeconomic management is a futile endeavor.

The transition of many countries from central planning to market-oriented economies has highlighted the importance of structural reforms in promoting long-term growth. In many countries, the transition, accompanied by sharp declines in (officially measured) output and high rates of inflation, has been far from painless. However, there appears to be little scope for expansionary policies to attenuate these declines, at least in

Eastern Europe (Chu and Schwartz 1994). A comparison of the experiences of the Eastern European countries with those that came out of the former Soviet Union (FSU) points to a positive relationship between macroeconomic adjustment and structural reform on the one hand and economic growth on the other. The experience of industrial and developing economies also indicates that stabilization and sustainable economic growth are promoted by sound macroeconomic policies accompanied by deep structural reforms.

10II.1   Economic Growth, Structural Reforms, and Employment

In recent years, major structural reforms have complemented the more traditional fiscal and monetary policies in stabilization efforts in many countries. Stabilization has attempted to create an environment of low inflation and balance of payments viability, while major structural reforms have tried to create the conditions for improved efficiency and sustained growth. Growth is, of course, necessary to create employment opportunities for the growing population and to raise real wages over the medium and long term for the employed.

The impact on employment of stabilization programs with structural reforms is clearer in the long run than in the short run. Structural reforms aim to increase productivity and, thus, to promote growth in per capita income. To the extent that these reforms succeed, the increase in productivity may be accompanied by short-run negative effects on employment and ambiguous effects on income distribution. Successful and deep structural reforms are likely to change the matrix of demand for different workers' skills. Those who have the newly required skills gain; others lose. At the same time, stabilization with particular but popular structural reforms leads to labor shedding by both the public and private sectors. The net short-run result can be an increase in unemployment. Of course, in time, economic growth will create more jobs and more demand for labor. However, some time may pass before these more positive effects become evident. This is a price that may need to be paid to have genuine restructuring of economies.

Okun's Law
Four decades ago Arthur Okun explored the empirical relationship between output and employment growth. In the context of the U.S. economy, Okun's law stipulated that a 3 percent increase in output was necessary to

bring about a 1 percent reduction in the unemployment rate.[1] Two basic mechanisms underlie this relationship: (1) labor hoarding by enterprises during recessions and (2) the discouraged worker effect. The first mechanism involves the relationship between output and employment growth; the second involves the relationship between the official labor force and official employment growth.[2]

Okun's law was postulated and discussed in a period (the 1960s) when the business cycle was thought to be the key determinant of output change and when there were no major structural changes. Aggregate demand was assumed to be the driving force in the economy. Okun and those who discussed his "law" did not contemplate the effects that major short-run structural changes could have on the growth-employment nexus, especially in the short run. The focus of this chapter is on these effects.

Many recent structural adjustment programs have introduced major changes in labor markets, increasing their flexibility and efficiency; in financial markets, making them less repressed; in foreign trade, opening the domestic markets to foreign competition; in the public sector, increasing its efficiency through privatization of public enterprises, and through reforms of civil service, tax systems, public expenditure, public pensions, and so forth. These reforms had the objective of increasing productivity and, thus, of promoting growth. The short-run impact of these reforms on employment is discussed below.

Okun's Law and Structural Reforms

What is the impact of major structural reforms on employment and the relationship between growth in output and growth in employment?[3] Major structural policies have three important effects on the allocation of resources.

First, structural reforms can bring about the sectoral reallocation of capital and labor between industries, often from nontraded (and often low-productivity activities) to traded goods. Factors of production will be drawn away from previously subsidized industries, which were probably characterized by labor hoarding. Because the reallocation of labor is likely to be associated with a need for new and scarce skills, the output growth in the short run in the new or expanding industries will be characterized by low employment growth, high productivity, and high wages. This will occur while labor is being shed by the losing activities.

Second, to the extent that the structural reforms include privatization of public enterprises and major reductions in public employment, many public sector employees will lose their jobs.

Third, a more open economy will lead to more rapid adoption of technical change through exposure to foreign competition, forcing previously protected firms to become more efficient. At least at the beginning of the adjustment, this will reduce their employment and the number of workers required to increase their output.

Within the context of our model, these three mechanisms can be understood as follows.

First, these will be changes in the structure of the demand for labor. Sectoral shifts increase the variance of the labor surplus across firms and industries. Because recruitment cannot be instantaneous—on account of the need for retraining and impediments to labor mobility—this surplus becomes negative in new industries. Industries that have a hard time attracting qualified labor will therefore produce at high productivity levels, with high wages and long hours.[4] Thus, firms with expanding output may create little employment. At the same time, if declining firms are allowed or even encouraged to shed surplus labor in order to become more efficient, then the overall impact on employment of a one-time major sectoral shift may well be negative in the short run.

Structural reforms may also involve labor market reforms that allow declining firms to shed labor more easily. This increased flexibility leads to a fall in Okun's coefficient while the major structural reforms are going on. Workers in declining industries may experience wage reductions; those who have the skills needed by the expanding industries will experience wage increases. In the medium term, which may extend over years, Okun's coefficient will begin to increase as labor is reallocated, flexibility in firing is maintained, and new skills are acquired.

The second area is that of privatization and civil service reform. Privatization can have a significant effect on employment. In past decades, public enterprises were often used as vehicles to create employment, and as a consequence, public enterprises often ended up with many redundant workers.[5] When these enterprises are privatized, they often go through a period of considerable labor shedding. If privatization is widespread in many public enterprises, this labor shedding can have significant effects on the unemployment rate.

As an example, consider Argentina, where privatization covered enterprises in telecommunications, electricity, water, petroleum, petrochemicals, steel, shipbuilding, ports, roads, and rail transportation. Between 1990 and 1992, public enterprise employment declined from 293,000 to 110,000 persons. Because of lack of relevant skills, or age, or presumed acquired poor working habits, those who lost their public sector jobs had difficulties in finding work in the private sector, thus contributing to a rise in unemployment.

In our model, privatization involves the elimination of excess labor in the affected enterprises and an instantaneous reduction in employment given the level of the output. This can happen as a result of the preprivatization restructuring of public enterprises, aimed at making them more productive, or as a result of postprivatization restructuring, provided that severance pay regulations are not prohibitive. The instantaneous adjustment implies a decrease in the value of Okun's coefficient during the period immediately following the restructuring of the economy.

In the medium term, after labor surpluses have been eliminated, employers have convinced themselves that the reforms are permanent, and fired workers have acquired new skills, the transition to a less onerous system of labor protection should increase Okun's coefficient and lead to employment growth. Thus, for industries where privatization implies a shift away from coverage by a civil service contract, Okun's coefficient should begin to increase in the medium term.

The third area is an increase in productivity in the traded sector. In their drive to industrialize over past decades, many developing countries created highly protected, but inefficient, industries. The productivity of labor in these protected industries was generally very low. When a country opens its market, some of these industries go out of existence; others are forced to become more productive by changing technologies and shedding labor. Production for export, or increased competition for domestic markets, leads to higher productivity growth through greater exposure to information about new technologies, economies of scale, reduction in X-inefficiency, and so forth. If protection had been high or other implicit or explicit subsidies had been large, this productivity impact could be substantial. Similar dynamic efficiency effects can be expected from the dismantling of subsidies for previously favored sectors. In the short run, the resulting improvement in productivity will also lead to a weakening of the output elasticity of employment.

To sum up, in the short run, adjustment programs with major structural reforms may lead to output gains that exceed employment gains. Countries may end up with growth without employment creation or even with growth in official unemployment rates.

Country Experiences
Many countries experienced rapid productivity growth following structural reforms. Edwards (1993) has provided evidence from many Latin

Table 10II.1
Growth in Employment and Output for Selected Countries

		Annual growth (percentage change)	
		employment	output
Argentina	1985–1990	1.98	−0.79
	1991–1993	2.75	7.86
China	1979–1982	3.69	7.9
	1983–1985	3.76	12.2
	1986–1990	2.69	9.08
Thailand	1978–1985	3.56	5.4
	1986–1988	2.09	13.6
	1989–1993	2.28	9.46

Sources: World Bank, *World Tables*; International Monetary Fund, *IFS*, various issues, and national publications.
Note: For Argentina, employment and output refer, respectively, to employment and GDP in the formal sector; for China and Thailand, they refer to employment and value-added in the manufacturing sector.

American countries that implemented major trade reforms.[6] He concluded that there is broad support to the position that those countries that have embarked on trade liberalization programs have experienced an acceleration in the rate of productivity growth (Dornbusch and Edwards 1995, p. 44). The evidence on employment growth is more mixed, as might be expected. Let us consider a few country examples in some detail.

Since 1989, Argentina has carried out an adjustment program with pervasive structural reforms, which included trade reform, tax reform, deregulation of shop hours and licensing, large-scale privatization, and civil service reform.[7] Output has increased significantly (see table 10II.1) due to the reforms and the availability of capital following the reforms, which allowed a rapid expansion of new production sectors. Although Argentina experienced substantial employment reductions following the rapid privatization of large public enterprises and the reform of the civil service, the fast expansion in output was accompanied by slow growth in aggregate employment. Table 10II.1 indicates that the annual growth of employment between 1990 and 1993 was marginally higher than in the 1985–1990 period, notwithstanding the large increase in the average annual growth rate from −0.8 percent to almost 8 percent in the more recent period. The unemployment rate doubled, from 6.3 percent in 1990 to 12.4 percent in October 1994.[8]

After the second oil shock, Thailand implemented a stabilization program that included a number of important structural policies, such as a reduction in the export tax on rice, tax reform, an annual ceiling of 2 percent on government employment growth, and a substantial real exchange rate depreciation (Sussangkarn 1994). After 1986, these reforms contributed to very high rates of growth in manufactured exports (30–40 percent annually).

Table 10II.1 shows that the period of take-off of manufactured exports (1986–1988) was characterized by very high rates of growth of output (13.6 percent) but small employment growth in the manufacturing sector (2 percent). Employment grew less rapidly over 1986 through 1988 than over 1975 through 1985 in spite of the sharp increase in the growth rate. The high growth rates in output were also associated with growing sectoral, regional, and income disparities.

The slowdown in government employment growth had an adverse effect on employment after 1984, particularly for those with a traditional university education and vocational training for whom government employment had constituted a very high fraction of total employment (56 percent and 41 percent of the total, respectively). The educational system could not respond quickly to the shift in labor demand from the public to the private sector. Therefore it continued to oversupply graduates in the humanities and social sciences who had normally gone to work for the government and undersupply those in sciences and management who were needed by the growing sectors. Deficiencies in the vocational system contributed to an unemployment rate at the vocational level as high as 11 percent in 1986, while shortages emerged for engineering and scientific manpower. Once again, in the short run, a fast rate of growth in output was accompanied by unemployment and labor scarcity for particular sectors.

The experience of Argentina and Thailand is repeated in China and in Peru. In China, very high rates of growth in output in recent years have not led to an equivalent growth in employment (see table 10II.1). Per capita real income growth averaged 7.9 percent between 1979 and 1993, and total employment grew by 3.4 percent per annum between 1978 and 1992. Between 1982 and 1985, when the initial phase of industrial reforms was undertaken, the Chinese economy experienced an increase in gross domestic product growth from 8 to 12 percent, with insignificant changes in employment growth (see table 10II.1). Further employment declines in loss-making state-owned enterprises (SOEs) were averted by the provision of subsidies to these SOEs. The lower employment elasticity was maintained between 1986 and 1990, a period when the imbalance between demand and supply for new skills widened, on account of the rapid expansion in nonfarm activities (Cornia 1994).

In Peru, the real growth of GDP averaged −0.8 percent in the 1985–1990 prereform period when the average unemployment rate was 6.6 percent. Real growth rose to more than 5 percent per year between 1991 and 1995, but the unemployment rate rose to 8.4 percent.[9]

10II.2   Growth, Structural Reforms, and Wealth Distribution

Adjustment programs with major structural reforms can have a large impact on the value of assets and on their distribution among the population of a country. A full discussion of this important but unexplored issue would require a specialized study. Here I address some of its more important aspects: the impact of structural adjustment on the distribution of human capital, shares in enterprises, agricultural land, urban land, industrial buildings and structures, machinery and equipment, houses, old cars and other durable consumer goods, foreign exchange and foreign deposits, and money.

As far as human capital is concerned, I have already argued that adjustment programs with major structural reforms are likely to create strong demands for workers with particular skills (computer experts, financial analysts, etc.) but declining demands for those with traditional skills. The change in the structure of production will bring about a change in the matrix of the demand for labor. The demand for and the wages of those who have the desired skills rise, sometimes substantially, while the demand for and the wages of those with traditional skills fall. Some of the latter will end up unemployed. As a consequence, the distribution of the wage income is likely to become less even in the short run.

In many countries, successful adjustment with major structural reforms has led to spectacular increases in the stock markets.[10] These increases have reflected the expectation of future higher rates of growth in the earnings of the enterprises. Thus, as a group, those who owned shares have done very well in the postadjustment period. In most countries, this is a relatively small group, and in developing countries, it is likely to be even smaller. There is, of course, a large variance in the behavior of the individual shares. Shares in companies that had been highly protected have done less well than shares in other companies.

Landownership is highly concentrated in some countries and much less concentrated in others. Thus, the impact of the increase in the value of land on wealth distribution will depend on the concentration index for landownership. The value of agricultural land, especially of land that produces export crops, can be expected to rise. The removal of disincentives against the agricultural sector (overvalued exchange rates, export taxes, low domestic prices for their crops, etc.) can be expected to raise the value of land, thus benefiting its owners.[11]

The value of urban land is also likely to rise as a result of the removal of many structural constraints on its use and the expected rise in income, which inevitably leads to greater demand for housing and construction in general. The move from a repressed economy to one that relies on the market can lead to spectacular increases in urban land value.[12] The housing and construction boom that often follows economic liberalization is likely to provide an economic bonanza to the lucky owners of these lands. Some of these owners find themselves very rich through no effort on their part.

The impact on existing structures that had been used for commercial and industrial activities is less easily predictable. In some cases, these structures may have been tied to specific uses that are no longer economic, for example, to production that was made profitable by very high tariffs. Thus, there will be a fall in the value of these structures unless they can be put to totally new uses. In Buenos Aires, for example, some of the buildings near the harbor that had been in a state of semiabandonment for years have been transformed into luxury apartments, shops, and hotels. Still, no obvious conclusions follow. Buildings and structures made obsolete by the structural reforms will lose value, at least in the short run. This will be particularly true for machinery and equipment that may lose much of its economic value when the opening of the economy removes the economic rationale for its use. Those who owned this machinery will suffer losses.

A more stable economic environment, with low inflation or at least with a less variable rate of inflation, rising incomes, and the removal of regulations that constrain the housing market (such as rent controls), will often raise the value of the housing stock, leading to economic benefits to those who own the houses. This group will gain in relative terms with respect to those who do not own houses and have to pay higher rents. Of course, home ownership is much more broadly distributed than, say, land or stocks, that the impact on the wealth distribution will be less significant.

A more open economy that allows more freely the importation of new cars and new durable consumer goods will probably reduce the value of the stock of old cars and existing durable consumer goods, thus leading to some losses for their owners. As a group, the latter may come from the higher levels of the income distribution.

Finally, low inflation and more realistic exchange rates often sharply increase the domestic value of financial assets held abroad or held in the country in dollars or in other currencies. They also increase the value of domestic currency because of the lower inflation tax on these balances.

From this discussion, it can be concluded that adjustment programs with major structural reforms are likely to bring about major changes in a country's distribution of wealth. Because the present value of the existing assets tends to reflect the discounted value of their expected future earnings, the expectation that the future rate of growth will be higher than in the past implies that the total value of all assets combined will rise, at times substantially. Thus, as a group, those who own these assets will gain. The discussion and scattered evidence suggest also that the distribution of wealth will become less even following major adjustment policies. This speculative conclusion deserves a more detailed study to be more fully supported.

An aspect worth mentioning is the relationship between the ownership of assets at the point in time when an adjustment program is introduced (let us call it time t_0) and past, rather than future, economic policies. Assume, for example, that many of the assets owned at time t_0 were acquired in periods when real interest rates were negative for those who could get credit, the exchange rate was overvalued for those who could get foreign exchange through official channels, and tax and credit incentives and favorable regulations were available to some well-connected individuals.

Under these circumstances, those who could get access to credit at negative (and sometimes at highly negative) real interest rates, foreign exchange at overvalued exchange rates, major investment incentives, and government's favors through special regulations (say, favorable zoning decisions for the use of land) might have acquired some of the assets they owned at t_0 at very low prices.[13] These are some of the same assets that will become much more valuable after a successful adjustment program. The so-called *nomenklaturnaya privatizatsia*, or privatization for communist party elites, is an example. If some individuals had acquired assets at highly favorable conditions before the structural adjustment programs were enacted, and then, because of the reforms in those programs, these assets greatly increased in value, these individuals would have gained twice.

Adjustment programs with major structural reforms may set in motion effects that lead to increases in the value of assets and, possibly, increased concentration of wealth. It is especially because of these effects that economic policies in the postadjustment period may be particularly important. If the initial conditions are such that some individuals start with far more assets than others and if social policy is indifferent to the distribution of income, growth may not be associated with equity.

10II.3   Growth, Structural Reforms, and Income Distribution

The overall impact of long-run growth on the distribution of income has been a controversial topic. Based on his analysis of historical data, Kuznets (1955) advanced the hypothesis of a U-shaped long-term relationship between economic development and income equality. He postulated that at low levels of economic development, growth would be associated with increasing income inequality, while sustained growth eventually would improve the distribution of income. Subsequent empirical studies—for example, by Chenery et al. (1974), Ahluwalia (1976), and Ahluwalia, Carter, and Chenery (1979)—provided some support for Kuznets's hypothesis. These studies also indicated that the improvement in income distribution, which should occur at higher per capita income levels, is not inevitable. Policy choices matter in whether long-term growth leads to an improvement or a worsening of the income distribution.[14]

If economic growth is accompanied by rising employment and real wages, the labor share of income may rise.[15] This helps improve the functional distribution of income. For example, the rapid and sustained growth of many East Asian economies, including Hong Kong, Singapore, South Korea, Taiwan Province of China, and, more recently, Malaysia and Thailand, appears to have been accompanied by an improvement in the functional distribution of income. Growth in these economies has been led by outward-oriented, labor-intensive manufacturing industries with higher productivity compared to the traditional agricultural sector. In addition, high rates of saving and investment in both physical and human capital have boosted overall labor productivity. Consequently, these economies experienced high employment growth and large real-wage increases as they took off.

Between the 1960s and the 1980s, all of the four "East Asian Dragons" (Hong Kong, South Korea, Singapore, and Taiwan, Province of China) had annual growth rates in per capita GDP that exceeded 6 percent.[16] They

Table 10II.2
Economic Growth, Real Labor Earnings, and Poverty

Region	Income growth, 1980–1990[a]	Real earnings[b]	Poverty[c]
Sub-Saharan Africa	−0.9	−12.3	47.8
East Asia	6.3	5.1	11.3
South Asia	3.1	4.7	49.0
Eastern Europe	0.9	—	7.1
Middle East and North Africa	−2.5	—	33.1
Latin America and the Caribbean	−0.5	−3.1	25.5

Sources: International Labor Office (various issues); World Bank (various issues).
a. Average annual percentage change in real per capita income.
b. Average annual percentage change in real earnings in manufacturing: 1980–1988 for sub-Saharan Africa, 1981–1990 for East Asia, 1981–1992 for Latin America and the Caribbean, and 1980–1985 for South Asia.
c. Percentage of population below the poverty line in 1990.

also experienced significant improvement in income distribution, as measured by declining Gini coefficients. In fact, they were part of the very small group of economies with both sustained high growth and low relative inequality. For these economies between 1965 and 1989, a period of sustained rapid growth, the ratios of the income share of the top quintile to that of the bottom quintile of the population fell below 10 (Birdsall and Sabot 1991).[17] Conversely, in much of Africa and Latin America during the 1980s, and more recently in the economies in transition in Eastern Europe and in the former Soviet Union, prolonged economic stagnation and output declines were all accompanied by declining demand for labor, rising unemployment, falling real wages, and increasing income inequality. Tables 10II.2 and 10II.3 provide data on key indicators on growth, employment, wages, poverty, and income distribution in developing regions or selected countries.

Although there are examples in which sustained growth and increased income equality have gone hand in hand, the opposite relationship can also be observed in countries that experienced fast growth over shorter periods. In some Latin American countries, such as Brazil in the 1960s and 1970s, episodes of rapid growth over shorter periods were accompanied by a worsening of income distribution and rising poverty (Fields et al. 1977; Fishlow 1972, 1982). In these countries, the initial conditions in terms of wealth distribution may not have been good.

In China, strong economic growth recently has led to unprecedented improvement in general living standards for much of China's population.

Table 10II.3
Growth, Employment, and Income Equality in Selected Countries

	Indicator	1980	1985	1990	1994
Argentina	GDP growth	1.5	−6.6	0.1	
	Unemployment	3.0	6.2	7.6.	
	Inequality[a]			0.461[b]	
Brazil	GDP growth	9.1	7.9	−4.1	
	Unemployment	6.5	5.3	5.2	
	Inequality	0.56	0.57[c]	0.637	
Chile	GDP growth	7.8	2.5	3.0	
	Unemployment	10.4	12.0	6.0	
	Inequality			0.579[b]	
Philippines	GDP growth	5.2	−7.3	2.7	
	Unemployment	4.8	6.1	8.1	
	Inequality	0.452[d]	0.450	0.407	
Thailand	GDP growth	4.8	3.5	10.0	
	Unemployment			3.9	
	Inequality	0.473[e]	0.474	0.488	0.515

Sources: IMF, *IFS* (for GDP growth); ILO (various issues) for unemployment; and Fields (1991) and the ILO (1993, for inequality).
a. The Gini coefficient.
b. 1989.
c. 1983.
d. 1975.
e. 1981.

The rapid reduction in absolute poverty—from 28 percent in 1978 to 8.6 percent in 1990—is even more impressive (table 10II.4). However, this more recent growth has also been associated with widening income inequality compared to the earlier, less reforming period. The Gini coefficient increased from 0.26 in 1978 to 0.31 in 1990 for the rural population and from 0.16 in 1980 to 0.23 in 1988 for the urban population. Regional inequality also increased, since economic reforms in the interior provinces lagged behind the coastal provinces in southeastern China and the former provinces enjoyed less foreign direct investment, private sector expansion, and export growth.

The unusually high income equality in prereform China was achieved at high efficiency costs, with direct state control of prices and wages, restrictions on the movements of individuals, and rationing of consumer goods and services. Inefficient, egalitarian distribution policies hurt work incentives and slowed improvements in living standards, thus leading to a high

Table 10II.4
China: Economic Growth and Income Distribution

	1978	1980	1982	1985	1988	1990	1992
Real GDP growth (percentage per annum)	11.7	7.9	8.8	12.8	11.3	4.1	13.0
Agriculture	8.1	1.4	11.3	3.4	3.9	7.6	6.4
Industry	13.5	9.3	7.8	21.4	20.8	7.8	27.5
Inflation rate	0.7	6.0	1.9	8.8	18.5	2.1	5.4
Urban real wage growth	6.0	6.1	1.3	5.3	−1.7	9.2	6.7
Urban unemployment rate	5.3	4.9	3.2	1.8	2.0	2.5	2.3
Per capita household income (in yuan)[a]							
Urban	316	439		685	1,119	1,387	1,826
Rural	134	191		398	545	686	784
Income inequality (Gini coefficient)							
Urban		0.16	0.26		0.23		
Rural	0.23	0.28	0.22	0.26	0.34	0.31	
Regional inequality[b]	50.3		43.7	45.6		35.2	
Poverty incidence: Total (in percent)	28.0		13.9	9.2	7.8	8.6	
Urban	4.4		0.9	0.4	0.2	0.4	
Rural	33.0	27.6	15.2	11.9	10.4	11.5	
Number of the people in poverty: Total (in millions)	270		142	97	87	98	
Urban	10		2	1	1	1	
Rural	260	218	140	96	86	97	
Infant morality rate (per 1,000 live births)	41	39	36	31	31		
School enrollment rate	124	112	101	114	126	129	123
Social expenditures: Total (as percentage of GDP)	6.0	9.4	10.7	10.8	10.7	11.3	10.3
Education and health	3.1	3.3	3.8	3.7	3.5	3.5	3.3
Consumer subsidies	0.3	2.6	3.3	3.1	2.3	2.2	1.3
Social security	2.6	3.5	3.6	4.0	4.9	5.6	5.7

Sources: Ahmad and Wang (1991), Cornia (1994), (1992), Hu (1995), People's Republic of China (1993), and World Bank, *Social Indicators of Development*.
a. Based on household survey data.
b. Ratio of the average income of the five poorest provinces to that of the five richest provinces.

incidence of absolute poverty. The fraction of the population living in poverty, predominantly in rural areas, did not change significantly over decades of central planning.

Policies to secure social development were successful in the prereform period. Government maintained adequate expenditures on basic education and health care, and made extensive use of subsidies and transfers to maintain income equality within both the urban and the rural populations. In all major social indicators, such as infant mortality rate, school enrollment, and life expectancy, China outperformed comparable developing countries.

Since the time when economic reforms gained momentum in the late 1970s, the Chinese economy has undergone profound structural changes (Hu 1994, 1995). The share of agriculture in GDP has fallen from 37 percent to 29 percent. Massive rural unemployment has been avoided through the creation of semiskilled jobs in labor-intensive manufacturing and service sectors for former peasants. This rise of rural industry has improved the economic status of a significant share of the rural population, especially the better educated. In addition, the move away from collective farming, which was equivalent to a major land distribution, and the increases in the agricultural prices boosted productivity and peasants' incomes. Living standards in the rural areas have gone up, and poverty has declined rapidly. However, the emergence of wage earners in high-productivity rural industry has also brought about more income variation within the rural population.

The other second major structural change in the Chinese economy has been the diminished economic importance of the state-owned sector, whose share of national industrial output fell from 78 percent in 1978 to 43 percent in 1993. Real-wage growth in the competitive nonstate sector has much exceeded that in the state sector. As a result, urban income inequality has also shown moderate increases.

In Thailand, there is evidence that the fast rate of growth in output in recent years has led to a less even distribution of income. According to estimates by the Bank of Thailand, the Gini coefficient rose from 0.474 in 1988 to 0.515 in 1992. The share of total income going to the top 20 percent of the population rose from 54.9 percent in 1988 to 58.5 percent in 1992. At the same time, the share going to the bottom 20 percent of the population dropped from 4.5 percent in 1988 to 3.7 percent in 1992. In 1992, the average income of the richest 20 percent of the population was almost sixteen times the average income of the poorest 20 percent.

In Peru, there is no evidence that the income distribution has become less even; the Gini coefficient was almost unchanged between 1991 and 1994. On the other hand, the losers, in a relative sense, from the major changes that occurred between 1991 and 1994 were the urban middle classes residing in metropolitan Lima. Those belonging to the seventh, eighth, and ninth deciles experienced far less of an increase in consumption or income than the rest of the population. At the same time, those with technical education or secondary school degrees experienced the biggest gains.[18]

To summarize, economic growth, necessary for growth in employment and reductions in absolute poverty, may not be sufficient to reduce unemployment and improve the distribution of income. Especially in the short run and after major structural reforms, growth, on the one hand, and employment and income distribution, on the other hand, may go in different directions. Government policies can help maximize employment gains associated with economic adjustment and prevent a major deterioration in the distribution of income and the standard of living of the poorest groups. In Argentina, China, Peru, and Thailand, employment growth has lagged behind economic growth, due in part to the short time frame and the labor productivity gains generated by the structural reforms. In these countries, employment gains may have been limited also by the slow response of the educational system in terms of training and education. In China, the spectacular output growth has significantly raised the living standards of its people and reduced poverty, although income inequality has increased.[19] The expansion of rural industry and private businesses has generated strong employment growth, while employment in the urban state-owned sector has been maintained at some efficiency cost. Redistributive policies, including social spending policies, subsidies, and transfers, seem to have made a difference in preventing greater increases in inequality. How the continuation of these policies will affect income distribution in the future remains to be seen.

10II.4 Employment, Income Distribution, and IMF Policy Advice

If adjustment programs, with major structural reforms, are successful, they will stabilize the economy and improve the allocation of resources. As a consequence, they will create the conditions for economic growth that will contribute to the eradication of absolute poverty. In the short run, the impact on employment may be neutral or even negative, while the distribution of wealth may become less even. In conclusion, if we divide the period in the preadjustment and the postadjustment periods, and if the adjustment program is successful in promoting growth, the initial conditions for the growth race that will follow the introduction of the adjustment program will not be such as to make all participants start the race with the same conditions or opportunities.[20] Because of more valuable assets or more valuable human capital, some will be better prepared than others for that race. This is inevitable and natural, but it raises the question as to the role that the government could play in this process.

Many countries have pursued adjustment programs with major structural reforms. Some did so in earlier years, others in later years. Some did it with the assistance of the IMF, others without such assistance. Therefore, by adjustment program, I do not necessarily mean an IMF-supported adjustment program. For this reason, it has not been necessary to mention the IMF up to this point. The policies necessary for successful adjustment are broadly the same whether recommended by the IMF or pursued independently by the countries. The earlier conclusions thus apply to all adjustment programs.[21] In this section, the focus is aspects of IMF involvement, with an emphasis on policies recommended by the IMF that have an important social component.

IMF policy advice to member countries has both a macroeconomic and a structural dimension. Each of these can have implications for growth, employment, and the distribution of income, in the short run and over time.

The impact on employment of structural reforms often advocated by the IMF can be seen in the context of section 10II.1, where it was shown that civil service and enterprise reform, trade reform, and policies associated with the sectoral reallocation of labor and capital can lead to a decline in the short run in the employment intensity of growth. This possible decline should be assessed in the context of the broader longer-term positive effect of that policy advice on growth, especially relative to the status quo.[22]

IMF policy advice explicitly addresses income distribution in a number of ways. First, the policy mix recommended is often designed to limit the effect of adjustment on the poor, for example, by spreading the tax burden more equitably or limiting unproductive expenditures while protecting spending aimed at the most vulnerable members of society. Second, transitory costs of adjustment that fall on the poor may be compensated by the strengthening of a country's social safety nets.

IMF-supported programs have focused on various aspects of expenditure policy, including civil service reform, wage policy, and public investment. Government expenditure composition can influence income distribution in a number of ways. Certain types of public expenditure may provide disproportionate benefits to particular income groups. Expenditures on primary health care or roads in rural areas, for example, may benefit the poor in developing economies, while expenditures on large urban hospitals or university education may benefit primarily the middle- and upper-income groups (see Tanzi 1974). Spending on higher public sector wages may similarly benefit the urban middle class. In addition, some expenditures—in particular, transfer payments and some elements of social insurance—are explicitly concerned with redistribution.

IMF advice on expenditure has also focused in part on improving the productivity of expenditures by focusing on activities that tend to have high rates of return. Many of these activities, such as basic public health and nutrition programs, primary education, and essential infrastructure, have beneficial effects on both growth and income distribution. There is substantial scope for improving the pattern of public expenditure because in many countries much public spending is neither conducive to economic growth nor of benefit to lower-income groups (see Tanzi 1974; Birdsall and James 1993).

The integration of targeted social safety nets into adjustment programs would appear to improve income distribution without negative effects on economic performance, to the extent that the safety nets are well designed and focused on the poorest. As part of the effort to make social safety nets better targeted, the IMF has recommended the elimination or reduction of generalized food subsidies, to be replaced with cash compensation or targeted subsidies. The effect of this shift would be to increase the incomes of rural farmers, who tend to be among the poorest in many countries, while protecting the truly poor urban consumers. It is plausible, however, that some near poor, especially in the cities, may fare the worst under certain reforms, which would tend to increase inequality as measured, say, by the Gini coefficient.

IMF advice on tax reform has focused on designing efficient, broad-based tax systems, consistent with the revenue needs of a country. An attempt has often been made to reduce reliance on the taxation of international trade and to increase reliance on domestic transactions and incomes. In addition, IMF-supported programs have included agreements to improve tax administration. All of this advice has aimed at reducing some of the disincentives associated with high tax rates and at making the tax system a more efficient instrument of public policy.

Finally, more generally, the kinds of reforms recommended by the IMF in areas other than the public finances tend to reduce the opportunities for rent seeking and, thus, over the longer run, tend to improve opportunities for all rather than just the well connected.

10II.5   Conclusions

Sustained economic growth is necessary for the creation of well-paying jobs and the growth of real per capita income so as to reduce poverty and improve standards of living. When a country's economy has stagnated because of distortions caused by poor economic policies, adjustment programs incorporating important structural reforms are often essential in providing the conditions for such growth. These programs change the status quo and create opportunities for gains on the part of many individuals. However, in the short run, they also inevitably affect some groups negatively, either by reducing their income by causing some to lose their jobs or by reducing the value of the assets of still others. The gains from these programs are thus not evenly distributed. This is the reason there is often vocal opposition to these programs.

This may be the price that must be paid to put a country in a position that makes it possible for it to grow over time, but the price may lead to strong enough opposition to the program and a reversal of policies. Such reversals are unfortunately quite common. The government can pursue social policies that reduce the chance that this will happen and correct for some negative effects of adjustment. The IMF has been paying particular attention to the development of such policies, which must have two aims: to protect, to the extent possible, the most vulnerable groups and to ensure that existing polices do not give unfair advantages to the better placed and the better connected. At the same time, they must preserve the incentives introduced by the adjustment programs.

There is much room, especially in fiscal policy, for reforms that are both pro-growth and pro-poor. Often many of the policies that benefit the lowest-income groups are also those with the highest social rate of return. Thus, the composition of public spending can be changed to eliminate unproductive spending and reduce spending that predominantly favors the urban middle classes and the better off. Spending that has a high rate of return and benefits the poor, such as spending on primary education and preventive health, must receive a greater share of the total. Often a disproportionate share of educational spending goes to higher education, which has a lower social rate of return and benefits mostly the better off, and a large share of health spending goes for large urban hospitals, which are rarely used by the truly poor, who are often rural poor.

In addition, efficient, well-targeted, and economical safety nets must be developed; while maintaining economic incentives for those who benefit from them, these safety nets must provide a floor below which the standard of living of individuals must not fall. This floor must be realistic, and it must be related to the country's per capita income and, possibly, to cultural or regional factors. The IMF has been doing a lot of work in this area and has been assisting several countries in developing these efficient safety nets. This work has been carried out to ensure the survivability of IMF-supported programs.

At the other end of the income distribution, some policy reforms may also reduce the chance that the better off and the better connected use the government to achieve unfair advantages. Thus, the IMF has discouraged the use of tax and credit incentives that rarely benefit the poor, regulations that may be used to establish monopolies, and large investment projects when there is no clear evidence that these projects have a high social rate of return. It has also paid close attention to the tax systems in order to remove or reduce clearly regressive taxes and to maintain some progressivity in an effective rather than just a statutory sense. At times, taxes on assets have been recommended to achieve this objective.

Over the years, we have become less naive about the wisdom of imposing highly progressive taxes to achieve redistribution and creating social spending that is not well targeted. The high progressive taxes tended to be progressive only on paper, and the social spending often became spending for everyone or, especially, for the urban middle classes. We now tend to judge policies by their results rather than by the declared intention. It would be a pity, however, if this attitude led us to the conclusion that a government cannot do much to ensure that a market economy is beneficial to all.

Notes

I greatly appreciate the assistance I received from Ke-young Chu, Sanjeev Gupta, Benedict Clements, Zuliu Hu, Jerry Schiff, and Caroline Van Rijckeghem.

1. Subsequent estimates reduced the relationship from three to two. See the comment by Stanley Fischer on William D. Nordhaus, "Macroconfusion: The Dilemmas of Economic Policy" in Tobin (1983).

2. Labor hoarding arises from explicit and implicit contractual commitments to maintain employment; transactions costs, including the cost of severance pay and future costs associated with new hiring, such as training costs; and technological factors, including indivisibil-

ities for specialists, clerical and sales personnel, and supervisors (Pechman 1983, p. 156). An increase in output (relative to potential), following a recession in which labor hoarding took place, leads to a lower increase in employment, because only firms without excess labor hire additional workers, while labor productivity increases (through an increase in hours worked per worker or an increase in productivity per hour).

The discouraged worker effect implies that participation rates increase when output growth increases because the availability of jobs tempts some potential workers to enter the workforce. In developing countries, the increased availability of jobs in the cities may accelerate migration from the rural areas, thus changing underemployment into open unemployment and leading to a further weakening of the link between the unemployment rate and output growth. Because I am focusing on employment, the output elasticity of employment is the most relevant relationship.

3. Consider a simple model in which output growth is exogenously determined for each firm (this is the view implicit in the work of Okun). Assume that due to labor hoarding or other reasons (regulations, etc.), firms cannot reduce their employment, and production shows constant returns to scale. For firms that do not hoard labor, the relationship between the growth rates of employment and output in a firm would be

$$\dot{E}_i = \dot{Q}_i - \dot{A}_i,$$

where E is employment, Q is output, A equals Q/E (surplus $= 0$) labor productivity reflecting the state of technology, and i denotes firm i. The dots on the variables denote change over time.

For firms with labor hoarding, the change in employment will be bounded from below by zero, while being equal to the above expression minus the preexisting labor surplus:

$$\dot{E}_i = \max[\dot{Q}_i - \dot{A}_i - S_i/E_i, 0],$$

where S is employment with zero marginal product or surplus equals $E - Q/A$, and t is time.

When S_i is high, the ratio between employment growth and output growth is low; growth may take place without any additional employment or with little additional employment. Assuming a constant rate of technological change, the above suggests the following equation:

$$\dot{E} = \alpha + \beta\dot{Q}.$$

β is Okun's coefficient, which corresponds to the inverse of the output elasticity of employment.

4. Also, new industries may be conservative in their hiring, especially soon after the structural reforms have taken place, because of the fear that these reforms may be reversed.

5. At times, they became parking lots for those who could not find jobs in the private sector.

6. Based in part on the extensive set of country studies in Papageorgiou et al.

7. This consisted of a reduction in the maximum statutory tariff ranging from 20 to 200 percent to a level ranging from 10 to 65 percent between 1986 and 1991 and the coverage of nontariff barrier ranging from 0.89 to 73.2 percent to a level ranging from 0 to 20 percent.

8. In 1994, 62 percent of the unemployed were unemployed because they had lost their jobs. The largest increase among the unemployed was in the fifty to sixty-four age bracket. Those who had the greatest difficulty in finding jobs were those over forty-five years of age (*Informe Económico* 1994).

9. Note that the quality of the employment statistics in Peru is rather low.

10. See espęcially IFC (1994). For example, in Argentina, the market capitalization in millions of U.S. dollars rose from, 3,268 in 1990 to 43,967 in 1993; in China, it rose from 2,028 in 1991 to 40,567 in 1993; in India, from 27,316 in 1989 to 97,976 in 1993; in Mexico, from 8,371 in 1987 to 200,671 in 1993.

11. The policies pursued by China in the late 1970s and early 1980s amounted to a major land reform. Therefore, most farmers benefited from the productivity gains in the agricultural sector.

12. See, for example, the *Economist* (1995).

13. This was part of the classic form of rent seeking often favored by special connections between those receiving special advantages and some government officials.

14. See Adelman and Robinson (1988) for a more recent and comprehensive survey.

15. In developed countries, this share is often much higher than in developing countries.

16. They represented a high proportion of the economies that have experienced sustained high rates of growth.

17. In these economies, the initial conditions related to the distribution of wealth were generally not associated with a great degree of inequality.

18. This information is derived from an unpublished study by Gustavo Yamada Fukusaki.

19. In the other countries discussed, growth also led to declines in absolute poverty at least for some periods, but to some deterioration in the income distribution.

20. The importance of the initial conditions for the future impact of growth on income and wealth distribution has been emphasized in various studies.

21. Of course, they are more relevant for countries that made more sudden changes in policies than for those where the good policies were pursued over many years.

22. In general, faster-growing countries reduce absolute poverty at a faster pace than slowly growing or stagnating countries.

References

Adelman, I., and Robinson, S. 1988. "Macroeconomic Adjustment and Income Distribution: Alternative Models Applied to Two Economies." *Journal of Development Economics.*

Ahluwalia, M. 1976. "Income Distribution and Development: Some Stylized Facts." *American Economic Review* 66 (1976): 128–135.

Ahluwalia, M., Nicholas G. Carter, and Hollis B. Chenery. 1979. *Growth and Poverty in Developing Countries.* Staff Working Paper no. 309. Revi. Washington, D.C.: World Bank.

Ahmad, E., and Wang Yan. 1991. *Inequality and Poverty in China: Institutional Change and Public Policy 1978–1988.* China Program no. 14. London: London School of Economics.

Birdsall, Nancy, and Estelle James. 1993. "Efficiency and Equity in Social Spending: How and Why Governments Misbehave." In Michael Lipton and Jacques van der Gaag, eds., *Including the Poor.* Washington, D.C.: World Bank.

Birdsall, Nancy, and R. Sabot. 1991. *Unfair Advantage: Labor Market Discrimination in Developing Countries.* Washington, D.C.: World Bank.

Blejer, Mario and Ke-young Chu. 1990. *Fiscal Policy, Labor Markets and the Poor*. Working Paper WP 90/62. Washington, D.C.: IMF.

Chenery, H., M. S. Ahluwalia, C. L. G. Bell, J. H. Duloy, and Richard Jolly. 1974. *Redistribution with Growth*. London: Oxford University Press.

Chu, Ke-young, and Gerd Schwartz. 1994. *Output Decline and Government Expenditures in European Transition Economies*. Working Paper WP 94/68. Washington, D.C.: IMF.

Cornia, G. A. 1994. *Income Distribution, Poverty and Welfare in Transitional Economies: A Comparison Between Eastern Europe and China*. Innocenti Occasional Papers, Economic Policy Series no. 44. Florence: UNICEF.

Dornbusch, R. 1995. "Progress Report on Argentina." In R. Dornbusch and S. Edwards, eds., *Reform, Recovery, and Growth: Latin America and the Middle East*. Chicago: University of Chicago Press.

Edwards, S. 1988. "Terms of Trade, Tariffs and Labor Market Adjustment in Developing Countries." *World Bank Economic Review* 2:165–183.

Edwards, S. 1993. "Openness, Trade Liberalization, and Growth in Developing Countries." *World Bank Economic Review* 31:1358–1393.

Edwards, Sebastian. 1995. "Trade Policy, Exchange Rates, and Growth." In Rudiger Dornbusch and Sebastian Edwards, eds., *Reform, Recovery, and Growth: Latin America and the Middle East*, pp. 13–52. Chicago: University of Chicago Press.

Fields, Gary. 1977. "Who Benefits from Economic Development?" *American Economic Review* 67:70–82.

Fields, Gary. 1991. "Growth and Income Distribution." In George Psacharopoulos, ed., *Essays on Poverty, Equity and Growth*, pp. 1–52. New York: Pergamon Press.

Fields, Gary, and Nohra Rey de Marulanda. 1976. *Intersectoral Wage Structure in Colombia*. New Haven, Conn.: Economic Growth Center, Yale University.

Fisher, Stanley. 1983. Comment on William D. Nordhaus, "Macroconfusion: The Dilemmas of Economic Policy." In James Tobin, ed., *Macroeconomics, Prices, and Quantities: Essays in Memory of Arthur M. Okun*, pp. 267–276. Washington D.C.: The Brookings Institution.

Fischer, Stanley. 1993. "The Role of Macroeconomic Factors in Growth." *Journal of Monetary Economics* 32:485–512.

Fishlow, Albert. 1972. "Brazilian Size Distribution of Income." *American Economic Review* 62: 391–402.

Fishlow, Albert. 1982. "United States and Brazil: the Case of the Missing Relationship" *Foreign Affairs*, 60:904–923 (Spring).

Friedman, Milton. 1968. "The Role of Monetary Policy." *American Economic Review* 58(1):1–17.

Hu, Z. 1994. *Social Protection, Labor Market Rigidity, and Enterprise Restructuring in China*. Paper on Policy Analysis and Assessment 94/22. Washington, D.C.: IMF, October.

Hu, Z. 1995. "The Role of Enterprises in Social Protection: The Case of China." Unpublished. Washington, D.C.: IMF.

International Finance Corporation. 1994. *Emerging Stock Market Factbook*.

International Labor Office. *Yearbook of Labor Statistics* (various issues).

International Labor Office. 1993. *The Incidence of Poverty in Developing Countries: An ILO Compendium of Data.*

Kuznets, Simon. 1955. "Economic Growth and Income Inequality." *American Economic Review* 45:1–28.

Okun, A. M. 1983a. "Potential GNP: Its Measurement and Significance." In J. A. Pechman, ed., *Economics for Policymaking: Selected Essays of Arthur M. Okun.* Cambridge, Mass.: MIT Press.

Okun, A. M. 1983b. "Upward Mobility in a High-Pressure Economy." In J. A. Pechman, ed., *Economics for Policymaking: Selected Essays of Arthur M. Okun.* Cambridge, Mass.: MIT Press.

Papageorgiou, Demetrios, Armeane Choksi, and Michael Micheely. 1990. *Liberalizing Foreign Trade in Developing Countries: The Lessons of Experience.* Washington, D.C.: World Bank.

Pechman, J. A., ed. 1983. *Economics for Policymaking: Selected Essays of Arthur M. Okun.* Cambridge, Mass.: MIT. Press.

People's Republic of China. 1993. *China Statistical Yearbook.* Beijing.

Phelps, E. 1967. "Phillips Curves, Expectations of Inflation and Optimal Unemployment over Time." *Economica* 34 (August): 254–281.

Republic of Argentina. 1994. Ministry of Economy, Public Works, and Public Services, *Informe Económico.* Buenos Aires.

Sussangkarn, C. 1994. "Thailand." In S. Horton, R. Kanbur, and D. Mazumdar, eds., *Labor Markets in an Era of Adjustment: Case Studies,* vol. 2. Washington, D.C.: World Bank.

Tanzi, Vito. 1974. "Redistributing Income Through the Budget in Latin America." *Banca Nazionale del Lavoro Quarterly Review.* 27:65–87.

Tanzi, Vito. 1989. "Fiscal Policy, Growth, and the Design of Stabilization Programs." In Mario I. Blejer and Ke-young Chu, eds., *Fiscal Policy, Stabilization, and Growth in Developing Countries.* Washington, D.C.: International Monetary Fund.

Tanzi, Vito. 1994. "The IMF and Tax Reform." In Amaresh Bagchi and Nicholas Stern, eds., *Tax Policy and Planning in Developing Countries.* Delhi: Oxford University Press.

Tobin, James, ed. 1983. *Macroeconomics, Prices, and Quantities: Essays in Memory of Arthur M. Okun.* Washington, D.C.: The Brookings Institution.

Comments

Ricardo Hausmann

Comments on Guitián

Guitián, in developing the relationship between monetary policy and equity, argues that monetary policy should seek price stability as its main objective. He bases his argument on monetary neutrality: that in the long run, money has no real effects; it affects only the price level. He concludes that monetary policy should be used to stabilize the price level, and no other objectives should be assigned to it. Other instruments are best used for equity purposes. Moreover, he stresses that market-friendly instruments are better than credit and interest rate controls in achieving the objectives of monetary policy.

Furthermore, Guitián argues that although monetary policy should not be used for purposes other than price stability, there really are no trade-offs between the objectives of monetary policy: low inflation and improved income distribution. The empirical evidence he presents suggests that the former is good for the latter. In particular, he provides some evidence indicating that inflation, and especially inflation volatility, is bad for income distribution—and even more so in lower-income countries.[1]

I will challenge Guitián's assertion that monetary policy should be concerned with only medium-term price stability and question his thoughts on the adequate balance between market-friendly and regulatory instruments in monetary policy.

Real Volatility and Monetary and Exchange Rate Arrangements
Guitián argues that monetary policy should seek medium-term price stability and balance of payments viability. In particular, expansionary monetary policies are not the answer, because they will not be sustainable and will require painful future adjustment. So far, we can all agree. He also points out that inflation volatility is bad for income distribution.

However, inflation volatility is not the consequence only, or even primarily, of monetary policy instability. It is related to real shocks that the economy must absorb. As the table shows, not all regions exhibit the same amount of macroeconomic volatility. Output and consumption are much more stable in the industrial and Asian countries than they are in Latin American, sub-Sahara African, Middle Eastern, and North African countries. Related to this difference in the instability of macroeconomic outcomes is the link with terms of trade volatility, a real source of external uncertainty that countries must face.

The last three regions in the table have between two and three times the terms of trade volatility of the first three.[2] They also exhibit more capital account volatility. In particular, Latin American countries have a capital account that is twice as volatile as that of the industrial and the East Asian miracle countries.

Inflation and recessions also seem to be related to aggregate volatility. Latin American and sub-Sahara African countries generate far more inflation, far deeper recessions, and more volatile real exchange rates than the industrial or Asian countries. Interestingly, Middle Eastern and North African countries do not suffer from the inflation problems or the real exchange rate volatility that characterize Latin American and sub-Sahara African countries, but they seem to generate more output volatility and far deeper recessions.

We should care about volatility for several reasons. Volatility reduces growth and hurts people (Rojas-Suárez and Weisbrod 1995b). Unstable countries grow less not just because they invest less but also because they get less out of their investments. Moreover, poorer countries and people suffer more in recessions because they have fewer means to smooth consumption.

Guitián takes too seriously the argument of monetary neutrality. He argues that monetary policy should be geared to medium-term price stability because money does not have real effects, except in the short term.[3] This is obviously an exaggeration in Guitián's own views since he argues that inflation caused by money is bad for growth, a long-run phenomenon. But more important, since money does have real short-term effects, we need to ask how these are related to the transmission of shocks to an economy, and hence to the ensuing volatility and its impact on growth, welfare, and equity.

In this respect, different monetary and exchange rate arrangements, all compatible with some form of medium-term price stability, will have different implications on how these shocks are transmitted into macroeconomic volatility. Hence, just stating that monetary policy should be solely concerned with medium-term price stability does not provide much useful guidance. The policy-relevant question is: What monetary and exchange rate arrangement provides optimal adjustment to shocks and limits damaging volatility without causing high or unstable inflation and without postponing needed policy reaction?

In principle, external uncertainty can be channeled into a mix of reserve, exchange rate, and interest rate uncertainty, where the mix will be a consequence of the exchange and monetary arrangement adopted. Hausmann and Gavin (1996) provide evidence that pegged exchange rates generate more stable real exchange rates, but at the cost of more output volatility.

Should reserves play a major shock-absorbing role? If this is the case, then there may be a trade-off between higher reserves and, hence, better self-insurance against shocks, on the one hand, and greater domestic investment, on the other. How large should reserves be to play this shock-absorbing role? And if reserves should play this role, how can we guarantee that they are used to minimize the costs of adjustment and not just to postpone adjustment inefficiently?

Reserves will be used depending on the type of exchange rate arrangement. In a pure float, they would never be used. In a fixed exchange rate regime, the amounts used will be determined endogenously, depending on fiscal and domestic credit policy. A mixed exchange rate system would lead to a combination of uncertainty over reserves and over the exchange rate. How much uncertainty should be left in the level of reserves and how much transmitted to the nominal exchange rate?[4] What amount of exchange rate flexibility should countries adopt? How is it related to the amount of shocks they receive? And how can countries guarantee price stability if the exchange rate is used as a shock absorber and, hence, cannot play the role of nominal anchor? Should the monetary and exchange rate arrangements of shock-prone countries be substantially different from other, more stable ones?

Furthermore, exchange rate volatility will affect both the level and the volatility of interest rates, in turn affecting the ability of financial markets to develop long-term unindexed instruments. Should central banks tolerate dollarization or promote indexation? Should somebody act as a lender of last resort of the banking system? What are the equity implications of the potential fiscal costs of banking crises or the benefits of the lender of last resort function?

The alternative answers to these questions have important equity implications, and Guitián's appeal to medium-term price stability provides little
or no guidance.

How Market Friendly Should Monetary Policy Be?

Another element with which I take issue is the view that market-friendly
instruments in monetary policy are always superior to more interven-
tionist approaches. If the debate is only on credit and interest rate controls, we can easily agree. These instruments are not efficient and are
best abandoned. Where I think there still is a major policy issue is on the
appropriate mix of reserve requirements and open-market operations as
instruments of monetary control.

The traditional view is that reserve requirements are an indirect and
inefficient form of taxation on financial intermediation,[5] while open-market
operations make explicit the fiscal costs of controlling monetary aggregates. In a world where only distortionary taxes exist, you may want to
use some reserve requirements and some open-market operations to opti-
mize excess burden of the fiscal impact.

A point that has not been made so clearly is the effects of using short-
term government paper as an instrument of open-market operations. Here
the issue becomes one of debt roll-over risk, which can be quite substantial, especially in shock-prone countries. If a country undergoes a negative
shock and has not yet had time to adopt adjustment measures, the simple
fact that a large stock of debt must be renewed may generate a bank-run
type of behavior on the part of investors. If each agent believes that the
other will not renew his bond, it is optimal for each agent not to renew it
himself. This may lead to extremely high interest rates that are likely to
cause an unsustainable fiscal deficit and prompt an inflationary attack. We
have just seen this scenario unfold in Mexico, a country that had zero
reserve requirements and a large stock of short-term public debt issued for
the purpose of monetary sterilization. With the benefit of hindsight, we
might conclude that Mexico would have been better advised to control
monetary aggregates during the period of capital inflows with less "market-
friendly" but safer increases in reserve requirements.

Attempting to do open-market operations with longer-term paper may
be very expensive from a fiscal point of view. The difference in cost is not
unrelated to the roll-over risk in the sense that as the maturity of the bond
lengthens, investors lose the option of deciding whether to stay, and they
will ask to be compensated for this through a larger yield.

Hence, the argument in favor of market-friendly monetary policy instruments needs qualification. In particular, I hope it is not meant to imply that reserve requirements should not be kept prudently high or that open-market operations should be conducted without concern about the potentially dangerous debt profile it generates.

A final point on market friendliness is on the degree of financial liberalization regarding international capital flows. Capital flows may be an important source of macroeconomic volatility (Gavin, Hausmann, and Leiderman 1995). It expresses itself not only in wild gyrations of stock and bond prices but, more important, in real exchange rates, real wages, unemployment, and growth. Some of the most conservative and prudent countries in Latin America, such as Chile and Colombia, have faced situations in which fiscal and monetary policy are overwhelmed by excessive inflows with their impact on overheating, real appreciation, and current account deterioration. In that context, they have resorted to regulation and implicit taxation of capital inflows as a means to insulate their economies from excessive external volatility. By doing so, they were able to endure much better the recent turmoil in financial markets, in comparison to more market-friendly players, such as Mexico and Argentina.

Comments on Tanzi

Tanzi starts by arguing that sustained growth is good for poverty and income distribution over the longer run. However, achieving sustained growth may require structural reforms to eliminate important distortions and obstacles, and these reforms may hurt employment in the short run. They will also have an impact on asset prices and cause redistribution of wealth. Different assets may be affected differently; the premium for certain skills may rise, stock markets may boom, and other assets, such as land and structures, may see their prices change, so reforms will generate both winners and losers in the short to medium term. These distributive effects may generate a political backlash that could threaten the reforms. Some redistributions may be necessary, and others may be inevitable, but government policy can help by maximizing employment gains associated with reform, adopting social safety nets, and improving the distributional effects of fiscal policies through tax, spending, and civil service reforms.

Tanzi recognizes the difficulties involved in incorporating equity considerations in the design of adjustment programs. Employment and asset price effects may have welfare implications that are important in themselves, but they may as well have the added complication of eroding the

Table 10.C.1
Standard Deviation of Major Economic Aggregates, 1970–1992 (in percentage)

	GDP	Private consumption	Inflation	Terms of trade	Capital account	Fiscal deficit	REER[a]	Decline in recessions[b]	International reserves
Industrial countries	2.2	2.1	3.9	8.9	1.7	2.4	4.8	−4.1	1.08
East Asian miracle countries	3.0	4.1	6.2	8.0	1.5	2.4	6.2	−1.1	2.28
South Asian countries	3.4	5.4	7.9	7.9	1.1	4.2	N.A.	−6.3	1.44
Latin American and Caribbean countries	4.7	5.6	463.5	15.1	2.8	4.7	13.4	−21.5	2.74
Sub-Saharan African countries	5.3	10.3	88.6	22.1	4.4	4.5	19.4	−23.5	3.23
Middle Eastern and North African countries	7.8	8.2	6.9	25.6	6.1	8.5	5.5	−36.9	5.66

Sources: World Bank World Tables; IFS; and IDB.
Note: Averages per region are population weighted.
a. The real effective exchange rate.
b. The sum of the decline in output in recession years between 1970 and 1992.

support for reform. In this respect, Tanzi breaks with the conventional wisdom of the 1980s, which was based on the Rybcynsky theorem, and argues that, in the long run, trade liberalization will lead to an increase in the relative price of the most abundant factor. Since unskilled labor was thought to be that factor, it was assumed that open trade would lead to improved income distribution.

Recent experience with trade liberalization suggests that the relationship is more complete and that the premium for skills may rise significantly in the medium term.

Employment Considerations and the Speed and Sequencing of Reform

In studying the relationship between growth in employment and growth in output, Tanzi notices that reform can bring serious changes in this link by causing labor reallocation to higher-productivity sectors, cuts in public sector employment, more rapid adoption of technical change, privatization, and civil service reform. Wage differentials and unemployment may rise even if growth performance is adequate.

The only way low-income countries can become high-income countries, however, is if output grows more than employment. This implies an increase in productivity, which is required to sustain higher real wages. Reforms, by eliminating serious distortions in resource allocation, will generate rapid increases in productivity in most sectors, especially in those where output contracts. The challenge is that if the aggregate result of all these reallocations does not produce very high rates of growth, then the gap between productivity increases and output growth may cause rising unemployment. This is the situation in Argentina, where unemployment increased substantially in the context of 7 percent growth. China was able to avoid rising unemployment by having double-digit growth while maintaining high subsidies to inefficient public sector firms.

The point here is that most reforming countries cannot achieve such high growth rates, especially at the start of a reform program. Growth performance in Eastern Europe, the former Soviet Union, and Mexico has varied from mediocre to dismal. On the other hand, productivity increases, certainly beneficial, may be relatively high, leading to rapidly rising unemployment. This situation leads to timing and sequencing issues in the design of reform programs. Should labor-shedding measures introduced be taken after some other activities have generated significant labor demand, even if the delay is costly from a fiscal point of view? Should policies that lead to high growth in tradables be undertaken before reforms that cause major declines in lagging sectors? Is there a lesson for Eastern Europe in China's sequencing and speed of reforms? Can China be emulated by highly urbanized economies, or are China's sequencing and speed of reforms those that only very rural countries can achieve? Should privatization and civil service reform lead or lag behind stabilization and trade reform? Should liberalization of export trade take place before full opening of imports? Are these sequencing issues technically possible, or is it more fine-tuning than most governments can manage, given both the technical and political constraints?

Resource-Based Development

The problem of job creation may become more acute in resource-rich countries, where labor-intensive development is an unlikely consequence of liberalization. Latin America, sub-Saharan Africa, North Africa, the Middle East, and much of the former Soviet Union tend to be resource rich relative to their endowments of labor, and consequently they are less likely to develop labor-intensive activities. This is an important contrast with East and South Asia.

In Bolivia, Colombia, Peru, Trinidad, Venezuela, Papua New Guinea, Kazakstan, and Russia, liberalization attracts investment in resource-based sectors. These sectors tend to be highly intensive in a form of capital that is put in place up-front in large, sunk installments. Hence, beyond the resources themselves, two aspects determine a country's advantage in these activities: the cost of capital and the efficiency with which the economy is able to install the new capacity. Since developing countries face a high cost of capital and tend to be inefficient in complex industrial construction, the resource-based economic rents tend to go into paying for the high cost of borrowed funds and the low efficiency of plant installation. All too often, little of the increased income goes into the rest of the economy, especially after the investment expenditures have been made.

Moreover, while the investment is taking place, capital inflows and increased domestic expenditures may lead to real appreciation, which may thwart the development of other, more labor-intensive, tradable sectors. This investment-related Dutch disease may have important distributional implications: Peasants may be displaced by real appreciation, while access to mining rents requires participation in urban social programs.

Furthermore, if sustained endogenous productivity growth is an important part of long-term growth and if resource sectors tend to get less of it, an initially large endowment in natural resources may lead to a low-growth equilibrium (Matsuyama 1992). This may be part of the explanation for the higher growth and better income distribution observed in a resource-poor East Asia.

Finally, resource abundance tends to generate a trade pattern that is subject to greater terms of trade volatility, a factor that may limit growth and cause important welfare costs.

What does resource abundance do to the employment impact of reform? Should resource-based development be encouraged at the start of reform, to make adjustment less painful, or should it be discouraged? Should minimum resource rents be set and captured by the government through taxes, or should they be forgone and left to act as an attractor of more capital? It may well be that excessive policy optimism on the social benefits of resource-based industries is leading many countries into beggar-thy-neighbor policies (e.g., through tax competition) so that rents get transferred abroad and development becomes inefficiently concentrated in resource-based industries.

Social Safety Nets: Motivation and Implication

In justifying social safety nets, Tanzi stresses the need to guarantee the survivability of reform programs from the opposition caused by its distributive consequences. He argues that well-targeted safety nets that protect the most vulnerable may be good for welfare and for political economy of reform. Moreover, if they are accompanied by a reallocation of expenditure from universities to elementary schools and from large city hospitals to primary care rural centers, welfare may be improved even more.

I argue a different point of view. First, the opposition to reform often comes not from the poor but from the middle class and from those living off the quasi-rents that are destroyed by market liberalization (Hausmann 1994). Hence, no matter how desirable they may be on equity grounds, safety nets may not be crucial for the survivability of reform. For example, Venezuela's large safety nets did not prevent major policy reversals.

Second, there is a trade-off between targeting, which focuses scarce public resources in the most vulnerable, and universality, which increases support for public programs. Targeted programs may help the poor but may complicate the politics of reform by forcing the middle class to accept higher taxes for public programs scientifically designed not to reach them.

Third, reforming spending priorities for education and health may consume much more political capital than it generates because it implies confronting large and well-organized constituencies. These reforms may be good for welfare and equity, and they should be done; however, they are likely to have negative political economy effects and consequently should not be done for a political payoff.

Fourth, new social transfer programs may be a distraction from the necessary reform of the core social ministries. By creating alternative structures that bypass the education and health bureaucracies, governments may avoid or postpone the need to deal with the major inefficiencies of these organizations. Social safety nets are usually adopted with short-term objectives but are too slow to be put in place in time to compensate for major stabilization measures, such as devaluations and price liberalizations.

In conclusion, safety nets may not be effective politically, may be too slow to compensate the losers, and may distract from other important social reform efforts. Serious reforms in education, health, and pensions and improvements in the efficiency and risk-sharing aspects of labor legislation may be more important social goals.

A Final Word

Tanzi and Guitián have offered important contributions on the road to understanding the relationship between equity and economic policy in an era of reform. As such, they are provocative in the sense that they open a debate and, more important, a line of research. We have always wanted economic policy to do good to people and have searched for ways to do so. However, we have always found that efficiency tends to be analytically more tractable than equity. As we proceed on the line of research suggested by these authors, we will get a better grasp of the real trade-offs and the issues that are involved in the design of equity-conscious economic policy.

Notes

1. Two questions can be leveled at the evidence presented. First is the issue of causality. Does inflation cause bad income distribution, or is it the other way around, with distributive problems causing fiscal deficits, which then generate inflation? On this point, see Tommasi and Velasco (1995). Second is the issue of robustness. Since Latin America is the region with both the highest volatility and the worst income distribution, is it driving the results? Or is it just a Latin America story?

2. Terms-of-trade volatility seems to be more important in resource-rich countries, since resources themselves, as opposed to labor or capital, tend to be product specific, making supply inelastic so that shocks are expressed mainly in price changes.

3. What I think Guitián means by monetary neutrality is that the long-run Philips curve is not downward sloping, but most likely is upward sloping (i.e., inflation and unemployment

are complements, not substitutes, in the long run). Money neutrality would imply a vertical Philips curve.

4. These issues are addressed in Rojas-Suárez and Weisbrod (1995a).

5. As with all taxes, reserve requirements will also tend to be avoided through off-balance operations. This effect can be limited by remunerating them.

References

Caballero, Ricardo, and Mohamed Hammour. 1995. "On the Ills of Adjustment." Mimeo. Cambridge, Mass.: MIT.

Cragg, Michael, and Mario Epelbaum. 1994. "The Premium for Skills in LDCs: Evidence from Mexico." Mimeo. New York: Columbia University.

Gavin, Michael. 1994. "Unemployment and the Economics of Gradualist Policy Reform." Mimeo. Washington, D.C.: Inter-American Development Bank.

Gavin, Michael, Ricardo Hausmann, and Leonardo Leiderman. 1995. *The Macroeconomics of Capital Flows to Latin America: Experience and Policy Issues.* Inter-American Development Bank, Office of the Chief Economist Working Paper Series no. 310. Washington, D.C.: Inter-American Development Bank.

Hausmann, Ricardo. 1994. "Sustaining Reform: What Role for Social Policy?" In Colin I. Bradford, ed., *Redefining the State in Latin America*, pp. 173–194. Paris: Organization for Economic Cooperation and Development.

Hausmann, Ricardo, and Michael Gavin. 1995. *Overcoming Volatility in Latin America.* International Monetary Fund Seminar Series (International), no. 1995–34. Washington, D.C.: International Monetary Fund.

Hausmann, Ricardo, and Michael Gavin. 1996. *Securing Stability and Growth in a Shock-Prone Region: The Policy Challenge for Latin America.* Inter-American Development Bank, Office of the Chief Economist Working Paper Series no. 315. Washington, D.C.: Inter-American Development Bank.

Inter-American Development Bank. Forthcoming. "Shocks and Growth: Assuring Stability in a Turbulent World." In *Economic and Social Progress Report.*

Matsuyama, Kiminori. 1992. "Agricultural Productivity, Comparative Advantage, and Economic Growth." *Journal of Economic Theory* 2(58) (December): 317–374.

Rojas-Suárez, Liliana, and Steven R. Weisbrod. 1995a. *Financial Fragilities in Latin America: The 1980s and 1990s.* Occasional Paper 132. Washington, D.C: IMF.

Rojas-Suárez, Liliana, and Steven R. Weisbrod. 1995b. *Achieving Stability in Latin American Financial Markets in the Presence of Volatile Capital Flows.* Inter-American Development Bank, Office of the Chief Economist Working Paper Series no. 304. Washington, D.C.: Inter-American Development Bank.

Tommasi, Mariano, and Andrés Velasco. 1995. "Where Are We in the Political Economy of Reform?" Paper presented at the Columbia University Conference on Economic Reform in Developing and Transition Economies, New York, May 12.

Comments

Arjun Sengupta

Output Implications of Monetary Policy

Guitián writes his chapter in a way that suggests that most of his policy propositions are self-evident and are universally accepted. That is not so, particularly the so-called principle on monetary neutrality, that is, that monetary policy is unable to change real output. Even if in the very long run this neutrality may hold, in the short and medium term—the period most relevant for the working out of the IMF-supported adjustment programs—it may not. But I agree with two of his main propositions: that monetary policy should focus mainly (Guitián says *uniquely*) on the medium-term objectives of price stability and that price stability or low inflation favors "an environment in which the distributional outcome is safe from the nonneutralities of adjustment and inflation-related costs." This second proposition is related to the IMF's policy advice but is essentially based on an almost universally accepted proposition that inflation, both anticipated and unanticipated, adversely affects income distribution.

Output Growth, Employment Growth, and Income Distribution

Tanzi is more general, talking about structural reforms as such, with a much broader sweep. He discusses some theoretical relations between output growth, employment growth, and income distribution, in the context of structural reform. He also examines some of the country experiences and brings out quite cogently the possibility that adjustment programs of this type, supported by the IMF and the World Bank under policies of structural reform, when they produce output growth, may end up with "growth without employment creation or even with growth in unemployment." The relation between structural adjustment under economic reforms, growth, and inequality of income is, however, very uncertain. Between the 1960s and the 1980s, the four East Asian tigers had high growth rates and significant improvement in income distribution (declining Gini coefficients). But Latin American countries and Eastern European countries during this reform period of the 1980s had both low growth in output and increasing income inequality. The case of China is even more interesting. China's rapid income growth associated with economic reforms showed a rapid reduction in absolute poverty from 28 percent in 1978 to 8.6 percent in 1990; the trend was quite steady over a long enough period. But the Gini coefficient, for both the rural and urban areas, increased steadily and significantly during this period.

The conclusion that I draw from Tanzi is that in the medium term, there is no unequivocal relationship between income growth and inequality or unemployment. It depends on the initial conditions, the nature of growth, and the nature of policy reforms. It is, of course, possible to argue that income growth is a necessary, though not a sufficient, condition for a sustainable reduction in inequality. But the relationship between economic reform and income growth is less certain, at least in the short to medium term and especially when economic reform is more in the nature of stabilization than of structural reform. And it is the short and medium terms that are the most relevant to the consideration of the sustainability of any policy programs. In theory, economic reforms may lead to economic growth and improved income distribution in the long run. But if income distribution deteriorates or poverty increases sharply in the short to medium term, there may be not only adverse effects on savings, investment, and growth but also a political economic disruption of the policy programs as such.

Desirable Policies

What kinds of policies could be adopted by an adjusting state or should be advised by the IMF to arrest the deterioration of the poverty index and equity of income distribution during the period of economic reform?

Income distribution policies must not nullify the basic thrusts of policy reform. If deregulations and market competitions are the essential elements of economic reform, nothing should be done to reverse the deregulations or affect the relative prices obstructing the path of allocation efficiency.

It is in this context that a suggestion that international financial institutions (IFIs) should subsidize the redistribution policies becomes relevant. Such subsidized financial assistance by IFIs would be like lump-sum transfers from abroad. Ideally these should come as grants; otherwise their repayment in the future would entail some taxation with distortionary effects. However, if the economy grew, which hopefully would be the case following economic reform, such repayment may not be too difficult, especially if the transfers were made in concessional terms.

If this suggestion were accepted, any IMF-supported reform program should be accompanied by a program of poverty alleviation and redistributive measures financed by transfers at concessional terms, if not by grants, from the IFIs. The IMF and World Bank should carefully work out such programs with the recipient countries' authorities, keeping in mind that the transfers should be properly targeted and have the maximum visible impact on poverty without neutralizing the relative price effects of the reform programs. For example, there should be no attempt to protect the industrial units or their labor, which lose out in competition. On the contrary, they should be helped to exit and, if possible, to retrain. It may sometimes be better to help programs that are not directly related to reforms, such as nutrition, primary education, women and child welfare, and urban and rural sanitation, where the impacts are visible and the deficit-reduction measures of the reform programs may entail substantial cuts in expenditure. Another highly visible and highly effective measure may be a well-targeted subsidized food distribution program, supporting the bottom 20 to 30 percent of the population below the poverty line. This may bring down the domestic market prices of food grains, with a favorable impact on real wages. If the food market were completely opened to international trade as a consequence of economic reforms, the border prices would determine the production effect in the food sector, insulating it from the targeted concessional food supply program affecting a fraction of the population.

It would be desirable to have as large as possible a program of such complementary redistributional and antipoverty measures to accompany the reform programs financed by international transfers. However, given the aid fatigue in the world today, it would be unrealistic to expect too large a support on this account, and it would be necessary to find domestic sources of finance for such programs. Here the main constraint would be the deficit-reduction programs of economic reforms, which could not be allowed to be relaxed. Then would come the main challenge to the designers of the reform programs: how to raise resources and target the reduced expenditure within the overall constraint of a low deficit-to-GDP ratio, to help implement programs that promote growth and redistribution, and protect—if not expand—antipoverty social programs. This would be difficult but possible if one keeps in mind all the trade-offs and uses all instruments available.

While keeping the target of deficit reduction in view, it will be necessary to identify measures to raise taxes. Since most reform programs press for a reduction in the rates of taxes and tariffs, the emphasis is mostly on tax administration and widening the tax nets. There are limits to this, and it will be necessary to look for areas where tax incidence can be raised. This will lead to raising taxes from those who have the ability to pay. Tanzi identifies several groups who will benefit most from the reform measures, especially among the asset holders. The problem here will be to balance the tax increase with the disincentive effects, especially for investment. However, in assessing these disincentives, one must consider the positive effects of the sustainability of reforms, increasing prospects of growth and credibility in the policies, which may result from the expenditure programs that need to be financed.

This brings us to the expenditure programs. The general tendency in most reforming countries is to reduce social expenditures and public investment without reducing many of the subsidies and revenue expenditures. This tendency should be arrested, but not because there is no fat in social expenditures and public investment; there is, but there is much more in other revenue expenditures and subsidies, which are protected by political lobbies and not economic rationale. Reducing social expenditures and public investment without touching these lobbies would send a signal that would work against the political economy of sustainability of reform. It would be much better to protect the level of social expenditures but redesign the expenditure programs for better targeting and better delivery. This should give the IMF and World Bank staff a lot of additional but fruitful work.

What about public investment? In most of the reforming economies, public and private investments need not be competing; they could be complementary, especially if public investment is focused on infrastructure and social sectors. It is still possible to argue in favor of public investment in many areas, as Joseph Stiglitz stated in chapter 3, with imperfections in capital markets and diverging social and private returns. The additional argument would be private investors' propensity to wait and watch until they have sufficient confidence in the sustainability of the reforms and the potential for growth. This is an externality related to government action, and public investment in areas that have large linkage effects, such as infrastructure, may be necessary to keep up the overall rate of investment and economic growth.

An increase in public investment need not be limited to public enterprises. Reform of the public enterprises, including their privatization, is a major element of any economic reform program. But the case for increasing public investment is based on different considerations and can be supported even without bringing in public enterprises. I give an example from the Indian experience. In Assam, the northeastern province of India, with limited roads and rails access, there is a lot of gas that is being flared because no enterprise is willing to consider heavy investment in the cracking of gas due to transport problems and the lack of downstream industries that could use the output. The government offered a 30 percent capital subsidy to any private sector party willing to invest in the gas-cracking plants and ensure the supply of gas to the public sector gas companies. Initially two private companies responded, and one was chosen on grounds of available technology and financing. As that project materialized, many downstream units also showed interest, and it became clear that the plant's output would not have to be transported to distant mainland units. This has made the economics of the project very attractive, and many other private investors are now coming forward with investment proposals. It should now be possible to reduce, or even remove, the capital subsidy.

There is a related proposal that some of us are considering in India; it is known as convertible equity, by which the government would offer a minority equity participation to private corporations investing in infrastructure. The investment rule would thus be shared, and the management and operations would be in the hands of the private companies. It would be convertible equity in the sense that the private majority partner would be given the option, after three to five years, to convert the equity into fixed coupon bonds owed to the government. This may be an effective way of persuading the private sector to invest in areas considered risky because of uncertainties related to growth and reform sustainability, even though the government is determined to carry out the reforms.

Possible IMF and World Bank Role

The IFIs, like the IMF, could be helpful when a government is determined to stick to reforms but the private investors (domestic and foreign) are waiting and watching. The lack of investment may reduce the growth potential and actually end up realizing private investors' fears, while public investment of the kind that I have just mentioned may play a role in mitigating this. But the IFIs, particularly the IMF, could help by establishing a special window of assistance that would be automatically available to a country that is sticking to its reforms and may be subject to exogenous shocks when, in the absence of any cushion, it may be forced to reverse some of the policies. For example, the IMF could establish a special first tranche for countries that are under an IMF program or are qualified for this tranche at the time of their Article IV consultation if they are not under a program. Accordingly, if the reserves of such a country were to fall below a trigger point related to their imports, the country could immediately draw on IMF resources to its entitlement under the first tranche. This would be insurance, which would not likely be invoked most of the time but would give the country's investors some assurance that the country has enough cushion to meet unforeseen demands without changing policies.

Contributors

Alberto Alesina
Professor, Harvard University

Jagdish Bhagwati
Professor, Columbia University

Nancy Birdsall
Executive vice president, Inter-
American Development Bank

Andrea Brandolini
Economist, Bank of Italy

Michael Bruno
Vice president and chief economist,
World Bank

James Buchanan
Professor and Nobel laureate in
economics for 1986, George
Mason University

Michel Camdessus
Managing director, International
Monetary Fund

Michael Deppler
Deputy director, European I
Department, International
Monetary Fund

John Flemming
Professor, Oxford University

Alberto Giovannini
Professor, Columbia University

Danuta Gotz-Kozierkiewicz
Alternate executive director,
International Monetary Fund

Manuel Guitián
Director, Monetary and Exchange
Affairs Department, International
Monetary Fund

Arnold C. Harberger
Professor, University of California
at Los Angeles

Ricardo Hausmann
Chief economist, Inter-American
Development Bank

Enrique Iglesias
President, Inter-American
Development Bank

Grzegorz Kolodko
Deputy prime minister and minister
of finance, Poland

Affiliations at the time of the conference (June 1–2, 1995)

Anne Krueger
Professor, Stanford University

Assar Lindbeck
Professor, University of Stockholm

Jiwei Lou
Director, State Commission, China

Jean-Claude Milleron
Undersecretary-general, United
Nations

Christian Morrison
Head of research, Organization
for Economic Cooperation and
Development

Jacob Mwanza
Governor, Bank of Zambia

Martin Ravallion
Lead economist, Policy Research
Department, World Bank

Dani Rodrik
Professor, Columbia University

Nicola Rossi
Professor, Universita Degli Studi di
Roma

Arjun Sengupta
Member secretary, Planning
Commission, India

Lyn Squire
Director, Policy Research
Department, World Bank

Nicholas Stern
Chief economist, European
Bank for Reconstruction and
Development

Joseph Stiglitz
Chairman, Council of Economic
Advisors, United States

Lawrence Summers
Deputy secretary, United States
Treasury Department

Vito Tanzi
Director, Fiscal Affairs Department,
International Monetary Fund

Naohiro Yashiro
Professor, Sophia University

Index

Acemoglu, D., 83
Adelman, Irma, 141, 321, 347, 372
Africa. *See also* North Africa
 capital flight, 157
 devaluation effects, 130
 education resources in francophone
  countries, 306
 IFIs' role in, 158
 inequality of income distribution, 118
 inflation volatility in sub-Sahara, 379–381
 lack of economic growth, 118, 120, 156
 linkage between equitable distribution and
  growth, 154, 155, 156, 158
 poverty, transition effects on, 130–131
 public employment benefits for the poor,
  307
 public investments, 311
 resource-based development in sub-Sahara,
  377
 results of economic stagnation and output
  declines during the 1980s, 362
Agell, J., 83
Aghion, P., 82, 83, 84
Agricultural extension and research programs, 24, 44
Agricultural sector. *See also* Landownership
 agricultural exports, 126
 land distribution effects on income
  distribution, 11, 162
 productivity relative to nonagricultural
  sectors, 126
 public expenditures in rural zones to
  increase productivity of agriculture, 245
Ahluwalia, Montek S., 119, 361
Akerlof, G., 47
Alam, M. S., 47
Albania
 health, transition effects on, 178

Alejandro, Carlos Diaz, 283
Alesina, Alberto, 14, 78, 80, 87, 100, 136–
 137, 301–302, 315, 318, 321–322
Alexander, William E., 347
Alvarez, C., 18
Amsden, Alice H., 47
Anand, Sudhir, 6, 141, 142
Angell, Alan, 308, 321
Argentina
 boom-and-bust syndrome, 209
 distribution of government benefits to the
  poor, 225
 employment growth lag behind economic
  growth, 366
 hyperinflation and, 7, 15
 income distribution, 5
 linkage between equitable distribution and
  growth, 15–16
 long-term growth effects on inequality, 13
 as market-friendly, 384
 populism, 210
 privatization effects, 354–355
 reduction in tax evasion, 313–314
 rise in real wages, 234
 skill differential, 11
 structural reform effects, 356
 unemployment increase despite growth,
  381
Armenia
 unemployment, 173, 175
Arrow, K. J., 46
Arrow-Debreu theorem, 27, 41, 63, 64, 65
Aspe, Pedro, 308
Asset redistribution, 133–134, 139. *See also*
 Land reform
Assets
 structural reform effects on value of, 360–
  361

DATE DUE